AS & A2
Sociology

Exam Board: AQA

Complete Revision
and Practice

AS-Level Contents

We deliberately haven't put answers in this book — because there are lots of valid ways to answer essay questions. Instead, we've put in a section about how to do well in your exam — which includes some sample 'A' grade exam answers.

Do Well in Your Exam

A2-Level Contents

We deliberately haven't put answers in this book — because there are lots of valid ways to answer essay questions. Instead, we've put in a section about how to do well in your exam — which includes some sample exam answers.

Published by Coordination Group Publications Ltd.

Editors:
Taissa Csáky, Gemma Hallam, Thomas Harte, Luke von Kotze, Katherine Reed

Contributors:
Ellen Bowness, Polly Cotterill, Charley Darbishire, Sam Datta-Paulin, Anna Hazeldine, Carol Potter, Rachael Powers, Sean Purcell, Kate Redmond, Neil Renton, Frances Rippin, Claire Thompson, Karl Thompson, Julie Wakeling, Andrew Walker

Proofreaders:
Sarah Acford-Palmer, Andy Park, Glenn Rogers

Acknowledgements:

Government Statistics or National Statistics reproduced under the Terms of the Click Use Licence

Source: National Statistics website: www.statistics.gov.uk. Crown copyright material is reproduced

with the permission of the Controller, Office of Public Sector Information (OPSI)

Census statistics: Source 2001 Census data supplied by the General Register Office of Scotland © Crown Copyright

Pages 36 and 108: © NatCen. Source: Kathleen Kiernan 'Men and women at work and at home' in Roger Jowell, Lindsay Brook, Gillian Prior and Bridget Taylor, editors (1992) 'British Social Attitudes: the 9th Report' Aldershot: Dartmouth Publishing Company

Page 38: Statistics Copyright © United Nations 2000-2008

Page 40: Statistics from the National Society for the Prevention of Cruelty to Children (NSPCC) © 2008 NSPCC

Page 42: Sunday Times Rich List © NI Syndication

Page 52: Graph Copyright © CASE 2005-2008

Page 69: Extract reprinted from 'The Lancet' Vol. 297/edition 7696, Julian Tudor Hart, 'The Inverse Care Law', Copyright (1971) with permission from Elsevier

Page 74: Extract from 'Limits to Medicine: Medical Nemesis, The Expropriation of Health' by Ivan Illich © Marion Boyars Publishers

Page 100: Extract from 'The God Delusion' by Richard Dawkins, published by Bantam Press. Reprinted by permission of The Random House Group Ltd.

Page 123: Photograph © KPA / Zuma / Rex Features

Page 124: Graph based on original © Philippe Rekacewicz, UNEP/GRID-Arendal

http://maps.grida.no/go/graphic/world_population_development

Page 129: Photograph © KPA / Zuma / Rex Features

Every effort has been made to locate copyright holders and obtain permission to reproduce sources. For those sources where it has been difficult to trace the originator of the work, we would be grateful for information. If any copyright holder would like us to make an amendment to the acknowledgements, please notify us and we will gladly update the book at the next reprint. Thank you.

ISBN: 978 1 84762 426 0

With thanks to Laura Jakubowski for the copyright research.

Groovy website: www.cgpbooks.co.uk
Jolly bits of clipart from CorelDRAW®
Printed by Elanders Hindson Ltd, Newcastle upon Tyne.

Based on the classic CGP style created by Richard Parsons.

AS-Level

Sociology

Exam Board: AQA

Culture and Identity

There are lots of different theories about how society shapes individuals — or how individuals shape society.   You need to have a decent idea of what functionalism, Marxism and interpretivism are.

Functionalism *Says the Individual is the Product of* Society

Emile Durkheim (1858-1917) was one of the founders of sociology. In his view, society is made up of various **institutions**, each of which has a useful **function**. So, Durkheim and his followers are known as **functionalists**. They looked at **how society was structured** — you can call functionalism a **structural theory**. Functionalists looked at how institutions in society work, and how they **affect individuals**. Here are some examples:

1) **The Family** — has the function of socialising children.

2) **Education** — has the function of preparing young people for adult society.

3) **Religion** — has the function of uniting society through shared beliefs.

Functionalists believe that the **structures** of society are set up to allow society to **run as smoothly as possible**. Durkheim was keen on the idea that individuals **internalise** the **norms** and **values** (the rules and ideas) of society. This means those norms and values **become a part of who you are** — your personality and your **identity**. The result is **consensus**, which means everyone sharing the **same norms and values**.

Durkheim called the **shared norms and values** that **hold society together** the "**collective consciousness of society**".

> **Definitions**
>
> **Structure** — the way **society operates as a whole**. Individuals have **almost no control** over this.
> **Identity** — an individual's **mental picture** of **herself / himself**.
> **Norms** — ways of **behaving** and / or **thinking** that are seen as **normal** in society.
> **Values** — **beliefs** about what things are **important** and what things are **right** and **wrong**.
> **Culture** — The **combined** effect of **norms** and **values** — a **way of life**.

Not Everyone **Agrees** with **Functionalist** Thinking

1) **Interpretivists** (also called **interactionists**) focus on the **individual** more than functionalists do. They say functionalism is **wrong to ignore the individual**. They think that individuals can choose how to behave, and aren't simply responding to social forces.

2) **Marxists** say functionalism ignores the **unequal power** of some groups. Marxists say the rich have the most influence in defining the norms, values and beliefs in society. They think structures in society are set up to **serve the interests of the rich**, not to keep society ticking along as smoothly as possible.

3) **Postmodernists** say **functionalism is outdated** because it's based on the idea that there's only one dominant or shared culture. Postmodernists argue that today there's a **complex and diverse range** of cultural norms and values.

Marxism *Says the Individual is the Product of* Economic Forces

Karl Marx

Karl Marx (1818-1883) was another of the founders of sociology. He focused on the **effects of capitalism**. He thought that the **economic system (infrastructure)** of a society determined the beliefs and values of that **society (the superstructure)**.

> **Marxists** believe that the most important force in society is **class conflict**

1) In **capitalist societies**, workers are employed to produce goods which are sold by their employers at a **profit**.

2) Only a bit of this profit ends up in the workers' wages — most of it's **kept by the employer**.

3) Marx said that if workers were allowed to **notice the unfairness** of this, they'd revolt. So, to **avoid revolution**, the **capitalist system shapes the superstructure** to make sure that the workers accept their lot in life.

4) **Institutions** like the family, education and religion **lead individuals** into **accepting** the **inequalities of capitalism**.

In other words, Marxists think people are **socialised** into a **culture** based on their **social class**. They think people's **identity** depends on their **class position** in the capitalist system.

Not Everyone **Agrees** with **Marx** either...

1) **Functionalists** say Marx put too much emphasis on the role of **economic structures** in shaping ideas and beliefs.

2) **Interpretivists** say he placed too much emphasis on **class** and not enough on individuals.

3) **Postmodernists** say social class doesn't have such an important influence on individual identity any more. They say people are defined by the choices they make, not by whether they're a worker or a boss.

Culture and Identity

Interpretivists Say Individual Actions are Most Important

Many sociologists say that culture is actually determined by the **behaviour and interaction of individuals**. Theories like this are called **action theories** because they emphasise the **action** of individuals, as opposed to **structural theories** like functionalism and Marxism, which are all about the big structures of society.

Interpretivist (or **interactionist**) theories start with the idea that all individuals **interpret** society around them — people **try to make sense** of society. Interpretivists say that culture comes from **people's own ideas** of how people **interact** with each other.

Interpretivists don't say structures aren't important, but they do suggest that each of us **responds** to social structures in our **own way**. We aren't just products of socialisation — we all have **free will** and make **choices**. An important point here is that the **results of individual choice** can be **large-scale social change**. For example, **Jonathan Gershuny (1992)** made an interpretivist analysis of gender roles in the home.

It's always good to bring an example in.

> 1) Some **women decided** they wanted to **work outside the home**. That's the **individual choice** bit.
>
> 2) Male partners then took on **more childcare** and housework. It became **acceptable** for men to adopt roles in the family that had been considered **feminine**. That's the **large-scale social change** bit.

Labelling Theory Says We're Given Labels which Affect our Behaviour

The **classic example** of labelling theory is the **self-fulfilling prophecy** of **educational failure**. This is where a child is **labelled** as a bad student and then goes on to actually **become** a bad student.

Very **strong labels**, e.g. "**criminal**" or "**pervert**", can take on what's called **master status**, which means they replace an individual's other labels. Someone labelled a criminal could be seen as just a criminal, and **nothing else**.

It's important to remember that labelling theory is a kind of **interpretivism** — it says that the **individual** can choose to accept or reject labels. In other words, being called a failure will only turn you into a failure if you choose to accept the label.

What do you know... Not Everyone Agrees with the Interpretivists either...

Marxists say interpretivists don't pay enough attention to **conflict** or to the fact that some social groups are more **powerful** than others. **Functionalists** say they don't acknowledge the importance of the **socialisation process**.

To **sum up** — here's a nice table showing the **main ideas** of functionalism, Marxism and interpretivism.

Functionalism	Marxism	Interpretivism
Dominant in 1940s and 1950s	Dominant in 1960s and 1970s	Influential in the 1970s
Culture is produced by social structure to create consensus.	Culture is produced by social structure to disguise class conflict.	Culture isn't produced by social structure. Culture is produced by individuals.

Practice Questions

Q1 What's the basic difference between structural and interpretivist approaches?
Q2 Which theorist believed in consensus?
Q3 Which theorist believed in class conflict?

Exam Question

Q1 Explain what is meant by "labelling theory". (2 marks)

Students of the world unite — all you have to lose is your brains...

*Social structure, social action, consensus and conflict are key sociological ideas. If you understand them, many other topics will make a lot more sense. So **learn these pages**. Make sure you can jot down a few sentences about what functionalists, Marxists and interpretivists think about the relationship between individuals and society. Then you'll know you've learnt it.*

Different Types of Culture

In the UK, there's more than one type of culture and there are lots of ways to look at culture — folk vs urban, high vs low, popular culture, global culture...

Culture is a *Way of Life*

Culture means the **language**, **beliefs**, **shared customs**, **values**, **knowledge**, **skills**, **roles** and **norms** in a society. It's the way of life of a **social group** or **society**. Culture is **socially transmitted**. That means it's **passed on** through **socialisation** (see p.10).

> A **subculture** is an identifiable **group** within a culture whose members share **values** and **behaviour patterns** which are **different** from **mainstream norms**, e.g. youth subcultures like punks and goths. Subcultures can be a form of **resistance** to mainstream culture (see p.61).

Mass Culture *replaces* Folk Culture

Folk culture is the culture of **pre-industrial society**. It includes things like folk dances, folk songs, fairy tales, old wives' tales, traditional folk medicine and agricultural rituals. It's mainly passed on through word of mouth. Sociologists have looked at the ways **culture changes** as people move from **villages** into **towns** and **cities**.

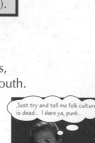

Just try and tell me folk culture is dead... I dare ya, punk...

1) **Robert Redfield (1947)** said that "**folk societies**" were based on strong extended families, **supportive communities** and a **local culture**. In **urban** societies these were **not present**.

2) **Georg Simmel (1950)** argued that **urban societies** showed a **reduced sense of community**, and that urban people were more **individualistic** and **selfish**.

3) Theorists from the **Frankfurt School** said that this reduced sense of community was linked to the development of a **mass culture**. They said that the **media** had become a **strong agent of socialisation**, and it was wiping out the differences between local cultures. Instead, it looked more and more like there was just **one big culture**, shared by **everyone**.

4) These days, the term **mass culture** is used not just to describe the effects of the **media**, but also to refer to **fashion** and other types of **consumption**, e.g. if you eat lunch in a famous burger chain, you're taking part in mass culture.

You can also *Divide* culture up into *"High Culture"* and *"Low Culture"*

The **elite** (better educated, with more money and power) tend to have a **distinct culture** from the **masses**.

1) Shakespeare, opera, sophisticated restaurants and arty French films are the type of things that are associated with "**high culture**".

2) Meanwhile, the masses enjoy **low culture** — e.g. soap operas, reality TV, musicals, fast food and Hollywood films.

This is all linked to the ideas of "class taste", cultural deprivation and cultural capital — see p.56-57.

3) High culture is generally considered more **difficult to appreciate** and the audience is seen as **educated** and having "**good taste**". Aspects of high culture are seen as **good for society**, though they don't make much money compared to a lot of low culture, so the government often **subsidises** them.

4) In recent years a lot of **funding for high culture** has come from a **low culture source** — the National Lottery®. Some customers have been hostile to the idea that the lottery is used to pay for "arty" dance and theatre companies. They suggest it's **elitist culture** — most lottery punters **wouldn't get to see it** and probably **wouldn't like it** if they did.

Many sociologists say there's *No Such Thing* as *"Low Culture"*

1) The ideas of **mass culture** and **low culture** are very **negative**. Some sociologists have argued that this view is based on an **elitist perspective**. For example, **Bourdieu (1984)** says the **whole idea** of "high culture" is just a way of giving **status** to **elite groups** — he says that status is maintained by passing on **cultural knowledge**.

2) Marxists argue that high culture is just ruling class culture, and that the ruling class have imposed their idea of culture on the rest of society, and defined it as "better" than working class culture. Some Marxists argue that so-called "low culture" is just as **complex** and **sophisticated** as "high culture". For that reason, they prefer to use the term "**popular culture**", which is more of a positive idea.

3) Important work on popular culture has been done by the **Centre for Contemporary Cultural Studies** (**CCCS**). They analyse popular culture products like TV, magazines and youth fashions, finding **meanings** within them.

Popular Culture *theorists emphasise that the* Audience is Active

"**Mass**" and "**Low**" culture are both concepts that are based on the idea of a **passive audience**. They assume that the audience is being **manipulated** by the media and doesn't have much control.

"**Popular**" culture is a concept that is based on the idea of an **active audience**. This audience shapes and changes the culture. The CCCS has done a lot of research into the way this happens in youth fashions and subcultures.

Different Types of Culture

There's also a *Global Culture*

Giddens (1990) says that **technological change** has led to globalisation. Goods can be **transported** to anywhere in the world, and **information** can be quickly transmitted across the globe. This has meant that cultures that were once local have become global. For example, British and American pop music is everywhere. American and Indian films are popular internationally.

1) **Klein (2000)** and **Sklair (1995)** point out that a few large **transnational corporations** (TNCs), e.g. Coca-Cola®, NIKE and TimeWarner, are involved in the majority of cultural production, making cultural goods that are consumed all over the world. **Sklair** argues that TNCs and the global media have **more power** than individual **nation states**.

2) Critics of globalisation worry that these TNCs will replace the world's current **cultural diversity** (the differences in people's lifestyles because of the society they live in) with Western culture. They refer to cultural globalisation as **cultural imperialism**. **Klein (2000)** says there's already a trend towards **cultural homogeneity** (everyone having the same culture, wearing the same trainers, eating the same burgers, drinking the same fizzy drinks).

3) Supporters of cultural globalisation argue that it's a **two-way process**. Western culture is transmitted to new societies, and other identities and cultures get passed back to Western societies — e.g. through **Bollywood films** shown in Western mainstream cinemas. With the movement of people from different countries and cultures to other parts of the world, many countries are now **multicultural societies**. Postmodernists argue that this allows people to consume a **plurality** of cultures — this is called **multiculturalism**. They think that globalisation leads to **hybridity** (a **pick and mix**) of cultures rather than one culture being imposed on another.

A *Cultural Industry* is... an *Industry* that *Creates Culture*

1) In pre-industrial times, people mostly **made their own things**, or made things for their **community**. They made their own folk culture — singing folk songs, telling stories round the fire, even... morris dancing.

2) In our capitalist industrial society, we **buy cultural goods** that have been made by the **cultural industries**. Buying goods has become part of the culture of modern, Western society — it's known as **consumer culture**.

3) Some of the most important examples of **cultural industries** are the fashion industry and various media industries such as film, news, music, advertising, broadcasting and the magazine industry. All of these industries create and sell things that fit into people's **cultural lives** — the stuff they **think about**, and **talk about**, and in many cases the stuff that helps them to **define who they are**. Some theorists, e.g. **Featherstone (1991)**, call this "**symbolic consumption**" — see below.

Symbolic Consumption means *Buying Things* that help *Define* who you are

1) In modern industrial societies, **hardly anyone** buys any product based on its **function** alone.

2) For example, most **trainers** are just comfortable shoes — so choosing a pair should be pretty easy, right... yeah, right. The thing is, when most people choose a pair of trainers, they have to make sure that they're the **right brand** and the **right style**. You don't just buy the shoes, you buy what the shoes **stand for** — their "**symbolic value**". What you're actually buying is part of your **identity**.

3) That means that **most industries** in the modern world have actually become **cultural industries**. They're selling things that have some kind of "**cultural meaning**" attached. Any industry that makes things with a **brand image** that **means something** to people, or **stands** for something, is involved in **cultural production**.

Practice Questions

Q1 What is folk culture?
Q2 What is mass culture?
Q3 What is globalisation?
Q4 Give an example of symbolic consumption.

Exam Question

Q1 Assess the view that high culture is elitist. (24 marks)

If I watch X factor on top of Ben Nevis, does that make it high culture?

Culture is everywhere, apparently. Even something as simple as choosing Coke® over PEPSI®, or BURGER KING® over McDonald's, is seen by sociologists as a case of symbolic consumption. In fact, a sociologist would probably see this very book as a cultural product. You need to be familiar with the terms on these pages, because you'll need them to analyse different views of culture in the exam.

Theories of Culture

Some approaches focus on the idea that those in power use popular culture to control those who aren't.

Cultural Decline approaches suggest everything is Getting Worse

The idea that culture is getting worse isn't new. Back in **1869**, **Matthew Arnold** argued that **low culture** (he called it "philistine culture") was **taking over**. Later on, the literary critic **F.R. Leavis (1930)** wrote a great deal about the idea that high culture was in decline. Like Arnold, he felt that **low culture** was **dominant**, and that this was leading to **serious social damage**.

You can still find people expressing Leavis's sort of idea in books and newspaper columns.

A lot of cultural criticism doesn't come from sociologists, but from <u>art critics</u> and <u>literary critics</u>.

The **cultural decline argument** says there's a **cycle of degradation**. It goes like this:

> 1) **High culture** is **refined** and improves its audience as people.
> 2) **Low culture** has **bad values**. It encourages **swearing, violence, uncouth behaviour** and general **lack of respect**.
> 3) Society gets worse because almost **nobody** is exposed to **high culture** and almost **everybody** is exposed to **low culture**.
> 4) As **society** gets **worse**, **low culture** gets **even worse** in response, and in turn brings society down **even further**.

Many critics feel that this is a **snobbish** and **elitist** perspective, which encourages the idea that some people in society are **naturally superior** to others. For example, **Marxists** have mostly been pretty **unsympathetic** to the cultural decline argument. On the other hand, some influential Marxists were very **pessimistic** about **low/mass culture** too, but for different reasons.

Marxism says that the working class are Oppressed by Capitalism via Culture

1) Many Marxists say it's all to do with **ideology**. They say everyone is **tricked** into accepting the idea that everything about society is **just fine**. Marxists from the **Frankfurt School** decided that the **mass media** were the main way of transmitting **capitalist ideology**. (The Frankfurt School began as a group of sociological thinkers in 1930s Germany.)

2) They argued that mass culture **helped capitalism** to oppress the working classes by **destroying community** and **individuality**. It also encouraged **acceptance of authority** and **discouraged** people from **thinking for themselves**.

3) In this way, capitalism used **mass culture** to **prevent revolution** from ever happening.

> Some examples the Frankfurt School pointed out were:
> - **Hollywood films** that distracted ordinary people from social issues, giving them **false dreams** of **glamour** and **adventure**.
> - **Newspaper horoscopes** which suggested that a person's life experiences were down to **luck** or **fate**, rather than social structures or personal actions.
> - TV and radio **advertising** that reinforced the values of capitalism.

Marxists said capitalism creates False Needs and Commodity Fetishism

1) **Capitalism** is based on **selling things**. According to Frankfurt School sociologists **Adorno and Horkheimer (1944)** mass culture encourages you to think you **"need"** to **buy things** which you don't need at all, such as a cupboard full of shoes, or an iPod®. You **don't** actually **need** these things in the same way you need **food** and **water** and **oxygen**, but it's **good for capitalism** if you **think** you do. That's **false need**.

2) Another Marxist idea is **commodity fetishism**. This is where false needs create **obsessions** and **desires** about consumer goods — **"must-have"** objects. An example of this is when a new mobile phone comes out and everyone wants it. **Golding and Murdock (1991)** suggest that people buy products because capitalism promotes goods via the media.

3) **Adorno and Horkheimer** said commodity fetishism was like a **religion**.

4) According to them, the really clever trick is that **capitalism creates desires** that **only capitalism can satisfy**. This means we all end up thinking **capitalism** is a **good** thing, because it gives us **exactly what we want**.

> So to sum up, the **Frankfurt School** took a **pessimistic** approach to mass culture:
> - Mass culture is used to **dull the minds** of the **working classes**.
> - Mass culture promotes **capitalist ideology**.
> - **Commodity fetishism** encourages **economic activity**.
> - The population are **passive victims** of mass culture.

Arnold liked his job, but had misunderstood when they had asked him to knead the bread.

Theories of Culture

Not All Marxists agree with the Frankfurt School

1) The Italian thinker **Antonio Gramsci** (1891-1937) said that the idea of a **single mass culture** was too **simplistic**.

2) **Gramsci (1971)** thought that capitalism creates a big **dominant culture**. He called this dominance **hegemony**.

3) Gramsci believed that **capitalism** had to **tolerate** some oppositional cultures, rather than stamp them out. By **allowing some opposition** to exist, he said, capitalism could create the **illusion** that it was a **fair** and **free** system.

4) He had a big influence on the work of Marxists like **Stuart Hall** of the **Centre for Contemporary Cultural Studies**. Hall says that **youth subcultures** help working class youths to **resist capitalist values**.

5) Hall, and other neo-Marxists who take a more positive, optimistic view of modern culture, prefer the term **popular culture** to mass culture.

> Gramsci wrote most of his theories in prison, in the 1930s. His prison notebooks were published much later. That's why the date of publication is well after he died.

Hegemony — nothing to do with dominant hedges. Apparently.

Feminism links popular culture to Socialisation and Patriarchy

Where Marxists see the mass media as promoting **capitalism**, feminists have concentrated on representations of **gender roles**. During the 1970s and 1980s, many feminists researched the relationship between **popular culture** and **gender socialisation**.

Most of these studies suggested that popular culture **stereotypes** women into roles — such as housewife or sex object. These roles are then **reinforced** in society.

1) **Ferguson (1983)** and **McRobbie (1978)** studied magazines, and found that they promoted traditional female roles.

2) **Radical feminists**, such as **Andrea Dworkin (1981)** in her study of pornography, suggest that many images of women in popular culture encourage and justify **violence** against women.

3) More recently, some feminists have argued that popular cultural representations of women can also be **empowering**. For example, **Camille Paglia** has written a lot about Madonna's public image as a strong female role model.

Practice Questions

Q1 Explain what is meant by "cultural decline".

Q2 How do the Frankfurt School view popular culture?

Q3 Explain how popular culture could be said to stereotype women.

Exam Question

Q1 Explain what is meant by 'commodity fetishism'. (2 marks)

Capitalism didn't tell me to want a new phone — the TV advert did...

According to the Frankfurt School, I didn't really need that Mina dress after all. If only Theodor Adorno could have texted me to tell me. Sigh. Anyway, make sure you know the nuts and bolts of these theoretical approaches, because you'll need them if you want to get top level marks. Without mentioning relevant theorists, you aren't going to win the examiner over.

Theories of Culture

Get ready for some hardcore theory. This is the stuff that really shows those examiners that you know what you're talking about. Modernism, pluralism and postmodernism — it can look brain-bursting to start with, but once you get the key ideas, it all just falls into place.

Modernist *sociologists believe society can be understood* Scientifically

Modernism is a word that's used to mean many different things. In sociology it refers to the "**classical sociological**" approaches of **Marx** and **Durkheim**. Those two certainly didn't agree about everything, but they had some similar **beliefs** which meant that they can both be seen as modernist.

- They both believed that society was a **structure** — an organised system.
- They both believed that **social structures controlled individuals**, never the other way around.
- They both believed in the idea of **progress** — society improving over time.
- They both believed a **scientific approach** could explain society.

Marxism and functionalism are also known as <u>structuralist</u> viewpoints because they focus on structure.

In Modernism *there are* Two Opposing Views *of* Culture

1) The **Marxist** perspectives start from the idea that culture creates **false consciousness**. Marxists believe culture is all set up to reinforce the **class structure** and to **distract** the working classes from realising that they're being **oppressed**. According to Marx, this helps prevent **revolution** from taking place.

2) Marx thought that the working classes would eventually **realise** that they were being tricked and the **false consciousness** created by capitalist culture would be replaced by **class consciousness**. Then **revolution** would come. The **Frankfurt School** perspective described on p.6 is a good example of Marxist modernism.

1) Durkheim's **functionalist** perspective describes culture as a kind of **social glue**. It bonds people together by creating shared interests and purposes.

2) It also helps to **socialise** people into appropriate behaviour. This prevents society from breaking down into chaos.

It should be pretty clear that **Marx** and **Durkheim** saw culture as doing basically the **same thing** — **controlling people**. The difference was, Marx thought that this was a bad thing, while Durkheim believed it was necessary and good.

Semiotic Analysis *looks for* Hidden Structures *of* Meaning

1) An important approach to popular culture is semiotics. This perspective is based on the ideas of the linguist **Ferdinand de Saussure** (1857-1913). Saussure was a **structuralist** — he thought that meaning was found in the **structure** of language, rather than in the **individual words** of a language.

2) According to semiotics, society is full of **signifiers** (words, symbols and images) — which create **meanings**.

3) Meanings can be either **denoted** or **connoted**. **Denoted** (or denotative) meanings are **obvious**. **Connoted** (or connotative) meanings are **suggested** — you don't see them right away, and may only notice them **subconsciously**.

4) For example, a **picture** of a gun **denotes** a gun. A picture of a gun **connotes** all sorts of things — **power**, **masculinity**, **death**, **gangsters**, **fear** and so on.

5) Quite a lot of **sociological work** on culture now involves **semiotic analysis**, looking for the **connotative** meanings of cultural objects. This can be from all kinds of perspectives. For example, **Dick Hebdige (1979)** took a **Marxist** approach to his semiotic analysis of **punk**, while **Ann DuCille's (1996)** analysis of the Barbie™ doll was focused on **feminism** and **ethnicity**.

Theories of Culture

Pluralists say we have Power through Choice

Pluralists think that popular culture **reflects society**.

1) They argue that there is a **range of consumer goods** available which gives people lots of **choice**, e.g. different magazines, different brands of trainers, different films to go and see.

2) People have the **power to choose** the products they like — this is called **consumer power**. Consumers are **active**, not passive.

3) The cultural industry **takes notice** of what consumers want — it's in their interests to **create products** that people will **buy**.

4) Therefore, it is the **consumers** who **shape popular culture** — not the other way round.

The chin-flator 5000. Surely a must-have?

However, not everyone agrees with the pluralists. For example, **Ien Ang (1991)** suggests that the **opinions** of consumers are largely **ignored** by the cultural industry.

Postmodernism argues that Culture is Diverse

1) Postmodernists reject the idea that culture helps to unify people in society. Instead they argue that **culture is increasingly diverse**.

2) Postmodernists like **Stuart Hall (1992)** say that this diversity results in **fragmented identities**. People can **construct their identity** from a range of different cultures. Layers of identity can include nationality, gender, ethnicity, religion and political beliefs.

3) Hall links this with the rise of **new social movements** such as feminism, black power, and the green movement. He also links this with **globalisation** — as a response to cultural globalisation, people have constructed new identities such as "Black British", "British Muslim", "Somali living in London" etc.

4) The way people **use culture** reflects their **fragmented identity**. Some sociologists have looked at the way that British Asians pick and mix aspects of traditional **Indian** and **Pakistani** culture, black **hip-hop culture** and British **urban** culture to make a **hybrid culture**.

Postmodernists say signifiers are more powerful than the things they signify

1) In other words, the **name** and **image** we give to something has more meaning than the thing itself.

2) There are lots of examples in popular culture — e.g. **brands**. Look at the counterfeit "label" goods on any street market in the country. The **only selling point** for a cheaply made, **fake Gucci watch** is the **name** on the product.

3) **Baudrillard (1981)** suggests that in the postmodern age **symbols** have become **commodities**, and that we no longer buy products for what they **are** but for the things they **represent**.

Practice Questions

Q1 What does modernism mean?

Q2 What is semiotic analysis?

Q3 What is consumer power?

Q4 What did Stuart Hall mean by "fragmented identities"?

Exam Question

Q1 Assess the view that culture helps to unify society. (24 marks)

What a load of Baudrillard...

The modernist viewpoints ought to be familiar — it's only old functionalism and Marxism all over again. Pluralists think ordinary people have some control over culture. Postmodernists are obsessed with symbolism. And Scientologists think that people were brought to Earth by the alien ruler Xenu in a spacecraft 75 million years ago... Fortunately you don't need to revise that last lot.

Socialisation and Social Roles

Most sociologists believe you have to learn how to fit into society, e.g. learn how to behave and what to believe. This process is called socialisation. It begins in childhood and continues throughout life. As usual in Sociology, there are different views about how it all works…

Socialisation is the passing on of Culture

1) **Culture** is a key term for this section. It means the **"way of life"** of a society — things like language, customs, knowledge, skills, roles, values and norms. Culture is **passed on** through **socialisation** from generation to generation.

2) **Norms** are **social rules** about **correct behaviour**. For example, by queuing in a shop or wearing formal clothes to a job interview, you're conforming to norms. **Laws** often reflect norms, but sometimes lawbreaking is the norm. Making illegal copies of CDs is a good example of this.

3) **Values** are more **generalised beliefs and goals**. Ideas like "freedom of speech", "respect for human life" or "equality" are all **values**.

4) **Culture, values and norms** are **not fixed**. They **vary** according to the time and place. For example, British culture is different from American culture, and today's culture is different from the culture of 30 years ago.

Sociologists say that through socialisation the **norms and values** of society are **internalised** — i.e. they become part of everyone's way of thinking.

There are two kinds of socialisation — **primary socialisation** and **secondary socialisation**.

There is only one Agent of Primary Socialisation — The Family

Primary socialisation comes first. In **early childhood**, individuals learn the **skills**, **knowledge**, **norms** and **values** of society. This all happens in three ways:

1) Children **internalise** norms and values by **imitating their parents / guardians**.

2) Children are **rewarded** for **socially acceptable behaviour**.

3) Children are **punished** for **socially "deviant" behaviour**.

> Children who are deprived of social contact during development often can't function as social adults. In 1970, an American girl known as "Genie" was discovered. She'd been locked up by her father for her first 13 years and never managed to recognise even basic social norms.

There are many Agents of Secondary Socialisation

Secondary socialisation comes after primary socialisation and **builds on it**. It's carried out by **various institutions**. The most important are **education**, **peer groups**, **religion** and the **mass media**.

Education

The education system aims to pass on **knowledge and skills** such as reading and numeracy. Learning these skills is a part of socialisation, but sociologists suggest that **education socialises individuals in other ways** as well:

1) **Functionalists**, like Durkheim, believe that school **promotes consensus** by **teaching norms and values**. They also say children learn to value belonging to a **larger group** through things like school uniform and assembly. All this is important for **fitting into society**.

2) **Marxists**, such as **Bowles and Gintis (1976)** believe education operates a **hidden curriculum** that socialises pupils into **ruling class cultures** and encourages them to **accept exploitation**. The curriculum is the **content** of education. Marxists reckon there are two sorts — the acknowledged curriculum (maths, English, geography etc.) and the hidden curriculum (doing as you're told and not questioning authority).

Peer Groups

Peer groups are made up of people of **similar social status**. The peer group can **influence norms and values**. This can be towards **conformity** or **deviance**. **Youth subcultures** sometimes encourage **deviant** behaviour, like joyriding.

> Conformity = doing what society likes
> Deviance = doing what society doesn't like

Religion

Religion often provides **social norms and values**. Most religions oppose theft and murder, and teach respect for elders.

Mass Media

The **mass media** are **powerful** in shaping norms and values in the audience. Some sociologists (e.g. Althusser) argue that the media have now **replaced religion** in secondary socialisation.

The Workplace

Workplace socialisation involves learning the norms and values that enable people to fit into the world of work, such as being on time and obeying the boss.

Socialisation and Social Roles

Individuals *have* Social Roles *and* Status

Like it says on the last page, **socialisation** is the process that turns individuals into members of a social culture. According to some sociological perspectives, an important result of socialisation is that each individual ends up with a number of **roles**. These are associated with different sorts of **status**. This is a bit tricky, so concentrate.

1)   Your **status** is your **position** in a **hierarchy**. You can have low status or high status. It's the respect and recognition others give to your position. The Queen is a **person**, but being Queen is a **status**.

2)   Your **roles** are the **behaviours and actions** you take on **because of your status**. In sociological terms, a role is a set of norms that go with a status. The Queen has to meet the public and show an interest, she has to speak to the nation on TV on Christmas Day, and she has to travel abroad and meet leaders of other countries. These are all **roles**.

Status can be ascribed or achieved

Ascribed status is fixed at **birth**. For example the Queen (this is the last time with that example, I promise) **inherited her status** from her father (who was King, not Queen, obviously) when he died.
Head teachers, on the other hand, have **achieved** status. This means they've **earned** it through **education** and **work**. This is a **very important difference** for sociological arguments about gender, class and ethnic identities.

Social *Behaviour is* Regulated *by* Social Control

1)   Socialisation puts **limits** on people's behaviour. The functionalist Durkheim called this **constraint** (it's also known as **social control**). If it weren't for internalised norms and values, people would **do what they liked**. Internalised norms and values are like having a **little police officer inside your head**, stopping you from doing wrong and crazy things.

2)   Functionalists say that socialisation creates a **consensus**, where everyone has the **same values and norms**.

3)   It's important for people to **conform** to the norms and values of society. When people conform to the expectations, they're **rewarded**. When people **don't conform** to social expectations, they're **punished**. Sociologists call these punishments **sanctions**. Sociologists call behaviour which doesn't conform to society's expectations **deviant**.

Society is Diverse

Functionalists say that there's a **consensus** of shared values and norms in society. It's true that many values and norms are shared across the whole of society, but there's actually a lot of **variation**. There are **many different cultures** in today's society — it's **multicultural**.

Postmodernists are big on the idea of **personal choice**. They say that in today's society people have a large amount of choice in their actions and behaviour — and in the values that they believe in.

Sociologists *argue that* Nurture *is* More Important *than* Nature

1)   Everyone agrees that you can inherit **physical characteristics** like eye colour from your **parents** — but it's **debatable** whether you can inherit **personality traits** like being good at Maths. This is called the **nature vs. nurture debate**.

2)   Most **sociologists** prefer the idea that it's **society** that **shapes** your **behaviour** and **personality**. They argue that it's the **process of socialisation** that makes you the person you are, e.g. the influence of family, peer groups and education.

3)   It's often **difficult to prove** whether **biology** or **socialisation** has resulted in a characteristic — both your genetic make-up and your social influences are **extremely complex**.

4)   It's likely that people are formed by a **mixture** of **biological** and **social influences**. For example, if parents are intelligent they will probably pass on the biological potential to be intelligent to their children, but they will also nurture them to be intelligent, e.g. through encouraging them to read and giving them educational toys.

Practice Questions

Q1   When in a person's life does socialisation occur: (a) in early childhood, (b) in adolescence, or (c) throughout life?

Q2   Name five agents of secondary socialisation.

Q3   What is a role?

Exam Question

Q1   Explain what is meant by ascribed status.

(2 marks)

And I thought socialisation was just something to do down the pub...

Socialisation is the process by which people learn to be members of society. The main things I remember learning when I was young are to only speak when spoken to, to always eat my greens, not to play with a football in the house, not to take sweets from strangers, not to pogo stick next to the cliff and not to offer myself as food to stray lions. Though I learnt that last one the hard way.

Class Identities

The following pages explore different aspects of social identity starting with class.

'Identity' is a tricky concept in Sociology

Identity can be a bit of a slippery concept, so best to nail it down right at the start...

1) At a basic level, your **personal identity** is the sort of stuff that would appear on an identity card — name, age, physical appearance, distinguishing marks, place of birth. These are **easily checked**, hard to change **facts** about who you are.

2) In **Sociology**, identity has a **deeper meaning**. It refers to the **way we see ourselves**, and the **way others see us**. This sort of identity comes from things that are more **complicated**, and sometimes **less fixed**, than the basic identity card stuff. Social class, ethnicity, friendships, work, gender, age and sexuality are all factors that contribute to your **social identity**.

3) Your social identity is often linked to **roles you perform** in society (e.g. daughter, student, volunteer, best friend) as well as the **social groups** you are a part of (e.g. female, middle class, Asian, teenager).

Societies are Stratified — Divided into Layers

1) **Social class** is an important part of **identity**. Most societies are **stratified** by social class.

2) **Stratification** is the division of societies into **layers**. The **richest** and **most powerful** are at the **top**, the **poorest** and **most powerless** are at the **bottom**. In between are lots of **strata** (which means layers, like the layers in rock) organised in a **hierarchy**. **Social class** is the main stratification system in **modern, Western capitalist societies**, such as the **contemporary UK**.

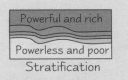

Powerful and rich

Powerless and poor

Stratification

There are Four Key Classes

For the **census** the **government** uses a scale called the **National Statistics Socio-Economic Classification** (NS-SEC). It has **eight classes** based on the **jobs** people do:

- higher management and professional
- lower management and professional (e.g. teacher, nurse)
- intermediate (jobs without managerial responsibilities, mostly in service industries)
- small employers and self-employed (e.g. restaurant-owner, plumber)
- lower supervisory and technical (e.g. builder's foreman, salesfloor supervisor)
- semiroutine (skilled services and manual work)
- routine (usually unskilled work)
- never worked / long-term unemployed.

Sociologists usually talk about just **four basic social classes**:

1) The **upper class** are **wealthy** and **powerful**. The original upper class was the **landowning aristocracy**. Their wealth is **passed on from generation to generation**. People who have made a lot of money from business or from the entertainment industry are also sometimes considered to be upper class.

2) The **middle class** earn their money from **non-manual work**. Teachers, doctors, managers and pretty much anyone who **earns their living sitting in an office** are middle class. The middle class is **getting bigger** because there are **more non-manual jobs** these days, and fewer manual jobs.

3) The **working class** make their money from **manual work**. Farm labourers and factory workers are working class. The working class have **poorer life chances** than the middle class.

4) The **underclass** get their money from **state benefits**. They include the long-term unemployed and the homeless. The underclass have **the poorest life chances**.

Sociologists have most often focused on the division between the **middle class** and the **working class**. Marx divided society into just two classes — the **proletariat** (the workers) and the **bourgeoisie** (the bosses).

Class Identities

Class Culture Affects Identity

Sociologists often link **identity** to **social class**. **Who you are** is connected to your **class culture** and **class identity**.

1) **Barry Sugarman (1970)** argued that middle class and working class children are socialised into **different norms and values**. **Middle class** children are encouraged to plan for the future (**deferred gratification**) whereas **working class children** are encouraged to live for the moment (**immediate gratification**). Deferred gratification is a big part of studying and training for a **professional career**.

2) **Charles Murray (1994)**, a New Right thinker, suggested that **certain values keep people poor**, for example believing in the **acceptability** of living on **state benefits**. He argued these values are **passed on** from one generation to the next.

3) **John Scott (1991)** looked at the ways the **upper class** use the **public school system** (this means the **top private schools** like Eton and Rugby) to create **social networks** which then follow through into **high status universities** (such as Oxford).

4) In the state education system, **middle class children** tend to form **pro-school subcultures** (such as homework clubs) and are more likely to be placed in top sets. **Working class children** are more likely to be **anti-school** and to find themselves in lower sets. (For further detail on this, see pages 56–57.)

Bourdieu said the Upper Class use Cultural Capital

1) **Pierre Bourdieu** argued that the upper class **maintains its position** (on top, that is) by passing on **cultural capital**. This means the **knowledge** and **social skills** you need to fit in to the top level of society. It includes things like knowing **which knife and fork to use**, knowing the **"right" way to speak** and having an appreciation of **high culture** such as opera and ballet.

2) He also said that **middle class** families try to **develop cultural capital** in their own children in order to **improve** their class position. These parents **encourage** their children to read "good" books, experience theatres, go to art galleries and so on.

3) By contrast, he said that **working class** families **don't develop** this form of **cultural capital**.

Many Sociologists say Class Isn't the Most Important Influence any more

1) Most sociologists agree that identity used to be based on how and where people **earned their money** (social class). Many **postmodernists** say that these days identity is based on how and where people **spend** their money (consumption).

2) They also claim that people's **leisure activities** are **no longer class based**.

3) Traditional **working class** activities included things like **bingo**, **darts** and the **pub**. The **middle classes** were associated with **DIY**, **dinner parties**, **golf** and **bridge**.

4) Nowadays, lifestyles are based more on **individual choice** than class background. Middle class people do traditional working class leisure activities and vice versa.

Postmodernists also argue that there isn't any difference between high and low culture any more — globalisation means people have access to a range of media images in an instant, resulting in a mass culture (see p 4)

1) **New Right** theorist **Peter Saunders (1990)** argues that today an individual's identity **isn't** based on social class. He claims that the old **divisions** between social classes have **disappeared** in our modern, **equal opportunities** society.

2) **Marshall (1988)** suggests that the working class still see themselves as working class, but they are more **fragmented** than in the past due to the **loss of traditional industries**. This has meant that traditional working class identities have weakened.

Practice Questions

Q1 What are the four social classes usually discussed in sociology?
Q2 What does the term 'immediate gratification' mean?
Q3 Briefly outline Charles Murray's views about culture and poverty.
Q4 According to Marshall, why have working class identities become fragmented?

Exam Questions

Q1 Explain what is meant by the term 'cultural capital'. (2 marks)

Some very classy pages to revise...

Most sociologists are keen on figuring out what makes the working class different from the middle class. Agents of socialisation like the family and social class (see p.10) are a common explanation. Postmodernists, on the other hand, argue that social class doesn't really exist in this twenty-first century world.

Gender Identities

Gender is about masculinity and femininity (as opposed to straightforward biological boy/girl differences).

Sex is Not the Same as Gender

In sociology, **sex** means the **biological differences** between men and women. **Gender** means the aspects of **masculinity** and **femininity** that are **not biological** but **cultural**. They are **learned through socialisation**.

Sociologists focus on **gender**. One reason for this is that there are **gender inequalities** in education and employment that **can't be explained** by the **biological** differences between men and women.

The Family is the Primary Agent of Gender Socialisation

Ann Oakley's (1974) research led her to identify **four** ways in which **family life** usually teaches children the **norms** and **values** associated with **masculinity** and **femininity**:

1) **Manipulation** — parents **often encourage** "normal" behaviour and interests for the child's sex and **discourage** what's seen as **deviant**. This **manipulates** the child's self-image — the child becomes interested in "normal" behaviours. For example, girls are often dressed up in pretty dresses so that being pretty becomes important to them. Girls are sometimes told off for being "unladylike" — shouting, playing loudly, getting mucky.

2) **Canalisation** — parents often **channel** their **children's interest** in particular directions. **Boys** may be given **construction toys** like LEGO® and **aggressive toys** like toy guns. **Girls** may be given **beauty toys** like toy jewellery and make-up, **mothering toys** like dolls and prams, or **housewife toys** like toy kitchens.

3) **Verbal appellation** — parents may **use language and names** to **define what's appropriate**. For example, "you're an angel" (girl) versus "you're a cheeky monkey" (boy), or "what a beautiful little girl" versus "what a big strong boy".

4) **Different activities** — parents may involve children in **different aspects** of the **household**. For example, girls help wash the dishes, boys help wash the car.

School is a Secondary Agent of Gender Socialisation...

For more on the experiences of boys and girls at school see p.60–61.

1) Girls and boys are treated **differently** in **education**. Sociologists say that education passes on **gender stereotyped assumptions** about how males and females should behave. Remember that gender stereotyped assumptions can **disadvantage boys** as well as girls.

2) There are still **gender differences** in **subject choice**. Boys are more likely to study science subjects (especially physics) and I.T. at AS / A2 level. Girls tend to dominate in art and English literature.

3) **Skelton (2002)** argues that schools both create gender stereotypes and maintain those learnt at home.

...and so are the Media

1) The **mass media** help to build gender roles. For example, **females** in Hollywood films are often presented as **weak**, in need of rescuing by a strong male hero.

2) **Angela McRobbie (1978)** has argued that teenage female magazines **reinforce conventional notions of femininity**, emphasising the importance of getting and keeping a man, being "beautiful" and so on.

Awww, kittens

3) **Wolf (1990)** suggests that **advertising** tends to present an unobtainable **'ideal image'** for women, reinforcing the notion that women should **look good** for **men**.

4) **Joan Smith**, in her 1997 book *Different for Girls*, also argued that **culture creates** and **perpetuates** gender differences.

Gender Stereotypes can Affect Employment Opportunities

1) **Traditional gender roles** can have an **impact** upon the **opportunities** and **experiences** of men and women in the workplace and at home. According to Social Trends 38 (2008), **19% of men** are employed as **managers or senior officials**, compared to **11% of women**.

2) It is still difficult for women to reach the **top levels** of **traditionally 'male' professions**. For example, the majority of **judges** are male.

Gender Identities

Gender Roles are Changing — for Females...

1) In the **1970s**, when Sue Sharpe first researched **teenage girls' attitudes**, she found they valued **marriage** and **motherhood**. When she repeated the research in the **1990s**, she found that this generation of teenage girls stressed their **career ambitions**.

2) **Diana Gittins (1993)** looked at the **rising divorce rate** and said this was evidence that women's **attitudes to marriage** had changed a great deal. They were much **less willing** to **accept** relationships they weren't happy with. This was a sign that the old **passive female gender roles** were a **thing of the past**.

3) One important factor is the fact that more women **go out to work**, and earn good money. It is now more common for women to be the **biggest earners** or only earners in their household than it was in the past. The increase in office-based work is referred to as the **feminisation of the workforce**.

4) There has also been an **increase** in **female deviant behaviour** — for example girl gangs, as studied by **Ann Campbell (1984)**.

...And for Males

1) Research by **Jonathan Gershuny (1992)** shows that **childcare** and **housework** are **shared** between men and women much more than in the past. The so-called **"new man"** does the dishes and changes the baby's nappies. Statistics show an increase in the number of **househusbands** — men who stay at home, cook, clean and care while their female partners go out to work.

2) One cause of men staying at home might be the **loss of traditional jobs** and **roles** for men. **Heavy industry has declined** and the majority of jobs now require **traditionally feminine skills** such as communication. Boys aren't socialised to have these skills as much as girls are, and girls are now socialised to be ambitious and dominant — traditionally masculine traits.

3) **Máirtín Mac an Ghaill (1994)** says these changes have led to a **crisis of masculinity** where **men no longer know** what their role should be. This idea says that men are **shut out** from their **traditional** roles, and **not adequately socialised** to be able to **fit into new roles**.

Masculinity in the Media has Become Feminised

1) **Rutherford (1996)** points out that images of men in the media are now being used in traditionally female ways — i.e. to be ogled at. Male stripper groups like the Chippendales are a good example. He also looks at the marketing of **men's cosmetics and toiletries**. There are far **more** of these products now than in the past, and the images used to advertise them are often of **half-naked male models**. These are signs that men's roles have moved closer to women's. Rutherford calls this the **feminisation of masculinity**.

2) **Wilkinson (1997)** suggested that increasingly male and female **values** are **coming together**, with both men and women **creating** their **own identities**.

Findings like this have led some sociologists to believe that **traditional ideas** of **masculinity** and **femininity** are now in **decline**. **Postmodernists** say that **both men and women** now see **consumption** and **leisure** as the **key factors** in shaping their **identity**, rather than masculinity and femininity.

Practice Questions

Q1 What is the difference between sex and gender?
Q2 Name two secondary agents of gender socialisation.
Q3 What did Rutherford mean by the "feminisation of masculinity"?

Exam Questions

Q1 Suggest two ways in which gender roles are changing. (4 marks)

Q2 Outline three ways that agents of socialisation influence femininity. (6 marks)

I never liked pink much anyway...

With these pages, you need to learn about traditional masculinity and femininity AND how these gender roles are changing as society changes. As usual, those postmodernists claim nothing matters any more except shopping and leisure. Wasters.

Ethnic Identities

British society includes many different ethnic groups. Ethnicity can be an important part of identity. Not to forget gender, religion, class, nationality and occupation. One thing you can say for identity — it ain't simple...

Sociologists Use the Term Ethnicity, not Race

Race is a way of classifying people by **visible biological features**, like skin colour or bone structure. The idea of race is linked to **racism**, the idea that some races are inferior to others.

That's one reason most sociologists agree **ethnicity** is a better term to use when you're talking about society. People from the same **ethnic group share** the **same culture** and **socialisation**.

Ethnic Minorities have Different Cultural Features

Ethnic minorities in the UK are mostly people whose families came here from former colonies like **Jamaica** and **India** in the **1950s and afterwards**. Statistics from the **2001 census** say **7.9% of the population** are from ethnic minorities.

> Ethnic minorities have distinctive **cultural features** from their countries and **cultures** of origin. This means stuff like **values**, **customs**, **religion**, **diet**, **language** and **clothing**. These **cultural features** give each ethnic minority its **ethnic identity**.

It's a long time since the 1950s, so Britain's ethnic minorities have been through a lot of **changes**. The way **ethnic identity changes over time**, from one generation to the next, is something a lot of sociologists study (see below).

Culture based on **shared origin** is still an **important influence** on **ethnic identity** though. Some ethnic groups work hard to keep distinctive cultural features going. For example, **Modood et al (1997)** suggested that cultural origins still play a key role in influencing the behaviour of Asians, particularly the older generation.

Children are Socialised into an Ethnic Identity

Quite a few studies have looked at the way **parents pass on ethnic identity** to their children. This is primary socialisation — the socialisation that takes place as part of family life.

1) **Rosemary Hill (1987)** found **the family** was very **important** in the Leicester Asian community. She also said that some children learned "Western" ideas about marriage, education, work and so on from white peers. Hill thought this led to **generational conflict** between parents and children from ethnic minorities.

2) **Roger Ballard (1994)** disagreed. He found that young Asians **negotiated** the two aspects of their lives (home and outside the home). That meant that at **home** they'd behave in **traditional** ways to fit in with their parents, but **outside** the home they'd "**act Western**".

3) **Shaun Hides (1995)** studied the use of **artefacts** in ethnic minority homes. He was interested in the way things like **furniture**, **pictures**, **ornaments** and **religious items** helped **reinforce** ethnic identity. Hides found that the wearing of **traditional dress** was a really important part of this. **Women** wore traditional dress **more often** than men, and Hides concluded that **women** had the most **important role** in keeping ethnic identity going.

Ethnic Identity is Also Created by Secondary Socialisation

1) **Racism** in British society can affect secondary socialisation. For example, studies by **David Gillborn (1990)** and **Cecile Wright (1992)** suggest that Afro-Caribbean pupils are often **labelled** as a **problem** by teachers. This can lead to a **self-fulfilling prophecy** where pupils form an **anti-school subculture** because that's what the school seems to **expect** them to do.

2) The **peer group** is important too. Academic **Tony Sewell** said in an interview in **2000** that he thinks young Afro-Caribbean males are too influenced by popular culture. He believes that they encourage each other to be interested in **expensive consumer goods** (e.g. cars, the latest mobile phones, clothes) instead of **education**.

Ethnic Identities

Some Sociologists Say that *Ethnic Identities* are a *Response to Racism*

1) When **Afro-Caribbean** and **Asian** families first arrived in Britain, they faced a lot of **prejudice** from the white population.

2) Some people from ethnic minorities felt there **wasn't any point** trying to **integrate** into the mainstream.

3) One way minorities responded to **discrimination** in work, housing and education was to **hold on** to their **ethnic identity** and **resist** full assimilation into the mainstream.

4) **Cashmore and Troyna (1990)** show how people in ethnic minorities turned to **each other** for **support**, for example in religious groups like the (mostly black) **Pentecostal Church**.

New Ethnic Identities are Emerging

1) **Stuart Hall (1996)** talks about **new ethnicities** which are very **varied**. He says that the **old ideas** of condensing ethnicity to **white / black** are being **challenged**. There are lots of **different kinds** of Asian ethnicity and black ethnicity. Hall also points out that for ethnic minority people, **gender** identity, **class** identity and **sexuality** can actually be **as important** or **more important** than ethnic identity.

2) Many sociologists argue that **young people** from **ethnic minority** backgrounds are developing **hybrid identities** — based on a mixture of influences. **Paul Gilroy (1987)** examined how black and white culture has become mixed together. **Maria Gillespie (1995)** looked at how young Sikhs brought bits of **mainstream popular culture** together with **Punjabi traditions**.

3) **Tariq Modood (1997)** found that **ethnic identities** were **changing**. Things like wearing **ethnic clothes** were **less important** for young people than for their parents. **Younger** people were more likely to be **political** and **upfront** about their **ethnic identity**. On the other hand, second generation immigrants were **more likely** to **see themselves** as **British** or partly British than first generation immigrants.

4) **Basit's (1997)** study suggested that ethnic identities are **dynamic** and **changeable**. Basit's interviews with British Asian schoolgirls suggested that they **combine elements** of both British and Asian cultures. They created their identity based on their Asian culture's **ethnicity**, **language** and **religion**, but in the **context** of a **British society**. This made their identity particularly **unique**, as the girls' parents thought that their daughters would not feel as **comfortable** if they were to go to Pakistan or Bangladesh to live, because of the **impact of British culture** upon them.

Practice Questions

Q1 What's the difference between 'race' and 'ethnicity'?

Q2 What makes ethnic minorities distinctive from the mainstream population?

Q3 How can secondary socialisation affect ethnic identity?

Q4 Briefly outline the view that ethnic identities are a response to racism.

Q5 What are Stuart Hall's views about the emergence of new ethnicities?

Q6 What are hybrid identities?

Exam Questions

Q1	Suggest two ways in which the family may influence ethnic identities.	(4 marks)
Q2	Examine sociological explanations for the emergence of new ethnic identities.	(24 marks)

So many identities, so little time...

Sociology is full of these "hot button" topics. Debates about racism, identity and multiculturalism come up in the newspapers and on the radio fairly often. For you as a sociology student, the important thing is to know the main theories about how ethnic identity is learnt by socialisation — and to know some key studies so you can quote them in your answers.

18

National Identities

Yup. Yet more aspects of identity.

National Identity is about Feeling you Belong to a Country and its People

Durkheim said that national identity (nationalism) has an important function. It makes **individuals** feel that they **belong** to a **larger group**. **Benedict Anderson (1983)** reckons that **nationalism has replaced religion** in giving people's lives meaning.

National identity can have **negative** effects. It can be used to **exclude** certain groups. For example, if someone defines being British as being **white**, then they are **excluding black and Asian British people**. When an organisation excludes ethnic minorities like this, it's called **institutional racism**.

1) **Symbols** and **rituals** are important to national identity. The symbols of a nation's identity include things like its **currency**, its **flag**, and its **national anthem**.

2) Every nation has its own **national rituals**. These are events when people are **expected** to **think** about what it **means** to be English, or Scottish or French, and so on. A good example from Britain is **Remembrance Sunday** when there are processions and ceremonies to remember British soldiers who died fighting in wars.

National Identity is a Product of Socialisation

Schudson (1994) says that individuals are **socialised** into a **national culture** and identity by agents of socialisation such as **education** and the **mass media**. For example, the National Curriculum says all children must learn about Shakespeare. The **hidden curriculum** also contributes by having school celebrations for national events such as the **Queen's Jubilee**, or letting pupils watch "important" national football matches at school.

The **media** are also very important in building up national identity. They do this by **broadcasting national rituals** — things like Royal funerals or the state opening of Parliament.

Stuart Hall (1992) writes about the way each country has its own collection of **stories** about itself. National identity is about **learning** and **sharing** these tales of **wars won**, **great sporting victories** and so on. These are **passed on** from one generation to the next.

Traditional National Identity is on the Decline

Some sociologists suggest that during the last 20 years, people have found it **harder** to **identify** with Britishness. British national identity isn't as strong as it was, and some would say it **doesn't exist** any more. There are a few reasons for this:

1) **Big business** is now **international**, and companies like the McDonald's fast food chain appear all around the world. People in Britain are often **working for companies** based in **Japan**, or **Germany** or the **USA**. Some **British companies** have been **bought by corporations** from **overseas**. Sociologists call this breaking down of national boundaries **globalisation**.

2) Mainstream **TV**, **fashion**, **music** and **film** are often dominated by **American products**. Many people think that the result of this is that Britain and other countries are **losing their own cultures**.

3) Britain today is **multi-ethnic**. It contains many **different** groups, religions and languages.

4) Britain has strong **regional differences**. Scotland, Wales and Northern Ireland have strong national identities of their own. Under the New Labour government, regional identities have been given a boost by **devolution** — regions being given **more political power** by central government, e.g. the creation of the National Assembly for Wales in 1998.

New National Identities are Being Formed

The old "Britishness" is partly being replaced by a **new multicultural national identity**. Things like food, fashion and music bring together **British traditions** with **multicultural influences** from **inside Britain** and **international influences** from the **rest of the world**. Our new "national dish", chicken tikka masala, is an example of this.

There are some **obstacles** to the creation of this new British identity, one of which is **racism**. A lot of the traditional British identity was based on the idea that the British were **different from** (and **better than**) the rest of the world. Some people may prefer this traditional view of "Britishness" and be **resistant** to the idea that British society and identity is changing.

Sexuality and Identity

Sexuality is another part of Identity

1) **Sexuality** means a person's **sexual orientation** — whether they are heterosexual, homosexual or bisexual. It also implies **sexual desire**. It is something which **society** can seek to **control**.

2) **Attitudes** towards sexuality **vary** between different cultures and over time. **Jeffrey Weeks (1986)** argued that sexuality is a **social** and **historical construct** — taking on **different meanings** depending on the society and time period.

3) In the past in the UK, **monogamous heterosexual relationships** were the **norm** in **mainstream culture** — and people who tried to live differently were often treated **very negatively**. People with different sexual orientations sometimes formed **subcultures** (see p.4) — **alternatives** to the mainstream.

4) **Agents of socialisation** such as religion, the media and education can **pass on attitudes** about sexuality.

Religion passes on ideologies that control sexuality

1) Religion tends to **promote** a **norm** of **heterosexuality** and **marriage**. Many religions forbid homosexuality and sex outside of marriage, e.g. Catholicism.

2) **Feminists** argue that religion **oppresses female sexuality** by imposing a **strict norm** of staying a **virgin until marriage**, only having sex to have babies and being **sexually passive**.

3) **Functionalists** think that the **control** and channelling of **sexuality** is crucial to the continuation of society. They think it's important to have a **stable family** for kids to be born into, and a monogamous sexual relationship between husband and wife to keep society stable.

4) The **New Right** claim that a **moral decline** caused by **secularisation** has encouraged homosexuality, abortion and pornography. They say these are **threats to social order**.

5) **Postmodernists** think this is all old hat and that religion doesn't have that big an influence on sexuality any more. They say individuals have choice in the **construction** of their **identity** — including **sexual identity**.

Representations of sexuality in the media can be stereotyped

1) **Homosexual** relationships and **heterosexual** relationships are often treated differently in the media. For example, **Coronation Street** and **EastEnders** have both had storylines involving a **gay kiss** which got widespread media attention. You don't get much outcry in the papers when a **man and woman** kiss on a soap opera.

2) There was a **prejudiced** aspect to **early media reporting** of **HIV/AIDS**. It was initially openly characterised as a "gay disease". Some tabloid newspapers in the 1980s referred to AIDS as a "gay plague".

3) Increasingly though, the way that the **media** has **represented gay people** has been **more positive**, for example the television series *Queer as Folk*, and the films *Beautiful Thing* and *Brokeback Mountain*.

Social attitudes towards sexuality are reflected in the law

1) Homosexuality used to be **illegal** in the UK. It was **decriminalised** in England and Wales in **1967** — but the **age of consent was 21**, higher than for heterosexual people.

2) In 1988, **Section 28** came into force. It **prevented** local authorities from **"promoting"** homosexuality, i.e. presenting gay relationships as acceptable. The scope of this law was ambiguous — but many **teachers** thought it meant they **weren't allowed** to **talk about homosexuality** with pupils.

3) Over the last decade, there have been moves towards **equality** — for example, Section 28 was repealed in 2003, the **age of consent** for gay men was **lowered to 16** in 2000, **civil partnerships** for gay couples were introduced in 2005, and the **Equality Act (Sexual Orientation) 2007** made it illegal to discriminate against gay men and women in the provision of goods and services. These all reflect **changing attitudes** in **society**.

Practice Questions

Q1 Give one example of a national symbol and one example of a national ritual.

Q2 Give three agents of socialisation that can pass on attitudes about sexuality.

Exam Question

Q1 Suggest two ways national identity has changed. (4 marks)

I'm having an identity crisis...

People don't just have one identity — they have blimmin' loads. Class, gender, ethnicity, nationality, sexuality... and there's more over the page. So gird your loins, square your shoulders and chin up — another 4 pages and you'll have polished off this section.

Age and Identity

The identity topic rolls on... Two more aspects of identity are age and disability.

Attitudes about Age **Vary** between **Cultures** and **Change Over Time**

1) Views about age **aren't universal** — they **change over time**, and vary between **different societies** and cultures. Age can be seen as a **social construct**.

2) Age is part of social **identity**. People are **socialised** to accept the **norms** and **values** of the **society** they live in. So the way a society **views** certain **age groups** affects **people's behaviour** and **treatment of each other**.

3) Assumptions about at **what age** someone becomes an **"adult"**, or at what age someone is **"old"** can vary between different societies and cultures.

4) For example, in **modern, British society** children are treated **differently** from **adults**. They have to go to school, they aren't allowed to do certain activities (e.g. smoking), and they are viewed as needing constant protection and care. But back in 1800, many children in the UK were treated like **mini-adults** and **worked full-time** as soon as they were physically able to do so (see p.40-41).

5) People who are **similar ages** and have lived through the same **cultural and political events** are often referred to as being from the same **generation**. It can be part of an individual's **identity** that they **feel part of a generation** — e.g. the 60s generation.

6) The **law** affects how different age groups are treated. For example, legally **65** is the **retirement age** in the UK. People over 70 **can't do jury service**.

7) **Bradley (1997)**, however, argues that age is **less important** to identity than other facts like class, gender and ethnicity. This is because people know that their age identity is **temporary** — they're not going to be a child, teenager or middle aged forever.

A social construct is something that's accepted as true in a particular society — but which isn't a scientific fact.

Her cooking wasn't up to much, but if you're going to insist on hiring a two-year-old chef...

The **Media** sometimes present **Stereotyped** views of different **Age Groups**

1) The way the media represent different age groups can **influence** social attitudes — and **reflect** them.

2) Some sociologists have found evidence of **ageist** attitudes in media products. **Simon Biggs (1993)** studied the way older people are presented on television entertainment programmes. He found they were often in stereotyped roles, e.g. "forceful", "vague" or "difficult" — especially in sitcoms.

3) **Lambert (1984)** found that **older men** were often portrayed in **positions of power**, e.g. newsreaders. But this was not the case for older women.

4) There are also media stereotypes of **young people**. Children are often represented as **innocent**. Teenage characters in TV soaps are often **a bit wild** — prone to drug-taking, petty crime, binge drinking and unplanned pregnancy.

Marxists think **Attitudes** to **Age** are influenced by **Capitalism**

1) Marxists suggest that age groups are defined by the **capitalist system**. For example, **adults** are people of **working age**, and the **elderly** are people who are **too old to work**.

2) **Phillipson (1982)** argues that capitalism views the **elderly** as a **burden on society**. This is because their **working life** has **ended**, and they usually have **less spending power**. Old age becomes a **stigmatised** identity.

Increasing Life Expectancy has changed attitudes to Old Age

1) The UK has an **ageing population**. The **Social Trends 33 (2003)** report said that between 1970 and 2001, the **number of people over 65** rose from **13%** to **16%**.

2) This is partly because people are **living longer**. According to **Social Trends 33 (2003)**, between 1971 and 2001, **life expectancy** in the UK **increased** from 69 years to 75 years for men, and from 75 years to 80 years for women.

3) **Giddens (1986)** argues that **longer life expectancy** has an **effect on family life**. For example, people are more likely to know their grandparents or great-grandparents. Families continue for much longer after the children have left home.

4) **Postmodernists** argue that **attitudes** to old age are **changing**. **Featherstone and Hepworth (1993)** found that magazines aimed at older people portray an image of "youthful" old age — enjoying holidays and sports, wearing fashionable clothes etc. They also argue that people can **mask their age** more than ever before, e.g. through cosmetic surgery.

Disability and Identity

Society puts Disabled People into a *Separate Category*

1) **Tom Shakespeare (1994)** argued that 'disability' is a label that society uses to **categorise people**. Being in the category of 'disabled' is often **more of a problem** than the disability itself. In this way, 'disability' can be seen as a **social construct**.

2) He argues that it is more useful to talk about disabilities as **impairments** — they don't make it **impossible** for people to do some tasks, they just make it **harder**. Since everyone's abilities are different, **everyone has some sort of impairment** — not just people traditionally defined as 'disabled'.

3) He also says that society should adapt so that **everyone** has access to the same services, regardless of how severe their impairments are.

There is sometimes *Prejudice* against *Disabled People*

1) There are **negative stereotypes** of disabled people as **weak** and **dependent on others**.

2) **Scott (1969)** studied the way that **blind people** were treated by **medical professionals**. He concluded that the blind people sometimes **learned helplessness** — they relied on sighted people for support because this was what the medical professionals **expected** them to do. Because they were **labelled** as dependent, it became a **self-fulfilling prophecy**.

3) Some people have challenged the idea that disabled people are unusual in being reliant on others. For example, **Marsh and Keating (2006)** argue that everyone is dependent on other people to some extent.

Disabled People are Under-represented in the Media

1) There's very **little representation** of **disabled people** in the **media**. **Roles** for disabled people are **limited**. Research by **Cumberbatch and Negrine (1992)** looking at British television over six weeks found the roles for disabled people were based on **pity** or **comedy**. They found that **disabled actors** never appeared **just as actors** playing a person who **just happened to have a disability**, only in roles **particularly about disability**. However, there are some positive portrayals of disabled people in films and TV — e.g. *Four Weddings and a Funeral*.

2) They also found that how people **interpreted** media messages about disability depended on their **personal experiences**. Those with real-life experience of disability were more likely to **reject unrealistic portrayals**, or to **reinterpret** them according to their own knowledge. This suggests that the media can only create **negative perceptions** amongst people who haven't already **formed their own ideas**.

Practice Questions

Q1 What characteristics have TV soap operas often given to teenage characters?
Q2 Give two examples of stereotypes about age groups that are sometimes presented by the media.
Q3 How do Marxists think that capitalism defines who society views as elderly?
Q4 What is Tom Shakespeare's view about how society should view disability?
Q5 How are disabled people usually portrayed in the media according to Cumberbatch and Negrine?

Exam Questions

Q1 Suggest two ways in which attitudes towards old age have changed.	(4 marks)
Q2 Assess the view that the media influence society's perception of disability.	(24 marks)

You want to retire with a pension at 17? — Oh, act your age...

Age is a flexible part of identity — everyone grows older and society's views of age change, often according to changes in the population within a single person's lifetime. On the other hand, disability is much more rigid — a person is unlikely to stop being disabled and society often unfairly views it as the most important attribute of an individual.

Leisure, Consumption and Identity

In a postmodern world, identity is all about shopping...

Identity *is influenced by* Popular Culture

1) Many theorists and researchers have looked at the ways in which **individual identity** is influenced by **popular culture**.

2) According to **Blumler and Katz (1974)**, people use the media to meet their needs. They called this the "**uses and gratifications model**". Individuals **decide** which media to use, based on what they **want** to experience.

3) They classified people's use of the media into categories. "Personal identity" and "social interaction" were two of their categories. For example, they found that some viewers of TV quizzes liked to **compare themselves** with the contestants (personal identity) and would **talk about** the shows **afterwards** (social interaction).

Morley (1980) studied reactions of different social groups to media

Morley showed the same episodes of the current affairs programme *Nationwide* to different social groups. He demonstrated that different social groups created **different semiotic readings** of the same product:

There's more about semiotics on p.8.

• **black** viewers were likely to see the programmes as **racist**.

• **union** organisers were likely to see them as **anti-union**.

• **management** trainees were likely to see them as **pro-union**.

• **university** students drew attention to the way the programmes were **constructed**.

The uses and gratifications model suggests that **popular culture** is **involved** in personal **identity**, but doesn't create it. Morley's *Nationwide* study points to the influence of a **range of factors** such class and ethnicity on the way individuals **engage** with **popular culture**.

Some argue that Identity *is increasingly linked to* Leisure

1) **Traditional patterns of employment** helped create a strong sense of identity through **work**, **family** and **location**. When people were often expected to stay in the same skilled or semi-skilled job for a lifetime, and when work was closely linked to family and community traditions, it was easier to build your sense of **identity** around your **job**.

2) People have become more **geographically** and **socially mobile**, jobs are **less secure**, and families (traditional, extended and nuclear) are **less stable**.

3) **Willis (1990)** suggests that work is now **less satisfying** because it often requires little **skill**. All of this leads to people using their **leisure time** to gain **satisfaction** and build their **identity**.

Postmodern *sociology says* Class, Gender *and* Ethnicity Don't Mean *so much*

1) Traditional sociology has looked at the way patterns of leisure and identity are linked to **social class**, or **gender**, or **ethnic** background.

2) In recent years, sociologists have suggested that people do not feel constrained by these social determinants, and are now much more likely to build their identities through **symbolic consumption** (see p.5).

3) Some examples of this include the "new man" (caring, sensitive, does the housework), "ladettes" (young women who take on some features of traditional masculine identity) and "wiggers" (white people adopting aspects of black identity). In all of these cases, individuals use **leisure time** and **products** from the **culture industries** to build **identities** for themselves.

4) Some sociologists, such as **Chris Rojek (1995)**, have concluded that **culture**, rather than social class, is the best way to understand patterns in leisure.

Leisure, Consumption and Identity

As *Leisure* expands, the *Culture Industries* also *Expand*

1) The **classic Marxist explanation** of this is that the cultural industries exist just to **make profits**. They **control** and **exploit** consumers in their free time, making them **think** that they need **expensive leisure pursuits and entertainment**. Workers keep working in order to buy cultural commodities and spend money on leisure.

2) The **cultural decline explanation** (see p.6) says that people are encouraged by popular culture to waste their time on **vulgar worthless activities** when they could be improving themselves with **education** and **high culture**. According to this view, greedy companies are making easy money by providing cheap, trashy entertainment.

3) **Willis (1990)** says that these two views are actually quite similar and **equally wrong**.

> Willis suggests that capitalism has acted exactly as you would expect — of course it's tried to **profit** from the increased desire for leisure in modern audiences. However, the audience **wants** all this material because it **needs to be creative**. Now that work is often **less creative** than it used to be, people find ways of being creative and finding identity through leisure. Willis refers to "**symbolic creativity**" — a pick and mix approach to the cultural industries that allows people to **construct their identity** from little bits of high culture and little bits of mass culture.

Symbolic Communities are constructed through Culture and Leisure

1) **Cohen (1985)** suggests that communities are now "**symbolic communities**". Instead of the traditional idea of a group of people **living near each other** and providing mutual support, a community can now be any group of people who are **connected** to each other. For example, supporters of a football team, work colleagues, users of a website.

2) **Jenkins (1996)** argues that groups such as **football supporters** use the symbols and rituals of the group to **define themselves** as people. He said that there are **three important elements** to this:

- Defining yourself and others as belonging to the group.
- Defining who is not a member of the group (the "other").
- Being defined by other people in the group as "one of us".

3) The idea of symbolic communities is closely connected to Willis's idea of **symbolic creativity**.

- **Lifestyle shopping** makes us feel like **individuals** — because we choose the products that we buy to express our identity. For example, you might feel that your limited edition Hello Kitty® bag really says something about **you**.
- **Lifestyle shopping** also helps us to belong to **symbolic communities** — because we choose products that have symbolic meanings which other people share. When you see another person in town with a limited edition Hello Kitty® bag, you might feel a sense of **kinship** with them.

Practice Questions

Q1 What is the "uses and gratifications" model?
Q2 What reason does Willis give for leisure becoming a more important factor in identity?
Q3 What are symbolic communities?

Exam Question

Q1 Assess the view that individuals now build their identities through their leisure time. (24 marks)

It says it's about leisure but it looks like work to me...

Phew... It's the end of the section. There's been a lot of heavy theory in this section — but if you've managed to get your head around it, you'll find the sections that follow much easier. The usual suspects — Marxists, functionalists, postmodernists, feminists and interpretivists — have an opinion about everything and turn up throughout the book...

The Nature and Role of Family in Society

The family is one of the most important social groups for Sociology because almost all people experience living in a family for some of their life.

Families and Households are Not Necessarily the Same Thing

A **household** is a group of people who **live together** who may or may not have family or kinship ties. The 2001 UK census recorded **24.4 million households** in the UK. **Families** make up the **majority** of households, but there are other types, e.g. **students** or **friends** sharing a house or flat. A recent **social trend** in Britain is the **increase** in the number of people **living alone**. (This information is from **Social Trends 33 (2003)** — a report by the Office for National Statistics.)

A **family** is a type of household where the people living together are **related**. Most commonly, a family is also a **kinship** group. Kinship means being related by **birth** or **blood** — parents, children, grandparents, cousins. Families also include non-kinship relationships — foster children, guardians, step-parents and stepchildren, mother-in-law etc.

Here are the main types of family:

1)   **Nuclear family**: Two generations living together (mother and father and dependent children).

2)   **Traditional extended family**: Three or more generations of the same family living together or close by, with frequent contact between grandparents, grandchildren, aunts, cousins etc.

3)   **Attenuated extended family**: Nuclear families that live apart from their extended family, but keep in regular contact, e.g. via phone or e-mail.

4)   **Single-parent families:** A single parent and their dependent children.

5)   **Reconstituted families:** New stepfamilies created when parts of two previous families are brought together. E.g. a reconstituted family may comprise of two new partners who bring children from former partners together to create a new family group.

Functionalists Emphasise the Positive Role of the Family

Functionalists see **every institution** in society as **essential** to the **smooth running** of society. A **key functionalist study** by **Murdock (1949)** concluded that the family is **so useful** to society that it is **inevitable** and **universal** — in other words you **can't avoid** having family units in a society, and societies **everywhere** have family units.

> "No society … has succeeded in finding an adequate substitute for the nuclear family … it is highly doubtful whether any society will succeed in such an attempt." Murdock, G.P. (1949) *Social Structure*, Macmillan, New York

Murdock (1949) looked at 250 societies in different cultures

Murdock argued that some form of the nuclear family existed in all of the 250 different societies he looked at.
He argued the family performed four basic functions – sexual, reproductive, economic and educational (social):

Sexual   Provides a **stable sexual relationship** for **adults**, and **controls** the sexual relationships of its members.

Reproductive Provides new babies — **new members of society**.

Economic   The family **pools resources** and **provides** for all its members, adults and children.

Educational   The family **teaches children** the **norms** and **values** of society, which keeps the values of society going.

In the 1950s, American sociologist **Talcott Parsons** argued that the family always has **two basic and irreducible** (vital) **functions**. These are the **primary socialisation of children** and the **stabilisation of adult personalities**.

1)   **Primary socialisation** is the process by which children **learn** and **accept** the **values** and **norms** of society. Parsons described families as **"factories"** where the next citizens are produced.

Remember: functionalists see the positive nature of the family as two-way — it's equally useful and beneficial to individuals and society.

2)   For adults, the family **stabilises personalities** through the **emotional** relationship between the parents. The emotional relationship gives the **support** and **security** needed to cope in the wider society. It's a **sanctuary** from the **stress** of everyday life.

Some Say Functionalists Ignore the Negative Aspects of Family Life

The functionalist perspective has been **criticised** for **idealising** the family — focusing on the good bits and blanking out the bad bits. **Morgan (1975)** points out that Murdock makes no reference to **alternative households** to the family or to **disharmony** and **problems** in **family relationships**.

The **functionalist** view of the family was **dominant** in sociology into the 1960s. Since then there's been **widespread criticism** that neither Murdock nor Parsons look at issues of **conflict**, **class** or **violence** in relation to the family. Some feminists argue that they also ignored the issue of **exploitation of women**.

The fact that functionalists **overlook negative aspects** of family life **makes their position look weak**.

The Nature and Role of Family in Society

Marxists See the Family as Meeting the Needs of the Capitalist System

Like functionalists, Marxists view the family as performing **essential functions** for modern industrial society. The key difference is that **Marxists** argue that the family **benefits** the minority **in power** (called the "**bourgeoisie**") and the economy, but **disadvantages** the **working class** majority (called the "**proletariat**").

1) **Engels (1884)** said the family had an **economic function** of keeping wealth within the **bourgeoisie** by passing it on to the next generation as **inheritance**. In other words, when a **rich person dies**, their **kids get their money**.

2) **Zaretsky (1976)** focused on how the family helped the capitalist economy. He argued that the family is one place in society where the **proletariat** can have **power** and **control**. When the **working man** gets home, he's **king of his own castle**. This relieves some of the **frustration** workers feel about their low status, which helps them to **accept** their **oppression** and exploitation as workers.

3) The role of women in the family in capitalist society as "**housewife**" means workers are **cared for** and **healthy**. This makes them **more productive** — a great benefit that the capitalist class (the employers) get for **free**.

4) The **family household** is a unit with the **desire** to **buy** the **goods** produced by capitalist industry, e.g. washing machines, cars, fridges. The family is a **unit of consumption**. The family buys the goods for more than they cost to produce and the **bourgeoisie get the profit**.

All in all, Marxists argue the family is a **very useful tool of capitalism**.

The Marxist View is Criticised for being too Negative

The Marxist view of the family is all about it being a **tool of capitalist oppression**, and **never mentions nice things**, like bedtime stories for the kids, or trips to the zoo.

Criticisms of the Marxist view of the family

1) Marxist sociology is entirely focused on **benefits to the economy**, and benefits to the working man's **boss**. It **ignores other benefits** to individuals and society.

2) Traditional Marxist sociology **assumes** that the worker is **male**, and that women are **housewives**.

3) There is **no Marxist explanation** for why the family flourishes as an institution in **non-capitalist** or **communist** societies and there is little Marxist research on **alternatives** to the family.

Functionalists and Marxists both see the family as having a **key role** in society in **reproducing social structure and order**. The **key sociological debate** between them is whether this is **positive** or **negative** and **who benefits**.

Practice Questions

Q1 What do sociologists define as a household?

Q2 What are the key functions of the family according to Parsons?

Q3 Explain the ways in which functionalist and Marxist perspectives on the role of the family are similar.

Q4 Explain the ways in which functionalist and Marxist perspectives on the role of the family are different.

Exam Questions

Q1	Suggest three functions that nuclear families might perform.	(6 marks)
Q2	Examine the view that the family performs the vital function of maintaining the 'status quo' in society.	(24 marks)

Cog in society's machine or tool of capitalist oppression — you decide...

If you're comparing functionalist and Marxist perspectives about the role of the family, make sure you cover the pros and cons of each view — and most importantly, make sure you answer the question. Remember, functionalists believe that the family is there to keep society chugging along smoothly, and Marxists believe it's there to help exploit the common worker.

The Nature and Role of Family in Society

There's a lot of different feminist theory about the family — it's generally left-wing and anti-traditional. But it's worth looking at recent right-wing pro-traditional ideas as well. And at the postmodernists — who say everyone can do what they like. Hooray.

Most *Feminists* Believe the *Family Exploits* and *Oppresses Women*

1) From a **feminist perspective**, the **family** helps to **maintain the existing social order**. (If that sounds familiar, it's because functionalists and Marxists also talk about keeping up the existing social order.)

2) Feminists call the existing social order **patriarchy**. Patriarchy is the **combination of systems, ideologies and cultural practices** which make sure that **men** have power.

3) Feminist theory argues that the family **supports** and reproduces **inequalities** between men and women.

4) The idea is that women are **oppressed** because they're **socialised** to be **dependent** on men — and to put themselves in second place to men. The **family** has a central role in this socialisation — **male and female roles** and **expectations** are **formed in the family** and then **carried on into wider society**.

5) Feminist sociologists say that there's an **ideology** about men's **roles** and women's **roles** in the family.   ← *An ideology is a set of ideas about the way things are and the way things ought to be.*

There are *Three Main Strands* of *Feminist Thought* on the *Family*

The three strands of feminist thought are **radical feminism**, **Marxist feminism** and **liberal feminism**.

The distinction between the three theories comes from what they see as the **root cause of patriarchy**. For radical feminists it's the **power dominance of men**, for Marxist feminists it's the **capitalist system** and for liberal feminists it's **cultural attitudes** and laws that allow **discrimination**.

All these theories generalise quite a bit.

Marxist feminism — key points

Marxist feminism sees the **exploitation of women** as essential to the success of **capitalism**. The family produces and cares for the next generation of workers for society at almost **no cost** to the capitalist system. It's cost-free because society accepts that **housework** should be **unpaid**. Men are paid for work outside the home, but **women aren't paid** for work **inside** the home. If this sounds outdated, remember evidence shows that even when women work outside the home they still do **most** of the domestic labour (see p.36). **Benston (1969)** points out that if housework were paid even at **minimum wage** levels it would **damage capitalist profits** hugely. **Ansley (1972)** thinks that men take out their frustration and stress from work on women, instead of challenging the capitalist system.

Radical feminism — key points

Radical feminist theory also highlights **housework** as an area of **exploitation of women**, but... and it's a big but... radical feminists don't see this as the fault of the capitalist system. Radical feminists see exploitation of women as being down to the **domination of men in society**. Radical feminism believes that **men will always oppress women**. **Delphy and Leonard (1992)** are radical feminists who see the family as a patriarchal institution in which **women do most of the work** and **men get most of the benefit**.

Liberal feminism — key points

Liberal feminists emphasise the **cultural norms** and **values** which are reinforced by the family and by other institutions in society. The family is only sexist because it **supports mainstream culture** which is sexist. Liberal feminists believe **social change is possible**. They try to put pressure on institutions such as the **legal system** and **government** to change laws and social policies which discriminate against women.

Feminist Theory has been *Criticised*

1) All strands of feminist theory have been **criticised** for portraying women as **too passive**. It plays down the ability of individual women to **make changes** and **improve** their situation.

2) Feminist sociology **doesn't acknowledge** that **power might be shared** within a family.

3) Some feminist theory has been criticised for **not considering** the households in society which **don't** feature a **man and woman partnership**, e.g. **lesbian** and **gay** relationships and **single-parent** households. The power structures in those families **don't get looked at**.

4) Some **black feminists** have pointed out that a lot of feminist theory doesn't address the fact that women from different **ethnic backgrounds** have different **life experiences**.

The Nature and Role of Family in Society

The **New Right** Believe the **Nuclear Family** is the **Bedrock of Society**

1) **New Right theory** developed in sociology in the **1980s**. It's based on the idea that the **traditional nuclear family** and its **values** (mum, dad and kids, parents married, dad in paid employment) are best for society.

2) New Right theorists reckon that **social policies** on family, children, divorce and welfare have **undermined** the **family**.

There's more about the New Right on page 64.

3) **Charles Murray** is a New Right sociologist who says the traditional family is under threat. **Murray (1989)** says that **welfare benefits** are **too high** and create a "**culture of dependency**" where an individual finds it easy and acceptable to take benefits rather than work.

4) New Right theorists are particularly concerned about giving lots of **welfare benefits** to **single mothers**. They also think that it's a very **bad idea** to have children brought up in families where adults aren't working.

5) New Right sociologists believe that the increase in **lone-parent** and **reconstituted** (step) families and the easier access to **divorce** have led to a **breakdown in traditional values**. They say that this causes social problems such as **crime** to increase.

6) Some politicians have made use of New Right theory. It's had an influence on **social policy** — making it **harder** for people to **get benefits**.

Pine cladding — that's the real bedrock of society

New Right theory has been **criticised** for "**blaming the victim**" for their problems.

Postmodernists Say **Diversity** in Family Structures is a **Good Thing**

1) The **central idea** of **postmodern views of the family** is that there's a much **wider range** of **living options** available these days — because of **social** and **cultural changes**. There are traditional nuclear families, stepfamilies, cohabiting unmarried couples, single people flatsharing, more divorced people etc.

2) Postmodern sociologist **Judith Stacey (1990)** reckons there's **such a diversity** of family types, relationships and lifestyles that there'll **never** be **one dominant type** of family in Western culture again. She says that "Western family arrangements are **diverse, fluid** and **unresolved**". This means a person can move from one family structure into another, and not get stuck with one fixed family structure.

3) Postmodernists say the **key thing** is the idea that contemporary living is so **flexible** that one individual can experience lots of different types of family in their lifetime. Postmodernists see this **diversity** and **flexibility** as **positive** — because it means individuals can always **choose** from several options depending on what suits their **personal needs** and lifestyle. People aren't hemmed in by tradition.

4) Sociological **criticism** of postmodern theory **questions** whether this "journey through many family types" is really all that typical. **O'Brien and Jones (1996)** concluded from their UK research that there was **less variety** in family types than Stacey reported, and that **most** individuals actually experienced **only one or two** different types of family in their lifetime.

Practice Questions

Q1 Identify three different strands of feminist thought about the family.
Q2 Give two characteristics of patriarchy.
Q3 What does Murray mean by a "culture of dependency"?
Q4 Why do postmodernists think there will never be one dominant type of family in Western culture again?

Exam Questions

Q1	Assess the view that men benefit from existing family structures while women suffer.	(24 marks)
Q2	Examine the view that the traditional nuclear family is under threat from a culture of dependency.	(24 marks)

If this is too difficult to learn, blame your family. Or blame society...

Another couple of pages all about different views of the family. Feminist theory is complicated because there are different varieties of feminism. Which one you go for depends on exactly how unfair you think family life is on women, and exactly whose fault you think it is. Don't forget to learn the reasons why sociologists say each theory might be wrong, or flawed.

Changes in Family Structure

The average family today doesn't have the same structure as the average family 250 years ago.
Sociologists suggest various reasons for this, mostly to do with people moving to cities to work in factories.

Industrialisation Changed Family Structure

1) There are **two basic types of family structure** you need to know: **extended** and **nuclear** (see p.24).

2) There are **two basic types of society** you need to know:

> **Pre-industrial society:** This means society before industrialisation. It is largely **agricultural** and work centres on home, **farm**, village and **market**.
>
> **Industrial society:** This means society during and after **industrialisation**. Work centres on **factories** and production of goods in **cities**.

Industrialisation is the process by which production becomes more mechanical and based outside the home in factories. People travel outside the home to work and urban centres (cities) are formed. Industrialisation in the UK started in the 18th century.

3) What you really, really need to know is **how these two affect each other**.

> In **pre-industrial** society the **extended** family is most common. Families **live and work together** producing goods and crops to live from, taking the surplus to market. This is where the term **cottage industry** comes from.
>
> In **industrial** society the **nuclear family** becomes dominant. There is a huge increase in individuals leaving the home to work for a wage. The key social change is that industrialisation **separates home and work**.

Remember — **industrialisation is historical fact** but the **nature** of the **social change** it created is **a subject of sociological debate**.

Functionalists Say Industrialisation Changed the Function of the Family

American sociologist **Talcott Parsons** studied the **impact of industrialisation** on **family structure** in American and British society. Parsons thought that the dominant family structure changed from extended to nuclear because it was **more useful** for industrial society — i.e. the **nuclear family** is the **best fit** for **industrial society**.

1) Lots of **functions** of the family in **pre-industrial** society are **taken over by the state** in industrial society — e.g. policing, healthcare, education.

2) The nuclear family can focus on its function of **socialisation**. The family socialises children into the roles, values and norms of industrialised society.

3) Parsons said the industrial nuclear family is "**isolated**" — meaning it has **few ties** with local **kinship** and economic systems. This means the family can up sticks and **move easily** — ideal for moving to where the work is.

> In short, **family structure adapts** to the **needs of society**.

Most functions of extended family taken over by state

Specialised for socialising children

Nuclear family — Mobile

Functionalists Say Industrialisation Changed Roles and Status in the Family

Status for an individual in **pre-industrial society** was **ascribed** — decided at birth by the family they were born into. Parsons reckoned that in industrial society an individual's status is **achieved** by their success in society **outside their family**.

The idea here is that the **nuclear family** is the **best** for allowing individuals to **achieve status** and position without **conflict**. It's OK for an individual to achieve higher or lower status than previous generations. This allows for greater **social mobility** in society. People can **better themselves**.

Parsons says that **specialised roles** for men and women develop within the family. He thought that men are **instrumental** (practical / planning) leaders and women are **expressive** (emotional) leaders in a family. As a **functionalist**, Parsons said these roles come about because they're **most effective** for society. **Feminists** and **conflict theorists** disagree — they say these roles come from **ideology** and **power**.

Other Sociologists say it's all More Complicated

Functionalists are **criticised** for seeing the modern nuclear family as **superior** — something that societies have to evolve into. They're also criticised for putting forward an **idealised** picture of history. **Historical evidence** suggests there was actually a **variety** of family forms in the past.

Sociologist **Peter Laslett (1972)** reckons that the **nuclear family** was the **most common** structure in Britain even before industrialisation. His evidence comes from **parish records**. Also, **Laslett and Anderson (1971)** say that the **extended family** actually was **significant** in industrial society. Anderson used the **1851 census** for evidence. He said that when people moved to the cities for industrial jobs, they lived with relatives from their extended family.

Changes in Family Structure

Willmott and Young Said Families Have Developed Through Three Stages

British sociologists **Willmott and Young (1960, 1973)** did two important studies looking at family structures in British society from the 1950s to the 1970s. They mainly studied families in different parts of London and Essex. Their work tested the theory that the nuclear family is the dominant form in modern industrial society.

You need to remember their conclusion, which was that **British families have developed through three stages**. (Initially, they set out four stages, but there wasn't a lot of evidence for the last stage, so they dropped it.)

Stage One: Pre-Industrial	Family works together as **economic production unit**. Work and home are combined.
Stage Two: Early Industrial	Extended family is broken up as individuals (mostly men) leave home to work. Women at home have strong **extended kinship** networks.
Stage Three: Privatised Nuclear	Family based on **consumption**, not **production** — buying things, not making things. Nuclear family is focused on its **personal relationships and lifestyle**. Called **"the symmetrical family"** — husband and wife have joint roles.
Stage Four: Asymmetrical	Husband and wife roles become **asymmetrical** as men spend more leisure time **away from the home** — in the pub for example. *this stage got dropped*

Husband and wife roles are called "conjugal roles" by sociologists.

Other Sociologists have Criticised Willmott and Young

1) Willmott and Young (and other functionalists) have been criticised for **assuming** that family life has got **better and better** as structure adapts to modern society. They're described as **"march of progress"** theorists.

2) Wilmott and Young **ignore** the **negative** aspects of the modern nuclear family. Domestic violence, child abuse and lack of care for the elderly and vulnerable are all problems in society today.

3) **Feminist** research (see p.26) suggests **equal roles** in the "symmetrical family" don't really exist.

Different Classes Might Have Different Family Structures

Willmott and Young's work in the **1960s** and **1970s** supported the **theory** that **working class** families had **closer extended kinship networks** than middle class families.

To get up to date, the British Social Attitude Surveys of **1986** and **1995** showed that **working class** families have **more frequent contact** and ties outside of their nuclear family.

Recent work by **Willmott (1988)** suggests that **extended family ties** are **still important** to the modern nuclear family but they're **held in reserve** for times of **crisis** rather than being part of everyday life. For example, if your house floods, you might go and stay with your sister, even if you don't usually spend loads of time with her. In Parsons' terminology this makes the modern family **"partially isolated nuclear"**.

Practice Questions

Q1 Give an example of social change caused by industrialisation.

Q2 What roles did Parsons believe men and women had within the nuclear family?

Q3 What is meant by the term "symmetrical family"?

Q4 Outline one criticism of Willmott and Young's "march of progress" theory.

Exam Questions

Q1	Examine the ways in which industrialisation changed the function of the family.	(24 marks)
Q2	Examine the view that the extended family remains an important aspect of modern industrial society.	(24 marks)

My mum works at Sellafield — we're a real nuclear family...

OK — here's something where it helps to have a vague idea about history, and about what this "industrialisation" business was. The idea is that when people went to live in cities and work in factories, society changed. Of course, it'd be far too much to expect sociologists to agree about it. Oh no. So you have another couple of pages of sociological debate...

Changes in Family Structure

Politicians sometimes try to promote certain family structures through their policies.

Governments try to Influence Family Structure through Social Policy

1) The UK government often makes **laws** that are designed to influence family life or family structure. These laws are part of **social policy**.

2) Social policy laws cover areas such as **divorce**, changes to the **benefit system** which affect family income, reforms to the **education** system, **adoption/fostering** and **employment**.

Social Policy has Changed Over Time

1) The way that governments tackle social policy has **changed** quite a lot in the period since the Second World War.

2) In the 1945–1979 period, the state's social policy was quite **interventionist**.

3) **The Welfare State** (see p.52), which was set up by a Labour government in 1948, supported families through benefits, public housing, family allowances and free health care.

4) People paid into a **national insurance** scheme to pay for the welfare state. It was **universal** — everyone had the same benefits and services.

The NHS even covered floating baby syndrome...

The 1979 Conservative Government Believed in Reduced State Intervention

The Conservative Party was elected in 1979 with **Margaret Thatcher** as their leader. Reacting to several years of political instability, they set about **reforming** the relationship between society and the state.

1) The Conservatives were influenced by **New Right** ideology. They believed that nuclear families were the **cornerstone of society**, but also thought that society as a whole should be **freed from interference** by the state as much as possible. They thought the UK had become a **"nanny state"** with too much government control over individual lives.

2) They set out to make individuals more **responsible** for their own lives and decisions — the state would **intervene much less** in private matters. So benefits were cut and **taxes lowered**. **Means testing** was introduced for some benefits with the aim of helping only those in **genuine need**. (Means testing is when you only get a benefit if your household income is below a set level.)

3) Mothers were encouraged to **stay at home** through preferential tax allowances. Families were pushed to take on more responsibility for **the elderly** through benefit cuts.

Mrs Thatcher's Conservatives echoed the concerns of Charles Murray, who first coined the phrase 'culture of dependency' (see page 27).

The Conservatives Legislated to Protect People in a Traditional Family

The Conservatives valued **traditional**, **nuclear families**. In 1988, Thatcher described the family as "the building block of society. It's a nursery, a school, a hospital, a leisure place, a place of refuge and a place of rest."

The Conservatives created several laws that enforced the **rights** and **responsibilities** of individuals in families.

1) The **Child Support Agency** was established in **1993** to force absent fathers and mothers to **pay** a fair amount towards the upkeep of their children.

2) The **Children Act 1989** outlined for the first time the rights of the child.

3) The Conservatives also considered a law to make **divorce more difficult** — a compulsory **cooling off** period of one year was proposed before a couple could divorce. In the end they abandoned this idea because they couldn't find a way to make it work in practice.

Changes in Family Structure

New Labour Promised a Compromise between the Old Ideologies

New Labour came to power in **1997** led by Tony Blair.

1) They based their ideology on '**The Third Way**' — a middle ground between **left-wing** and **right-wing** politics. Their policies were designed to be **more pragmatic** and **less ideological** than either the 1979 Conservative government or previous Labour governments.

2) In their 1998 consultation paper '**Supporting Families**', they made it clear that **marriage** is their preferred basis for family life.

3) However they have shown an awareness of, and concern for, **diversity** of family life.

4) In 2005 they introduced **civil partnerships**, a union a lot like marriage that is available to gay couples.

5) They've also introduced laws allowing any type of cohabiting couple to **adopt children**.

6) They have adopted some **New Right ideas** when it comes to **family policy** — e.g. they've cut lone parent family benefits, supported means-tested benefits and are opposed to universal benefits.

Feminists Believe that Social Policy is Designed to Protect Patriarchy

1) **Feminists** believe that the **New Right** want to reinforce a **sexist and exploitative** model of the family by keeping women in the home and making them the main support for their children.

2) They also think that social policies continue to support a **patriarchal** society even under New Labour — for example the differences in maternity and paternity leave reinforce the idea that the mother is the **primary carer** and the father is the **earner and provider**.

Marxists Argue that Social Policy is Designed to Protect Capitalism

1) Marxists also **oppose** the policies of the **New Right**. They argue that reducing benefits to the poor only **makes them poorer**, and that **means testing** for benefits is **degrading** for the claimant and likely to dissuade worthy applicants.

2) They believe that social policies tend to be designed to **maintain the capitalist system**. By reinforcing traditional gender roles, **social policy** moulds women into a **reserve army of labour** which can be drawn on in times of crisis.

Practice Questions

Q1 What is social policy?

Q2 Give two examples of Conservative policies in the 1980s that affected family life.

Q3 What has been New Labour's attitude towards family diversity?

Q4 Give two criticisms of the New Right's attitude towards social policy.

Exam Questions

Q1 Suggest two ways that social policy has influenced family life in the UK since 1997. (4 marks)

Q2 Examine the view that social policies in the UK have sustained inequality both inside and outside the family. (24 marks)

My social policy — Thursday is the new Friday...

Politicians usually want to support the traditional nuclear family, but since 1979 they've generally also wanted to reduce state intervention in people's private lives. Marxists think that New Right ideas about the family prop up capitalism while feminists think they help exploit women. Think of a way to remember that if you can.

Family Diversity — Changing Family Patterns

These pages are about which family types are getting more common, and which are getting less common.

Social Trends Indicate More Variety of Families and Households

Official **Social Trends** statistics clearly show that the **variety** of family types has **increased** in Britain since the **mid 20th century**. There's now no such thing as "the British family" — there are several kinds of family structure out there.

Look at the evidence:

1) There were **24.4 million** households in the UK in 2002 — up by a third since 1971.

2) The **average size** of households is getting **smaller**. The number of households made up of **5 or more** people has **fallen** from **14% in 1971** to **7% in 2002**.

3) You might think that more small households means more nuclear families. However, the percentage of households which are **nuclear families** has **fallen** from **33%** in **1971** to **25%** in **2002**.

4) Two of the biggest **increases** have been in **single-person** households and **lone-parent family** households. This explains why the average size of households has got smaller.

5) There's been an increase in the **proportion** of families which are **reconstituted** families — also known as **stepfamilies**. There are **more stepfamilies** now that there's **more divorce**. In 2001-2, **8%** of all households were **reconstituted families**.

6) **Weeks, Donovan et al (1999)** found that there had been an increase in the number of **gay** or **lesbian** households since the 1980s. This is due to changes in attitudes and legislation.

7) There has been a rise in the number of people **cohabiting** without marrying — it is estimated this will reach **3 million** couples by 2020.

8) The number of children born **outside marriage** has increased to **40%** of all births.

The stats in points 1–5 are from "Social Trends 33 (2003)".

The two **overall patterns** are:

1) There's been an **increase** in the **diversity** of families in the UK. There are more **different kinds** of family.

2) **The nuclear family** is still the most **common** type of family, even though the **proportion** of nuclear families is going down. In 2002, **78%** of children lived in nuclear families.

Rapoport and Rapoport (1982) Identified Five Types of Family Diversity

Organisational diversity	Differences in the way families are **structured**, e.g. whether they're nuclear, extended, reconstituted or any other form.
Cultural diversity	Differences that arise from the different norms and values of **different cultures.**
Class diversity	Different views are often held by **different parts of society** concerning families. For example, more affluent families are more likely to send their children to boarding school than poorer families, leading to a different relationship between the parents and children.
Life-course diversity	Diversity caused by the **different stages** people have reached in their lives. E.g. family relationships tend to be different for childless couples, newly-weds with children and people with grown-up children.
Cohort diversity	Differences created by the **historical periods** the family have lived through. For example, children who reached maturity in the 1980s may have remained dependent on their parents for longer due to high unemployment.

Class, Ethnicity and Sexuality Affect Which Types of Family You Experience

Eversley and Bonnerjea (1982) found **middle class** areas in the UK have a **higher** than average proportion of **nuclear families**. Inner-city **working class areas** are more likely to have a higher proportion of **lone-parent households**.

Lesbian and **gay** families have been hidden from the statistics. The **official definition** of a couple has only included **same-sex couples** since 1998.

The study of **ethnic minorities** by **Modood et al (1997)** found that:

1) Whites and Afro-Caribbeans were most likely to be **divorced**. Indians, Pakistanis, Bangladeshis and African Asians were most likely to be **married**.

2) Afro-Caribbean households were the most likely to be **single-parent families**.

3) **South Asian** families are traditionally **extended** families, but there are more **nuclear family** households than in the past. **Extended kinship links** stay strong and often reach back to India, Pakistan or Bangladesh.

4) There's **diversity** within each ethnic group though.

Family Diversity — Changing Family Patterns

Fewer People Marry and More People Live Together Instead

In 2001 the **lowest** number of **marriages** took place in the UK since records began.

This does NOT mean a decline in family life, though:

1) Over the same period of time there was an **increase** in the number of adults living with a partner (**cohabiting**). In 2001-2 a **quarter** of all non-married adults aged 16-59 were **cohabiting**.

2) **Social trends statistics** show that living with a partner doesn't mean you **won't** get married — it often just means a **delay** in tying the knot. A **third** of people who cohabited with a partner went on to **marry** them.

3) The **majority** of people in the UK do marry, but the **proportion** who are **married at any one time** has **fallen**.

4) **Men** tend to **die** before women. **Elderly widows** make up a lot of **single-person households**. There are **more old people** these days, so this helps explain why there are so many single-person households.

The UK has one of the Highest Divorce Rates in Europe

1) There's been a **steady rise** in the **divorce rate** in most **modern industrial societies**.

2) The **divorce rate** is defined as the **number of people per 1000 of the married population** who get **divorced** per year. In 2000, Britain's divorce rate was **2.6** compared to the European average of **1.9**.

3) **Actual divorces** in the UK rose from **25,000** in **1961** to **146,000** in **1997**.

4) The **proportion** of the population who were **divorced** at any one time was **1%** in **1971** and **9%** in **2000**.

5) The average **length** of a marriage that ends in divorce has remained **about the same** — **12 years** in **1963**, **11 years** in **2000** (source — Census 2001 report).

6) Although the divorce rate is increasing, divorced people are **marrying again**. In 2001, **40%** of all marriages were **re-marriages**.

You don't have to learn all of these statistics, but if you can learn some of them off by heart and quote them in your essays, you'll look very bright and shiny.

There are several **social**, **cultural** and **political** factors you **need to know about** when you're explaining why divorce is increasing in the UK.

1) Divorce has become **easier to obtain**.
2) Divorce is more **socially acceptable**.
3) Women may have **higher expectations** of marriage, and **better employment opportunities** may make them less financially dependent on their husbands.
4) Marriages are increasingly focused on **individual emotional fulfilment**.
5) The New Right believe that marriage is **less supported by the state** these days.

Availability and acceptability are the buzz words in the debate on divorce.

Remember — the **link** between divorce and marriage breakdown isn't completely straightforward. Some couples separate but never actually go through with the divorce procedure.

You **can't assume** marriage was **happier** in the past because there were **fewer divorces**. A marriage can break down but with the couple still **staying married** and living together. This is called an **empty-shell marriage**.

Practice Questions

Q1 Which household types have increased in the UK in recent years?
Q2 Give five types of family diversity.
Q3 What evidence is there that divorce has increased in the UK in recent times?

Exam Question

Q1 Assess the view that divorce rates have risen because divorces are now easier to obtain. (24 marks)

86% of people get bored of reading about divorce statistics...

Sometimes I wonder what sociologists would do without the Office for National Statistics, and their Social Trends reports. Anyway, jot down your own list of trends in the size of the family, the number of single person households, the number of divorces and the number of people cohabiting. You have to know which are going up and which are going down.

Family Diversity — Changing Family Patterns

There have been some trends in family diversity that almost everyone agrees on. But not everyone agrees on their causes.

People are Having **Fewer Children** and Having them **Later in Life**

One very clear change in British family life is the **decrease** in the **average number of children** people have.

1) People are having **fewer children**. The average number of children per family was **2.4** in **1971**, compared to **1.6** in **2001** (the lowest ever recorded).

2) Women are having children **later**. The average age of women at the birth of their first child was **24** in **1971**, compared to **27** in **2001**.

3) More people are **not having children at all** — **9%** of women born in **1945** were childless at age **45**, compared to **15%** of women born in **1955**.

Social changes have influenced these trends. **Contraception** is more readily available and **women's roles are changing**. The emphasis on the **individual in post-industrial society** is a key factor. Children are expensive and time-consuming, and couples may choose to spend their time and money in other ways. The **conflict** between wanting a **successful working life** and being a **mum** has made many women **put off having kids until later**.

New Technologies have Created New Family Structures

1) **Macionis and Plummer (1997)** highlighted the ability of new fertility treatments to allow family structures that were previously impossible.

2) Treatments such as **in vitro fertilisation** allow an egg to be fertilised in a **test tube** and then medically implanted into the womb of a surrogate mother who may not have been the original egg donor.

3) In 1991, **Arlette Schweitzer** acted as a surrogate mother using a fertilised egg originally taken from her own daughter. So it's arguable that the child is both her **daughter** and her **granddaughter**.

4) Fertility treatments have allowed **gay and lesbian** couples, and **single and older women**, to have children when they wouldn't have been able to before. This means that family structures exist that were **impossible** in the past.

Eversley and Bonnerjea (1982) found Regional Variations in Family Structure

Eversley and Bonnerjea (1982) found that some types of family structure were more likely to be found in certain types of area:

> **Inner cities** have higher concentrations of **single-parent** and **ethnic minority** families.

> **Southern England** has a high number of **two-parent**, upwardly-mobile families.

> **Coastal areas** are home to a large number of **retired couples** without dependent children.

> **Rural areas** tend to be characterised by **extended families** and strong external patterns of **kinship**.

> **Declining industrial areas** have a large number of **traditional families**, but also show a high amount of **diversity**.

The **New Right** think that Family Diversity is **Caused** by Falling Moral Standards

1) **New Right** theorists believe that family diversity is the result of a **decline** in traditional values. They see it as a **threat** to the traditional nuclear family and blame it for **antisocial behaviour** and **crime**.

2) **Murray (1989)** suggests that **single-mother** families are a principle cause of crime and social decay, because of the **lack** of a **male role model** and authority figure in the home.

3) The New Right believe that state benefits should be cut and social policy targeted to **discourage** family diversity and **promote** marriage and the nuclear family.

The New Right have been criticised for their 'blame the victim' approach.

Family Diversity — Changing Family Patterns

Functionalists *Think that the Growth in Diversity has been* **Exaggerated**

1) The functionalist **Robert Chester (1985)** admits that there has been **some growth** in family diversity, but believes that the **nuclear family** remains the dominant family structure.

2) He argues that statistics show a **greater increase** in diversity than is actually happening. This is because **UK society** has an **ageing population** (see p.20). **Death rates** are **decreasing**, e.g. in 1971, the death rate for men was 12.1 per 1000, but by 2006 it had fallen to 8.6 per 1000 (Social Trends 38, 2008). This means the **distribution of ages** in society is changing so that the proportion of older people is **increasing**. This increases the number of people who are at a stage in their life when they're **not in a nuclear family**.

Death rates have fallen for several reasons, e.g. improving standards of living, advances in health care and a decrease in manual, heavy labour jobs (Social Trends 38, 2008).

3) Chester has also suggested that nuclear families are becoming **less traditional** and **more symmetrical** (see page 29) to better fit modern living.

Postmodernists *see Diversity and Fragmentation as the New* **Norm**

1) Postmodernists claim that there is no longer a single dominant family structure — postmodern society is **highly diverse** and its diversity is **increasing**.

2) Improvements in **women's rights** and the availability of **contraception** have resulted in people having far more **choice** in their type of relationship.

Postmodernists emphasise the rise of individualism as a crucial feature of postmodern society.

3) People now tend to create their relationships to **suit their own needs** rather than following the traditional values of religion or the government.

4) Their relationships only last as long as their needs are **met** — creating even greater **diversity** and **instability**.

Beck (1992) identified the "negotiated family"

1) The postmodernist Beck believes that many people now live in **"negotiated families"** — family units that vary according to the changing needs of the people in them.

2) Negotiated families are **more equal** than traditional nuclear families, but are **less stable**.

3) **Weeks, Donovan et al (1999)** suggested that family commitment is now viewed as a matter of **ongoing negotiation** rather than something that lasts forever once entered into.

Jeffrey Weeks (2000) *says there's Increased* **Choice** *in* **Morality**

1) **Jeffrey Weeks (2000)** believes that personal **morality** has become an **individual choice** — rather than a set of values influenced by **religion** or dictated by **society**.

2) He sees modern **liberal attitudes** towards marriage, divorce, cohabitation and homosexuality as a major cause of **irreversible** diversity.

Practice Questions

Q1 Give two reasons for the decrease in the average number of children people have.
Q2 Explain why family structures are now possible that were impossible in the past.
Q3 Outline how region can affect family diversity.
Q4 On what grounds do New Right theorists oppose family diversity?
Q5 Give two reasons that postmodernists give for the growth of family diversity.
Q6 Explain how the decline in the influence of religion may have affected family diversity.

Exam Questions

Q1 Suggest three reasons for increasing family diversity. (6 marks)

Q2 Assess the view that people have become less idealistic in their attitudes towards family structure. (24 marks)

Have you met the nuclear family? They make you feel right at-om...

Postmodernists think family diversity is the new rule, the New Right think it's the result of falling standards and Jeffrey Weeks thinks that everyone just makes their own mind up. At least everyone agrees that diversity is increasing. Well, except functionalists.

Roles and Relationships Within the Family

As well as studying the place of the family unit in wider society, sociologists also research what happens within the family. The key focus is on the different roles and expectations of men, women and children within the family.

The **Rise** of the **Nuclear Family** led to **Joint Conjugal Roles**

Conjugal roles are the roles of **husband and wife** (or partner and partner) within the home. **Elizabeth Bott (1957)** studied how **jobs and roles within the family** were **allocated** to **men and women** in modern industrial Britain.

Sure, her study is **old**, but it's a **good foundation** for the debate, so don't dismiss it — **learn it**.

Bott (1957) identified two ways household jobs can be shared

Segregated roles	Husbands and wives lead separate lives with clear and **distinct responsibilities** within the family. The man goes out to work and does DIY. The woman stays home, looks after the kids and does all the emotional stuff.
Joint roles	Husband and wife roles are **more flexible** and shared, with less defined tasks for each. Usually leisure time is shared. Responsibility for making decisions is also shared.

Willmott and Young (1973) studied the changing structure of the British family from extended to nuclear (see p.29). They reckoned that the increase in the nuclear family meant that **joint conjugal roles** would develop. They predicted that **equal** and **shared responsibilities** would be the **future norm** in British families.

Willmott and Young's picture of **widespread equality** in marriage was **criticised** as soon as it was published.

Oakley (1974) pointed out that their study only required men to do a **few things round the house** to qualify as having joint roles. Their **methodology** overlooked the **amount of time** spent on housework — making 10 minutes' washing-up equivalent to an hour's hoovering, an hour's ironing and all the rest of the housework too. Oakley's research found it was **pretty rare** for men to do a lot of housework.

Conjugal Roles are Still Unequal Although Most Women have Paid Jobs

Since the early studies by Bott, and Willmott and Young, **new family structures** have developed. There are now lots **more families** where **both partners work outside the home**. Sociological evidence shows that an **equal share** of **paid employment** hasn't led to an **equal share** of **domestic labour**.

1) Edgell (1980) tested Willmott and Young's theory and found none of his sample families had joint conjugal roles in relation to housework. However, he did find increased sharing of childcare between men and women.

2) Oakley (1974) found that women took on a double burden — taking on paid jobs and still keeping the traditional responsibilities for home and children.

3) Boulton (1983) concluded that men may help out with specific bits of childcare like nappy-changing, but women are still primarily responsible for children.

4) Ferri and Smith (1996) found that two thirds of full-time working mothers said they were responsible for cooking and cleaning. Four fifths of the same group said they were responsible for laundry.

These are all **small-scale studies** — it's important to look at research using a much **larger sample**. The **British Social Attitudes Survey 1991** was a **large-scale study** that questioned about **1,000 people** about housework. It showed a very **clear division of labour** — **women** did **most of the housework**. For example, washing and ironing was mainly done by women in 84% of households, shared equally in 12%, and mainly done by men in 3%.

Industrialisation led to the Creation of the "Housewife"

1) **Oakley** thinks that the role of the **housewife** was **socially constructed** by the **social changes** of the **Industrial Revolution**, when people started **going to work in factories** instead of working at home.

2) **Married women** were often **not allowed** to work in factories. A new role of **housewife** was created for married women.

3) Middle class households had female **servants** to do domestic work. Working class women did it themselves.

4) The **cultural values** that said women should be in charge of housework were **so dominant** that domestic work came to be seen as "**naturally**" (biologically) the role of women.

Roles and Relationships Within the Family

Decision-Making and Sharing of Resources can be Unequal

As well as looking at the **division of labour** and tasks in the home, sociologists have researched how **power is shared** in the home. The traditional role of the **man** holding **power to make decisions** was **so widespread** that the phrase "**who wears the trousers**" is often used to mean who's in charge.

Edgell (1980) interviewed middle class couples

He found that **men** had **decision-making control** over things both husband and wife saw as important, whilst women had control over minor decisions. Half of husbands and two thirds of wives expressed a view that sexual **equality** was a **bad thing**.

Alas, no one knows who was wearing these trousers. It's a mystery.

Pahl (1989, 1993) researched money management by 100 dual-income couples

She concluded that the most common form of financial management was "**husband-controlled pooling**", which she defined as: the money is shared but the husband has the dominant role in how it's spent.

Explanations for Inequality are based on Theories About Power in Society

Guess what? There are **functionalist**, **Marxist** and **feminist** theories on power in society.

1) For **functionalists**, men and women still largely perform **different tasks** and **roles** within the family because it's the **most effective way** of keeping society **running smoothly**.

2) **Marxist** sociologists interpret the fact that men and women have different roles as evidence of the **power of capitalism** to **control** family life. They say women and men have unequal roles because **capitalism works best that way**. Even with more women working outside the home for equal hours to men, the capitalist class needs to **promote women** as "naturally" **caring** and **nurturing** to ensure workers are kept fit, healthy and happy. This role for women is maintained **ideologically** through the **media**, e.g. in adverts.

3) From a **feminist** perspective, inequality in household roles demonstrates **inequality in power** between men and women. A **patriarchal** society will produce **unequal conjugal relationships** because society's **systems** and **values** will **inevitably** benefit men at the expense of women.

So, all explanations of conjugal roles lead back to **different theories** about **power in society**.

These explanations all agree that different roles for men and women in the family help to **maintain the status quo** (keep things the way they are at the moment) in society — the disagreement between them is over **who benefits**.

Practice Questions

Q1 Define the term "conjugal roles".
Q2 Describe the differences between joint and segregated conjugal roles.
Q3 What is meant by the "double burden" of women in modern society?
Q4 How was the role of "housewife" socially constructed, according to Oakley?
Q5 Identify two areas of inequality in conjugal relationships other than household chores.

Exam Questions

Q1 Evaluate the evidence that conjugal roles are still unequal in modern British society. (24 marks)

Q2 Assess the view that power is the key to understanding relationships within the family. (24 marks)

I'll have a cup of tea while you're on your feet, love....

This is mainly about inequality in the family. You know, who does the housework, that sort of thing. Some sociologists look on the bright side and say that things are getting more equal. Others say they still aren't equal enough. Remember to look at the possible causes and social construction of inequality. And learn some of the statistics — it gets you more marks.

Roles and Relationships Within the Family

This page examines emotional work within families and the dark side of family life — domestic violence and child abuse.

Women *in Families can be Responsible for all the* Emotional Work

Doing **emotional work** in a family means **reacting** and **responding** to other family members' emotions, **alleviating** pain and distress, and **responding** to and **managing** anger and frustration.

1) **Diane Bell (1990)** suggested that there is an "**economy of emotion**" within all families and that running the economy is the responsibility of women.

2) She says managing family emotions is a bit like **bookkeeping** — the woman's role being to balance the family's **emotional budget**.

1) **Duncombe and Marsden (1995)** found that women in families are often required to do **housework and childcare, paid employment** and **emotional work** — amounting to a "**triple shift**" of work.

2) They found that married women were **happier** when their husbands **shared** some of the burden of emotional work.

3) But they also found that emotional work is predominantly **gendered** — women have the **main responsibility** for managing the whole family's emotions.

1) **Gillian Dunne (1999)** studied **lesbian households**. She found that the **distribution** of **responsibilities** such as childcare and housework tended to be **equal** between the partners. The couples were **flexible** and fair in the way they **shared work**.

2) Dunne thought that in **heterosexual relationships**, the division of work in the household was usually **less fair** because of traditional ideas about **masculinity** and **femininity**.

Some Sociologists See Child Abuse *in Terms of* Power

Sociologists study the issue of **child abuse** by parents and carers in terms of **power relationships**. You need to be able to **explain abuse** as a **form of power** rather than explore **details** of abuse itself.

A parent or carer is able to abuse a child by **manipulating** the **responsibilities and trust** which go along with the role of parent or carer. Families are **private** and separate from the rest of society. This makes it less likely for children to report abuse.

Social policies have been **adapted** to give some **protection** to children. The **Children Act 1989** was set up so the state can **intervene** in families if social workers are **concerned** about children's safety.

Domestic Violence *Affects Many Families in the UK*

Research by Professor **Elizabeth Stanko (2000)** found that:

1) A woman is **killed** by her current or former partner **every three days** in England and Wales.

2) There are 570 000 cases of **domestic violence** reported in the UK every year.

3) An incident of domestic violence occurs in the UK every **6-20 seconds.**

The Home Office estimates that **16% of all violent crime** in the **UK** is domestic violence.

The fourth **United Nations Women's Conference in 1995** reported that **25%** of women worldwide experience domestic violence.

Roles and Relationships Within the Family

Radical Feminists See Domestic Violence as a Form of Patriarchal Control

Radical feminist theory says violence against women is treated differently to other violent crime.

1) Dobash and Dobash's first UK study (1979) found the police usually didn't record violent crime by husbands against their wives.

2) Since 1979 the police have set up specialist domestic violence units, but still the conviction rate is low compared to other forms of assault.

3) Before 1991, British law said a husband was entitled to have sex with his wife against her will. In 1991 the rape law changed to say that a husband could be charged with raping his wife.

4) Evidence like that above is used by radical feminists to support their argument that laws and social policies in society have traditionally worked to control women and keep men's power in society going.

Radical feminists believe that violence against women within the family is a form of power and control.

> "Violence was used by the men they lived with to silence them, to 'win' arguments, to express dissatisfaction, to deter future behaviour and to merely demonstrate dominance."
> — Family Violence Professional Education Taskforce 1991, *Family Violence: Everybody's Business, Somebody's Life*, Page 116, Federation Press, Sydney. By permission of the publisher.

The social climate helps to maintain this situation by making women feel ashamed and stigmatised if they talk about the violence. The shame and stigma are part of the ideology of patriarchy — the school of thought that says women should know their place.

Remember, not all feminists agree with the radical feminist view.

Shame also comes from the idea that women should know better — not get involved with violent men in the first place. There's a tendency to blame the victim.

Dobash and Dobash found that most women who left violent partners returned in the end. This was because of fear of being stigmatised — and because they were financially dependent on their partner.

Abusive partners often condition their victim into thinking that nobody cares and there's nowhere to go. The pressure not to leave an abusive partner comes from the relationship as well as from society.

Radical Feminism is Criticised for Overemphasising the Power of Men

There are two main criticisms of radical feminist theory of the family:

1) It overemphasises the place of domestic violence in family life. Functionalists argue that most families operate harmoniously, while postmodern theory argues that individuals have much more choice and control to avoid, leave or reshape their family relationships.

2) It presents men as all-powerful and women as powerless when in reality women often hold some power over men. The journalist Melanie Phillips (2003) highlights the fact that women abuse men too and male victims are often ignored by society and the police. The pressure group Families Need Fathers campaigns for men to have equal rights in family and child law.

Practice Questions

Q1 What is meant by 'emotional work' in families?

Q2 What proportion of women worldwide experience domestic violence?

Q3 What do radical feminists think is the cause of domestic violence?

Q4 Give two criticisms of the radical feminist view of domestic violence.

Exam Questions

| Q1 | Assess the view that domestic violence is part of the ideology and practice of patriarchy. | (24 marks) |

| Q2 | Examine the ways in which feminist sociologists have contributed to our understanding of family roles and relationships. | (24 marks) |

Brrrr... not pleasant, is it...

You'd be forgiven for thinking that this stuff is all a bit depressing. But abuse does happen and you need to know how society deals with it and the different explanations people have for it, fair or unfair.

Childhood

These pages examine the social construction of childhood, the position of children in today's society, and the future of childhood.

Childhood is Partly a **Social Construct**

1) Sociologists say **childhood** is not only a **biological stage of development** but a **social construct** as well. The idea of how children are **different** from adults in their **values**, **behaviour** and **attitudes** isn't the same everywhere in the world, and it hasn't been the same for all times. In other words, it's **not universal** — different societies, with different cultures and values, can view childhood in different ways.

2) An example of this is how the school leaving age in Britain has moved from 12 to 16 in the last century. It would now be not only **socially unacceptable**, but also **illegal**, to leave school and work full-time at the age of 12. Effectively, the age at which childhood ends and adulthood begins has moved in line with social attitudes.

3) **Jane Pilcher (1995)** highlighted the **separateness** of childhood from other life phases. Children have different rights and duties from adults, and are regulated and protected by special laws.

Ariès says a **Cult of Childhood** Developed After Industrialisation

Sociologist Philippe Ariès' work on the construction of childhood is a classic study.

<u>Ariès (1962) looked at paintings</u>

Ariès said that the concept of **childhood** in Western European society has only existed in the **last 300 years**. Before this, in medieval society, a child took on the role of an adult as soon as it was physically able. Children in medieval paintings look like mini-adults.

With **industrialisation** social attitudes changed and people began to value children as needing specialised care and nurturing. The importance of the child reinforced the importance of the role of the **housewife** — it was the housewife's job to look after children.

This '**cult of the child**,' as Ariès referred to it, first developed in the middle classes and over time has become a part of working class values.

> You need to be aware that although Ariès' work is very important, he has been criticised. E.g. Pollack says that Ariès' work looks weak because it uses paintings for its main evidence.

Children are Protected by **Special Laws**

1) Children are subject to laws that restrict their **sexual behaviour**, their **access to alcohol and tobacco**, and the amount of **paid work** they can perform. These laws act **in addition** to the laws that affect adults.

2) They are offered **additional protection** by the **Children Act 1989**, which allows them to be **taken away from their parents** by the state if it judges the parents to be **incapable** or **unsuitable**.

3) They are given **price reductions** on many **goods and services**, e.g. they pay less on **public transport** and don't have to pay **VAT on clothing**.

4) But organisations such as the **National Society for the Prevention of Cruelty to Children** (the **NSPCC**) argue that they need greater protection. An NSPCC report by **Cawson et al (2000)** said that **16%** of children aged under 16 have experienced **sexual abuse** during childhood, and **25%** of children have experienced **physical violence**.

British Society in the 21st century is **More Child Focused** than Ever

1) There's now lots of **social policy** related to childhood. Children are recognised as having unique **human rights**. The **United Nations Convention on the Rights of the Child** was ratified (agreed to) in 1990 by all the UN members (except the USA and Somalia).

2) In Britain the Child Support Act 1991 established the **Child Support Agency**. This gave children the legal right to be **financially supported** by their parents, whether the parents are **living with the child or not**. This Act also made courts have to ask for the **child's point of view** in custody cases and take the child's view into consideration.

3) Children also hold more **power** in modern British society than at any other time in history. This has been identified by advertisers who recognise the **financial power** of children — this is often referred to as "**pester power**". Advertisers advertise a product to children because they know the children will **pester** their parents to buy the product.

Childhood

Functionalists See the Position of Children in Society as a Sign of Progress

Some functionalist sociologists, including **Shorter**, make the "**march of progress**" argument:
1) Society has a functional need for **better**-educated citizens and **lower** infant mortality rates.
2) So school leaving ages have **gone up** and child protection has **improved**.
3) That means that the current position of children is the result of **positive progression** from the past.

Childhood Varies according to Class, Gender and Ethnicity

Some sociologists suggest that the experience of childhood varies depending on class, gender and ethnicity:
1) Children living in **poverty** tend to suffer poorer health, a lack of basic necessities, lower achievement in school, poorer life chances, and higher incidences of neglect and abuse.
2) **June Statham and Charlie Owens (2007)** found that black and dual-heritage children were more likely to end up in care than white or Asian children.
3) **Julia Brannen (1994)** said that Asian families were much stricter with their daughters than their sons.
4) **Hillman (1993)** found that parents generally give **boys** more **freedom** than **girls**.

Child Liberationists Believe that Society Oppresses Children

Diana Gittins (1985) argues that there is an "age patriarchy" — adults maintain authority over children. They achieve this using enforced dependency through 'protection' from paid employment, legal controls over what children can and can't do, and in extreme cases abuse and neglect.

Hockey and James (1993) noted that childhood was a stage that most children wished to escape from and which many resisted.

Sociologists Disagree over the Future of Childhood

1) **Neil Postman (1994)** believes that childhood is **disappearing**.
2) Children grow up **very quickly** and experience things only open to adults in the past.
3) He argues that our definitions of 'childhood' and 'adulthood' will need to be **changed** soon.

1) **Nick Lee (2005)** disagrees with Postman.
2) He agrees that childhood has become an **ambiguous** area, but argues that parents have **financial control** and children can only spend as much as their parents allow.
3) So the **paradox of childhood** is one of **dependence** and **independence** at the same time.

Practice Questions

Q1 Explain the view that childhood is partly a social construct.
Q2 Give two ways in which 21st century British society could be said to be more child focused than before.
Q3 Describe how functionalists see the role of children in society.
Q4 How do class, ethnicity and gender influence a person's experience of childhood? Give examples.
Q5 What arguments have been put forward to support the view that childhood is disappearing?

Exam Question

Q1 Assess the reasons for the change in status of children since industrialisation. (24 marks)

Here's looking at you, kid...

The main idea on these pages is that childhood is partly socially constructed and that theories about it are not universally accepted. Remember that it's not enough to say that something is a "social construct" — you need to say how and why.

Poverty and Welfare

The sociological questions here are: "Which groups have the most / least?", "Is inequality increasing or decreasing?", "How much should the State help the poor?" and "Why does poverty exist at all?" So, that's all pretty straightforward then.

Wealth *is the* Value *of a* Person's Possessions

Wealth is defined in official statistics as the **value of all the possessions** of an individual **minus** any **debt**. It includes houses, land, money in the bank, shares and personal goods.

Wealth can be divided into **marketable wealth** and **non-marketable wealth**. **Marketable wealth** means **things you can sell**. **Non-marketable wealth** means things like your **salary** or a **pension fund**.

Percentage of marketable wealth owned by:	
The richest **1%** of society	**22%**
The richest **5%** of society	**42%**
The richest **10%** of society	**54%**
The richest **25%** of society	**75%**
The richest **50%** of society	**94%**

These figures come from the Social Trends 33 (2003) report by the Office of National Statistics. The pattern's pretty consistent over the last 25 years, by the way.

1) Every year government statistics on wealth in the UK are published in the Social Trends report.

2) The table shows that over half of the country's wealth is owned by a small percentage of the population. The less well off 50% of the population share only 6% of the country's wealth. These dramatic patterns show a society where a few people are extremely wealthy.

3) Wealth largely results from ownership of business and property. Most of this gets passed down to the next generation, so wealth stays in the same families for years. However, lots of the richest people in Britain have generated their own wealth (see below).

The *Sunday Times* publishes a list of the 1000 richest individuals in the UK every year.

1) The 2003 list revealed that the super-rich are mostly men. Only 77 out of 1000 were women.

2) 753 of them were self-made millionaires, 247 inherited their wealth. The ten richest individuals had money from business and land. The wealthiest individual in Britain in 2003 was the Duke of Westminster, but in 2007 it was Lakshmi Mittal, a self-made billionaire who trades in steel. (Sunday Times Rich List © The Times, London 2003, 2007)

Income *is the* Money *a Person Receives on a* Monthly *or* Yearly Basis

1) The vast **majority** of the British population **doesn't have significant wealth**. For most individuals their money comes from an **income**. Income is defined as the **personal funds an individual receives** on a **monthly / yearly basis**. This is usually from a **job** but can be from **benefits**, or **interest** on a savings account.

2) Household **disposable income per head** has **grown steadily** in the UK since the early 1980s. This reflects **overall growth in the economy**, and could be said to show that **everyone is getting richer** to some extent.

3) On the other hand, the **gap** between **rich and poor** has **widened** in recent years (according to Social Trends 2004). This means that the rich are getting richer whilst the poor are getting **relatively** poorer. Ahhh... the stuff sociology is made of...

£9.18 a month just doesn't go as far as it did in my day.

There are Patterns *of* Which Social Groups *are likely to* Earn *the* Least

The **Social Trends** report shows how many people have an income of **less than 60% of the median income** (the government measure of poverty). The **median** income is the **middle** income. **Half** the population **earn more** than the median, **half** of them **earn less**.

1) Households where adults are **unemployed** are **most likely** to have an **income below 60%** of the median. Which makes sense — you don't earn a lot of money when you're unemployed.

2) In 2001, **22%** of pensioners lived in households with **incomes of less than 60%** of the median. Which makes sense — you don't earn a lot of money when you're **retired**, either.

Poverty and Welfare

Income Also Seems to be Related to Ethnicity

The **Social Trends 33 (2003)** report also includes statistics about how **ethnicity and income** are related.

1) Overall, people in **ethnic minority households** were **more likely** than people in white households to be in the **lowest earning category**.

2) **White, Afro-Caribbean** and **Indian** households were pretty much equally likely to be the **highest earners**.

3) **64% of Pakistani and Bangladeshi households** were in the **lowest earning category**.

4) **White and Afro-Caribbean** households were **fairly well spread** across **all income groups**.

Absolute Poverty is a Lack of the Minimum Requirements for Survival

1) An individual is in absolute **poverty** if they don't have the income to afford the basic necessities — **food**, **warmth** and **shelter**. By this definition there are **very few individuals in the UK in poverty**.

2) **Rowntree (1871-1956)** set up the first major studies of poverty in the UK in **1899** and measured it in absolute terms. He made a **list of essentials** needed for life and recorded how many families could **afford** them. Those whose income was **too low** were classed as **in poverty**. He found **33%** of the population in York were in poverty.

3) There are criticisms of Rowntree's study. His definition of poverty didn't allow for any wasted food and it assumed the **cheapest** options were **always available**. The lists of essentials were compiled by **experts** and **didn't match the lifestyle** of the folk he surveyed. He did listen to his critics though, and for two further studies, (published in 1941 and 1951), he **added more items** to the list of essentials. By this time, **more people** could afford the basics on the list. His conclusion was that **poverty was disappearing fast** in 20th century Britain.

4) Another **study of poverty in absolute terms** is **Drewnowski and Scott (1966)**. They devised a "**level of living index**" which worked out the income needed for **basic needs**, adding **cultural needs** to the list. However, it's debatable whether cultural needs like TV should be included in a study of **absolute** poverty.

Bradshaw (1990) Devised the Budget Standard Measure of Poverty

1) **Bradshaw (1990)** used an approach similar to Rowntree's idea of **absolute poverty**. He studied the **spending patterns** of the least wealthy and used those patterns to calculate an **adequate budget**. Anyone earning less than the adequate budget was classed as "**poor**".

2) The main difference between Bradshaw's approach and Rowntree's was that Bradshaw studied how people **actually spend their money** whereas Rowntree assumed that if people earnt more than the **usual total cost of essential items** then they weren't poor.

3) Because Bradshaw's test isn't relative (see p. 44), it gives clear and unambiguous statistics that are easy to **compare** between different studies.

4) Critics have argued that Bradshaw set a **very low 'adequate budget'**, so his conclusions are not a **true reflection of deprivation** in society.

Practice Questions

Q1 Give a one-sentence definition of each of the following: wealth, income and absolute poverty.

Q2 How much of marketable wealth is owned by the richest 1% in British society, according to Social Trends, 2003? And how much is owned by the poorest 50%?

Q3 How did Bradshaw's work differ from Rowntree's?

Exam Question

Q1 Explain the meaning of the term 'income'. (2 marks)

We can all dream of being rich...

Most rows between married couples are about money. It's troublesome stuff, but you can't live without it. Learn the basic pattern of wealth distribution — if you can learn a couple of figures as well, that'd be useful. And learn how Bradshaw advanced the methods of Rowntree — they both used absolute figures but Bradshaw factored spending patterns into his calculations.

Poverty and Welfare

Not all sociologists agree with the absolute definition of poverty — they prefer relative definitions of poverty.

Relative Poverty is a Comparison with the Average Standard of Living

Many sociologists (especially left-wing ones) favour the **relative** definition of poverty.
Relative poverty shows whether an individual is rich or poor **in relation to the other people**
they **share** their **society** with, rather than whether people have the basics like food and shelter.

Townsend (1979) Introduced the Concept of Relative Deprivation

1) **Townsend (1979)** devised a **"deprivation index"** — a list of 60 things **central to life** in the UK. The list included **social activities**, such as inviting other people over for meals, and **possessions**, such as owning a refrigerator.

2) From his list of 60 things, he selected **12** that he thought were **equally essential to the whole population**.

3) He then gave each household a **deprivation score** based on whether or not they had the items on his shortlist of 12 items.

4) Looking at his statistics, he found that the deprivation score **went up rapidly** after wealth dropped **below a certain threshold**. The threshold was about 150% of the 1979 basic supplementary benefit levels (now called income support).

5) So he classified all households that **earnt below the threshold** as **"suffering from poverty"**.

6) Using his measure, Townsend calculated that **22.9%** of the population were suffering from relative poverty.

Barney was well stocked in all his essential life items.

1) **Piachaud (1987)** has argued that Townsend's deprivation index is too **subjective** and **culturally biased**, citing shortlist items such as having **cooked breakfasts** and **Sunday joints**.

2) **Wedderburn** also criticised Townsend's method for creating the deprivation index. She argued that he should have carried out **research** into the customary behaviour of people in society. It seemed to her as though he had just picked items based on his own **cultural opinions**.

Mack and Lansley (1985) Measured Poverty using a Consensual Approach

1) **Mack and Lansley (1985)** measured poverty in a similar way to Townsend, but acted on some of the criticisms his work had received. They defined poverty to be "an **enforced lack** of **socially perceived necessities**".

2) They used a **survey** to determine which items to include on their list of perceived necessities. They asked respondents what they considered to be the necessities. Any items that were classified as essential by **over 50%** of the respondents were added to their list. They ended up with a list of **22 items**.

3) They then surveyed households to find out which necessities they lacked. Households could answer that they had the item, wanted but couldn't afford the item or didn't want the item. Only those that said they **wanted but couldn't afford the item** were considered to be **deprived**. Mack and Lansley therefore argued that their figures would only reflect **involuntary** deprivation.

4) If a household involuntarily lacked **three or more items** from the list of necessities then they were classified as **poor**.

5) They reported that **14%** of the population were living in poverty in **1983**. When they repeated the study in **1990**, they found that this figure had risen to **21%**.

6) A more recent study by **Gordon et al (2000)** found that **24%** of the population were living in poverty in 1999 according to the test set by Mack and Lansley.

Poverty and Welfare

Mack and Lansley's Studies Have Been Criticised

1) Critics have argued that because the 1990 survey and the 1983 survey didn't produce **the same list of necessities**, their results are not **directly comparable**.

2) They also argue that as long as **some difference** exists between the richest and poorest, some of the poorest will be **relatively deprived**.

The Different Definitions of Poverty have Advantages and Disadvantages

	Advantages	Disadvantages
Defining poverty absolutely	1) Absolute poverty is always measured on the **same scale** — no matter what group you're looking at. That makes it easy to **compare** statistics between groups. 2) It gives a better idea of the standard of life in **developed countries**, where people who are relatively poor may still have more than enough wealth to **meet their basic needs**.	1) Measuring absolute poverty means making some assumptions about people's **basic needs.** 2) It also assumes that everyone has **the same** basic needs. It disregards information about occupation, gender, age and culture that might be relevant to deciding someone's **basic needs**.
Defining poverty relatively	1) Relative poverty takes into account **people's expectations** and the **subjective quality** of their lives. 2) So it gives a **more realistic** picture of the **relative** deprivation that is caused by **inequalities in society**.	1) As long as there is **any difference** between people in society, some of them will **appear to be "poor"** in a relative poverty study. 2) If the rich are getting richer **more quickly** than the poor are getting richer, then relative poverty will **increase** even though the lives of the poor are **improving**.

How much poverty there is out there really depends on how it's **defined** and **measured**.
With an **absolute** definition of poverty, Rowntree concluded **poverty** was soon to be a **thing of the past**.
Studies based on the **relative** definition of poverty suggest that poverty **persists** in the UK.

But then again, it always will because it's <u>relative</u>.

Practice Questions

Q1 Give two advantages of defining poverty absolutely.
Q2 What was Townsend's deprivation index?
Q3 How did Mack and Lansley's work differ from Townend's?
Q4 What is the difference between measuring absolute poverty and measuring relative poverty?

Exam Question

Q1 Assess the problems involved in defining and measuring poverty. (24 marks)

Poverty is a bad thing, no matter how you measure it...

Make sure you understand the difference between relative poverty and absolute poverty and between voluntary and involuntary deprivation. Townsend studied poverty by looking at what households lacked. Mack and Lansley's work was similar, but they used surveys to work out what society thinks a household should possess, and allowed for voluntary deprivation.

Explanations of Wealth Distribution

Evidence shows that wealth is distributed unequally, and that incomes vary from small to huge. To sociologists, a pattern like this needs explanation — and of course there are lots of different explanations for the way that wealth is shared out.

Early Theories **Blamed the Poor** for Being Poor

1) The first theories of poverty **blamed the individual** for the poverty they were in.

2) The **19th century** sociologist **Herbert Spencer** said the **poor** were those in society who had **failed** to do the best for themselves. He suggested that they were immoral, lazy and more interested in booze than an honest day's work.

3) Spencer said the **state shouldn't intervene** to help the poor because the poor are a useful **example to others** not to follow that way of life.

Functionalists Say **Unequal Distribution** of **Wealth** is **Good** for Society

Functionalism says some people are richer / poorer than others because **society functions that way**. **Functionalist theory** argues that as societies develop, they have to find a way of allocating people to suitable roles and jobs. The most **important jobs** need to be **rewarded more highly than others** to motivate **intelligent people** to **train** and **qualify** for them. The key study to know here is *Some Principles of Stratification* (**Davis and Moore 1949**). Don't worry that it's old — it's classical functionalism.

Functionalist arguments have been **criticised** — they assume the best jobs are allocated on the basis of **talent** when in reality **discrimination** by social class, age, ethnicity and gender often influences who gets the top jobs. **Tumin (1967)** reckons that Davis and Moore **ignore all the talent and ability in the working class** which society doesn't use.

Weberians Say Distribution of Wealth is Based on **Market Situation**

1) Weberian sociologists (followers of **Max Weber**) say that the distribution of wealth and income is based on what they call **market situation**.

2) An individual's market situation is how **valuable** their **skills** are for society and how **scarce** their skills are. It's about **supply and demand** of skills. High demand for your skills makes them worth more.

3) For example, currently **plumbers** can earn **higher wages** than other skilled manual workers, because there's a **shortage** of plumbers and people **need their skills**. So plumbers have a good market situation at the moment.

4) Weberians say **poor people** have a **poor market situation**.

5) There **isn't always the same demand** for the **same skills** — the same people don't always have the best market situation. This means there's always some **movement of wealth in society**.

6) Individuals **compete** to improve their market situation. **Powerful people** like judges, politicians and the directors of big companies can do the most to keep themselves in a good market situation.

Car mechanics are always in demand in the tiger economies.

Marxists Blame Capitalism for Inequalities in Wealth and Income

1) Marxists say that the social groups which have **low levels of wealth** and **income** are the ones which are **powerless** in society.

2) According to Marx and his followers, **capitalism thrives** on **inequality of income** — if there were equal distribution of wealth there wouldn't be any profit for the capitalists. The capitalist class **needs profit** to keep up its **power in society**.

3) Marxism says **exploitation** is an **essential part of capitalism** — and inequalities in wealth and income are a central part of that exploitation.

4) Marx predicted that as capitalism develops, **more oppression** of the proletariat (working class) is needed. Marxists say the current **widening gap between rich and poor** is evidence of this.

As you may have noticed, the Marxist explanations for most things are quite similar. Capitalism, exploitation, etc., etc...

Explanations of Wealth Distribution

Recent *Changes in Society* Have *Increased* the *Gap* between *Rich* and *Poor*

1) The gap between the income of the rich and the income of the poor **went down** in the **1970s**.
Under the **Labour government (1974-1979)**, **benefits** given to the poor **went up** and taxes paid
by the rich were **very high**.

2) In the **1980s**, under the Conservative government, the **gap widened**. The top rate of tax went down
so the **rich kept more of their earnings**. Taxes that everyone pays like **VAT** and **fuel tax** went up.
The economy did well, so rich people earned more money on their **investments**. **Benefits** went **down**.

3) **Adonis and Pollard (1997)** reported that the gap continued to widen into the 1990s. In addition to policies introduced
during the 1980s, they identified the **increase in private education** as a factor affecting wealth distribution.

4) An **Office of National Statistics** report by **Penny Babb (2004)** based on the 2001 census suggested that the gap
between rich and poor continued to grow under New Labour.

5) There has been an **increase** in the number of **single parent households**. Single parent households
tend to have less money (see below) and this means the statistics show **more poorer households**.

6) There are also more **two earner households** — e.g. families where both parents work.
Income is measured by household, so a **household with two people** in good jobs is
relatively rich. This contributes to the statistics showing an **increase in rich households**.

Some Social Groups are *More Likely to be Poor* Than Others

For these statistics, poverty is defined as having an income that's less than 60% of the median income.

> **Women** — in 1992, there were **5.2 million women** living in **poverty** in the UK, compared to **4.2 million men**.
>
> **Older people** — in 1992, **32%** of households where the **main adult was over 60** were poor.
>
> **Single parents** — in 1992, **58%** of **single parents** had an income of less than half the average.
>
> **Disabled people** — in 1996, **47%** of **disabled** people had an income of less than half the average.
>
> **Ethnic minorities** — in 1997, the Policy Studies Institute said that overall UK ethnic minorities are **more likely**
> to be poor. **Pakistani and Bangladeshi** households are the most likely to have **low income**.

1) Women tend to be poorer than men **partly** because they're **more likely** to be **single parents** than men.
Working mums are more likely to be in **part-time jobs** that fit in with childcare, but that pay less.

2) Older people tend to be poorer because they're **retired** — some retired people only get a **basic state pension**.

3) **Single-parent** families tend to be poor because it's hard to get **good work** and **look after kids** at the same time.

4) **Disabled** people face **discrimination** in the job market. Disabled people, and people with long-term illnesses who
can't work, live on **incapacity benefit** and **disability benefit**, which means they have a fixed, relatively low income.

5) **Some ethnic minorities** tend to be **richer / poorer** than others — and there's **variation** in the
level of income within ethnic minority groups. It's not as clear-cut as the statistics suggests.

Practice Questions

Q1 Why did Spencer argue inequality of income is good for society?

Q2 How does an individual's market situation affect their wealth?

Q3 Did the gap between rich and poor decrease or increase in the 1980s?

Q4 Write down five groups in British society who are more likely to be poor than others.

Exam Questions

Q1	Examine the view that "Inequality in wealth is beneficial to society".	(24 marks)
Q2	Examine the social composition of the poor in British society.	(24 marks)

Ever seen how much plumbers charge...

Remember that the gap between rich and poor went down, then up again. It's mainly related to tax and benefits. Learn those functionalist, Weberian and Marxist explanations for the distribution of wealth. You can probably guess the functionalist one: "it's all for the best" and the Marxist: "it's cos of evil capitalism, grr". Watch out for those Weberians and their plumber though.

Why Does Poverty Exist?

Unsurprisingly, different schools of sociological thought have different explanations of why poverty exists.

Oscar Lewis said Culture was the Cause of Poverty

Lewis (1959, 1961, 1966) studied the poor in Mexico and Puerto Rico

Lewis thought that the **values**, **norms** and **behaviour** of the **poor** were **different** to the rest of society and these values were passed on from generation to generation.

He said individuals learn how to be poor and learn to expect to be poor through the subculture of poverty they're socialised into.

He reckoned that this **culture** of resignation, apathy and lack of participation in wider society initially starts as a response to poverty but then becomes a culture which keeps people in poverty. He called it a '**design for life**'.

1) Lewis's work was **controversial** and **criticised** from the start. Similar research done at the same time found **highly organised community facilities** and **political involvement**.

2) **Schwartz (1975)** concluded that the poor **weren't culturally different** from the well-off.

1) Situational Constraints theory says that the poor have the **same values and norms** as the **rest of society** and any difference in the **behaviour** of the poor is because they're **limited** by their **poverty**. For example, unemployment restricts lifestyle options.

2) **Coates and Silburn (1970)** studied poor areas of Nottingham. They found that **some people** in poor areas **did feel resigned to being poor**, and that it wasn't worth trying to get out of poverty. But... they said this was actually a **realistic assessment** of an individual's situation. It **wasn't proof** of some kind of **alternative value system**.

3) Coates and Silburn's research supported the idea that **poverty leads to other forms of deprivation** which can trap people into a **cycle of deprivation**. This means poverty is **practically hard to get out of**, not culturally hard to get out of.

Different Reasons have been Given for the Growth of Poverty

1) **Brewer and Gregg (2002)** argued that **changes in the economy** have caused a growth in poverty rates.

2) They identified an increase in the number of households with **no working adults** at one end of the scale and an increase in the number of households with **two working adults** at the other. These changes have led to an increase in the **gap** between **high earning households** and **low earning households**.

3) They also found that **reductions in income tax** for employed people had been **greater than raises in benefits** for unemployed people. This caused an **increase in relative poverty**.

1) **Smith, Smith and Wright (1997)** think that **modern educational policy** reinforces current trends in poverty.

2) They say that **market-driven educational reforms** (see p. 64) favour middle class children. So working class children are more likely to end up in **failing schools**.

3) They also found that the **abolition of maintenance grants** in 1998 means that working class children are less likely to consider **going to university**.

4) They argue that a **poorer education** leads to **poorer work opportunities**, reinforcing the **gap in earnings** between rich and poor.

New Right Theorists Blame Dependency on Welfare for Poverty

1) **Charles Murray (1993)** described a sector of society which he thought had a **culture of dependency on the state** and an **unwillingness to work**. He called this group the **underclass**.

2) Murray identified the **rising number** of **single-parent families**, **rising crime**, and **attitudes** of **resistance to work**. Murray accepts that not all poor people are work-shy but he thinks a significant group just don't want to work.

3) In Murray's opinion, **Welfare State benefits** are **too high**. He says this means there's not much encouragement to get off welfare and get a job.

4) Another right-wing sociologist, **Marsland (1989)**, thinks that the **level of poverty** is **exaggerated** by other writers. He says society should **keep a small level of poverty** to **motivate** others to work. Marsland agrees with Murray that the **Welfare State is too generous** and encourages a **culture of non-work** amongst some groups.

Sociological **criticism** of Murray says his **evidence** for the existence of an underclass is **too weak**. **Walker (1990)** found **very little evidence** of **different values** and **behaviour** among the poor. His opinion was that **blaming** the poor **distracts** from the **real causes** of poverty such as the **failure of social policy**.

SECTION THREE — WEALTH, POVERTY AND WELFARE

Why Does Poverty Exist?

Weberian Sociologists Blame Inequalities in the Labour Market

1) **Max Weber** thought that an individual's **position in the labour market** was the key to their life chances, wealth and status. The people whose skills were most **valued** and **needed** would always be the **wealthiest**.

2) **Dean and Taylor-Gooby (1992)** think that **changes in the UK labour market** have led to increased poverty. There are more casual and temporary jobs, but less job security and far fewer "jobs for life". Dean and Taylor-Gooby say this means more people are likely to experience poverty at some point.

3) **Townsend (1970, 1979)** has the view that the key **explanation for poverty** is the **low status** of some workers, which doesn't give them much power to improve their labour market situation.

Marxists Blame the Capitalist System for Poverty

Marxists think that the working class tends to be poor because of capitalist exploitation. They say it's a mistake to focus on the poor as a **separate group** — poverty comes from **class structure**, so sociologists should focus on the **working class** instead.

They think that **poverty exists** because it **serves the needs of the capitalist class** in society. **Kincaid (1973)** explains it like this:

1) The low-paid provide a **cheap labour supply** for the **capitalist class**, which keeps **profits high**.

2) The varying pay levels within the working class keep individuals **competing** against each other to get the best jobs. This **divides the working class**. Marxism says that if the working class all **united together** they'd be a **threat** to capitalism — so it's in the **interests of capitalism** to keep the **working class divided**.

3) Kincaid believes poverty is **not an accident** — he thinks it's an **inbuilt part** of the capitalist system.

Marxists say welfare benefits don't do much good

1) Marxist sociologists **Westergaard and Resler (1976)** argue that state benefits only **blunt the extremes** of poverty.

2) They say that **welfare benefits stay low** so that people **still need to sell their labour** even if their wages are low.

3) They also argue that most of the **money paid out in welfare benefits** has been **paid in by the working class in tax** or **subsidised by their low wages**. The working class are getting their own money back, not money from the rich.

Marxist Explanations of Poverty Have Been Criticised

1) Marxist explanations of poverty **don't explain** why some groups in society are much more likely to experience poverty than others. Marxists treat poverty (and just about everything else) as a **characteristic of capitalism**, and as something that the **working class as a whole** suffers. They don't look for much **detail** about the experience of poverty for **individuals** or **groups**.

2) Marxism **ignores** the effects of **gender** and **ethnicity** on poverty. It doesn't explain why women are more likely to be poor than men, or why Bangladeshi households are more likely to be poor than Afro-Caribbean households.

3) **Townsend (1970, 1979) rejects** the argument that the Welfare State (e.g. state benefits) doesn't do much good. He believes that **social policy can and should improve standards of living** even within a capitalist system.

4) **Capitalism** creates **wealth** in the economy. This increase in wealth contributes to the **reduction of absolute poverty**.

Practice Questions

Q1   Give an example of an attitude and a behaviour which Lewis (1959, 1961, 1966) argues causes poverty.

Q2   What does Murray (1993) identify as the key processes which create an underclass?

Q3   Give an example of how poverty is helpful to the capitalist class, from a Marxist perspective.

Exam Question

Q1   Assess the view that the poor are to blame for their poverty.   (24 marks)

Blame the victim or blame the system...

It's not as easy as you might think to explain why people get stuck in poverty. Each of these theories makes some sense, but they don't all look at the big picture. When you're answering an exam question that asks you to "critically examine the arguments" bear that in mind — remember the downsides of each theory. Use one theory to criticise another.

Social Policy and Poverty

You need to know what kind of things governments do to sort out poverty.

The **New Right** believes in the Reduction of the **Welfare State**

1) The **New Right** think that a **generous welfare state** actually **makes people poorer**.

2) British New Right thinker **Marsland (1989)** thinks all **universal benefits** (paid to everyone regardless of wealth) should be abolished because they **encourage dependency**. He says that benefits should only exist to support those in the most desperate need for the shortest possible time. He argues that this will encourage people to "stand on their own two feet".

3) **Right wing policy** encourages **business** so that **wealth will be created**. Right wing politicians would prefer everyone to make their own money and decide how to spend it, instead of paying lots of tax or getting benefits from the state.

4) American sociologist **Murray (1993)** recommended a "**moral**" benefits system to discourage people from forming **single-parent families**. He thought that unmarried mums should get no benefit at all.

> In the UK, the most recent Conservative governments (1979-1997) were influenced by New Right theory. They **reduced spending** on welfare by removing some universal benefits and having benefits **only for the poorest**. They made it clear that they wanted to **get rid of the dependency culture** by **reducing benefits** and **allowances**.
>
> The idea was that people would be **better off working**.
>
> The idea was also that resources freed up by these welfare cuts would **boost the economy**, which would benefit society as a whole. Conservatives said the money at the top would "**trickle down**" to make **everyone** in society wealthier.

Examples of Conservative welfare reforms

1) **Stopped paying benefits** to **16-18** year olds.

2) **Replaced grants** for basic necessities with **loans**.

3) **Abolished** entitlement of **students** to **benefits** in the **academic holiday**.

4) Introduced the **Child Support Agency** — forcing **absent parents** to pay for the support of children, rather than the state.

People on low incomes used to be able to get a "social fund" grant to buy things like a new cooker. Nowadays they can get a loan, which they have to pay back.

So, some of the **New Right solutions to poverty** have **been tried** in the UK. They've been criticised by some sociologists for **increasing** relative poverty.

Social Democrats Believe **Social Policy Reforms** Could Solve Poverty

Social Democrats see **institutions** in society as the cause of poverty. They believe **inequality** in **wealth and income** is the root cause of poverty, so they want government policy to **redistribute wealth** and resources from **rich** to **poor**.

The big idea is that the state **should** work to stamp out poverty — and that the state **can** work to stamp out poverty.

1) Social democratic theory says **increasing welfare provision** will help to **solve poverty**.

2) **Mack and Lansley (1985)** suggest a big increase in benefits. They conducted a public opinion poll in which British people said they were **prepared to pay higher taxes** to get rid of poverty.

3) **Townsend** sees the solution to poverty in the **labour market**. He says **social policy** must have the job of **reducing inequalities** in the labour market.

4) The poor are most often unemployed or low-paid. This means **policies** are needed to **improve wages** and conditions and to **protect workers' rights**. The **National Minimum Wage** and **Working Families' Tax Credit** brought in under the New Labour government are examples of this kind of intervention.

5) British sociologists **Walker and Walker (1994)** argue for an "active employment strategy" where the government would actually **create work** for the unemployed.

> Social democratic theory has been **criticised** by people on the **right wing** and on the **left wing**.
>
> 1) **New Right** theorists say the social democratic policy of **strengthening the Welfare State** and increasing the power of social policy would be an **absolute disaster** in terms of solving poverty. The New Right say these things led to the increase in poverty in the first place.
>
> 2) Left wing **Marxists** say the **state** will always **serve the interests** of those in **power**, which means that nothing the government does can make a big difference to poverty in capitalist society.

Social Policy and Poverty

Since 1997, the *New Labour* Government has had a *"Third Way"* Approach

When New Labour took power in Britain in 1997, it claimed its social policies would reduce poverty significantly. Their philosophy **combines** both the **New Right** and the **social democratic** theories — so it was called "**the third way**".

The theme was that the poor need "**a hand up not a handout**". The "hand up" part means the state should have **social policies** which **help the poor** — rather like the social democratic theory. The "not a handout" part means people **shouldn't depend** on benefits — rather like **New Right theory**.

They say the state has a responsibility to **help people in real need**, and individuals have a **responsibility to help themselves**. The "**New Welfare Contract**" of 1998 says that the **government** has to **help people find work**, make **work pay**, help with **childcare**, help the **poorest** old people and help those who really **can't work**. It says that **individuals** have to look for work, be as **independent as possible**, support their own family, save for retirement and not defraud the taxpayer by claiming benefit when they shouldn't.

Don't worry — you don't need to know all the New Labour social reforms in detail. Here are some examples which help show the ideology behind them.

Reforms to remove dependency on benefits — so working pays more than benefits...

1) **Working Families' Tax Credit** — tax reductions for the **low-paid but working**.

2) **National Minimum Wage** — to ensure every employer **pays more than benefit levels**.

3) **New Deal** — a **training** and **support** package for people **returning to work** from benefits.

4) **Welfare to Work** — a series of opportunities for **young, unemployed people** paid for by tax on profits of privatised gas and electricity companies.

5) **Income Tax cuts** — they halved the **starter rate** (the lowest rate), meaning that poorer families **keep more** of what they **earn**.

6) **Educational Maintenance Allowance** — extra money for **students** from poorer backgrounds who stay in education after they're 16. By keeping people in education for longer, New Labour hope that they'll be less likely to need benefits later on.

Reforms to make the poor less socially excluded and isolated

1) **Social Exclusion Unit** — launched to provide support to **reintegrate excluded people** back into society.

2) The concept of **stakeholders** — individuals could own a stake in organisations which affect them, either in financial terms or voting power.

3) **Childcare costs** paid for or subsidised by the government.

There is conflicting evidence as to whether the government has achieved a reduction in poverty since 1997. The Social Trends 33 (2003) report showed that the distribution of wealth had changed little over the past 28 years. The number of people classed as unemployed had fallen though.

Marxists say *Nothing* Will Work Except the *Overthrow of Capitalism*

1) Marxists believe that the root cause of poverty is the **inequality** central to the **capitalist system**. Therefore, the Marxist solution to poverty is the **removal** of the **capitalist system**.

2) Marxists say that while the capitalist system keeps on going, poverty will still be around — **no matter** what **social policy** you throw at it. **Westergaard and Resler (1976)** think no big **redistribution of wealth** can happen until capitalism is overthrown and replaced by a **socialist** society where **wealth is communally owned**.

3) The most **common criticism** of the Marxist approach is the **evidence** that **socialist** and **communist** **societies haven't eradicated poverty**. People were poor in Soviet Russia and there is poverty in Cuba.

Practice Questions

Q1 Why do the New Right think that the Welfare State can be too generous?

Q2 Give an example of a social policy which could be used to lessen poverty.

Q3 Explain how Marxist theory argues poverty could be eradicated in Britain.

Exam Question

Q1 Assess the view that ideology lies behind all solutions to poverty. (24 marks)

Sounds great on paper — but will it work in real life?

Although the four theories here are different, they all make some kind of sense on paper. It'd probably be great if everyone earned enough money to buy the best kind of private welfare. It'd probably be great if the state provided really good public welfare for everybody. In real life it's hard to make things work. At the moment, the jury's still out on the Third Way idea.

Welfare Provision

Welfare means all the institutions that look after people — whether they're state-provided or not.

Four Sectors provide Welfare — Public, Private, Voluntary and Informal

Public Sector

These are **state services** which are **funded**, **regulated** and **run by the state**. Examples — the **NHS**, the free **education system** and the **benefits system**. Most services are **free at the point of delivery** and are **funded by taxes** and **national insurance**.

Private Sector

These services are **run by companies for profit**. They often offer **alternatives** to state services — e.g. **private hospitals**, **schools** and **nurseries**. There's no state funding but they have to **meet state regulations**. The individual **pays for these services directly**.

Voluntary Sector

These services are provided by **charity**. They often provide **extra** facilities and services beyond what the state provides. E.g. the **hospice** movement and **Help the Aged**. They have to **conform to state regulations**. Voluntary services **may get some state funding**. The individual receives these services **free** or at a **subsidised low cost**.

Informal Sector

This means services and help provided by **friends and family** as and when needed. The informal sector often provides services **in addition to state services** or when there **isn't enough state provision**. Examples — **family carers**, **family childminders**. There's **little** or **no state funding** or **regulation**. It's usually **free** to the individual but **costs the provider money**.

1) The **combination** of all four types of welfare provision is known as **welfare pluralism**.

2) The British system is based on welfare pluralism. Since the 1979 Conservative government, there has been a **steady growth** in **private**, **voluntary** and **informal sector welfare** and a **relative decline** in **public sector welfare**.

The Welfare State — Health, Housing, Education, Social Work and Benefits

1) The British **Welfare State** was set up in the **1940s** after the **Beveridge Report** was published. The Welfare State was designed to wipe out the social problems of society. Beveridge defined these as the "**five evils**".

Ignorance (poor education)	⟹ **1944 Education Act**
Disease (poor health)	⟹ **NHS set up in 1946**
Want (poverty)	⟹ **National Insurance Act**
Idleness (unemployment)	⟹ **National Assistance Act**
Squalor (poor housing)	⟹ **Council Housing Programme**

2) People in work would pay into a **national insurance scheme** which would **pay for the Welfare State**. The Welfare State was designed to be free at the point where you actually needed it. For example, going to the doctor = free.

3) The British Welfare State is **universal**. This means all benefits and services are given to **everyone** rather than **selectively** to the poorest. **Checking** that people are **poor enough** to get a selective benefit is called **means testing**.

4) The **cost of the Welfare State** has **risen a lot**. (This graph is based on information from the **Centre for Analysis of Social Exclusion**, CASEbrief 5, April **1998**).

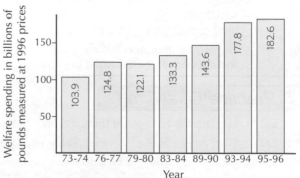

Welfare spending in billions of pounds measured at 1996 prices

Year	Spending
73-74	103.9
76-77	124.8
79-80	122.1
83-84	133.3
89-90	143.6
93-94	177.8
95-96	182.6

There have been a lot of **Conservative reforms** to **reduce the size** of the Welfare State and **cut costs**.

1) **Increase** in **selective benefits** — e.g. 1980 Housing Act, 1988 Social Security Act.

2) **Reduction** in **universal benefits** — e.g. general entitlement to free eye tests abolished.

3) **Privatisation** of welfare provision — e.g. local authority care homes closed, replaced by private care homes.

4) **Increase** in **voluntary** and **charitable** welfare provision — e.g. housing associations taking over council houses.

Under **New Labour** there's been an emphasis on trying to make the NHS and social security more **efficient** to **save money**. Most benefits and services cut by the Conservative governments **haven't been reintroduced**.

Welfare Provision

Social Democrats *believe the* Welfare State *can* Reduce Inequality

The founders of the Welfare State thought it'd **reduce inequality** because the rich and poor would all get the **same benefits** and **services**. Resources would be shared out more **equally**. Part of the vision of the Welfare State was that these policies would help create a society where all people had **equal opportunities**. But...

...There's research demonstrating **persistent hard-to-shift inequality** in all five areas of welfare — **health, education, housing, unemployment** and **poverty**. A good overall study by **Le Grand (1982)** found not much evidence of redistribution of resources. Le Grand found that **middle class** families were more likely to use the free services of the welfare state — not the working class, or the poor.

Marxist sociologists **Westergaard and Resler (1976)** argue that the welfare state has failed to reduce inequality between social classes in Britain. Their research focused on **tax** and **benefits**, and concluded that the **working class contributed most** as a **proportion** of their **income** and that the **middle class benefited the most**. However, the middle classes as a group pay most in terms of the total tax received by the government. Some sociologists have argued that by focusing on the contribution as a proportion of total income, **Westergaard and Resler** emphasised the inequality aspect.

The New Right *Prefer* Selective Benefits *and* Means Testing

1) Remember, the New Right theory blames poverty on an **overgenerous welfare state**.

2) So, from the New Right point of view, the ideal welfare state has a **small range** of **minimal benefits** which are only selectively available to the very **poorest**.

3) Selective benefits would be **means-tested** — the government would only provide them to people whose incomes were below a certain level.

4) The New Right say that governments must focus on creating a **strong economy**. In a strong economy **private welfare providers** can compete giving individuals **choice** and **value**. New Right thinkers reckon the **free market economy** is the **best way** to ensure services are provided at the **lowest prices** and the **best quality**.

5) The New Right think that a **strong market** will encourage individual endeavour, leading to an increase in standards of living for everybody. The Welfare State would only be needed as an **emergency back-up**.

For Marxists *the* Welfare State Reproduces *and* Legitimises Capitalism

1) According to Marxists, the Welfare State makes sure the capitalist class always has a **healthy workforce** through the NHS. For Marxists, they don't do this to be **nice** to the individual worker but to **keep them working**, which is essential to keep **making profits**.

2) The Welfare State helps to portray the image of a **caring society** where the state **cares** for the individual. Marxists say this is **useful** to the capitalist class because it **hides** the real **oppressive** nature of capitalism and **keeps the working class quiet** — which prevents a revolution.

3) Not all Marxists agree, mind you. An **alternative Marxist view** is that the **Welfare State exists** because it was **fought for** by **workers' struggle** and the capitalist class wouldn't have provided it otherwise.

Practice Questions

Q1   Name four sectors which provide welfare.

Q2   What were the key social problems the Welfare State was founded to address?

Q3   List four Conservative reforms of welfare provision.

Q4   Outline the findings of Le Grand (1982)

Exam Questions

Q1 Explain the difference between public sector and private sector welfare.	(4 marks)
Q2 Examine the Marxist theory of the Welfare State.	(24 marks)

Shall we give the poor some money, or shall we not bother...

You might think that the New Right theorists are all mean old grumpyboots with no heart, or that Marxists are just dreamers with no grip on reality. The thing is, they both genuinely believe they're doing the best for everyone. With these social policies, it's hard to tell who's wrong and who's right, but you can look at real-life examples — most of these ideas have been tried somewhere.

The Role of the Education System

Different theories try to explain the role or function of education in society. Some of them look at the positive functions. Some look at how education oppresses pupils and maintains inequality. Some look at pupil interaction in the classroom. Some say we should get rid of school altogether... Yay.

Functionalism *Says Education Has* Three Functions *that Help Society*

1) Education teaches the **skills** needed in **work** and by the **economy**.
2) Education **sifts and sorts people** for the **appropriate jobs**. This is called the **allocation** function.
3) Education plays a part in **secondary socialisation**, passing on **core values**.

1) **Durkheim** said that education passes on **norms** and **values** in order to **integrate** individuals into society. Education helps to **create social order** based on cohesion and value **consensus**.

2) **Parsons** describes school as a bridge between the family and adult roles of society. Schools pass on a **universal value** of **achievement**. Parsons says that education **selects** children into **appropriate roles** because it's **meritocratic** (meaning that the best students rise to the top). He agrees with Durkheim that education helps to make people agree about norms and values.

3) **Davis and Moore (1945)** say that every society sorts its members into different positions. They think that there are **rules** for how education does this — called "**principles of stratification**". They believe that there has to be a system of **unequal rewards** (more money or status) to **motivate** people to train for the top positions.

The **functionalist** perspective says that education is **meritocratic**. A **meritocracy** is when social **rewards** are allocated by **talent** and **effort** rather than because of a position someone was **born** into.

Talent + motivation + equal opportunity = qualifications and a high position in society

Marxism *Says* Education Legitimises Inequality *through* Ideology

1) Education **prepares children** for the **world of work** by giving them **skills** and **values** they'll need.
2) Education **justifies inequality**.
3) Education passes on **ruling class ideology** that **supports capitalism**.

1) The neo-Marxist **Althusser** sees education as part of the "ideological state apparatus". In other words, it's a tool of capitalism which is used to pass on the belief that society is fair. Althusser thinks education produces a **docile and obedient workforce**.

2) **Bowles and Gintis (1976)** say that there is a close link between school and work. They say that there's a **correspondence** between **pupil experiences of school** and **adult work**:
   - Pupils are taught to accept the **hierarchy** at school. Work also has a hierarchy.
   - Pupils are **motivated by grades** to do **boring work**. Workers are **rewarded with pay** to do **boring work**.
   - The **school day** is broken into **small units**. So is the **work day**.
   - At school and work **subservience** (following the rules) is **rewarded**.

   Bowles and Gintis say that the '**hidden curriculum**' (things like being on time for lessons, and doing your homework) **prepares people for work**. They also say that meritocracy is a **myth** which is used to **blame individuals** for not succeeding.

3) **Willis (1977)** says that education **doesn't turn out** an **obedient workforce**. Some kids form an **anti-school subculture** and cope with school and then adult work by mucking about.

4) **Bourdieu** used the concept of **cultural capital** (language, skills, knowledge and attitudes) to explain how the middle class get into the top positions. There's **plenty** on this on p.57.

Radicals *like* Illich *Want to* Get Rid Of School Completely

Illich (1971) believes that education has four functions:

Illich agrees with functionalists about the functions of school — but he thinks the functions aren't good enough. So we should give up school as a bad idea.

1) Education **looks after kids** during the day.
2) Education **sorts pupils into job roles**.
3) Education **passes on dominant values**.
4) Education helps people learn **skills and knowledge**.

The problem for Illich is that schools **don't create equality** or **develop creativity**. Illich wants to "**deschool society**". He wants everyone to have **access to education throughout their lives** according to what they need.

The Role of the Education System

There are **Problems** with **Functionalist** and **Marxist Views**

Criticisms of Functionalism

1) Evidence of **differential achievement** in terms of class, gender and ethnicity suggests that education is **not meritocratic**.

2) **"Who you know"** is still more important than "what you know" in some parts of society. So the allocation function isn't working properly.

3) It can be argued that the education system **doesn't prepare people** adequately for **work**. For example, the lack of engineering graduates indicates education is failing to produce what **employers** and the **economy** needs.

4) Functionalism doesn't look at how education may serve the interests of particular groups in terms of **ideology** and **values**. It **doesn't explain conflict**.

Criticisms of Marxism

1) Marxism assumes people are **passive victims**. It **exaggerates** how much working class students are **socialised** into **obedience**. Willis showed how students actually resist authority.

2) Most people are **aware of the inequality** in education. Most people don't believe that society is fair.

The problem with both approaches is that they don't look at interaction and social processes within the school.

There are **Similarities** and **Differences** Between **Functionalist** and **Marxist Views**

1) Both functionalism and Marxism look at the **big picture** — institutions and the whole structure of society. They tend to **ignore social interaction** — with the exception of Willis. Both say education has a **huge impact** on the individual and that there's a **close link** with the **economy** and **work**.

2) The biggest **difference** is how they see **inequality**. Marxists say education helps to **maintain inequality** and **make people accept inequality**. Functionalists say education passes on the value of **meritocracy** and lets people **better themselves**.

Feminists say that the Education System is **Patriarchal**

1) Some feminists argue that the hidden curriculum unofficially **reinforces gender differences**.

2) There are still **gender differences** in **subject choice** in schools. Gender stereotyping may still exist.

3) Girls are now outperforming boys at school — but **boys** still **demand more attention** from the teacher.

4) **Men** seem to dominate the top positions in schools (**head teacher**, **deputy head**) and even more so in universities.

Liberal feminists want **equal access to education for both sexes**.

Radical feminists believe men are a bad influence, and want **female-centred education** for girls.

Marxist feminists want to consider gender inequalities **combined with inequalities** of **class** and **ethnicity**.

Practice Questions

Q1 Name three functions that the education system performs according to functionalists.

Q2 Name two functionalist studies of education.

Q3 What is meant by meritocracy?

Q4 What did Bowles and Gintis say pupils' experience of education had a close correspondence with?

Q5 Give two problems with the Marxist theory of education.

Q6 What is the difference between Marxist and functionalist approaches to education?

Exam Questions

Q1 Identify two ways in which schooling in capitalist societies mirrors the working world. (4 marks)

Q2 Examine the Marxist view that the function of the education system is to pass on ideology and reproduce the existing class structure. (20 marks)

Getting rid of school sounds good, but what'd you have instead?

Mmm, there's lots of theory here. If you know what Marxism, functionalism and feminism are, then their views of school **shouldn't come as a big shock**. *Functionalists think education brings social harmony. Marxists say school is there to produce an obedient workforce. Feminists think school reinforces gender inequality and difference. They're so predictable.*

Class and Differential Achievement in Education

Sociologists have investigated how social class affects how well people do at school. Financial and cultural factors are studied, as well as in-school factors like streaming.

Social Class *tends to Affect* Educational Achievement

1) Pupils from **professional** backgrounds are significantly **more likely** to enter **higher education** than those from unskilled backgrounds.

2) Pupils from **middle class** backgrounds are more likely to study for **A-Levels**, whereas **working class** pupils are more likely to take **vocational** subjects.

3) Pupils from disadvantaged backgrounds are **more likely** to **leave school at 16** and **less likely** to start school being able to **read**.

4) Pupils from **unskilled backgrounds** on average achieve **lower scores** on SATs and in GCSEs and are more likely to be placed in **lower streams** or **bands**.

I wonder if class affects how well you do in a school of fish...

Some sociologists have suggested that the relative intelligence levels of different socio-economic and ethnic groups account for discrepancies in educational attainment (**Eysenck (1971)** and others). But it is difficult to determine whether IQ or social factors are more important to educational achievement.

Processes Inside School — *Labelling, Streaming and Subcultures are Factors*

1) **Negative labelling** of students can lead to a **self-fulfilling prophecy of failure**. **Becker (1971)** and **Keddie (1971)** say that teachers tend to evaluate pupils in terms of an **ideal student**, by looking at appearance, personality, speech and social class.

2) Negative labelling can mean students get put into **lower streams or bands**. **Ball (1981)** found that the pupils in the top bands were from **higher social classes**. Teachers had **higher expectations** of them and they were **taught in different ways**. Keddie found that teachers allowed pupils in the top streams access to higher levels of knowledge. Working class students didn't get this knowledge.

3) As a response to negative labelling and frustration with low status, pupils may form **anti-school subcultures**. **Hargreaves (1975)** found that those in the **bottom streams** were more likely to be non-conformist. **Woods (1983)** responded by saying that there are lots of different reactions to school, but **non-conformist** reactions were more likely to come from **working class** students.

These explanations are useful when looking at day-to-day experiences in schools. The problem is that they don't explain how **factors outside of school** (e.g. poverty, cultural deprivation) can influence achievement.

Labelling theory is also too **deterministic** — it says that once you're negatively labelled that's it, you're more likely to fail. This isn't always the case.

Material Deprivation Outside School *Can Affect Achievement*

The theory of **material deprivation** says that **economic poverty** is a big factor in low achievement at school.

1) In 1997, the **Joseph Rowntree Foundation** classified **one in ten** children as **poor** — which was defined as being in a family that couldn't afford at least three things other families took for granted.

2) **Halsey (1980)** found that the **most important factor** preventing working class students staying on at school was a **lack of financial support**.

3) **Douglas (1964)** found that children in **unsatisfactory living conditions** (poor housing, lack of nutritious food, overcrowding) didn't do very well in ability tests compared to kids from comfortable backgrounds.

4) **Unemployment** or **low income** means less money for books, internet access and school trips. Low income families can't afford **nurseries** and **private schools** and they can't afford to support their kids through **uni**.

5) Poverty and unsatisfactory living standards may cause **health problems** and **absence from school**.

Cultural Deprivation Outside School *Can Affect Achievement*

The theory of **cultural deprivation** says that **working class culture** and **parenting** aren't aimed at educational success.

1) **Douglas (1964)** thought the **level of parental interest** was the most important factor in affecting achievement. For example, middle class parents are more likely to visit schools for open evenings. Bear in mind though that **working class parents** may not go to open evenings because they work **inconvenient shifts** — not because they aren't interested.

2) Some sociologists say that working class kids don't have the **knowledge** and **values** that help achievement. **Museum visits**, **books** and **parental knowledge of education** may help middle class pupils to succeed.

3) Some **styles of parenting** emphasise the importance of education more than others.

Class and Differential Achievement in Education

Some Sociologists say Class Affects Attitudes to Education

1) **Sugarman (1970)** said that pupils from non-manual backgrounds and manual backgrounds have **different outlooks**. The pupils from **manual** backgrounds lived for **immediate gratification**. The pupils from **non-manual backgrounds** were **ambitious** and **deferred their gratification** — they invested time in studying and planned for the future.

2) **Hyman (1967)** said that the **values** of the working class are a **self-imposed barrier** to improving their position. He said that the working class tend to place a **low value** on education.

> *ethnocentric = believing your group/nation/culture is superior to others.*

But...

Material and cultural deprivation theories **don't** explain how **factors inside school** affect achievement.

Cultural deprivation theory **generalises a lot** about differences between middle class and working class life. It **ignores** working class families who **do** place a high value on education, and tends to **assume** that working class families have **no culture** at all, or that working class culture can't be **relevant** to school. This is **ethnocentric**.

The **method** may be **unsound**, e.g. attending parents' evenings might not be a good measure of parental interest.

The two Bs (Bernstein and Bourdieu) — Investigated Differences in Achievement

1) **Bernstein (1970)** found that working class pupils in the East End of London weren't comfortable with the style of language required by school. They used a restricted code — short forms of speech.

2) **Middle class students** knew how to use the same elaborated code as the teachers — a much more wordy style of speech with everything made very explicit.

3) In terms of language, the working class kids were at a disadvantage.

    1) **Bourdieu (1971, 1974)** reckons middle class students are at an advantage because they have the right kind of "**cultural capital**" — the right language, skills, knowledge and attitudes.

    2) He thought that the more cultural capital you have, the more successful you'll be in education — and he believed that working class pupils don't have access to cultural capital.

    3) Middle class families pass on cultural capital and expectations from parents to children. This is called cultural reproduction.

Problems with Bernstein's theory	Problems with Bourdieu's theory
There are **variations within** the middle class and working class. Different sections of these groups **vary** in how they use the **elaborate code** — the "posh language" of teachers.	**Halsey (1980)** found that **material factors** are important. **Lack of money** may **stop kids staying on at school** or **getting to university**.
Some sociologists have developed his ideas to say working class speech patterns are inferior or somehow "wrong" — controversial... **Labov (1973)** thinks the elaborated speech code is just **different**.	**Not all working class students fail**, even if they don't have cultural capital.

Recent Studies Suggest that Social Class Remains a Factor in Achievement

1) **Willmott and Hutchinson (1992)** studied inner-city schools in Manchester and Liverpool and identified an increase in the number of students leaving school with **no GCSE passes**. They linked the increase to **deprived social backgrounds**.

2) **Leon Feinstein (2003)** found that social class continued to have a **significant impact** on educational achievement. He argued that **redistributive policies** like Sure Start (see p. 64) should carry on throughout a **student's entire education**, rather than being restricted to their pre-school years.

Practice Questions

Q1   Give two facts about the links between social class and educational achievement.

Q2   Explain how processes outside school can cause underachievement by children from working class backgrounds.

Q3   What is cultural capital and who does it help in education?

Exam Question

Q1   Outline some of the sociological explanations for the underachievement of children from lower social classes.   (12 marks)

Immediate gratification sounds good to me...

A warning — the exam might ask something like "Assess how factors inside and outside school affect achievement". To answer, you'd need to look at home and school factors for ethnicity, gender AND class. So revise pages 58-61 as well as these ones.

Ethnicity and Differential Achievement in Education

Ethnicity is another factor that can influence how well people do at school.
Quick reminder — ethnicity means the shared cultural traditions and history which are distinct from other groups
in society. Modern Britain is said to be a multicultural society made up of many different ethnic groups.

Some *Ethnic Groups* Do *Better* Than *Others*

These figures are from **Modood et al (1997)** — the Policy Studies Institute's fourth survey of ethnic minorities in Britain.

All these statistics are averages. If you look at someone and say "she does well cos she's Chinese" you might be wrong.

Higher levels of achievement

1) The survey found that **Chinese, African Asians** and **Indian** groups were more qualified than whites. **Afro-Caribbean women** were more likely to have **A-levels** than white women.

2) Ethnic minorities were **more likely than white pupils** to continue into **further education** (from ages 16-19).

3) People from ethnic minorities who were **born in the UK** had much **higher qualifications** than people who moved to the UK from abroad.

Lower levels of achievement

1) **Bangladeshi** and **Pakistani women** were least well qualified. **Afro-Caribbean, Pakistani** and **Bangladeshi men** were least qualified.

2) **Pakistani** and **Afro-Caribbean** groups were **less likely** to get onto **university** courses, and **more likely** to get into **less prestigious universities**.

3) **Afro-Caribbean boys** are **more likely** to be **excluded from school**, more likely to be put in **lower streams** and more likely to do **vocational** courses.

African Asians means people of Indian origin who lived in Kenya and Uganda and then moved to Britain in the 1970s.

There are big **variations** between the **average achievement level** of different ethnic minority groups. There must be something behind it all — probably more than one factor, and probably some **social** and **economic** factors.

Some people say that **intelligence is inherited** — i.e. people underachieve because they've inherited low IQ.

HOWEVER... **IQ tests** can be **biased**. Sometimes they ask things that aren't really a test of brains, but really a test of **cultural knowledge**. The **Swann Report (1985)** found that if you took into account social and economic factors there were **no significant differences in IQ** whatsoever between different **ethnic groups**.

Processes Inside School — *Labelling, Curriculum* and *Prejudice* are Factors

Labelling theory says that teachers have **different expectations of different ethnic minority groups**. **Gillborn (1990)** found that teachers sometimes **negatively label black students**. Afro-Caribbean students were seen as a **challenge** to school **authority** — and were more likely to be excluded from school. Gillborn calls this the "myth of the black challenge". Teachers had high expectations of Asian students, which could lead to a self-fulfilling prophecy of **success**. In contrast, negative labelling could result in a **self-fulfilling prophecy of failure**.

There's also an issue about whether the school curriculum is **ethnocentric** — i.e. that it might fit the mainstream, white, middle class culture better than other ethnicities. It could be **Europe-centred** too. Languages in the National Curriculum are mainly **European** — kids usually learn French and German, not Gujarati or Chinese. **Assemblies, school holidays** and even **history lessons** may not fit with the culture and history of particular groups.

Some sociologists see British education as **"institutionally racist"**. This is where **policies** and **attitudes** unintentionally discriminate against ethnic minority groups. **Wright (1992)** found that even though members of staff said they were **committed to equal opportunities**, Asian girls got **less attention** from teachers and felt their cultural traditions were disapproved of (e.g. they might get told off for wearing a headscarf if it isn't part of the school uniform). **Afro-Caribbean boys** were more likely to be punished and **sent out of class**.

Some sociologists say that these factors may lead to **low self-esteem** for ethnic minorities. **Coard (1971)** said that black students are made to feel inferior in British schools.

Low Self-Esteem Exists — But it Isn't Really All That Widespread

1) **Mirza (1992)** found that black girls had **positive self-esteem** and **high aspirations**. The girls experienced discrimination but had **strategies** to minimise the effects of racism. It **wasn't low self-esteem** that affected their achievement — it was being **unwilling to ask for help**, or unwilling to **choose certain subjects**.

2) **Fuller (1980)** found Afro-Caribbean girls in London **resisted negative labelling** and **worked hard** to gain **success**.

3) Negative labelling and racism can affect pupils' reactions to school. Pupils may use either a **pro-school subculture** or an **anti-school subculture** to maintain their self-esteem.

Ethnicity and Differential Achievement in Education

Factors Outside School — *Language Difference* Affects Achievement

1) **Language** was a barrier for kids from **Asian** and **Afro-Caribbean immigrant families** when they **first arrived** in the UK.
2) The **Swann Report** found that **language didn't affect progress** for **later generations**.
3) **Driver and Ballard (1981)** also found Asian children whose **first language** was **not English** were **as good at English** as their **classmates** by the age of 16.
4) **Labelling theorists** would say that language might not be a barrier, but **dialects** or having an **accent** might **influence teacher expectations** and lead to **negative labelling**. For example, a teacher might **assume** that a child isn't good at English because they have a foreign accent and put them in a lower set.

Factors Outside School — *Family Difference* Affects Achievement

1) Some studies say that **family life varies** for different groups and this can influence achievement.
2) **Driver and Ballard (1981)** say that the **close-knit extended families** and **high parental expectations** increase levels of achievement in **Asian communities**.
3) Some sociologists say the relatively high levels of **divorce** and **single-parenthood** in Afro-Caribbean households could result in **material deprivation**. On the other hand, the **independence** of **Afro-Caribbean women** can mean that girls get **positive role models**.

Ethnicity Combines with *Social Class* to Affect Achievement

On their own, the factors inside and outside of school may not seem all that convincing. If you bring **social class** and **material factors** into the equation you get a more complex picture.

1) The **Swann Report** found that **socio-economic** status was a factor in the lower levels of achievement of **Afro-Caribbean** pupils.
2) **Pakistani, Bangladeshi** and **Afro-Caribbean** groups are more likely to be in **lower class positions** such as routine occupations (assembly line workers, factory workers) and elementary occupations (cleaners, labourers). This may result in poor housing, periods of unemployment, poverty and **material deprivation**.
3) **Chinese, African Asian** and **Indian** groups are more likely to be in **higher class** positions and **less likely** to experience material deprivation.

Leon Tikly (2005) Says That *Dual-Heritage* Children Face *Unique Problems*

1) **Dual-heritage** children are children whose parents are from **different ethnicities**. Around **7.3%** of London school pupils and **3.3%** of all UK school pupils are dual heritage.
2) **Tikly (2005)** observed that the **level of achievement** for dual-heritage children is **below average** and that they are **more likely** to be **excluded from school** — especially if they're **male**.
3) He suggested that the problems might stem from the facts that dual-heritage children often live in families with **lower income levels**, are more likely to come from **single-parent families** and face **more racism** from other students.
4) He also found that teachers often classified dual-heritage children as "black" and did not consider their **unique needs**.

Practice Questions

Q1 Give two facts about the links between ethnicity and educational achievement.
Q2 Why do sociologists dislike genetic explanations of intelligence and educational success?
Q3 Name one factor inside school that explains the underachievement of some ethnic minority groups.
Q4 Give an example of how social class combines with ethnicity to affect achievement.

Exam Question

Q1 Assess the significance of factors inside school in explaining the educational achievement of different ethnic minority groups.
(20 marks)

It's more complicated than you might have thought...

Remember that not all ethnic minorities underachieve — so don't go storming into your exam answer with a pre-prepared rant that it's all about white / black racism. There are always several different factors that affect each ethnic group.

Gender and Differential Achievement in Education

Gender is another factor that can influence how well people do at school.
Since the 1980s, things have changed. Sociologists used to talk about female underachievement.
Now there are worries that boys are falling behind. Geez Louise, make your minds up...

Here are **Six Facts** about **Gender** and **Differential Educational Achievement**

1) Girls get better results at all levels in National Curriculum tests.

2) Girls get better results in most subjects at GCSE.

3) Girls are more likely to pass their A-levels.

4) Women are more likely to go on to university.

5) Men seem to have most success at the highest levels of university.
A higher proportion of male students get first class degrees and PhDs.

6) Girls tend to go for communication-based subjects like English and sociology
and boys tend to go for technical ones like maths and physics.

Don't be tricked by these facts into thinking that boys are doomed.
You could say that there's been a bit of a '**moral panic**' about males underperforming.

Factors Inside School Explain Why Females Now Do Better

1) **Mitsos and Browne (1998)** say teaching has been **feminised**. Women are **more likely to be classroom teachers**, especially in primary schools. This gives girls **positive role models**.

2) **Textbooks** and **teaching resources** have changed and are less likely to **stereotype girls** into passive roles.

3) The National Curriculum **forced** girls to do **traditionally "male"** subjects. For example, more girls started to do **science**. Other Local Education Authority and government initiatives tried to encourage girls to do these subjects, e.g. WISE (Women In Science and Engineering) and GIST (Girls Into Science and Technology).

4) **GCSEs** include more **coursework** than earlier qualifications. Some people argue that coursework suits girls better because they put in **more effort**, are **better organised** and can **concentrate** for longer than boys (that's quite a sweeping generalisation though...)

5) **Swann and Graddol (1993)** think that high female achievement is a result of the **quality of interaction** they have with their **teachers**. Most of the time teachers spend with girls is used to **help with their work** but most teacher time spent with boys is focused on **behaviour management**.

6) **Jackson (1998)** says that schools label boys **negatively**. Boys are associated with poor behaviour, which gives the school a bad name, and with **low achievement**, which lowers the school's **league table position**. This negative label becomes a **self-fulfilling prophecy**.

Factors Outside School Explain Why Females Now Do Better

1) Policies such as the **Equal Pay Act** and **Sex Discrimination Act** have helped to create **more equal opportunities** in the wider society. This has **changed the values** of society and attitudes in school.

> The Equal Pay Act (1971) makes it illegal to pay men and women different wages for the same work. The Sex Discrimination Act 1975 means employers can't discriminate on the basis of gender.

2) **Sue Sharpe (1994)** found that girls' priorities have changed. They now want **careers** — and qualifications. More women go out to work, so girls see lots of **positive role models** in work. Girls nowadays often want to be **financially independent** — they don't just want to marry a rich man any more.

3) **Boys** tend to spend their leisure time being **physically active**. **Girls** are more likely to spend their leisure time **reading** and **communicating**. This means girls develop **language skills** that are useful for most subjects.

4) The **feminist** movement caused a **change in female expectations**, and made more people **aware of inequality**. People are now more careful about negative stereotyping, sex discrimination and patriarchy.

Archer (2006) says that Females Still Face Problems at School

1) **Archer (2006)** argues that the current **underachievement** by boys in education masks the **continuing problems** that girls still face.

2) She claims that **high-achieving Asian** and **Chinese** girls get negatively labelled by teachers as **robots** who are **incapable of independent thought**.

3) She also argues that **high-achieving black working class girls** get negatively labelled by teachers as **loud and aggressive**.

4) She concludes that the ongoing achievement of girls is **"fragile and problematic"**.

Gender and Differential Achievement in Education

Here are Some *Reasons* Why *Some Boys Underachieve*

1) Boys may be having an **identity crisis**. The rise of **female independence**, the decline of the **breadwinner** role for men and the rise in **male unemployment** might mean that boys don't see the point of education. This may lead to anti-school subcultures.

2) **Interpretivists** say that teachers have **lower expectations of boys**. Teacher expectations may lead to a **self-fulfilling prophecy** of poor behaviour. **Negative labelling** may explain why they're more disruptive. Boys are more likely to be **excluded** from school.

3) The **feminisation** of **teaching** means that boys don't have as many **role models** in school.

4) **Reading** is often seen as "uncool" or "girly". Boys who **avoid books** like the plague won't develop important **communication skills**.

Burly men in Santa hats can read books, too.

Subcultures help to Explain *Gender* and *Achievement*

Negative labelling and putting students into different **streams** or bands can cause some pupils to rebel against school's values. They form **subcultures**. These can be either **pro-** or **anti-school** subcultures.

1) In the 1970s **Willis** looked at why working class kids get working class jobs. He studied a group of boys later called "Willis's lads". The lads **rejected school** and formed an **anti-school subculture**. They **coped** with their own underachievement by having a **subculture where education didn't matter**, and where having a laugh was more important.

2) **Mac an Ghaill (1994)** says that **subcultures are complicated**. There are **lots of different types**. Boys may join a **macho lad subculture** because of a crisis of masculinity. But boys could also join **pro-school subcultures** and be proud of academic achievement.

3) **Fuller (1980)** found that **Afro-Caribbean girls** in **London** formed a **subculture** that worked hard to prove negative labelling wrong.

There are *Different Ways* to Explain *Gender* and *Subject Choice*

Girls tend to go for **arts and humanities**. Boys tend to go for **science and technology**.

1) **Subject choice** may still be influenced by **gender socialisation**. The ideas of **femininity** and **masculinity** create different **expectations** and **stereotypes** of what to study. Kids often see biology as "the science that it's OK for girls to do" and girls who do physics as "super hardcore science chicks" (or "geeky girls who do physics").

2) **Kelly (1987)** found that **science** is seen as a **masculine subject**. Boys dominate the science classroom.

3) **Parental expectations** and **teacher expectations** may encourage girls to follow what they see as the traditional "**normal**" choice for their gender. There's a pressure to **conform** to a social norm.

Practice Questions

Q1 Give two facts about the links between gender and educational achievement.
Q2 Name one factor inside school that helps explain why girls now do better than boys.
Q3 Give two reasons why subcultures are formed by some school pupils.
Q4 Give one reason why boys and girls choose different subjects.

Exam Questions

Q1 Explain what is meant by the 'feminisation of teaching'.	(2 marks)
Q2 Identify three educational policies that have led to improvements in girls' performance.	(6 marks)

Girls are DOOMED... no wait, boys are DOOMED... no wait... ah, forget it...

*Once again, you can't look at gender without looking at class and ethnicity. Working class girls don't do as well as middle class girls. Also remember that there's a **lot of generalisation** with these sociological theories. Of course not all girls prefer coursework to exams. I bet they prefer lounging around on the beach to doing exams though. Pity they don't test that.*

State Policy and Education

*All governments are interested in education. The 1870 Forster Education Act introduced elementary schooling
for 5–10 year olds in England and Wales. Since then there have been some major changes. Place your votes, please.*

The **1944 Education Act** Introduced the **Tripartite System** and the **11+**

By the time of the Second World War, the main problem in education was that there was a **huge divide** between the types of
secondary education available for the rich and poor. The **1944** Act (often called the **Butler Act** after the man who introduced it)
tried to create education for all — secondary schools were made free for all and the school leaving age was raised to 15.
You took the **11+ exam** (like an IQ test) at the end of primary school and then went to one of three types of school:

> 1) **Grammar schools** were for the able kids who passed the 11+. Pupils were taught
>   traditional subjects ready for **university**. About **20% of kids** got in to grammar school.
>
> 2) **Secondary modern schools** were for the **75-80%** of pupils **who failed** the 11+.
>   Secondary moderns offered **basic education**.
>
> 3) **Technical schools** were meant to provide a more **vocationally-minded** education for
>   those pupils with aptitude for **practical subjects**.

This **tripartite system** aimed to improve the education of all children, but several problems remained:

1) The **11+ didn't necessarily measure your intelligence**. It was **culturally biased**,
   and suited the middle class more than the working class.

2) **Few technical schools were built**, so the vocational part of the plan didn't work especially well.

3) Most children ended up either at grammar or secondary modern schools. These schools were supposed to have "**parity
   of esteem**" — they were supposed to be considered as having **equal value**. The problem was that grammar schools
   were seen as the best. Not a surprise since which school you went to was decided by how well you did in an exam.

4) Kids who failed the 11+ were **labelled as failures**, which sometimes turned them off education.

5) If well-off middle class pupils failed, their parents could still afford to send them to **private schools**.

In **1965** the Labour Government made Schools **Comprehensive**

The Labour government insisted that Local Education Authorities (LEAs) **reorganised most schools** so that everyone had
equality of opportunity. "**Comprehensive school**" means it's universal — everyone's meant to get the same deal.

Positive aspects of the comprehensive system	Criticisms of the comprehensive system
There's no 11+, so 80% of the school population don't get labelled as failures.	Comprehensive schools still stream pupils into sets depending on test scores. (So it's still possible to feel like a failure without the 11+.)
High-ability pupils generally still do well with this system. Lower ability pupils do better in comprehensive schools than in the old secondary moderns.	Schools in working class areas have lower pass rates than those in middle class areas.

The comprehensive system has not achieved equality of opportunity. Schools tend to be 'single-class', depending on the local
area. Where people can afford to live (and whether there are good schools nearby) is important in educational attainment.

In **1976** the Push for **Vocational Education** Started

Labour Prime Minister James Callaghan thought British education and industry was in decline because
schools didn't teach people the **skills they needed in work**. All governments since then have had
policies to create a closer link between school and work. This is called **vocationalism**.

> 1) **Youth Training Schemes (YTS)** started in 1983.
>
> 2) In 1993, **GNVQs** and **NVQs** were introduced — **practical qualifications**. ← *YTS were job training schemes for 16-17 year old kids leaving school.*
>
> 3) The introduction of the **New Deal** in 1997 means people on benefits must attend courses if they don't accept work.
>
> 4) Recently, **key skills** qualifications have started. These are supposed to be useful for all jobs.
>
> 5) **Curriculum 2000**, a reform of post-16 education, included the introduction of the **vocational A-Level** —
>   a qualification intended to be of equal worth to a traditional, academic A-Level.

There are some **problems** with vocational education:

1) Some sociologists argue that vocational education aims to teach **good work discipline**, not skills.

2) Some Marxist sociologists say that vocational training provides **cheap labour** and that governments encourage people
   into training schemes to **lower unemployment statistics**.

3) Lots of **young people** have **part-time jobs**, so they **already have work skills**.

4) Vocational qualifications often aren't regarded as highly as academic qualifications by universities and employers.

State Policy and Education

The 1988 Education Reform Act — Choice, Inspections and More Tests

In the late 1980s, the **Conservative** government introduced some **major reforms** in education.

Education should link to the economy

The government introduced **more vocational courses** and more **work placement schemes**.

There should be better standards in education

1) The government introduced a **National Curriculum** of **compulsory subjects** for all **5 to 16 year olds**.

2) **OFSTED** (Office for Standards in Education) was set up to **inspect** schools and make sure they were doing a **decent job**. You might have seen **teachers** getting somewhat **frantic** before an inspection.

3) Schools could **opt out** of their local education authority and become **grant-maintained schools**. This means that they got money **straight from the government** and could **spend it how they liked**. The government believed this would **improve standards**.

There should be a system of choice and competition

1) Parents could **choose** which school to send their child to — if the school had **space**.

2) Parents could use **league tables** to help them choose. **League tables** show **how many** kids at each school **pass their exams**, and how many get **good grades**.

3) Schools worked like **businesses** and **advertised** for students.

There should be more testing and more exams

Pupils had to sit **SATs** at **7, 11 and 14**, and **GCSEs** at **16**.

New Labour Try to Mix Some of the Old Ideas Together

In 1997, New Labour took over. They wanted to do something about **inequality**, but they also said there should be **choice** and **diversity** in education. It's a bit like the old Labour policies and the Conservative policies **mixed up together** — it's called "**third way politics**".

The government has made some changes since 1997:

1) They've **reduced infant class sizes** to a maximum of **30**.

2) They've introduced **numeracy hour** and **literacy hour** in **primary schools**.

3) New Labour have allowed **faith schools** and **specialist status schools**.

4) They've set up **Education Action Zones** to help in areas of deprivation.

5) They've tried to **increase** the **number of people going to university**.

A big change in 16-18 year olds' education came in 2000. Policy changed to make A-level education broader. Students now have to do **AS/A2s** and **key skills**, and there are more **vocational courses**.

The government are also keen on **citizenship education** to make pupils more **aware of politics**.

Practice Questions

Q1 What was the aim of the 1944 Education Act?

Q2 Name the three types of school in the tripartite system.

Q3 Briefly explain two problems with comprehensive schools.

Q4 Briefly describe two changes brought about by the 1988 Education Reform Act.

Q5 Name two changes in schools brought about by New Labour.

Exam Questions

Q1 Outline some of the ways in which state policies have influenced educational attainment. (12 marks)

Q2 Examine the ways in which social policies in education may reproduce and legitimise social class inequalities. (20 marks)

They'll never make their minds up...

Governments have been trying to "Sort Out Education Once And For All" and "Shake Up Britain's Failing Schools" for ages. But whatever happens, kids go to school, teachers teach 'em things, and there are exams at the end of it all...

State Policy and Education

These pages examine and evaluate the motivation behind recent state policies in education.

Some Policies Aim to **Reduce Class Inequality**

Compensatory education tries to make up for **material** and **cultural deprivation**, by giving **extra help** to those who need it.

1) **Sure Start** began in 1999. It's a government programme to improve early education and childcare in England. It now offers up to two years of **free childcare** and **early education** to all three and four year olds.

2) The **Educational Maintenance Allowance (EMA)** gives up to £30 per week to students who stay on in education after they're 16. A series of **bonuses** are available for good attendance and progress. EMA is **means-tested** so only children from poorer families benefit from it.

3) Other education policies designed to reduce class inequality include **free school meals**, **breakfast clubs** and **bursaries** for university places.

Some people have criticised the **methods** by which compensatory education is **implemented**.

1) They claim that the policies are **unfair** to students just **outside of the criteria for inclusion** — e.g. if their parents earn just over the limit that makes them eligible for EMA.

2) They also say that the policies are only **token gestures** towards solving the issues they identify — they rarely address **underlying problems**.

Some Policies Aim to **Promote Gender Equality**

Female underachievement used to be a problem

1) The **1988 National Curriculum** gave all pupils equal entitlement to all subjects for the first time. This has been credited with the increased achievement of girls in the last 20 years.

2) Initiatives such as the **Computer Club for Girls** (CC4G) and **Women Into Science and Engineering** (WISE) encourage girls to get involved with subjects they have **traditionally avoided**.

Recent policies have focused on boys' underachievement

1) In 1999 the government gave **grants** to primary schools to hold **extra writing classes** for boys to help push up their **SATs scores**.

2) In 2005 the **Breakthrough Programme** introduced **mentoring**, **after-school classes** and **e-tutorials** for teenage boys in an attempt to improve their exam performance.

The **New Right** has Influenced Many Modern Policies

1) The **New Right** believe in the introduction of **market principles** to all aspects of social and economic life. This includes **less central control** from the government, and encouraging **more competition**. They argue that this makes services **more efficient** while **reducing dependence** on the state.

2) Policies such as the introduction of school **league tables**, **Ofsted** inspections and **performance-related pay** have tried to create a '**market**' in schools — by creating incentives for schools and teachers to try to **outperform** each other.

3) Ideas such as **local management of school budgets**, **grant-maintained schools** and **academies** are attempts to reduce the amount of **centralised control** over education.

State Policy and Education

Chubb and Moe (1990) Proposed a Voucher System

1) **Chubb and Moe (1990)** suggested a scheme under which parents would be given a voucher to pay for the education of their children.

2) They'd have **free choice** over where to spend their vouchers — including deciding between the **private sector** or **existing state schools**.

3) Schools which provide **poor value for money** would lose customers and **close**. Schools which provide **good value for money** would attract customers and **grow**.

4) So competition would **drive up standards** in education.

Even the New Right Wants Some State Involvement in Education

1) **New Right** thinkers value the importance of education in **socialisation** — the process by which children learn the norms and values of society.

2) They believe education can help socialise children through **religious assemblies** and the **National Curriculum**, e.g. **citizenship lessons**.

The New Right has been Criticised for Distorting Educational Practices

1) Opponents of the New Right's market reforms argue that schools have become **more concerned with league tables** than the individual needs of pupils.

2) They also argue that the New Right's preferred "norms and values" are **ethnocentric** and **aren't representative** of the diversity of values and beliefs in society.

New Labour Policies Follow Third Way ideas

1) The '**Third Way**' is a **middle ground** between New Right ideas on **marketisation** and the left wing policies of **government intervention**.

2) New Labour have continued the process of **market reforms** begun by the previous Conservative government. For example, they've allowed schools to **specialise** in certain subjects — e.g. by becoming Music Colleges or Science Colleges — to try to **create diversity** and **increase choice for parents**.

3) They've also pursued some interventionist policies, such as setting up **Educational Action Zones** in areas of high deprivation.

> **New Labour have been criticised**
>
> 1) **New Right** thinkers have **criticised** New Labour for not giving parents **greater choice** in which schools they send their children to.
>
> 2) **Left wing** sociologists such as **Geoff Whitty** have argued that market-oriented educational reforms **create greater social divisions** by benefiting middle class families more than working class families.

Practice Questions

Q1 Give three examples of social policies designed to reduce educational inequalities.

Q2 Give four examples of social policies influenced by New Right thinking.

Q3 Give three criticisms of New Right educational policies.

Q4 Describe and evaluate two New Labour educational social policies.

Exam Questions

Q1 Identify **three** policies which have attempted to introduce market forces into schools. (6 marks)

Q2 Assess the ways in which social policies may reproduce and legitimise social class inequalities in education. (20 marks)

My educational policy is to revise everything...

Girls used to underachieve compared to boys, but now it's the other way round. That seems to be evidence that policies can affect equality, if nothing else. The New Right want policies that give everyone choice and give the market a chance to drive up standards, the left want the state to intervene and directly correct problems where they arise. And New Labour want both.

Definitions of Health

Most people believe they're unwell if they don't feel like they normally do. Sociologists see health as more than just not feeling poorly.

There are Two main Perspectives on Health

1) The **biomedical model** (favoured by **scientists**) says that health and illness are caused by factors **within** the body.

2) The **social model** (favoured by **sociologists**) says that health and illness are caused by factors **outside** the body.

The Biomedical Model says Health and Disease are Natural, Physical Things

Health professionals generally follow the **biomedical model of health**. This model has three key characteristics:

Key characteristics of the biomedical model

1) Health is seen as the **absence of biological abnormality**.

2) The human body is likened to a **machine** in that it needs to be **repaired** by treatment when it breaks down.

3) The health of society is regarded as dependent on the **state of medical knowledge**.

Nikky Hart (1985) identifies **five features** of the **biomedical model**:

1)	Disease is **physical**	The **biomedical model** concentrates on **physical symptoms** of disease, not social and environmental factors. Disease happens in an **individual's body**, not as part of society.
2)	**Doctors** are an **elite**	The **medical elite** (doctors) are the only people sufficiently **qualified** and **skilled** to **identify** and **treat** illness.
3)	Medicine is **curative**	The body can be **repaired** with drugs and surgery.
4)	Illness is **temporary**	Illness can be cured by the medical elite. **Wellness** is the **normal** state of affairs.
5)	**Treatment** is **special**	Treatment of disease takes place in **recognised healthcare environments** (e.g. doctors' surgeries, hospitals), which are **distinct** from the environment where the patient got ill.

Example: A **biomedical view of disability**.

The biomedical model **looks in** at the patient and tries to **fix** the disability through medical practice.

Medical practice is **interventionist** — it's something that's **done to** the patient.

Doctors → ← Physiotherapy
→ Surgery
Medical hardware (calipers, braces etc.) → ← Wheelchair

The Biomedical Model has been Criticised

1) Some sociologists, e.g. **McKeown (1976)**, say that **improved nutrition and hygiene** have been more important in improving health — starting with 19th and 20th century public health reforms.

2) **Ivan Illich (1975)** and others have argued that modern medicine actually **creates disease** (see p. 74).

3) **Marxist sociologists** in the 1970s accused biomedicine of distracting attention away from what they see as the real causes of illness — the **social causes**.

4) The biomedical approach can be viewed as **stigmatising** people who have an illness or disability — it views illness or disability as something **abnormal** that should be **fixed**.

5) **Tom Shakespeare (2000)** said that traditional approaches **medicalise** and **individualise** disability. They deal with the symptoms of each case separately and **ignore** social patterns.

Definitions of Health

The **Social Model** says that health and disease are **Social Constructs**

A "social construct" is an **idea that's created by a society** — as opposed to an idea that's based on objective and testable **facts**. It's specific to the **values and behaviour** of that society — it's not universal. *But* people living in that society will usually accept it as **natural** and "**common sense.**"

1) **The medical elite** (doctors) **haven't always dominated** the definition and treatment of illness and disease — it's a modern phenomenon. For example, in the 1700s, mental illness was often thought to be caused by evil spirits — a religious thing, not a medical thing.

2) In modern society illness is only recognised as serious if it has been **diagnosed** by the medical elite. The **social model** says **definitions of health and illness** are "social constructs" — not actually always related to real physical symptoms.

3) A **social model of health** would look to see which **environmental, social and behavioural factors** have contributed to make an individual person ill.

Example: A social view of disability.

The social model looks outwards from the individual to the environmental and social factors which disable an individual, e.g. lack of access, rights and opportunities.

A person using a wheelchair might feel more disabled by the lack of a wheelchair ramp than the fact that they can't use their legs to walk.

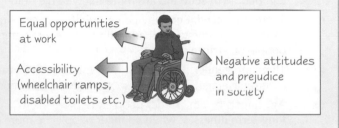

Equal opportunities at work

Accessibility (wheelchair ramps, disabled toilets etc.)

Negative attitudes and prejudice in society

The social model of health **challenges** the idea that **wellness** is the normal state of affairs. Individuals with an illness are seen as **"living with"** their condition instead of having something **"wrong"** with them.

Senior and Viveash (1998) say there is a **Social Process** of becoming Ill

Senior and Viveash (1998) argue that the **six stages** of getting ill are:

1) **Social factors** (such as diet, housing or stress) make some people more likely to become ill than others.

2) An individual develops **symptoms** — these can be **physical** (for example, throwing up), **psychological** (for example, feeling depressed) or **social** (for example, feeling that your marriage is collapsing).

3) The individual interprets their symptoms as an **illness**. Whether you **decide** you have an illness or not will depend on many influences, such as past experience, the mass media, family, culture and gender.

4) The individual decides to visit a **doctor**. This stage **differs** from one **social group** to another. For example, research by **Pui-Ling and Logan (1999)** showed that British Chinese people were less likely to report mental health problems because of social stigma.

5) The patient is **labelled** as **ill**. Although the doctor is powerful at this stage, patients can also be influential in persuading the doctor to label them.

6) **Statistics** are created based on information from doctors. These morbidity statistics are used to form **government policies** for **healthcare**. However, a very large amount of illness goes unreported. According to **Last (1963)** as much as 94% of illness is not reported to doctors. This phenomenon is known as the **clinical iceberg**.

Practice Questions

Q1 Why are doctors seen as part of a "medical elite"?

Q2 List the five features of the biomedical model of health and illness identified by Hart.

Q3 According to Senior and Viveash (1998), what are the six stages of the social process of becoming ill?

Exam Questions

Q1 Outline some of the features of the social process of becoming ill. (12 marks)

Q2 Assess the view that the biomedical model can completely explain health and illness. (24 marks)

All I care about is why I feel ill...

Hmm... the social model of illness seems a bit odd at first — how can it be society's fault that I've got a sore throat... But when you look into it, you have to admit that things like clean water, proper sewers and a good diet are at least relevant to health. As always, you're expected to know the key points of each theory, as well as their faults and pitfalls.

Inequalities in Health

Your chances of staying healthy, and of recovering if you do get ill, depend on which social group you belong to. Sociologists have given various explanations for this.

Health *has an Uneven* Social Distribution

1) The **working class** have a **higher infant mortality rate** than the national average.
The **wealthiest social groups** have **lower infant mortality rates** than the national average.

2) **Working class** people are statistically **more likely** to suffer from **serious medical conditions** such as heart disease, strokes and cancer.

3) **Working class** people are more likely to **die before retirement** age than the national average.

4) According to government statistics, people born in **social class 1** (professional) can expect to live for **seven years longer** than people born in **social class 5** (manual workers).

> Morbidity is another word for sickness. Mortality is another word for death.

5) **Morbidity** and **mortality** rates vary between different **regions** of Britain.
E.g. people in **Scotland** are more likely to die of lung cancer than people in **England**.

6) There is a **correlation** between **ethnicity** and **certain illnesses**. Some ethnic groups are genetically prone to particular illnesses — for example, **sickle-cell anaemia** is most common in people of **African** origin.

7) There are **gender** differences — women live **five years** longer than men on average. But they also **go to the doctor** more often.

> Points 1–8 are based on statistics from the Social Trends 33 (2003) report produced by the Office of National Statistics.

8) **Age** affects health. Older people are more likely to develop **long-term illnesses**, while younger people are more likely to be involved in **accidents** or other **violent incidents**.

9) There are large variations in health **internationally**. **Developing** countries tend to have higher morbidity rates than **developed** countries. And there are differences between the developed countries too — in **2005** the **British Medical Journal** reported research showing that the traditional diet in **Greece** and other Mediterranean countries was linked to **longer life expectancy**.

Cultural Explanations *Blame Bad Health on* Variations *in Attitude*

Some sociologists attribute **differences in health** to the **values** held and choices made by **different social groups**. These are called cultural explanations. **Cultural deprivation theory** is a cultural explanation that looks at differences between social classes.

1) **Cultural deprivation theory** says that the **working class** lead **relatively unhealthy lifestyles** with relatively poor diets, more smoking, less exercise and more drinking.

2) It also says that the working class are less likely to take advantage of NHS **public health measures** such as **vaccinations**, **health screening** and **antenatal care**.

3) **Howlett and Ashley (1991)** found that **middle class** people are better **informed** about health, with more **understanding** of health issues. Therefore, they tend to follow **healthier lifestyles**.

Cultural deprivation theory suggests that society needs better **health education** to make people more **aware** of health issues. It's resulted in lots of **government initiatives** through the **Health Education Authority** — trying to get people to give up smoking, eat less fatty food, etc.

Structural Approaches *link Health Inequalities to* Material Deprivation

Many sociologists **disagree** with cultural explanations. Instead they believe that differences in health and illness are caused by the way **society is structured**. The **middle class** is healthier than the **working class** because society gives the poor **less access** to things that could keep them healthy.

1) **Healthier diets** can **cost more**, and **gyms** are often **very expensive**.

2) **Smoking and drinking** may be related to **stressful lives**, not **cultural values**.

3) Working class people are **less likely** to be able to afford **private health care**.

4) The fact that working class people often **don't take advantage** of **public health facilities** has also been blamed on feeling **intimidated** by health care and **health care professionals**. Health care professionals are **mostly middle class** and health care in general can seem like it's set up to suit middle class people.

Work it, baybee, work it.

Inequalities in Health

Health Inequalities are Strongly Linked to Social Class

Most sociologists **agree** that **economic deprivation** is probably the **major factor** causing health inequalities, even if they don't agree exactly **why**.

A major government survey, '**Inequalities in Health Working Group Report (1980)**' (also known as the **Black Report**) confirmed that the poorer you are, the less healthy you're likely to be. It also found that those with the **most** need for health care get **least**, and those with the **least** need get **most**. This is called the **Inverse Care Law**.

> The **Inverse Care Law** was first defined by **Julian Tudor Hart (1971)**.
> He wrote that "The availability of good medical care tends to **vary inversely** with the **need** for it in the population served".

The Artefact Explanation Argues that Patterns of Inequality Don't Exist

1) Different people belong to different **social classes**, have different **ethnic backgrounds**, live in different **regions of the country**, have different **ages** and can be either **male or female**. The factors affecting health could be any combination of these variables.

2) The **artefact explanation** argues that the **patterns of inequality** in health are an **illusion** created by statistics, and don't really exist. There are so many variables involved that it would be impossible to prove that one factor was **causing** health inequalities.

3) The Black Report (see above) **tested** this explanation, and concluded that it **isn't true**.

Social Selection Explanations have a different approach

According to the **social selection** model, poor health **causes** low social status. People who suffer from physical or mental illnesses **sink to the bottom** classes of society, while those who are physically and mentally strong **rise to the top**.

> Social selection explanations have been criticised
>
> **Senior and Viveash (1998)** say that there is some truth in the idea that being healthy can **help individuals achieve status** and that being unhealthy can be a **barrier to success**. But they also point out that a lot of healthy people **fail to move upwards** in society and a lot of people with health problems **do not move downwards**. In many cases other factors, such as **family background**, are more important in determining social status.

Practice Questions

Q1 According to research, why are people from Mediterranean countries often healthier?
Q2 What is meant by the Inverse Care Law?
Q3 How do social selection explanations account for the link between illness and poverty?

Exam Questions

Q1 Suggest two ways in which social class can affect health. (4 marks)

Q2 Assess the view that inequalities in health are caused by cultural factors. (20 marks)

Everyone blames someone...

An awful lot of this sociology business is about blaming some system or other for the World's problems. Usual scapegoats are "working class values" and "unequal health provision". And some people just blame the statisticians for making everyone else blame each other. Make sure you know what the Inverse Care Law is — it's important for this whole module.

Access to Health Care

The National Health Service was set up to give free and equal health care for all. It was mostly a success. Mostly.

There are **Inequalities** in the Health Care **Provided** by the **NHS**

The **NHS** was set up in 1948. It aimed to provide **free** and **equal** health care for **everyone** in the country. Unfortunately, although the NHS was **generally a success**, it **doesn't give 100% equal health care** to all.

1)   NHS **money** is **shared out unequally** between different areas of the country.

2)   NHS money is **spent differently** in different areas of the country.

3)   **Specialist** hospitals, e.g. heart hospitals, **aren't spread out equally** across the country.

4)   There's a **north-south divide** in the **supply of health care**, as well as in people's health.

Sociologists and politicians often claim that there's a **two-tier system** in the NHS — which means that it provides a **lower level of care** to some, and a **higher level of care** to others.

Politicians have introduced **lots of reforms** to try to **make the NHS work better** and **make it cost less money**.

The **Internal Market** in the NHS had **Good** and **Bad Consequences**

In the **1980s**, Mrs Thatcher's Conservative government tried to **reform** the NHS to make it **more efficient** and **less expensive** (a lot of taxpayers' money is spent on the NHS). They introduced an **internal market**.

This meant that **health care providers** would **compete** with each other to provide services, and **GPs** would be **responsible for their own budgets**. The idea is that **competition drives prices down**. It's an **economics** thing. More **hospital management** was brought in to manage and supervise these changes.

The government **encouraged private hospitals** and **private health insurance schemes**. This was to take some of the **pressure** off the NHS by getting people who could afford private care to go private.

Like most things in sociology, there are pros and cons, and lots of different opinions.

Positive Consequences

1)   There's **more choice** for some "health care consumers" (patients).

2)   **Competition** tends to **drive down costs**.

3)   In some cases, health care became **more responsive to local needs**.

Negative consequences

1)   **Inner city GPs** look after **more people** and **sicker people** than GPs in **middle class** areas. **Money has to go further**, so inner city GPs can't afford the same quality of treatment — it's a **two-tier system**.

2)   Increased numbers of **NHS managers** and **accountants** could be a big **waste** of money.

3)   **Competition** between health care providers means that **two hospitals very close together** might offer almost exactly the **same services**. This can also be seen as a **waste** of money.

Foundation Trusts Have Been Criticised for **Increasing Inequality**

1)   In 2003, **New Labour** introduced **Foundation Trusts** to the NHS. Hospitals run by a Foundation Trust are often called **Foundation Hospitals**.

2)   The government's target is that all NHS Trusts will have foundation status as soon as possible.

3)   Unlike traditional NHS Trusts, Foundation Trusts are **independent legal entities** owned by their members. They can **opt out** of **government guidelines**, **raise their own money**, and **set their own priorities** for how to **treat patients**.

4)   Critics point out that the **top hospitals** are better at **attracting investment**, so they have more money and **attract better staff**. They argue that this creates a **two-tier system** — the **best hospitals** collect more money to **get even better**.

Most Health Care in the UK is Provided by **Women**

1)   Around **75%** of all **NHS workers** are **women**.

2)   However, only **25% of doctors** and **13% of consultants** are **women**.

3)   **Over 90%** of **nurses** are **women**.

4)   Studies have also discovered that the vast majority of **informal care** of **children** and **elderly relatives** is carried out by women.

Radical feminists think the NHS is a **patriarchal institution** — in other words, one where men dominate.

Access to Health Care

The *Inverse Care Law* can be Applied *Today* to *Inequalities* in *Health*

Remember the Inverse Care Law from page 69.

The **Inverse Care Law (Tudor Hart 1971)** states that people whose **need** for health care is **greatest** are actually **least likely** to get it.

Julian Le Grand's survey (2003)

Le Grand's conclusion was that the **middle class** get far **more benefit** from the **NHS** than the working class. The benefit the middle classes got wasn't in proportion to their actual health needs.

Le Grand found that the middle class were 40% more likely to get a **heart bypass** operation than the working class. Also, the working class were 20% less likely to get a hip replacement despite being 30% more likely to need one.

Even with something as simple as **consultation times** in GPs' surgeries, Le Grand found that professionals were likely to get on average two minutes more of a doctor's time than working class patients.

Working class areas tend to have the worst health facilities, the **fewest doctors** and the **fewest hospitals**.

This evidence supports the idea that the health care system is biased towards middle class people.

Research by **Cartwright and O'Brien (1976)** suggests that **middle class patients** tend to have a **better relationship** with their **doctor** than working class patients. Working class patients said they **felt** like the **doctor doesn't listen**.

The *Inverse Care Law* Could Also Apply to *Ethnic Minority Groups*

Ethnic minority health needs were identified as **relatively high** in a report published by the **Department of Health in 1992**. Remember, "**relatively high**" doesn't mean "shockingly sky-high" or "loads higher than the white population". It means anything from a **tiny bit more** to a **lot more** than the **average population**.

1) The rate of heart disease is significantly higher in men and women of **Indian** origin.
2) **Afro-Caribbean** people have a higher incidence of stroke, **HIV/AIDS infection** and **schizophrenia**.
3) **Suicide** rates are relatively high amongst **Asian** women.

Some sociologists think that **ethnic minorities** have **relatively poor health** because they're **less likely** to get the **full benefit** from NHS services. **Various possible reasons** have been suggested for this:

1) The cultural values of the NHS might be **different** from those of some ethnic minority groups. Some advisers say the NHS **needs to adapt** to **fit** the cultural values of ethnic groups.
2) Some people from ethnic minorities, especially the elderly, **might not speak enough English** to communicate well with health care staff.
3) There's some evidence that discrimination and racism affect access to health care. E.g. research in the 1980s found that **Asian women** in family planning clinics experienced racism.
4) **Some ethnic minority groups** tend to see illness and disease as a part of life you can't do much about — and **don't bother** to go to the doctor.

Practice Questions

Q1 List the advantages and disadvantages of an internal market in health care.
Q2 What are foundation trusts?
Q3 Give three ways in which it can be said that the Inverse Care Law operates in today's NHS.

Exam Question

Q1 Assess the view that the people who need health care the most are least likely to get it. (20 marks)

In the great drought of 1811 they introduced a two-tear system...

See, there's that Inverse Care Law again. There's still inequality in people's access to health care. Some think it's getting better, others think it's not. Sociologists are most concerned about a two-tier NHS, and about discrimination within the NHS. Governments keep trying to tweak NHS policy to make the NHS work better, or to make it cost less, or both.

Mental Illness

These pages cover different perspectives on mental health in the UK.

Mental Illness in UK Society is Unequally Distributed

Sociologists and psychiatrists can't agree whether mental disorders have **physical causes** or **social causes**.

Sociologists have tended to favour the view that there is a **social basis** for mental illness. Given the **social inequality** in who has good or bad mental health, maybe the sociologists have a point. For example:

1) **Afro-Caribbean individuals** in the UK are **more likely** to be **admitted to a psychiatric hospital** than other ethnic groups. They're more likely to be "**sectioned**" under the Mental Health Act — **admitted against their will**. Afro-Caribbean men are more likely to be diagnosed with **schizophrenia**.

2) Women are statistically more likely to be diagnosed with **depression** or **acute stress** than men. They're also much more likely to be on **drug treatments** for **mental illness** — antidepressants etc.

3) **Working class** men and women are statistically **more likely** to be diagnosed with mental illness than **middle class** people.

4) **Single women** have **better mental health** than **married women**.

There are **different perspectives** on these trends, including **medical**, **feminist** and **interpretivist** approaches.

The Medical Approach is to Treat Mental Health as a Biomedical Condition

1) The medical approach to mental illness focuses on the **abnormal individual** rather than the **environment** that the individual lives in. It concentrates on the **physical symptoms** of mental illness. For example, a **medical approach to schizophrenia** would say it's caused by a **chemical imbalance in the brain**.

Compare this with the key features of the biomedical model of illness on page 66.

2) The medical approach is **cure-orientated**. It emphasises the importance of treatments involving **drugs or surgery** for depression.

3) The medical approach suggests that treatment is best carried out in the **medical environment** (e.g. a hospital rather than the community) and should always be carried out by the **qualified elite** (e.g. doctors).

> 1) In the 1930s, mental disturbance was sometimes treated **surgically**. Doctors actually **severed** neural connections between certain parts of the **brain**. This is called a **lobotomy**. It often had unwanted side effects, such as adverse effects on the patient's **intellect**. Lobotomies aren't done any more, although more refined brain surgery is sometimes used in extremely severe cases.
>
> 2) In the 1940s, **electroconvulsive therapy** (**ECT**) was used to treat depression. It's still sometimes used to treat very severe depression. In ECT, an **electric current** is passed through the patient's **brain**, to create a **seizure** a bit like an epileptic fit.
>
> 3) **Drugs** are used to treat all sorts of mental illness. Some drugs have **severe side effects**.
>
> 4) Mental illness is also treated by **psychotherapy**, where the patient **talks** to a **therapist** who tries to get them thinking in a more healthy way.

Feminists see Women's Mental Illness as a Result of Patriarchy

Joan Busfield (2001) thinks that women might be diagnosed with more than their fair share of mental health problems because of **sexism** in the **male-dominated medical elite**. She thinks that doctors **label** and **interpret** behaviour differently depending on whether it's a man or a woman doing it. For instance, an **angry, stressed, upset woman** might be labelled **mentally ill** but an **angry, stressed, upset man** might just be "**overworked**".

Psychologist **Paula Nicolson (1998)** thinks that **postnatal depression** is more a **social thing** than a **physical thing**. She disagrees with the standard medical view that postnatal depression is a **mental disorder**, and that it's **normal** to be a **happy new mum**. Nicolson argues that it's **natural** for women to get **depressed** after having a baby.

Marxist feminists think that women's mental illness is caused by their "**dual oppression**" as **housewife** and **worker**.
Radical feminists suggest mental illness in women is a consequence of **patriarchal society** in which women have **low social status**, the **stress** of **housework** and **childcare** and the stress of **social isolation**.

Mental Illness

Inequalities in Ethnicity and Mental Health have Different Explanations

1) Some sociologists use **interpretivist thinking** to explain inequalities in **ethnicity and mental health**. **Littlewood and Lipsedge (1982)** found that psychiatric doctors and nurses were more likely to use sedatives with **black** patients. They suggested that this was because the medical staff were **mostly white** and did not understand how to speak to patients who were **culturally different**. They looked to drugs as an **easy solution**.

2) Others have offered structural explanations. **James Nazroo (1997)** found that ill health in ethnic minorities in general was linked to **poor housing**, **stress**, **low status** and **poverty**. Mental health differences could be part of the **same pattern**.

The Interpretivist Approach Sees Mental Health as a Social Construct

Thomas Szasz (1971) reckoned that **mental illness doesn't really exist**.

1) He thought that what we call "mental illness" is really just another **"social construct"** — a **label** society uses to **control non-conformist behaviours**. He said that people who behave in a way that the rest of society sees as **unacceptable** or **dangerous** are defined as "mentally ill".

2) People who are labelled as "mentally ill" can be admitted into psychiatric hospitals against their will. Szasz compared **forced treatment in mental hospitals** to the **persecution of witches** in the Middle Ages.

3) Szasz prefers a **system** where individuals are **free** to get psychotherapy **if they want to**. He says it's important that there's **no threat of force**, coercion or **loss of liberty**.

R.D. Laing was a psychiatrist who wrote in the late 1960s. He believed that "mental illness" is really a natural response to being in an unbearable situation. He also thought that mental illness needn't always be a negative thing. He had an idea that **mental breakdowns** could turn into **mental breakthroughs**.

1) **Erving Goffman (1961, 1970)** saw mental illness as a **stigma** caused by **negative labelling**.

2) Goffman was particularly **harsh** on the **role of mental institutions** in **reinforcing these labels**.

3) He thought that individuals in psychiatric institutions have to learn to **conform** to their label as "mentally ill". He said they **lose their old identities** in the process. Goffman calls this process a **"deviant career"**.

Goffman (1961) studied patients and staff in psychiatric institutions

Goffman described how patients respond to being labelled "mentally ill".

Withdrawal — Patient doesn't communicate with other patients — doesn't believe he / she belongs with them.

Rebellion — Patient refuses to cooperate with staff.

Cooperation — Patient plays along with the staff idea of how a mental patient behaves. Patient starts to act crazy.

The staff respond to the patient's "crazy" behaviour by **punishing** the patient — they take away the patient's liberty and privacy and they don't let the patient make choices. This is called **"mortification of the self"**. It ends up with the patient losing their personality.

The patient becomes **institutionalised**, which means they can't manage on their own outside the institution. After this, the staff can start from scratch, building up a "sane" conformist personality.

If a patient said, "I don't belong here — I'm not mad", the staff might think, "that's just what a mad person would say — you must be mad".

This is what happens to Jack Nicholson's character in the film One Flew over the Cuckoo's Nest.

Practice Questions

Q1 Which social groups are statistically most vulnerable to mental illness?

Q2 How would a "medical approach" define and treat disorders such as depression or schizophrenia?

Q3 According to Szasz, what is mental illness?

Exam Questions

Q1 Outline some of the features of the medical approach to mental illness.	(12 marks)
Q2 Assess the view that mental health is a social construct.	(20 marks)

If you say you're sane, it's proof you're not...

Mental illness is particularly interesting for some sociologists because it can be as much about social deviance as it is about mental health. In Stalinist Russia, you could get locked up as insane just for saying something the authorities didn't like. It's scary to think of. Learn about the medical treatments for mental health, the gender inequalities, and the negative labelling bit.

The Role of Medicine and Health Care Professionals

There are sociologists who dispute the role of the medical elite in improving public health in modern times. Some even say doctors are the cause of much illness and disease. Blimey.

Medical Intervention Hasn't Done a Lot of Good — According to McKeown

1) **McKeown (1976)** claims that **medical intervention** by the biomedical elite **hasn't had much impact** on improvements in health over the last 200 years.

2) McKeown thinks that the big health improvements have been mainly down to **social factors** — things like **sewage disposal**, supply of **clean water** and **improved diets.**

3) The **social changes** that McKeown says changed people's health all happened in the **19th century** — before the medical elite came to dominate health.

4) McKeown uses evidence like **life expectancy** and **infant mortality statistics**. He points out that life expectancy went up and infant mortality went down **before** biomedical techniques came in. For instance, mass immunisation for TB (a biomedical approach) only happened after the death rate for the disease had already gone down.

The bathroom — where social health <u>really happens</u>.

Illich Says the Medical Elite Actually Cause Bad Health

1) **Illich (1975)** defines **health** as the **capacity** to cope with the **human reality** of **death**, **pain** and **sickness**. This is a very different definition to the mainstream biomedical definition.

2) Illich believes that medicine has **gone too far**, and started to **"play God"** — trying to **wipe out** death, pain and sickness. OK so far... he then says that **trying to control death and illness** is a bad move which **turns people into consumers** or even objects. In his opinion, this messes up people's natural capacity for health and **makes people ill**.

3) Illich uses the word **iatrogenesis** to mean this kind of illness that's caused by modern medicine. He says there are **three types of iatrogenesis**:

> 1) **Clinical iatrogenesis** — the **harm** done to patients by **ineffective** treatments, **unsafe** treatments or getting the **wrong diagnosis**.
>
> 2) **Social iatrogenesis** — the idea that **doctors** have **taken over control** of people's lives, and individuals can't make decisions about their problems. More and more of people's problems are seen as **suitable** for **medical intervention**. This is called the **medicalisation of social life**.
>
> 3) **Cultural iatrogenesis** — the **destruction** of **traditional ways** of **dealing** with and making sense of **death**, **pain** and **sickness**.

Illich thinks the **worst** is **cultural iatrogenesis**. He puts it like this:

> "A society's image of death reveals the level of independence of its people, their personal relatedness, self-reliance, and aliveness."
> Illich (1975) *Limits to Medicine: Medical Nemesis, The Expropriation of Health*

According to Illich's view, dying has become the ultimate form of **consumer resistance** (when you're dead, you can't buy any more NIKE trainers, I'd imagine). **Death** isn't seen as something normal. It's become a **taboo**.

Functionalists See Illness as Deviant — Doctors Control this Deviance

1) According to **functionalists** like **Talcott Parsons (1951)**, doctors have an **important function in society** — they control the amount of time people take off **work** and **family duties**.

2) Illness is **"deviant behaviour"** which **disrupts** work and home life — you're not supposed to take time off sick.

3) Parsons said that sick people take on a **"sick role"**. While a person is sick, they're allowed to stop functioning in their **normal role**. They don't have responsibility for making themselves better — but they are **expected** to **want to get better**, and to do whatever the doctor tells them.

4) Doctors are in charge of **confirming** that the patient is **actually ill**. Doctors **allow** the sick person to take limited time off, and **make them better** by using their **expert medical knowledge**. Parsons thought that doctors always put the patient's needs before their own needs.

Critics of Parsons say the medical profession don't always put patients first — they say private medicine is proof that doctors are self-interested. However, it **can't be denied** that doctors really do give people **sick notes** so they can take sick leave.

The Role of Medicine and Health Care Professionals

Marxists see Medicine as an Institution which Supports Capitalism

Marxists believe that the medical profession only do good for the **capitalist** class — they **keep class inequalities going**. Marxists say that the medical profession have a **conservative** role in society.

1) Doctors keep the workforce **healthy** and **productive**. **Healthy** workers can **work harder** and won't have to take **time off sick**. This means **more profits** for the capitalist class.

2) Doctors **check** that **workers** aren't spending **too much time on sick leave**. They say **how long** a worker can **stay off work**.

3) Marxists believe that doctors **hide the real social causes of illness** (poverty, class inequality etc.) by focusing on the individual and their physical symptoms.

Some Marxists think that **doctors** are **agents** of **large drugs corporations** — they believe that health care exists mainly to produce **profits** for drugs companies.

Weberians see the Medical Profession as Self-Serving

Weberians think that doctors **arrange** things so that they **keep** their **high status** in society.

> A Weberian is a follower of German sociologist, historian and economist Max Weber (1864-1920).

They suggest that the medical profession is **self-serving**.

They argue that the medical profession has managed to **shut out** other forms of healing such as homeopathy, aromatherapy, faith healing and other types of **alternative medicine**. This gives modern medicine a monopoly.

Feminists see the Medical Profession as serving Patriarchal Interests

1) Some feminists say that most **contraceptive methods** (e.g. the pill and IUDs) are designed for men rather than women. This doesn't mean men are supposed to use them — it means they have **significant health risks** for women that **men would never put up with**.

2) **Oakley (1984)** has said that the process of childbirth has been "**medicalised**". In other words, women giving birth are treated like there's **something wrong with them**. **Control** over giving birth is taken away from women and given to **men**. Male doctors are often in charge, not midwives or the women who are actually giving birth.

3) Women tend to have **subordinate** roles in medicine — **nurses** and **auxiliaries** tend to be **women**, **consultants** tend to be **men**. Some feminists think that the role of being a nurse has been made to look like being a "doctor's handmaid" — a female servant obeying the male doctor.

4) **Cosmetic surgery** is criticised by some feminists as the "medicalisation of beauty", and also as a **social control** over women.

5) Feminists see the diagnosis and treatment of **depression** in women as another kind of **social control**.

> Of course, not everyone agrees that drugs for depression are prescribed to make women shut up and stop whingeing. It depends on your ideological viewpoint...

Practice Questions

Q1 What does McKeown claim is responsible for improvements in health in the last 200 years?
Q2 What does iatrogenesis mean?
Q3 What three types of iatrogenesis does Illich identify?

Exam Questions

Q1 Outline some of the ways in which the medical profession can be seen as patriarchal. (12 marks)

Q2 Assess the view that health and sickness are defined by the powerful. (20 marks)

If doctors make you ill, do teachers make you thick...

Blimey, this iatrogenesis idea is a bit radical — it's actually the doctors' fault that we're ill... Still, you can kind of see some reasoning behind it. Oh, and as ever, you need to be able to compare and contrast functionalist (all for the best), Marxist (all set up for the benefit of the bosses), Weberian (all for the benefit of doctors) and feminist (all unfair to women) views. It's a right laugh.

Key Issues in Research and Methods

Sociologists do research to get evidence which helps them understand society.
Unfortunately, it's not all that straightforward to study human behaviour. If only we were ants in an ant farm.

Sociologists Have Three Aims When Collecting and Using Data

1) Sociologists try to make their research **valid** and **reliable**. Research is **valid** when it gives a **true picture** of what's being measured. Research is **reliable** if other sociologists using the **same methods** get the **same data**.

2) You can't research the whole population. You have to take a **sample** (see page 80). Sociologists try to make sure that their **sample represents the population** — it needs similar proportions of different ages, genders, classes and ethnic groups. If a sample is **representative** then sociologists can **generalise** — i.e. conclude that the results are likely to apply to the entire population.

3) Sociologists aim to be **objective** and **avoid bias**.

> If a study focuses on a particular group, e.g. teenagers or working class people, researchers must still ensure that their sample is representative of that particular group.

Sociologists get data from different sources

1) **Primary sources of data** involve **first-hand research** — things like interviews, focus groups, questionnaires or observations (see page 80-83).
2) **Secondary data** includes things like **official statistics**.

Data can be either quantitative or qualitative

1) **Quantitative data** is **numbers** and **statistics**. You can easily put quantitative data into a graph or a chart.
2) **Qualitative data** gives a detailed picture of what people do, think and feel. It's **subjective** — it involves **opinions**, **meanings** and **interpretations**. You can't turn qualitative data into a list of numbers or a graph.

Positivists Use Reliable Methods That Give Quantitative Data

1) **Positivists** say behaviour is influenced by **external social factors**.
2) They think sociology should be **scientific** and **analyse social facts**. Social facts are things that **affect behaviour** and can be **easily measured**. They're **external** things like laws, **not internal** things like people's opinions.
3) So positivists measure human behaviour using **quantitative data** — data that turns everything into **numbers**.
4) They use **statistics** to measure the **relationships** between different factors. They're interested in **cause and effect** relationships, e.g. the factors that cause underachievement in schools.
5) They use sources like **questionnaires** and **official statistics**. These are **objective** and **reliable**.

Interpretivists Use Valid Methods That Give Qualitative Data

1) **Interpretivists** (also called **interactionists**) believe that you can only really **understand** human behaviour using **empathy** — by putting yourself in **other people's shoes**. They think that it is important to uncover and understand the **meaning** individuals give to **their actions** and to **the actions of others**.

2) **Interpretivist sociologists** use methods that let them discover the **meanings**, **motives** and **reasons** behind **human behaviour** and **social interaction**.

> Participant observation means being actively involved in the research as both participant and observer.

3) Interpretivists reckon that the **scientific** methods used in **positivist** research **don't tell you much** about how **individual people** act in society.

4) Interpretivists say you can't count meanings and opinions and turn them into statistical charts. They reckon **sociology isn't scientific** because **humans can't be measured** like ants in an ant farm. People don't always understand questions in questionnaires and they don't always tell the truth to researchers.

5) Interpretivists like to use methods that produce **qualitative** data — they try to understand human behaviour from the point of view of the **individual person**. They use methods like **participant observation** and **unstructured interviews** to build up a **rapport** (a feeling of mutual trust and understanding) with individuals, so they can produce a valid and detailed picture of what they think.

6) **Max Weber** said it's important to use **empathy** to **get inside a person's head** to figure out **why** they're doing what they're doing. He called this "**Verstehen**". Interpretivists take this idea very seriously — they're big on empathy.

> **Positivism** looks at the **institutions** in society. It's called **macrosociology**.
> **Interpretivist sociology** looks at the **individual**. It's called **microsociology**.

Key Issues in Research and Methods

Theoretical Background Affects Your Choice of Method

Theoretical background	Positivism	Interpretivism
Explanation of behaviour	It's determined by **social forces beyond people's control**.	Humans **make sense** of **social situations** during human interaction.
Aims of sociology	Sociology should discover **what causes what**.	It should **describe** and **explain** how people **make sense** of situations — using **empathy**.
Research methods	**Questionnaires** and **structured interviews** — they give **quantitative data** and they're **reliable** and **objective**.	**Observations** and **unstructured interviews** — they give **qualitative data** and a more **valid insight** into society.

Ethical Factors Affect Your Choice of Method

Ethical considerations can be grouped into **four main areas**:

1) **Consent** — all participants must have openly agreed to take part.

2) **Confidentiality** — the details of all participants and their actions must remain confidential and private.

3) **Avoidance** of **harm** — participants should not be physically or psychologically harmed by the research process.

4) **Avoidance** of **deception** — researchers should be open and honest about the study and its implications.

The **British Sociological Association** gives **ethical guidelines** for research. Researchers should use **informed consent** — people should know who's doing the research, why they're doing it and what it's about. **Covert participant observation**, where people don't know a sociologist is watching them, should only be used when there's **absolutely no other way** of getting data.

> Researchers studying **sensitive issues** like domestic violence often choose to use **informal interviews** to put the person answering the questions **at ease**.

Practical Factors Affect Your Choice of Method

1) **Time** — Some methods need more time. **Covert participant observation** takes a **long time**. The researcher has to get into the group they're studying and win their trust before starting the actual research. A **social survey** doesn't need the researcher to participate all the time and the **workload can be shared** in a team.

2) **Money** — This affects the **length** and **method** of the research. Money is needed to **pay the researcher**, for **transportation** to interviews, and to pay for **resources** like computers. **Large-scale social surveys** are **expensive**. The 1991 census cost £135 million. A small focus group will cost a lot less.

3) **Characteristics and skills of the researcher** — It'd be difficult for a **female** researcher to be involved in a participant observation of **monks** in a monastery. Some researchers may be OK with **dangerous situations** and others may prefer to **stay at their desk** and do **detailed analysis** of statistics.

4) **Access and opportunity** — If researchers **don't have access** to certain groups to carry out interviews or observations then they have to turn to **secondary sources**.

Practice Questions

Q1 What is the difference between quantitative and qualitative data?
Q2 Name two characteristics of positivism.
Q3 What type of data do interpretivists prefer?
Q4 Briefly explain how practical factors can affect your choice of research method.

Exam Question

Q1 Suggest two factors which may influence a sociologist's choice of research method. (4 marks)

Ready, aim, research...

Sociologists use different methods to produce different types of data. Positivists and interpretivists prefer different research methods. There are also ethical and practical factors which influence which method you choose. Remember that funding is a huge factor — sociologists don't work for nowt, y'know.

Key Issues in Research and Methods

The first step in sociological research is figuring out what you're going to research. The second step is condensing your topic down into a single question, or a single hypothesis.

Sociologists pick a **Topic** based on their own **Preference** and **Knowledge**

Well, obviously. But there's slightly more to it than the obvious, so here you go.

1) Sociologists often **specialise** in different fields of the subject and therefore will often choose a topic that they have experience or knowledge of — for example, **Steve Bruce** specialises in **religion**.

2) Sociologists try to pick a topic that they think they'll find **enjoyable** and **interesting** to research.

3) Also, certain topics become popular in sociology at different times. For example, research in the **mid twentieth century** focused on **stratification** and the **class system**. **Nowadays**, the focus of sociologists has moved on to other topics such as **world sociology** and **medical sociology**. To gain **prestige**, **funding** and public or academic **interest**, sociologists are more likely to focus their research on topics that are currently **in vogue**.

4) Sociologists and other academics who want to make a **change** in society prefer research that could help develop **solutions** to **social problems**.

5) Sociologists may feel that a particular issue is **neglected** by other researchers, so they'll research the issue to try to **"plug the gap"** — and encourage others to embrace the issue as well.

Funding and *Cooperation* for *Research* have an impact on the choice of *Topic*

1) There are a wide range of potential **sources of funding**. Some research is funded by **charities**, e.g. the Joseph Rowntree Foundation. Some is funded by **industry**. Some is funded by the **Government**. A lot of quantitative studies are done **directly** by **government agencies**.

2) The organisation which funds the research often likes to have some say in the **choice of topic**, or the **way** that the topic is **researched**. Government agencies often do research into areas covered by current or proposed **government policy**. **Industrial** grant providers tend to fund research that is likely to give their industry some **practical benefit**.

3) Additionally, a researcher needs to decide whether they will be able to get the **cooperation** of the groups they'll be studying if they choose a particular topic. If potential subjects refuse to give their help for the research, then the topic may not be viable.

The researcher's **Career** in **Sociology** is another factor in selecting a topic

1) Sociologists have their eye on their **careers**, just like everyone else. Researchers would jump at the chance to conduct a study that improves their **employability**. Interesting, original or popular topics that are well researched, with good clear results, improve an academic's chance of having their work **published**. Getting work published, particularly in one of the **big sociological journals**, really **improves a researcher's standing** in academia.

2) A quick way for a sociologist to progress in their career is to respond to another sociologist's work. The aim can be either to **prove** the other sociologist **wrong**, or to **add something** to their research. Practically speaking, this could mean investigating the same topic, but using slightly different methods, or investigating a different group of people.

3) This can mean that particular social groups are researched a lot. For example, **routine office workers** are frequently researched in order to test out **theories of stratification** — some systems classify them as working class and some as middle class. Each sociologist who wants to **disprove** or **add to** earlier research on classification has to research **yet another** bunch of routine office workers. Beekeepers **never** get this level of interest from sociologists.

Reviewing the Field is crucial to a good research topic

1) **Reviewing** and **critiquing** existing **data** and **literature** is an important feature in any sociological report. It requires the researcher to spend time reading **articles**, **publications** and other sources of information already produced on the subject.

2) The researcher then **analyses** this material to help clarify the issues around the subject.

3) Reviewing the field gives the researcher useful information on the types of **methodology** used in **previous studies**. They can see whether specific methods, e.g. structured interviews, worked in the past. They can see if research samples were big enough, and form ideas about how big their own sample should be.

Not many research opportunities in this field.

Key Issues in Research and Methods

Research Questions give Focus to sociological research

1) Once the researcher has chosen a broad topic area, they need to **narrow down** the focus of their research so they don't spread their work out too thinly and end up with not enough detail. They do this by coming up with a **single research question** that their research aims to **answer**.

2) A good research question should focus on **one part** of the topic, and it should be **clear** and **easy** to **research**.

3) Questions should be as **value-free** as possible. In other words they shouldn't be **biased**, or **suggest potential social changes**. So, "Should governments provide vocational education to 14-year-olds?" isn't a good research question because it asks for a **value judgement** on social policy. "What are the attitudes of employers, parents and teachers towards vocational education for 14-year-olds?" is **better**.

Hypotheses are Statements that make Predictions that can be Tested

1) A hypothesis is a **statement** that makes a **prediction**. A hypothesis acts as a **starting point** for research. The research will aim to either **show that the hypothesis is true**, or **show that it's false**.

2) A hypothesis states a **relationship** between **two factors** — e.g. "sociology teachers wear corduroy trousers" or "material deprivation causes educational underachievement".

Terms like "democracy" need to be Operationalised — i.e. Made Measurable

1) Sociology prides itself on giving names to **concepts** and **ideas** that aren't **easily explained** or measured. For example, it's **tricky** to measure things like "democracy", "development" and "culture".

2) You end up measuring these concepts by measuring **something else** that's **linked** to it — sociologists call this an **indicator**. This is called "**operationalising**" a concept. It means making it operational, or workable, by finding a way to measure it.

3) Researchers do this **every time** they conduct a piece of research, because you **can't research** something if you **can't measure** it. Each difficult concept needs an **indicator**, e.g. electoral participation or diversity of electoral results for democracy.

4) Researchers need to be able to **justify** how they **operationalised** their concepts in their final report. This is often a **subjective** process and the way a researcher operationalises may be **criticised** by other sociologists.

Triangulation is when you Combine Methods or Data

Triangulation is when sociologists try to combine different methods or data to **get the best out of all of them**.

1) Triangulation gives a more **detailed picture** than when you only use one method, so it's more **valid**.

2) When you triangulate, you can check different sets of data against each other, so it's more memorable.

3) Triangulation combines **strengths** and **weaknesses** of different types of data.

4) It can be **expensive** and **time-consuming** to do the same research by lots of methods. Sometimes it's **not possible** to use triangulation — there's only one viable method to get the data.

Practice Questions

Q1 Give three factors to consider when choosing a topic for research.

Q2 Why is reviewing the field useful?

Q3 What is the "operationalisation of concepts"?

Exam Question

Q1 Assess the various factors to be considered when choosing a research topic. (20 marks)

The scarecrow award — for being outstanding in your field...

Now you know how sociologists plan research — they pick a topic, find funding, check out previous studies, formulate a research question, make some hypotheses and operationalise all the concepts. If I'd known it was that easy, I'd never have gone into publishing. Revise these pages and do well in your exam and maybe you can become the sociologist I can only dream of being.

Surveys

Sociologists can choose from many research methods when they carry out social research. Some methods produce quantitative data. Others produce qualitative data. There are lots of different methods and lots of different problems.

Before You Can Start — You Need a Sample

1) It's **too expensive** and **time-consuming** for sociologists to involve the **whole population** in their research. They select a **sample**. Only the census includes everyone.

2) When they select the sample they usually try to make it **represent the population** — with similar proportions of people in terms of age, class, ethnicity and gender.

3) If the population is **homogenous** (all the same) the sample needs to be homogenous. If the population is **heterogeneous** (all different), the sample needs to be heterogeneous.

4) **Random sampling** is where names are selected at random from a list of names called a **sampling frame**. Random sampling is often more representative than non-random sampling.

How to do random sampling

1) **Simple random sample** — Pick names **randomly** from a list. Everyone has an **equal chance** of being selected.

2) **Stratified sample** — Divide the population into groups and make a **random selection** with the **right proportions** (if 60% of the population is male, 60% of the sample must be male).

How to do non-random sampling

1) **Snowball sample** — Find an **initial contact** and get them to **give you more names** for your research.

2) **Quota sample** — Pick people who fit into a certain **category** (say, 15 people between ages 30 and 40).

A Pilot Study Lets You Have a Practice Run

1) A pilot study is a **small-scale** piece of research used as a **practice run**. You might want to **test** the **accuracy** of your **questions**, or **check** to see if there are any **technical problems** in your research design. You do this to make the study **more valid** and **more reliable**.

2) You can also **test how long** the research will take, **train** your **interviewers** and get **research funding** — once you show your project is useful.

3) Pilot studies can be **time-consuming** and **expensive** and they can create a **lot of work**.

Social Surveys Give Quantitative Data

1) **Social surveys** collect information about a large population, using **standardised questionnaires** or **structured interviews**.

2) Social surveys tend to be used by **positivists** as a **primary source** of **quantitative data**.

3) Standard questionnaires and structured interviews are **reliable**. They're used by **government agencies** and **research companies**.

4) Data collected using surveys can be analysed to discover overall **patterns** and **trends**.

Townsend used a 39-page questionnaire in his 1979 research on poverty.

Longitudinal Studies are Social Surveys over a Period of Time

Longitudinal studies are done at **regular intervals** over a **long period of time**. They're often **large-scale quantitative** surveys, and they tend to be used by **positivists**. However, some studies like the TV programme *Seven Up* are more **qualitative**.

Seven Up was a TV documentary that asked 14 kids aged 7 what they thought about life, and what they wanted to be when they grew up. The programme makers came back to interview the children every seven years. The latest instalment was Forty-Nine Up.

Strengths of longitudinal studies

1) You can **analyse changes** and **make comparisons** over time.

2) You can study how the **attitudes** of the sample **change** with time.

Limitations of longitudinal studies

1) It's **hard** to recruit a **committed sample** who'll want to **stay** with the study.

2) It's **hard to keep contact** with the sample, which may make the study less valid.

3) You need **long-term funding** and you need to **keep the research team together**.

4) Longitudinal studies rely on **interviews** and **questionnaires** which might not be **valid** or **reliable**.

Surveys

Questionnaires Mainly Give Quantitative Data

Questionnaires mainly use **closed questions** and standardised **multiple-choice answers** —
e.g. "What's your favourite fish? Tick *cod, haddock, salmon, sea bass, tuna* or *other*".
Don't forget though that some questionnaires use **open-ended** questions.

Questionnaires mainly give you **quantitative** data which positivists like. **Standardised questions** make them **reliable**.
A questionnaire with **open-ended questions** can give you some insight into **meanings** and **motives**. They give you
qualitative data. The **reliability** and **validity** of a questionnaire depends on **how it's designed**.

Questionnaires should...

1) Use **clear, simple questions** which are **easy to understand**.
2) Give **clear instructions** and make it **easy** for the respondent.
3) Have a nice **clear layout** that doesn't **intimidate** people.
4) Give a **range of options** on **multiple-choice** questions.
5) **Measure** what **you want to measure**.

The person answering the questionnaire is called the respondent.

Questionnaires shouldn't...

1) Ask **embarrassing, threatening** or **complex** questions.
2) Ask **two questions instead of one**.
3) Be **too long**.
4) Use **sociological** terms that **no one understands**.
5) **Lead** the respondent to **answer a question** in a **particular way**.

Strengths of questionnaires

1) They're **quick** and **cheap**, and they can reach lots of respondents.
2) They're **reliable** because the questions are **standardised**.
3) They're **easy to analyse** with computer programs.
4) There's **no interviewer** to **affect** people's answers.
5) You can **spot patterns** in the answers and **make comparisons**.

Limitations of questionnaires

1) Respondents **may not tell the truth**.
2) Questions may be **misleading** or **mean different things** to **different people**. They may not measure what you actually **want to measure**.
3) Postal questionnaires have a **low response rate**. If it's **too low** it won't give a **representative** sample.
4) **Open-ended questions** make it **hard to quantify the data** into nice neat **numbers**.
5) No one can **explain** the questions if the respondent doesn't understand them.

1) Questionnaires can be used to investigate topics such as **TV viewing habits**, **purchasing habits**, **voting behaviour** and **experiences of crime**.

2) The **British Crime Survey** is a questionnaire that is carried out **continually** by the British government. They survey about **50,000** people a year and publish new results **annually**.

3) The **British Social Attitudes Survey** is carried out annually by the **National Centre for Social Research**. Each year they select around **3,300** British adults at random and send them a questionnaire.

Practice Questions

Q1 Why do sociologists select a sample?
Q2 Briefly explain two types of sampling procedure.
Q3 What are the benefits of carrying out a pilot study?

Exam Question

Q1 Examine some of the reasons why sociologists use surveys. (20 marks)

I had to give a sample at the doctor's — don't say I need one here as well...

*Pick your sample first, then do a pilot study. Check that what you're doing is really as valid and reliable as you'd like it to
be. Questionnaires are harder to design than you might think — you've got to give sensible options for multiple-choice
questions, and you've got to make the questions really clear and easy to understand.*

Interviews and Observations

These pages are about getting primary data from interviews and observation.

An **Interview** is a **Conversation** Between a **Researcher** and a **Respondent**

1) An **interview** is a **conversation** between a **researcher** and an **interviewee** where the researcher asks a set of questions.

2) You have to pick the **sample**, organise the **interview**, select / train your **interviewers**, **ask the questions** and **record the answers**. **Bias** can get in the way at each stage. An interviewer should create a **friendly relaxed atmosphere**.

3) An **interview effect** is when the **response** given isn't what the interviewee **really thinks**. This can be caused by the **gender**, **age**, **class** or **personality** of the interviewer. The **opinions** of the **researcher** and **interviewer** can **influence** the interviewee.

Structured **Interviews** = Quantitative Data, Unstructured ones = Qualitative Data

1) **Structured interviews** ask the **same standardised questions** each time. The questions are closed questions, with set **multiple-choice answers**.

2) They give **quantitative data** and they're very **reliable**.

3) They're used in **large-scale social surveys**.

4) The interviewer can **explain** and **clarify** the questions.

5) Structured interviews can ask the **same questions** as a questionnaire, but they get a much **higher response rate**. People tend to agree to be interviewed.

6) They're **more expensive** than questionnaires — you need to **pay for the interviewer**.

7) The interviewer has to **follow the list of questions** so they **can't ask for more detail** if the respondent says something **particularly interesting**.

1) **Unstructured interviews** are **informal**, with **no rigid structure**.

2) They're good for researching **sensitive issues** where the interviewer has to gain the respondent's **trust** — for example sexuality, domestic violence or crime.

3) They use **open-ended questions** and give **qualitative** data. They're quite **valid**.

4) The interviewer needs to have **skill** so they can **probe** to **find out more detail** about the interviewee's **beliefs** and **opinions**.

5) They're used with **smaller samples**, which means they're **not very representative**.

6) There are a lot of **interviewer effects** in an unstructured interview. The interviewee may say what they **think the researcher wants to hear**.

7) It takes a **long time** to write up an **unstructured interview** — you have to write down a **whole conversation**, not just the **codes** for particular **multiple-choice answers**.

Ethnography Studies the **Way of Life** of a Group

1) **Ethnography** is the scientific description of a specific culture by someone with first-hand experience of observing that culture. It was first used by **anthropologists** to study **traditional societies**. They joined the community, learnt the language, and noted their observations.

Anthropology is the study of humans.

2) It is based on small-scale fieldwork that tends to produce **qualitative** data. It's **valid** because you can study behaviour in **natural settings**.

3) You can use all sorts of methods to get **primary data**. You can use **unstructured interviews**. You can **observe** a community and see what they get up to.

4) **Case studies** are in-depth studies of **particular events** like **demonstrations**.

5) You can find out an **individual's life history** with **interviews** and **observations**.

6) **Time budgeting** is where you ask people to keep a **detailed diary** of their activities during a specified time. This can create **qualitative** and **quantitative** data.

7) Researchers may also analyse **diaries** and **letters**, which are **secondary data**.

- Ethnography is **in-depth research** which gives **inside knowledge** about a community.
- You get a **valid** picture from ethnography, but it relies on the **researcher's interpretations** of what people do and say.
- It's **difficult** to **make generalisations** from small-scale research.

Interviews and Observations

Observation is Watching Behaviour in Real-Life Settings

1) In **covert observation**, the researcher **doesn't tell the group** they're being observed. The British Sociological Association (BSA) advise that you should only use covert participant observation when there's **no other way** of obtaining the data. For example, **Nigel Fielding (1993)** used covert observation when researching the National Front (a far right-wing political party) because he believed he would encounter hostility if they knew he was a sociologist.

2) **Overt observation** (direct observation) is when the group is aware of the research and they know who the researcher is. For example, **Beverley Skeggs (1991)** used overt observation when studying female sexuality among students at a college.

3) **Participant observation** is when the researcher **actively involves themselves in the group**.

4) **Non-participant observation** is when the researcher **observes** the group but isn't actively part of the group.

> Interpretivists prefer observation because the researcher can get to the action.
> It tends to produce qualitative data that's more valid than questionnaires.

Participant and Non-Participant Observation Have Pros and Cons

Participant observation

1) Participant observation gets the researcher **right to where the action** is — so they can **check out the dynamics of a group** from **close up**.

2) **Participant observation** allows you to research the workings of deviant groups.

3) The researcher gets **first-hand insight** of people in **natural real-life settings**.

4) If it's **covert**, people **can't mislead** the researcher.

But...

1) The researcher may get too involved and find it **hard to stand back** and **objectively observe** the group.

2) **Overt research** may **influence** the behaviour of the group.

3) The researcher in a **covert observation** may join in with illegal acts if they're in a deviant group.

4) You **can't repeat the research**. It **lacks reliability**. A covert observer may find it difficult to remember all the events and accurately record them.

5) There are **ethical** and **practical** problems in **getting in**, **staying in** and **getting out** of the group.

6) The research usually includes a **small group** so it's not **representative** of the population.

7) It is **hard work**, **time-consuming** and **expensive**.

Non-participant observation

1) In **non-participant** observation, the researcher **isn't drawn into the group** so they can be more **objective** about the group's behaviour.

2) If you want to observe **deviant** groups, you have to be very **inconspicuous**.

But...

1) **Observing from the outside** stops you from getting to where the **action** is.

2) **Overt research** may **influence** the **behaviour** of the group.

Practice Questions

Q1 Give two differences between structured and unstructured interviews.

Q2 What is ethnography?

Q3 What research methods could you use to carry out ethnographic research?

Q4 What is the difference between covert and overt observation?

Q5 Briefly explain two strengths of participant observation.

Exam Question

Q1 Assess the usefulness of unstructured interviews to the sociologist. (20 marks)

Sociologists could be everywhere, watching us... shhhh...

It's annoying, this tendency people have to say what they think the researcher wants to hear. Can you really trust anything someone says in an interview...? I dunno. Participant observation gives access to people, but it's difficult to do and you won't necessarily get the same results twice. I don't think I'd want to do a participant observation of serial killers.

Experiments

You can use experiments to give you quantitative primary data.
You can get quantitative secondary data from statistics, and qualitative secondary data from documents.

Experiments Let You Find Cause and Effect

1) Experiments are used by **natural scientists** — biologists, chemists etc.
2) The researcher starts with a **hypothesis** and they use the experiment to **test** it out.
3) All the variables are kept constant, apart from the one you're interested in — the **independent variable**. Scientists **change the independent variable** and observe the effects on the **dependent variable**. If you were testing the effects of temperature on electrical resistance, **temperature** would be the **independent variable** which **you control** and **electrical resistance** would be the **dependent variable** which you **measure**.
4) The results are **turned into numbers** — the scientist looks for **patterns** and **cause-and-effect** relationships.
5) This method has been developed and used by **social scientists** to look for **social** causes and effects.

> Forming a hypothesis and testing it with an experiment is how science works, according to the hypothetico-deductive model.

There are Three Kinds of Experiment

1) **Lab experiments** are done in a **controlled environment**. The researcher **changes** the **independent variable**. The researcher observes the effect on the **dependent variable**. The researcher usually uses a **control group**, which is **left alone** to see what happens if you **don't do anything** to the **independent variable**. This method is often used by psychologists.
2) **Field experiments** are a response to the criticisms of lab experiments. They take place outside of the lab in **real social settings**, and those involved are often **unaware**. This method is used by **interpretivist** sociologists.
3) **Natural experiments** are not set up artificially. An example would be **twin studies**, but these are quite rare.

Strengths of lab experiments

1) The **researcher** has **control** over the experiment.
2) You get **quantitative** data.
3) You can **replicate** the research.

Limitations of lab experiments

1) It's **hard** to **reproduce real social situations** in a lab — lab experiments are **artificial**.
2) It is **difficult** to **isolate single variables**. **Social behaviour** is influenced by **many factors**.
3) There are often **moral** and **ethical** issues in lab experiments.
4) People may feel **intimidated** or **act differently** in the lab.

> Twin studies are where you study genetically identical twins in different situations, to see whether something's caused by genetics or if it's caused by socialisation.

> Researchers can measure things in a biased way if they have expectations about the results.

Strengths of field experiments

1) They're done in **natural social settings** and are more like **real life**.
2) They can show the **hidden meanings of everyday social interaction**.

Limitations of field experiments

1) You **can't control the variables** like you can in lab experiments.
2) If people **know they're being studied** they may **change** their **behaviour**.
3) There's an **ethical problem** in carrying out experiments when the subjects **aren't aware** that they are taking part in an experiment.

When People Know They're Being Studied, They Sometimes Act Differently

1) When people are more **interested** in something, they **try harder**. They may try harder at what they're doing because they know they're being observed and want to appear in a good light. This is called the **Hawthorne effect**.
2) People usually have an idea of what kind of **response** the **researchers** want. People often either give the researchers the **response they think they want** or the **exact opposite** — depending on whether they want to please the researchers or whether they want to be stubborn.
3) People usually try to show themselves in the **best possible light**. They may say they **wouldn't commit crime** when **really they would**. They may say they **recycle all their rubbish** when **really they don't**.
4) These effects mean data from experiments may not be **valid**.

Secondary Data

Statistics are a Source of Secondary Data

Official statistics are a source of secondary data. They're produced by local governments, central government and government agencies.

1) **Hard statistics** are **objective**. Politicians can't fiddle with them. Statistics on births and marriages are hard statistics.

2) **Soft statistics** are more **subjective**. Politicians can fiddle with them. Statistics on **crime**, **poverty** and **unemployment** are soft statistics. In the 1980s and 1990s, the government **changed the method** used to **measure unemployment** over 20 times.

3) **Social Trends** is a collection of **regular government surveys** published every year. It's a **great source** of **secondary data**.

4) The **census** is a survey of every household every 10 years. Every household has to fill in the form **by law**.

5) The **British Crime Survey** looks at victims of crime. The data is collected by a questionnaire.

Documents and Mass Media are a Source of Secondary Data

1) A document is **written text**. Documents can be **personal** — like **letters**, **diaries**, **autobiographies**, **memoirs** and **suicide notes**. Documents can also be **official**, like **school** records, **health** records, **church** records and **social work** records.

2) Documents can be **expressive** — more to do with **meanings**, like a **suicide note**. Documents can be **formal** — like **official documents**. **Interpretivists** prefer **expressive** documents because they're a big source of **qualitative data**.

3) **Max Weber** used **historical documents** when he was studying how the **religious** beliefs of Calvinism brought about a **social change**. **Michel Foucault** used **historical documents** to analyse changes in **social control** and **punishment**.

4) **Content analysis** is a method of **systematically** analysing a communication (e.g. a speech, film or letter) to understand its **meanings**. It is often used to study the mass media, e.g. research by the Glasgow University Media Group.

5) There are **problems** with documents. They can be **difficult to understand** if they're old. They might be **fakes**. They might contain **lies** — especially personal documents.

Sociologists Compare Different Secondary Documents

1) Sociologists look for **similarities** and **differences** between secondary documents. They can compare different **times**, different **cultures** and different **groups** within society by looking at secondary data.

2) Researchers can analyse real social behaviour and make comparisons without having to set up artificial experiments.

3) Durkheim used this **comparative method** in his famous 1897 study of suicide. He looked at the rates of suicide in different European societies. He found that the suicide rate was **consistent over time**, **but varied between societies** and varied for **different groups** within society.

Practice Questions

Q1 Name two advantages of field experiments over laboratory experiments.

Q2 What is the Hawthorne effect?

Q3 What is the difference between hard and soft statistics?

Exam Question

Q1 Explain what is meant by the term 'independent variable'. (2 marks)

Anyone up for an experiment on how people cope with being millionaires...

If you're not really into science, this business about dependent and independent variables might seem a tad confusing. Don't be too confused — just remember that the dependent variable is the one you measure to see how it's changed. All the stuff on secondary data is fairly straightforward, I reckon — it's about what kind of secondary data sociologists use.

Interpreting Data

You can interpret, analyse and evaluate data in lots of different ways.

Check Data's **Reliable**, **Valid** and **Representative**

Valid = data is a **true picture** of **what you're measuring**.

Reliable = you can use the **same method again** under the **same conditions** and get the **same results**.

Representative = the **sample** has the **same proportions** as the **population**.

Look for **Correlations** and Patterns in **Quantitative** Data

Correlation is where one variable is related to another.

% GCSE attainment by parents' socio-economic classification, 2002

	5 GCSE grades A*-C	1-4 GCSE grades A*-C	5 GCSE grades D-G	1-4 GCSE grades D-G	None reported
Higher professional	77	13	6	...	3
Lower professional	64	21	11	2	2
Intermediate	52	25	17	2	4
Lower supervisory	35	30	27	4	4
Routine	32	32	25	5	6
Other	32	29	26	4	9

Published in *Social Trends 34 (2004)*. Source: Youth Cohort Study by the Department for Education and Skills

If you were **analysing this data**, you would have to:

1) See **what the table's about**. The **title** tells you that this table is about how **educational achievement** is related to **parents' socio-economic position**.

2) Find out **where it's from**. It says *Social Trends*. This is a collection of government research. It's possible that there could be political **bias** here.

3) Look for a **correlation** between the variables. In this table, high socio-economic class seems to go with lots of GCSEs at grades A*-C.

4) Identify **patterns** in the data — it says that children with parents in higher socio-economic positions achieve a **higher percentage** of top grades. Those with parents in **routine** occupations achieve a **higher percentage** of grades **D-G**.

5) Ask if the data is **valid**. The relationship you can **see** might not be the **only one** there. There's a **correlation**, but you can't conclude that the parents' socio-economic class is the **cause** of their children's attainment level. Some sociologists would say that **material deprivation** is the cause but there might be **other causes** that the table just doesn't show.

6) Find out about the **sample**. It's from the **Youth Cohort** study, which has a **large** sample — so you could make **generalisations** about the **population** as a **whole**.

7) Find out about **how** the data was collected. The Youth Cohort study gets its data from school records. You could repeat this study again and get the same results.

The appendix of Social Trends tells you that the Youth Cohort study had 35 000 respondents.

If you've got a hypothesis about educational achievement and class, you can use the figures to test it out.

Question the **Method** and the **Sample** with **Qualitative** Data

"I always leave the quiet ones to just get on with their work. Girls are OK in the class too. It's the boys you have to be tough on. They are usually the troublemakers."

Imagine you got this quote from an **unstructured interview** with a teacher. You would have to:

1) Ask yourself whether the interviewee might have said it because of something to do with the **method**. A **different method** might produce a **different response**, so it might not be very **reliable**.

2) Ask yourself if it's **really what the interviewee believes** or whether they said what they **thought** the **interviewer wanted to hear**. This quote might not be a **true reflection** of how this teacher really acts.

3) See if the sample is **representative**. The research might use a **small** or **untypical sample** — which doesn't tell you much about **teachers in general**.

4) Find out **who carried out the research**. A researcher might have a particular **political** or **sociological point of view**. They can present the research in a way that suits their theories. This is **bias**.

5) Figure out what it **means**. The quote tells us something about processes like **labelling** that go on in schools.

Interpreting Data

Analyse *Official Statistics* — *They're* Not as *Objective* as they *Seem* at First

Official statistics are a **really useful** source of **existing information**. Some sociologists love them because they're **cheap** and **available** (fnar, fnar...). With **official statistics**, you can look at **trends** over **time**. The sample sizes tend to be **huge**, so at least you know they're **representative**. Official stats are sometimes your **only source of information**. There are some **problems** with official statistics, though — they don't always **measure** what they **say** they measure.

1) **Positivists** like official stats — they think official stats are a source of **objective, reliable** data. They **analyse** the relationship between social **variables** and look for **correlations** and **cause-and-effect relationships**.

2) **Marxists** say that **official statistics** are government statistics. They think all official stats are **politically biased** to serve the **interests of the ruling class**, and **designed** to **avoid political embarrassment**.

3) **Interpretivists** say that **official statistics** are **not hard facts**. They are **not as objective** as they **seem at first**. Interpretivists say **statistics** are **social constructions** and don't tell you about **meanings** and **motives**.

> **Example** — **crime statistics** don't tell you an **objective figure** of how many **crimes** are committed.
>
> The police **don't know about all crimes** that are committed. Some criminals get **let off**. Some people **don't trust the police** enough to tell them about a crime. Some people might not **realise** they're a victim of crime. So — there's crime that we **plain don't know about** if we use **official statistics**.

Analyse *Content* of *Documents* and the *Mass Media* — but *Take Care...*

1) Traditional **quantitative content analysis** produces **statistical data**.

2) For example, you can **count** the **number of times something happens** in a **TV programme** — like the number of times girls are in a passive role.

3) The research is **reliable** and **easy to obtain**, and you can **make comparisons**.

4) The problem is that the **researchers' interpretations** may be **biased**. Researchers **might not agree** on exactly what counts as a "passive role", for example.

5) You still have a lot of **explaining** to do even if you have a **clear result** like "ethnic minorities are under-represented in TV programmes". You have to explain **how** and **why**.

> **Qualitative analysis** (e.g. semiotic analysis) looks for **themes** and **meanings** in media and documents. **Interpretivists** prefer this method because it **uncovers hidden meanings**. It's more **valid** than quantitative analysis. The downside is that the researcher can **interpret** the sources in **different ways**. It's not very **reliable**.

John Scott (1990) thinks sociologists should be **really careful** when **analysing secondary sources**.

1) Documents might **not** be **authentic** — they might be **fakes**.
2) They might **not** be **credible** — the author might not be telling the **truth**.
3) They might **not** be **representative**.
4) They might be **difficult to understand** — full of **old-fashioned** meanings.

Practice Questions

Q1 How are the methods used to analyse quantitative data different to those used for qualitative data?
Q2 Name a strength of official statistics.
Q3 How would interpretivists criticise official statistics?
Q4 What does John Scott (1990) say about analysing documents?

Exam Questions

Q1 Explain what is meant by the 'reliability' of a set of data. (2 marks)

Q2 Examine the advantages and disadvantages of official statistics as a source of data for the sociologist. (20 marks)

I'm looking for patterns in an Argyle jumper...

Case studies don't always include numbers, but it's useful to know how to deal with them if you get them. Always look at how data's collected, the sample size, bias, validity and reliability. Don't get validity and reliability confused, will you. People seem to get them mixed up in the exam, and it'll lose you marks.

Limitations of Research

Research has its limits — it can't tell you everything. Here are all the pros and cons of different kinds of data.

Primary Data is Collected First-Hand — it has Good Points and Bad Points

The researcher collects primary information first-hand — they find it themselves. You could use methods like **interviews**, **questionnaires**, **observations** or **experiments**. You gather quantitative or qualitative data.

1) Primary data is obtained from **first-hand research**. It doesn't rely on **another sociologist's research** and you can carefully **choose your method** to make your data as valid and reliable as possible.
2) Primary data is always **brand new** and **bang up to date**.
3) **Some methods** of getting primary data can be **expensive** and **time-consuming**.
4) **Some methods** may put the researcher in a **dangerous situation**.
5) **Some methods** may be **unethical** if you don't give **informed consent**.
6) The **researcher's own values** may mess with the research process. This creates **bias**.
7) You **can't always get access** to the group you want to study.

Secondary Data is Existing Information — it has Pros and Cons

Secondary data sources include **official statistics**, **diaries**, **letters**, **memoirs**, **emails**, **TV documentaries** and **newspapers**. You gather the data together and analyse it, but you don't generate the data.

1) You can **quickly** and easily collect secondary data.
2) You can **easily** use **secondary data** to **compare different societies**.
3) With secondary data you can study **past events and societies**. You can **compare past** and **present**.
4) You don't have to worry about **informed consent**.
5) The **existing data** may not be **valid** or **reliable** — you're **stuck** with the way the research was **originally done**.
6) Documents may not be **authentic**, **representative** or **credible**. Official statistics can be **biased**.
7) You **might not be able to find** the information that you need from existing data.
8) **Your values** don't influence the **collection** of the data (though they might influence your **choice of sources**), but the **researcher's values** might have ruined the validity of the **original research**. **Your values** can get in the way of **how you analyse** the data.

Quantitative Data Can be Reliable but Not Very Valid

1) With quantitative data, you can **test your hypothesis** and look for **cause and effect** relationships.
2) You can **compare** your statistics against existing statistics, and look for **trends over time** and between societies.
3) It's **easy** to **analyse tables**, **charts** and **graphs** — especially line charts, bar graphs and pie charts.
4) You can **repeat** questionnaires and structured interviews to **test reliability**.
5) Quantitative methods allow **large samples**, so the findings can **represent** the **general population**.
6) **Statistics** can **hide reality**. **Categories** in **interviews** or **questionnaires** can **distort** the truth.
7) Statistics don't tell you anything about the **meanings**, **motives** and **reasons** behind behaviour — there's not much **depth** and **insight** into **social interaction**.
8) Statistics can be **politically biased**. The method may have been chosen in order to get the "right" data.

Qualitative Data can be Valid but Not Very Reliable

1) **Qualitative sociological data** gives **insight** into **social interaction**. It's a **detailed description** of social behaviour.
2) Qualitative data lets you find out the **meanings** and **motives** behind behaviour.
3) You don't have to **force** people into **artificial categories** like in questionnaires.
4) Qualitative methods let you build up **trust** and research **sensitive topics**.
5) Qualitative methods are **difficult to repeat** — they **aren't very reliable**.
6) The research is often on a **small scale** — so the findings might not **represent** the whole population.
7) **Positivists** say qualitative results **lack credibility** because they're **subjective** and open to interpretation.
8) The **researcher** can get the **wrong end of the stick** and **misinterpret** the group or individual they're studying.

Limitations of Research

Sociology *is* More Subjective *than* Traditional Science

1) **Objective knowledge** is the **same** no matter what your **point of view**. **Objective** methods provide **facts** that can be easily **verified** or **falsified**. Objective research is also **value-free** (see below), and doesn't have any bias.

2) **Subjective knowledge** depends on your **point of view**. **Subjective** methods give data that **can't** be easily tested. Subjective research requires **interpretation**.

3) Sociology is **more subjective** than the physical **sciences**, but it aims to be at least partly objective.

Positivist Sociology *tries to be as* Objective *as* Possible

1) Positivists (see p. 76) think sociology should be scientific and analyse social facts. Social facts can be directly observed and measured, e.g. the number of followers of Christianity in Britain.

2) Positivists look for correlations in data, and cause-and-effect relationships. To do this, they use quantitative methods like questionnaires (see p. 81) and official statistics, which are objective and reliable.

1) Interpretivist sociologists (see p. 76) reckon sociology doesn't suit scientific methods.

2) They try to understand human behaviour from the point of view of the individual, so they use methods that let them discover the meanings, motives and reasons behind human behaviour and social interaction.

There's Debate *over whether* Research *can be* Value-free

1) **Value-free research** is research that doesn't make **value judgements**, e.g. judgements about whether the things it researches are **good** or **bad**.

2) Value-free research doesn't let the **researcher's own beliefs** get in the way. For example, questionnaires mustn't ask questions that **lead** the respondent towards a particular answer.

3) In order for this idea of **value freedom** to work, the researcher must **interpret** all data **objectively**.

4) Value freedom means that the **end use** of the research **shouldn't matter**. Research should come up with knowledge, and how that knowledge is used isn't up to the researcher.

Some sociologists say **sociology can't be value-free**.

1) The decision to research in the first place is **value-laden** — someone has to decide that the research is worth spending money on. Some say that research which the **state** or **businesses** want to see is most likely to get funding.

2) It's difficult to **completely avoid bias** and interview effects (see p. 82).

3) Some Marxist and feminist sociologists **deliberately choose research** with an **end use** that they **approve** of. They believe that sociology **should** make **value judgements** about society and **suggest** ways it could be **better**.

Practice Questions

Q1 Give two strengths of primary data.

Q2 Give two criticisms of qualitative data.

Q3 How are interpretivists different from positivists?

Q4 Why do some feminists reject the idea of value freedom in sociological research?

Exam Question

Q1 Examine the problems some sociologists may find when using qualitative data in their research. (20 marks)

Research can't tell you everything...

When you discuss a method in the exam, try to include some examples of studies which used it. This shows the examiner that you understand what kind of research the method works best for. It'll also give you a chance to show off your wider sociological knowledge, which always goes down well with the examiners — it might even get you a few extra marks.

Application of Research Methods to Education

These pages give some examples of research into the sociology of education.

Rosenthal and Jacobson (1968) Tested Self-Fulfilling Prophecies

1) **Rosenthal and Jacobson (1968)** went to a school in San Francisco and gave every student an **IQ test** that they said could predict **intellectual blooming**. They kept the results **secret**.

2) They took a **random sample** of 20% of the students and **reported to the school** that the students in the random sample had been identified as the **bloomers** — those who were likely to show the **biggest gains** in IQ during the year.

3) A year later they went back to the school and **retested** all the students.

4) The results of the two IQ tests showed that the students they'd **randomly identified** as high scoring had made the most **intellectual progress** in the year between the tests.

5) They concluded that the teachers must have been communicating a **positive label** to this group — that they had successfully created a **self-fulfilling prophecy**.

Advantages of Rosenthal and Jacobson's research method

1) The children were researched in a **natural, real-life setting** — giving a greater chance of **validity**.

2) Studying IQ creates **quantified data**, which makes the patterns easy to assess.

Disadvantages of Rosenthal and Jacobson's research method

1) The children and teachers may have acted differently because they **knew they were being observed**.

2) **Misleading** the teachers at the school is arguably **ethically incorrect**, because it involves **deceiving** some of the subjects of the study.

3) Rosenthal and Jacobson were unable to **control all the variables** — there are many factors which could have **contributed** to changes in IQ over the year besides the treatment of students by their teachers.

4) The entire study relied on **IQ tests**, which some sociologists criticise as a **bad measure** of intelligence — e.g. they claim that IQ tests are **culturally biased** in a way that favours some people.

Paul Willis (1977) Studied Anti-school Culture

1) **Paul Willis (1977)** studied a group of 12 working class boys as they made their **transition from school to the workplace**, using a mixture of **observation**, **group interviews** and **individual interviews**.

2) He found that the group had formed an **anti-school culture** that **rejected trying hard** in favour of **disruptive behaviour**. The group had decided not to try to **achieve qualifications**, even if they were **intellectually capable**.

3) Willis found that they transferred the same **anti-authority culture** to their **workplace**. Most of them found work as shop-floor staff in factories.

4) Willis claimed that their anti-authority nature was something they **created themselves** and not something that was **transmitted to them** by school or society.

Advantages of Willis's research method

1) Most human interactions are **instinctive** and best studied in **real situations**. Willis used **direct observation** to see how the group acted in school and in their workplace, **group interviews** to see how they acted in each other's company, and **individual interviews** so that he could get an idea of what each subject was like on their own.

2) Individual interviews gave Willis a chance to **build a rapport** with the boys, allowing him to gain an **in-depth understanding** of their behaviour.

Disadvantages of Willis's research method

1) A sample of just **12** working class boys is **unlikely** to be **representative**. It would be misleading to generalise about all working class boys from these results.

2) However, performing the same study with a larger group of boys would be **very expensive**.

Application of Research Methods to Education

William Labov (1972) Assessed Linguistic Deprivation

1) **Bernstein (1971)** suggested that "**linguistic deprivation**" is a cause of **underachievement** of **working class and ethnic minority children**.

2) **William Labov (1972)** tested Bernstein's theory using **informal, unstructured interviews**.

3) Labov discovered that when **black working class children** were interviewed by a **white person** in a **formal interview**, they **became tense** and **spoke nervously**, appearing to be **linguistically deprived**.

4) When they were interviewed by a **black person** in an **informal setting**, they became much more **articulate**.

5) So the **apparent linguistic deprivation** seemed to be a reaction to a **perceived hostile environment** rather than a genuine feature of the children's **communication methods**.

"Linguistic deprivation" means a lack of ability with Standard English. The theory is that working class children tend to describe things in a condensed way and use more slang. This causes them to underachieve in education even though they may be expressing the same ideas as high achievers.

Advantages of Labov's research method

1) Informal, unstructured interviews are likely to offer **greater validity** than formal, structured interviews because they give the interviewer a chance to **adapt their questioning to their subject**.

2) **Sensitive or interesting issues** can be researched at greater depth in an informal interview because the interviewer doesn't have to stick to a **fixed questionnaire**.

3) The subject is more likely to **be at ease** in an informal situation, as the interviewer has a chance to build up a **rapport**. So they're less likely to **hide information**, potentially giving a **greater insight** into their thoughts and feelings.

Disadvantages of Labov's research method

1) All interviews depend on the questions and the skill of the **interviewer**. So results may be different **from one interviewer to the next**. This is known as "**interviewer bias**".

2) The possibility of "interviewer bias" also means that if the **same study** is carried out a **second time** then it can easily produce **completely different results** — it **isn't reliable**.

3) Data collected through informal, unstructured interviews is **difficult to quantify** — subjects may not have all been asked **the same questions**.

4) As the questions aren't all **planned in advance**, there is a risk that the interviewer will ask **biased** or **leading questions**, or just keep asking **similar questions** without realising.

5) The subject may give the reply they think the interviewer **wants to hear** to try to please them, possibly **without realising** that they're doing it (**social desirability effect**).

6) Unstructured interviews are **time-consuming** and **relatively expensive**.

Practice Questions

Q1 Describe Rosenthal and Jacobson's research method.
Q2 Give two disadvantages of Rosenthal and Jacobson's research method.
Q3 Describe Paul Willis's research method.
Q4 Give two advantages of Willis's research method.
Q5 Describe William Labov's research method.
Q6 Give three disadvantages of Labov's research method.

Exam Question

Q1 Suggest an advantage and a disadvantage for sociologists of using direct observation. (4 marks)

So many studies, so little time...

It's unlikely that these specific studies will come up in the exam — but you do need to understand how sociological methods can be applied to education. There's more about doing well in the exam on pages 94–96.

Application of Research Methods to Health

These pages show how some of the methods can be used to research health.

The **English Longitudinal Study of Ageing** Explored **Ageing, Health and Class**

1) The **English Longitudinal Study of Ageing (ELSA)** was set up by **Michael Marmot**. It follows a group of **over 8,500** people from all social classes who were **born before 1952**.

2) The ELSA is partially funded by **central government**.

3) The subjects have had to fill in a questionnaire **every two years** since **2002** about their health, work, experience of healthcare, cognitive abilities and income. In 2004, the questionnaire was combined with **a visit from a nurse** to measure things such as **blood pressure** and **lung function**.

4) A new report on the study is **published** after every set of questionnaires.

5) In 2006 the study showed that people in their 50s from the **poorest 20%** of the population are over **ten times** more likely to die than those in the **richest 20%**.

6) It also showed that there is a **strong relationship** between levels of wealth and **mortality and morbidity**.

Longitudinal studies are ones that follow the same group of subjects over a long period of time.

Advantages of Marmot's research method

1) The study has generated a **huge amount** of **quantitative data**, which is helpful for **scientific** and **positivist** research.

2) **Longitudinal studies** are the most **reliable** way to analyse **changes over time** as they eliminate the possibility of **different sample groups** each being **unrepresentative** in **different ways**.

Disadvantages of Marmot's research method

1) Longitudinal studies are **very expensive** and **time-consuming** — long-term funding is essential.

2) Some of the original group inevitably **leave the study** as time progresses — either **by choice** or just because they **die** or become **impossible to contact**. This affects the **reliability** of the research.

Dalrymple and Appleby (2000) Studied the **Attitudes of Epileptics**

1) **Jamie Dalrymple and John Appleby (2000)** used **anonymous questionnaires** to investigate the accuracy with which people suffering epilepsy **reported seizures** to their GPs.

2) Their questionnaires asked for **quantifiable data** and were filled in by **122 respondents** from **31 practices**.

3) They found that **one sixth** of their respondents **hadn't reported** a recent seizure to their GP.

4) They also found that patients who had experienced a recent seizure were also likely to be **suffering from depression** due to reasons such as **loss of driving rights**, **loss of employment** and **fear of discrimination**.

Advantages of Dalrymple and Appleby's research method

1) The use of questionnaires from patients that Dalrymple and Appleby had **never met** meant that the study was **detached**. It eliminated the possibility of **interviewer bias**.

2) The use of **quantifiable** data made it **objective**.

3) The study was **quick** and **cheap**, but collected results from a **large number** of people.

4) The fairly large size of the study means that it was likely to be **representative** of all epilepsy sufferers.

Disadvantages of Dalrymple and Appleby's research method

1) Questionnaires are **inflexible** and there is no real opportunity for **follow-up questions**.

2) Questionnaires depend on respondents **telling the truth**. Some may have been **embarrassed** about not reporting seizures, so may have **deliberately provided untruthful answers**.

3) **Interpretivists** think that questionnaires are **too detached** to produce **valid results** — they think that they don't provide a **true picture**.

Application of Research Methods to Health

Quirk and Lelliott *Observed* Acute Psychiatric Ward Patients

1) **Alan Quirk and Paul Lelliott** studied **acute psychiatric wards** in London hospitals. Their data was collected over **three years** of **participant observation**.

2) Alan Quirk **immersed himself** in the life of the ward, taking part in activities including **occupational therapy**, **ward rounds** and **treatment sessions**.

3) He often sat in TV rooms and corridors to try to **observe** what was going on and to **talk to patients**.

4) The study produced a large amount of **qualitative data** about how patients **interact with each other** and with **medical staff**.

5) One of the conclusions they drew was that **Goffman's 1961** characterisation of mental health institutions as total or closed institutions is no longer relevant — patients **maintain contact** with the outside world, tend to only stay for **short periods** and there is a **high turnover** in medical staff.

Advantages of Quirk and Lelliott's research method

1) Their data is likely to be **valid** — they gained a **large amount** of data, and had time to develop a **thorough understanding** of the interactions between patients and staff.

2) Their method gave them **access** to a group that is **difficult** to research with other methods.

Disadvantages of Quirk and Lelliott's research method

1) The study took **three years**, making it **time-consuming** and **expensive**.

2) It's unlikely that a **shorter study** with the **same methods** would produce reliable results because of the difficulty of **being accepted** by the group being studied.

3) It can be difficult to get **consent** from hospital trusts and their **ethics committees** for research of this nature due to the **unpredictable** and **dangerous environment** of acute psychiatric wards.

4) The research cannot **be repeated easily**, meaning that it **lacks reliability**.

Practice Questions

Q1 What is a longitudinal study?

Q2 Give two disadvantages of a longitudinal study.

Q3 What were the advantages of Dalrymple and Appleby's use of questionnaires?

Q4 What were the disadvantages of Dalrymple and Appleby's use of questionnaires?

Q5 Describe the research methods of Quirk and Lelliott.

Q6 Give three disadvantages of Quirk and Lelliott's research methods.

Exam Questions

Q1 Explain what is meant by 'validity' of data. (2 marks)

Q2 Suggest two reasons why sociologists might use questionnaires. (4 marks)

This last question's for one million — would you like to ask the audience...

Studying lots of people seems to mean either using questionnaires, which are very detached, or spending a great deal of money on interviews. And the latter may only produce qualitative data, which isn't always helpful for scientific analysis. In some cases it may not really be possible to do either, and sociologists like Quirk just have to observe as much as possible.

Do Well in Your Exam

These pages describe what the sample exam papers for the new specification are like. We can't predict exactly what the new exam papers will be like though — there may be a few changes. So it's important that when you take the exams, you **read the instructions and questions really carefully**. Don't assume they'll always follow the same pattern.

Unit 1 is worth 40% of the AS-level

1) The **Unit 1** exam is **1 hour** long. It's worth **60 marks** — **40% of the AS-level** or **20% of a full A-level**.

2) **Unit 1** has **three topic areas**: 'Culture and Identity', 'Families and Households', and 'Wealth, Poverty and Welfare'.

3) There's **one section** about **each topic area**. You only have to do **one** of these sections. It might sound obvious — but make sure you **choose** an **area** which you have been **taught and revised**.

4) Each section has **one large question** broken down into **five parts** — (a) to (e).

5) There are usually two **items** (short texts about the topic) to **read at the start**. The items usually highlight some of the **themes** or **theories** within the topic. Some of the question parts will **refer to the items** — so you **have to read them**.

6) The first **three parts** of the question **(a-c)** are likely to be **short-answer questions** worth about 2, 4 or 6 marks. The second **two parts** of the question **(d-e)** are likely to be **longer essay questions** worth about 24 marks each.

Unit 2 is worth 60% of the AS-level

1) The exam is **2 hours** long and it's worth **90 marks** — **60% of the AS-level** or **30% of a full A-level**.

2) **Unit 2** covers **three areas**: 'Education', 'Health' and 'Sociological Methods'. All students study 'Sociological Methods' and at least one of 'Education' and 'Health'.

3) The exam has **two sections** — not three like you might expect. This is because **'Sociological Methods'** is **combined** with the 'Health' and 'Education' topics. The two sections of the exam are called: **'Education with Research Methods'** and **'Health with Research Methods'**.

4) You only have to do **one section**. You have to answer **all parts** of the section you choose. Again, make sure you **choose the topic** that you have **been taught and revised the most**.

5) Each **section** contains **three questions**. Each of these questions will be broken down into **sub-parts**.

- The first question is worth **40 marks**, and is about either 'Health' or 'Education' depending on which section you're doing. You'll probably be given an **item to read**. The sample exam advises you spend **50 minutes** on this question.

- The second question is worth **20 marks**, and requires you to **apply** knowledge and understanding of **sociological research methods** to the topic of 'Health' or 'Education'. You're advised to spend about **25 minutes** on this.

- The third question is worth **30 marks**. Like question 2, it focuses on **sociological research methods** but you can use knowledge from **any area of sociology** to answer it. You're advised to spend about **40 minutes** on this.

You Get Marks For...

AO just means 'Assessment Objective'

You Get Marks for:
AO1 — Knowledge and Understanding shown through Clear and Effective Communication
AO2 — Application, Analysis, Interpretation and Evaluation

Short-answer questions are questions that **don't require an essay** or a **detailed description** for their answer — they're all the questions that are usually worth 2, 4 or 6 marks. They mainly test **AO1 skills**.

Essay questions and questions requiring **more detail** test **AO1 skills** *and* **AO2 skills**. They're usually worth 20 or 24 marks.

For **AO2** marks you need to do things like:

1) **Evaluate** a theory / study / method — discuss its **strengths and weaknesses**.

2) Present **alternative** explanations / interpretations of findings.

3) **Identify** and **evaluate** social trends.

4) Organise your essay so that it's got a **coherent argument** and **structure**.

5) Use **evidence** to **back up** your points.

And don't forget about the basics:
- Write as **neatly** as you can.
- Use good **grammar** and **punctuation**.
- Check your **spelling** — especially of words to do with sociology.
- Make sure you **answer the question**.

Do Well in Your Exam

Here are some Hints for Short-Answer Questions

1) If you're asked for **two** things, give **two** things. **Not one.** Not three. Or four. Five is **right out**.

2) If you're asked for two things, spend **equal time and effort** on **both**. You **won't** get as many marks for a **lopsided** answer.

3) Give **examples** from **sociological studies** and from **statistics** to **back up** your points.

4) Refer to **theories** like Marxism, functionalism and interpretivism — but **only** if they're **relevant**.

5) Use the **number of marks** as a **guide** for **how long you should spend on each question**. The more marks a question is worth, the longer you should spend answering it.

Here are some Example Exam Questions and Answers

A Couple of 2-mark Questions and Answers to Show You What to Aim for:

(a) What is a pilot study?   (2 marks)

(a)   A pilot study is a small-scale study carried out before the main research to test the method being used. For example, a researcher might give their questionnaire to a small group to ensure the questions can be easily understood.

> Explain the term

> Give a short example.

(a) What is meant by 'labelling theory'?   (2 marks)

(a)   Labelling theory is the idea that the labels given to people affect their behaviour. For example, someone labelled in school as 'disruptive' may internalise that label and start to believe it, causing them to actually become disruptive.

A Couple of 4-mark Questions and Answers to Show You What to Aim for:

(b) Suggest two ways in which industrialisation affects the family.   (4 marks)

(b)   Family structure changes as a result of industrialisation. Nuclear families become the norm, instead of extended families. Talcott Parsons argued that this is because the nuclear family is better suited to industrial society.
      Roles within the family are also affected. In pre-industrial society, men and women usually work together in the home. In early industrial society, many men leave the home to work, for example in factories. Women are more likely to remain working in the home.

> Don't waste time writing more reasons — two is enough.

(b) Suggest two ways in which an individual might be socialised into femininity.   (4 marks)

(b)   The family can socialise girls to behave in a feminine way, for example through verbal appellation. They might call a girl "pretty", "sweet" and "lovely", whereas a boy might be called "a big, strong boy" and "a cheeky monkey".
      The media can act as a secondary agent of gender socialisation. For example, Angela McRobbie argued that magazines aimed at teenage girls reinforce conventional ideas of femininity.

> Briefly mentioning relevant studies is good.

A Couple of 6-mark Questions and Answers to Show You What to Aim for:

> Don't waffle at the start. Get straight in there with your suggestions.

(c) Suggest three reasons why boys achieve slightly less highly than girls in education.   (6 marks)

(c)   Traditionally "male" employment sectors such as heavy industry and factory work have declined. It can be argued that this has left boys with greater uncertainty over what they can aim for in life — some are disillusioned and feel no incentive to work hard at school.
      The number of female teachers has increased. This means that boys have fewer role models at school than before, which arguably means they are less likely to try to push themselves to achieve.
      The trend is also likely to be partly self-perpetuating. Boys are considered to be underachievers, so some teachers negatively label them. That negative labelling can become a self-fulfilling prophecy, causing boys to continue to underachieve.

(c) Suggest three ways in which children are treated differently than adults in modern UK society.   (6 marks)

(c)   Children are banned from buying many harmful substances, such as alcohol and tobacco. This represents an extra protection for children — it works in addition to the various laws that govern adults.
      Children are not expected to work and are financially supported by their parents. This is different from most adults, who are required to earn enough money to support themselves.
      Children are also protected by the state from abuse by their parents or carers. So the state offers additional protection to children in the family, above the protection that other members of society receive.

> A new paragraph for each new point makes it clear you've suggested three things.

Do Well in Your Exam

Here's an Example 20-mark Question and Answer:

Here's an example of a **longer exam question** based on a short **text**. It's the kind of question you'll get in the **Unit 2 exam** — it combines sociological methods with another topic.

---

2   For this question, you need to apply your knowledge and understanding of sociological methods to a specific area in the topic of 'Education'.

You should read Item B and then answer the question below.

Item B: Investigating social class and educational achievement

Sociologists have studied the extent to which there is a link between social class and standards of achievement in education. For instance, Willis (1977) investigated how an anti-school subculture among 12 working class boys contributed to low educational achievement. More recently, Willmott and Hutchinson (1992) studied the link between deprived social backgrounds and an increasing number of children leaving school with no GCSE passes in inner-city Manchester and Liverpool.

Sociologists researching this topic have been interested in finding the reasons behind patterns of achievement. They have investigated the effect of negative labelling on students, and the extent to which cultural differences between social classes affect educational achievement. Other research has focused on material deprivation as a factor affecting education.

Read the text carefully. It'll give you ideas for what to write about.

Using material from Item B and elsewhere, assess the benefits and drawbacks of **one** of the following sociological research methods in the study of social class and educational achievement.

(i)   unstructured interviews
(ii)   official statistics   (20 marks)

---

(2)(i)   Unstructured interviews take the form of an unrestricted, free-flowing conversation between the researcher and subject.

Give a brief description of the research method you're discussing.

A key benefit of using unstructured interviews for researching social class and educational achievement is that they allow the researcher to build up a rapport with the interviewee. This makes the interviewee more likely to open up and be honest in their answers, resulting in valid data. Another advantage of unstructured interviews is that they allow the researcher to follow up any ambiguous or unusual responses, to gain greater clarity and detail. Unstructured interviews are most appropriate for interpretivist research which is focused on empathising with individuals and discovering the motivations and emotions behind their behaviour.

Some sociologists argue that differences in educational achievement by social class are a result of cultural differences in attitudes. Unstructured interviews are a good way to research individuals' attitudes. For example, Willis (1977) used a range of methods, including unstructured interviews, to research the male, working class anti-school subculture referred to in Item B. The boys in this subculture had very negative attitudes towards education and were disruptive in school. The unstructured interviews allowed him to build a rapport with the boys and gain an insight into their motivations and beliefs. This opportunity for rapport wouldn't have been possible using quantitative methods, for example official statistics or questionnaires.

Apply the information about methods to specific studies.

Another advantage of unstructured interviews for researching this topic is that it is a sensitive and subtle approach. For example, Labov used this method when investigating whether "linguistic deprivation" might be a factor in working class children underachieving in education. A different approach, such as formal, structured interviews, may have been intimidating to the interviewees.

On the other hand, there are some disadvantages of unstructured interviews as a research method. The results are not reliable. For example, if another sociologist repeated Willis's research with a different group of working class boys, they would probably get different results. The research sample tends to be small because it's a time-consuming and expensive method. For example, Willis used a sample of only 12 boys. It's difficult to generalise from the results, because answers tend to be specific to individual subjects. This also makes it difficult to make direct comparisons between one interviewee and another.

Discuss both strengths and weaknesses.

Positivist researchers would find alternative methods more appropriate, for example a survey of a large sample would be more likely to provide reliable, quantitative data that could be used to make generalised conclusions. An investigation such as Willmott and Hutchinson's into a possible correlation between social deprivation and educational failure might be easier to research using a positivist approach.

In conclusion, unstructured interviews are a useful research method for the topic of social class and educational achievement to some extent. In particular, they would be appropriate for interpretivist sociologists researching individuals' attitudes, motivations and emotions. They would be less useful for large-scale research.

Sum up with a short conclusion.

A2-Level
Sociology

Exam Board: AQA

Theories of Ideology

*These pages are about the many different ways people have used the concept of **ideology**. It's an important concept in Sociology — but unfortunately it doesn't have one agreed definition. So there's lots to learn.*

The term **"Ideology"** has several meanings

Antoine Destutt de Tracy first used the word **ideology** in 1796 to describe what he called a new '**science of ideas**' which he saw emerging after the French Revolution. Since then the term has been used in several different ways.

> **Ideology has been defined in a large variety of ways**
>
> 1) As a set of **political beliefs**, e.g. socialism, liberalism.
> 2) As the **ideas** and **beliefs** of a **particular social class**.
> 3) As the **dominant ideas** and **beliefs** of the **ruling class**.
> 4) As the **official beliefs** of a **political system**, e.g. in totalitarian (dictatorial) regimes like Hitler's Germany.
> 5) As a set of beliefs that represent a **total view of reality**, e.g. religious fundamentalism.

It's not easy to **pin down** just one workable definition for 'ideology' — but it's important you understand how the word has been used by some **prominent thinkers**.

Your **Social** and **Political** perspective **Influences** how you define **Ideology**

When someone uses the word 'ideology' their **perspective** will give you a clue as to what they mean. E.g.

Marxists	See ideology as the set of ruling ideas that **keep workers in their place**.
Feminists	See ideology as both the set of ideas that **keep women oppressed** (patriarchal ideology), and a potentially **liberating set of beliefs** (feminism).
Liberals (pluralists)	Tend to see ideology as **totalitarian** and **oppressive** — e.g. Stalin's Russia and Hitler's Germany both had official ideologies which were repressive. Pluralists **reject** the idea that there can be a **monopoly of truth**.

Karl Marx said **Ideology** was a **False Picture** imposed by the **Ruling Class**

Karl Marx (1818-1883) believed the most important force in society was **class conflict** between the workers and the ruling class. In *The German Ideology* (1970, New York: International Publishers, written 1845) Marx and Engels said: "The **ideas** of the **ruling class** are in every epoch the **ruling ideas**."

> 1) In capitalist societies, workers are employed to **produce goods** which are sold by their employers for a **profit**.
> 2) Only a **bit** of this profit ends up in the **workers' wages** — most of it's **kept** by the employer.
> 3) Marx said if workers were allowed to notice the **unfairness** of this they'd **revolt**.
> 4) Ruling ideas (or **ideology**) are needed by the ruling class to make a grossly unfair system **appear fair** and **legitimate** and therefore keep it going.
> 5) Marx claimed that ideology creates a '**false consciousness**' for the workers. It gets them to **believe** that the system and their **position** within it are both **fair** and **just** by **mystifying** and **falsifying** their picture of reality.
> 6) The function of ideology for Marx then was to keep the workers in their place and **stop them rebelling**.
> 7) According to Marx only the ruling class has an ideology because only they have the need to **create illusions**.

Cissie was sure she'd never <u>knowingly</u> mystified the proletariat.

Theories of Ideology

The **Marxist** view of **Ideology** was developed by **Gramsci**

Antonio Gramsci (1891-1937) was a Marxist who called the domination of ruling class ideology in society '**hegemony**'.

1) Hegemonic ideas don't just rule — they **dominate**. Other values and ideas still exist in society, but **don't** get taken **seriously**. Ruling class ideas become '**the common sense of the age**'.

2) Nobody questions 'common sense' and so **nobody questions** the **ruling class's right to rule**. Gramsci argued that the ruling class's ideology becomes **entrenched** in all areas of social life — e.g. religion, art, law, language, education. This makes it difficult to challenge.

   "....the ruling class not only justifies and maintains its dominance, but manages to maintain the active consent of those over whom it rules." (**Gramsci**, 1971, *Selections from the Prison Notebooks*, London: Lawrence and Wishart).

3) The **struggle** against hegemony for Gramsci had to be an **intellectual** one with socialist thinkers developing an alternative '**proletarian hegemony**' (proletarian = working class).

> Gramsci wrote most of his theories in prison, in the 1930s. His prison notebooks were published much later. That's why the date of publication is well after he died.

Althusser argued there were **Ideological State Apparatuses**

1) The neo-Marxist **Althusser** argued that elements of society like the education system, mass media and religion were **Ideological State Apparatuses** (ISAs).

2) The ISAs are a tool of capitalism used to **justify**, **maintain** and **reproduce** class inequalities.

3) For example, according to Althusser, education **transmits** and **reproduces** an ideology about what it means to be working class, what it means to be middle class, and what everyone's **place in society** ought to be.

Karl Mannheim identified **Two** types of **Ideology**

Mannheim (1929) argued that ideology can be defined in two ways.

1) A set of beliefs used to **justify** and **perpetuate** an existing social order (a ruling class ideology).

2) A **utopian** set of beliefs about how the world **could be organised** in the **future**. Utopian ideologies tend to be formed by **oppressed groups** who want **radical change**.

According to Mannheim both types of ideology **distort reality** — the former is a distortion to create the illusion of **fairness** in society, the latter is just a '**wish image**' of what the future might be like.

- **Marxism** could be seen as a **utopian ideology** with its vision of an ideal future society after the ruling class has been overthrown. The ideal vision is used to **criticise existing society**.

- **Functionalism** (see p.204) could be seen as a **ruling class ideology** as it seeks to **justify existing society** with its emphasis on **agreement**, **consensus** and **stability**.

Benji's idea of rebranding their petrochemical products organisation as "Benji's Bag o' Fun™" was little more than a wish image.

Practice Questions

Q1 List four different ways in which the word ideology has been used.

Q2 According to Marx, what is the purpose of ruling class ideology?

Q3 Explain what is meant by false consciousness.

Q4 Why aren't hegemonic ideas challenged in capitalist society, according to Gramsci?

Q5 What two types of ideology does Mannheim identify?

Exam Question

Q1 Assess the view that Marxism is a utopian ideology. (18 marks)

Explain the different theories — and get top Marx...

The trick is to remember that ideology doesn't have just one definition that you can reel off, but is used in lots of different ways by different sociologists depending on their... er,... ideological perspective.

Theories of Science

*These pages examine theories of science in relation to other types of **belief system**, and discuss the debates surrounding their similarities and differences.*

The **Traditional View** is that **Science** is **Objective** and **Evidence-Based**

Many scientists claim there is a clear **distinction** between **science** and other ways of viewing the world. A recent example is **Richard Dawkins**, who in *The God Delusion* (2006) made the following observations about science and religion:

"Fundamentalists know they are right because they have read the truth in a holy book... The truth of the holy book is an axiom, not the end product of a process of reasoning. The book is true, and if the evidence seems to contradict it, it is the evidence that must be thrown out, not the book. By contrast, what I, as a scientist, believe... I believe not because of reading a holy book but because I have studied the evidence... When a science book is wrong, somebody eventually discovers the mistake and it is corrected in subsequent books. That conspicuously doesn't happen with holy books."

Exhibit A: not painted blue due to the outcome of an evidence-based enquiry.

> **The traditional view of science**
>
> 1) **Science is objective** — the scientist is **neutral**.
> 2) Scientific enquiry is **evidence-based** — conclusions are based on evidence, not **preconceived ideas**.
> 3) Scientific enquiry is **'open'** — ideas which are **tested** and proved wrong are rejected and **more accurate** ideas replace them.

This **Traditional View** of science has been **Challenged**

Michael Lynch (1983) argued that science is **far less objective** than scientists claim.

1) Lynch studied scientists experimenting on lab rats and concluded that the scientists were more **influenced** by their **existing theories** than may have been expected.

2) When **'anomalies'** occurred — i.e. results they were not expecting — the scientists often put them down to **errors** in the photographs they were studying, rather than seeing them as **evidence** towards a new theory or hypothesis.

Science can be viewed as a **Belief System** like **Religion**

Polanyi (1958) suggested that a **belief system** was made up of **three factors**. Science can be viewed as fitting this model.

> 1) **A circularity of beliefs** — each idea within the belief system is explained in **relation to others**. If one is challenged or fails it is **defended** by reference to another, to **avoid changing** the belief system.
> 2) **Supporting explanations are given for difficult situations** — if any **evidence** is shown to **contradict** the belief there will be a reason to explain it (as with the anomalies in the experiments Lynch observed).
> 3) **No alternative belief systems can be tolerated** — a **sweeping rejection** of religion could be seen as an example of this.

Sociology can be treated as a **Science**

Positivists like Comte believe that sociology is scientific. It consists of **gathering information** about the social world, **classifying data**, and **drawing conclusions** about **'the social laws'** which govern human society.

The positivist **Durkheim** claimed that by using the technique of **multivariate analysis**, 'social facts' could be uncovered.

1) Multivariate analysis is the attempt to **isolate** the impact of **independent variables** (the factors affecting something) on the dependent variable (the thing being affected).

2) For instance, the level of working class achievement in school might be the **dependent** variable, and material deprivation and teacher labelling the **independent** variables.

3) Durkheim believed that by complex, in-depth **statistical analysis** the independent variables could be measured and a **social law established**.

The early positivists used an **inductive** approach. This means they first **collected data on their topic**, which they **studied** and **analysed**. From this they composed a **theory** or **hypothesis**. They then **tested** their hypothesis and drew **conclusions**. If their results were **repeatable** (i.e. if people repeated their experiment and got the same results), the hypothesis was considered a **social fact**.

Theories of Science

Popper *said scientists should use the* Deductive Approach *and* Falsification

The **deductive approach** is similar to the inductive approach, only in reverse — it starts with the theory, which then leads to the investigation. **Karl Popper (1959, 1963)** argued that theories or hypotheses could spring from anywhere, such as **flashes of inspiration** ('eureka moments') or even from **dreams**.

Popper said the positivists were **wrong** in their belief that theories could be **proved** to be **true**. He had a different idea of scientific method —

1) Popper rejected the idea that there are **permanent social laws** governing human behaviour. He claimed that any 'law' could at some point be **falsified** (proved wrong), no matter how many times it has been 'proved' correct in the past.

2) The famous example he gave was the hypothesis '**all swans are white**,' which can be 'proved' thousands of times until you encounter a **black swan**.

3) Popper said the aim of science and social science should be to constantly **strive to falsify** theories. This '**falsification**' of theories arguably distinguishes science from religion and other supernatural belief systems.

"Don't believe the hype."

Gomm *argued that scientists' work should be viewed in its* Social Context

Roger Gomm (1982) argued that the theories scientists produce are in part a product of their **social context**, and that scientists tend to try and **prove** rather than falsify their theories.

Gomm gave the example of **Darwin** and his **theory of evolution** to explain this.

1) Gomm suggests Darwin's theories of **natural selection** and the **competitive struggle** for the survival of the fittest were **not supported by all of the evidence**.

2) Darwin therefore missed the opportunity to '**falsify**' aspects of his theories. Gomm suggests the reason for this was **ideological** rather than scientific.

3) Gomm argued that the '**survival of the fittest theory**' slotted neatly into the **Victorian capitalist ideology** of free market economics, individualism, and the minimalist approach to welfare of the time. Gomm therefore emphasised the importance of placing 'science' in its **social context**. Scientific knowledge can be seen, at least in part, as **socially constructed**.

Kuhn *challenged the idea that science is* Objective

Thomas Kuhn (1962) introduced the idea that scientists, at certain times in history, work in a **paradigm**.

1) A paradigm, according to Kuhn, refers to the **framework** of **accepted ideas** in which scientists operate. It might include ideas on **truth**, **validity** and **methodology**.

2) Kuhn argued that scientists will tend to work within the paradigm and so seek evidence which **supports** it. This will continue until **anomalies** are so strong as to trigger a **paradigm shift** or **scientific revolution**.

3) When this happens, a new '**normal science paradigm**' is established and the process begins again.

Working within the paradigm can be seen as similar to Polanyi's first factor of a belief system — circularity of beliefs (see p. 100).

Practice Questions

Q1 According to Dawkins, what distinguishes science from religion?

Q2 What are the three factors which make up a belief system, according to Polanyi?

Q3 What is the difference between an inductive and a deductive scientific approach?

Q4 What is meant by falsification?

Exam Questions

Q1 What does Kuhn mean by a paradigm, and how is it important in the theory of science?   (18 marks)

Q2 To what extent can religion and science be seen as different varieties of belief system?   (33 marks)

Study this page — it'll help you do your experiments Popper-ly...

...or perhaps not. You see, science is a funny thing — you think it's a clean break from the superstition and mummery of the past, and yet it all turns out to be the product of inspiration and whimsy. I wonder what Richard Dawkins dreams of...

Theories of Religion

Sociologists disagree about religion. Some think it's great and stops society descending into chaos — others think it's just there to oppress people. God doesn't seem to have much to do with it.

Marx said Religion helps to Oppress Workers and Inhibits Social Change

1) Karl Marx said that in **capitalist** society there was a **conflict of interests** between the **ruling class** and the **working class** because the ruling class **exploit** the working class to get the most profit out of them (see p. 98).

2) But — there's **something stopping** the working class from **uniting** and **overthrowing** the ruling class. Marx argued that the working class are in a state of **false consciousness**. This means they're **not aware** of **how unfair** society is.

3) This is where **religion** comes in. Marx is **very critical** of religion. He said it's one of the things that **keeps** the working class in a state of **false consciousness**. He said, "**Religion is the opium of the people**" (1971, *Critique of Hegel's 'Philosophy of the Right'* Cambridge: Cambridge University Press, written 1843). This means that it **dulls the pain** of oppression like **opium** — a **drug** which kills pain. It doesn't take the oppression away, though.

Marx said that religion is used to justify social inequality

1) People have **the afterlife** to **look forward** to if they're **good**, so they **don't break the rules** and don't challenge the capitalist system.

2) Religion **consoles** people with the **promise of life after death** and so they **put up** with their **suffering** here **on Earth** more easily.

3) Religion often tells people that their **position is decided by God**. This encourages false consciousness by blaming God instead of **blaming capitalism**.

4) If **God is all-powerful** he could **do something** about the suffering **if he wanted to**. He **doesn't** do anything — so people think this must be **how society is meant to be**.

Marx believed religion was both a way of oppressing people and a way of cushioning the effects of oppression.

Marxism says that religion **passes on beliefs** that **oppress the working class**. It argues that religion is a **conservative** force which prevents revolution — it keeps things the same. The **rich stay rich** and the **poor** keep on working. It's a neat **social control**.

But... there are problems with applying this Marxist view to today's society. Fewer people go to a place of worship than in the past — if people **don't go to worship**, it's **hard** for them to be duped by formal religious ideology. Also, religion can bring about **change**, but traditional Marxists tend to ignore this.

Functionalists see religion as Maintaining Harmony and Social Cohesion

Functionalists also see religion as something that **inhibits change** and helps **keep society as it is**. But they think this is a positive role, which creates **social order** based on **value consensus**.

1) **Durkheim** studied **Aboriginal** society and suggested that the **sacred worship of totems** was equivalent to **worshipping society itself**. Durkheim said that sacred religious worship encourages shared values.

2) **Malinowski (1954)** looked at how religion deals with situations of **emotional stress** that **threaten social order**. Unpredictable or stressful events like births and deaths create **disruption**. Religion **manages these tensions** and promotes stability.

Religions have ceremonies for dealing with birth and death.

3) **Parsons** wrote in the 1930s and 1940s that religion provides **guidelines** for human action in terms of "**core values**". Religion helps to **integrate** people into a value consensus and allows them to **make sense of their lives**.

4) Functionalist **Bellah (1967)** suggested the idea of **Civil Religion**, which is when secular (non-religious) symbols and rituals create **social cohesion** in a similar way to religion. **Flags**, famous **political figures** and even **royal deaths** bring about some kind of **collective feeling** that generates **order** and **stability**.

Functionalism ignores **dysfunctional** aspects of religion. There are **religious conflicts** all over the world. Religion can be a source of **oppression**. Religion can also bring about **change**, and functionalism ignores that as well.

But in some cases Religion can Encourage Social Change

1) Marx's good pal **Engels** reckoned that in **some circumstances** religion could actually be a **revolutionary** force. Sometimes **religion** is the **only means of change** because all other routes have been blocked.

2) **Early Christian sects** opposed Roman rule and brought about change. **Jesus** himself encouraged social change.

3) In the 1960s and 1970s, **Catholic priests** in **Latin America** criticised the bourgeoisie and preached **liberation theology** — using religion to free people from oppression. This led to **resistance** and **social change** — in 1979, revolutionaries threw out the oppressive government in **Nicaragua**. Neo-Marxist **Otto Maduro** (**1982**, *Religion and Social Conflicts* New York: Orbis Books**)** studied liberation theology. He said religion is "often one of the main available channels to bring about a social revolution".

4) Reverend **Martin Luther King** and the **Southern Baptist Church** resisted oppression and segregation, bringing about **political** and **social rights** for black people in **1960s America**.

5) In Iran, **Islamic fundamentalism** encouraged **social change**. In 1979, there was a **revolution** against the Shah, led by followers of the Shia Ayatollah **Khomeini**. Khomeini set up a **religious government** that followed Sharia law.

Theories of Religion

Weber said that Religion can Create a Capitalist Work Ethic

Weber's book *The Protestant Work Ethic and Spirit of Capitalism* looked at how the **religious** ideas of **Calvinism** brought about social change. Weber spotted **two important things** in Calvinism:

1) **Predestination:** This is the idea that your **life** and whether you're going to heaven are **predetermined** by **God**. Calvinists believed only a **few** were **chosen** for heaven. This created **anxiety** — no one knew if they were chosen.

2) **Ascetic Ideal: Working hard** in your job was a **solution** to this anxiety. Success might be a sign that you were chosen for heaven. Early Calvinists lived a **strict** and **disciplined** life of hard work and simple pleasures.

Weber claimed that the ascetic ideal helped create an ethic of **disciplined hard work**. This is the **spirit of capitalism**. Not only was there a build-up of **capital**, there was the right **work ethic** for capitalism. Religion **indirectly** brought about change.

However, **Eisenstadt (1967)** contradicts Weber's theory by claiming that capitalism occurred in **Catholic** countries like Italy **before** the **Protestant Reformation happened** and before the ideas of **Calvin ever came out**.

Feminists point out the Sexism in Religion

However, menstruation is seen as taboo in many religions.

1) Women's capacity to **have babies** gives women an **important role** within religion, in terms of bringing **new life** into the world. Women's role as **primary caregiver** is seen as **important** by traditional religion — it's the job of a mother to raise her children to **believe in God** and worship God. Feminists say this **traps** women in **traditional** roles.

2) Because women are **sexually attractive** to men they're perceived to be **distractions** from worship. Many religions believe in giving worship to God through a denial of sexuality (e.g. priests in the Roman Catholic Church have to be **celibate**). Religions have historically seen women as "**temptresses**" of men — think of Eve and the apple.

3) Women are **excluded from power** in many religious organisations.

4) Feminists argue that religious texts **transmit messages** to readers through stories that reflect and uphold a **patriarchal** society. This patriarchal ideology says that women are part of the profane and imperfect, and maintains the **conformity** and **submission** of women.

profane = opposite of sacred or holy

5) **Simone de Beauvoir (1953)** saw religion as **exploitative** and **oppressive** towards women. She thought that religion promotes the idea that if women **suffer** in their present lives, then they'll receive **equality in heaven**, which allows women to **put up with** being treated as **inferior** to men in the hope of gaining in the afterlife. Spot the **similarity** to **Marx's** ideas on religion — just swap "women" for "working class" and you're there.

There are Problems with Feminist Anti-Religious Views

1) Women are not necessarily **passive victims** of religious oppression. Women may **actively resist** oppression — e.g. in **Afghanistan** under the Taliban it was forbidden for girls to go to school, so women educated girls in secret.

2) Religion **isn't necessarily patriarchal**. For example, **veiling** can have **positive functions** for Muslim women. The veil can **affirm Muslim identity** and **protect** women from sexual harassment in public.

3) Patriarchy within a society may be transmitted by other social and cultural activities, not by religion.

Practice Questions

Q1 In what ways does Marx say religion is used to justify social inequality?

Q2 What is the role of religion, according to functionalists?

Q3 What two aspects of Calvinism favoured a strong work ethic, according to Weber?

Q4 Give three examples of feminist views of sexism in religion.

Exam Question

Q1 Evaluate the view that there is sexism in religion. (33 marks)

The function of religion is to give you someone to pray to before exams...

There's an awful lot to learn here, I'll be honest. To make it easy on yourself, take each kind of theory individually. Once you've read it through, what Marxists and functionalists think about religion ought to be no big surprise. The next step is to learn the key names and studies. Cover up each subsection and work on it until you can remember the names and ideas.

Religious Organisations

Religious groups organise themselves into different forms. They differ in leadership, relationship to the state and politics, how they worship and who they appeal to. Sociologists have put forward different classifications of religious organisations.

There are **Four Key Concepts** in the Study of Religion

Religious Belief	Thinking that the world is controlled by supernatural forces — normally a god or group of gods.
Religious Commitment	Carrying out religious actions, such as praying or singing religious songs.
Religious Membership	Being part of a formal religious institution — a church, sect, cult, etc.
Religiosity	The level of an individual's connection with all aspects of religion — belief, commitment and membership.

1) A person's religiosity is the **balance** between their **religious experience** and their **religious beliefs**.

2) Some people attend church for social reasons, even though they don't believe in a god — their religiosity emphasises **membership** and **commitment**.

3) Others believe in a god but never go to church — their religiosity emphasises **belief**.

A **Church** is a well-established **Religious Organisation**

Sociologists often use a **typology** (a set of **"ideal types"**) to categorise and analyse religious organisations, e.g. 'church', 'sect', and 'denomination'. It is important to remember that these are **ideal** types — perfect **pure** models. **Real** religious organisations may include features of **more than one type**.

Social historian **Ernst Troeltsch (1912)** distinguished between different types of religious organisation, and used the word **church** to mean a **large religious organisation**. He said churches usually have four main features:

1) A church claims **monopoly over the truth** — it says its claims are **absolutely true** and others are **false**.

2) Churches have a **complex rigid hierarchy** and a **bureaucratic structure** with lots of **rules and regulations**.

3) Churches often have a **close relationship** to the **state**. Some nations have an official national religion (e.g. Islam is the national religion of Egypt) — Weber used the term **"ecclesia"** for this.

4) They are closely integrated into **mainstream society**. Churches act as a **conservative** force, resisting change. This is why the **upper classes** are more likely to join — even though churches are **universal** and **inclusive in principle**.

Examples of churches include the **Roman Catholic Church**, the **Church of England** and the **Episcopal Church**.

Troeltsch studied churches in **16th century** Europe. **Steve Bruce (1995)** says that Troeltsch's points don't always apply to today's churches because there's **religious pluralism** these days. Nowadays, the Church of England doesn't claim a monopoly over the truth and it isn't always conservative. ⟵

Religious pluralism = lots of different types of religious groups.

Sects are Small, Radical Religious Movements

Troeltsch defined sects as being almost the **opposite of churches**. Few religious groups fall into the category of sect.

People who are **dissatisfied** with mainstream religion can be attracted to a sect. Sects are often formed by people **splitting off from a church** because they **disagree** with the church's **practices** or **theology**.

1) Sects claim a **monopoly over the truth** and are intolerant towards other religious organisations.

2) Sects have **no complex hierarchy**. They often have a **charismatic leader** who **persuades** members to **follow his or her teaching**.

3) Sects are **small**. Their members follow with **total commitment**, and they can be **manipulated** by the sect's leader.

4) Sects are separate from the state — they're in **opposition** to mainstream society. Sects can sometimes offer an alternative way of life for **deprived** and **marginal** groups.

Examples of sects include the **early Methodists** and **Calvinists** (although over time these have become more mainstream). This category also includes **extremist** groups like the **People's Temple** in America who were led to mass suicide by Jim Jones, or the **Branch Davidians** led by David Koresh.

These extremist groups are generally called cults in everyday language. Watch out though — in sociology, cult means something else...

Religious Organisations

Denominations are Subsets of Churches

Troeltsch **originally classified** religious organisations into **churches** and **sects**.
The term "**denomination**" was added later.

1) Denominations don't usually claim **a monopoly over the truth**. They see themselves as a **possible route to the truth**. They are **tolerant** towards other religious organisations.

2) Like a church, they have a **hierarchy** and **bureaucratic structure**, but it isn't as complex.

3) They have a reasonably **large membership**, but not as large as an established church.

4) Members of denominations are usually **not as loyal** as members of churches.

5) Denominations **aren't closely connected to the state**. They get involved in society and **comment** on **current events**.

Denominations don't usually claim a monopoly over the truth — in general they prefer chess.

Examples of denominations are **modern Methodists** and **Baptists**.

Cults are Mystic Movements — Often Wrongly Defined

Bruce (1995) defined cults as movements without a fixed set of beliefs. They emphasise the **inner power** of the **individual** and **mysticism**. Cults are usually loosely knit and don't have a hierarchy.

Fundamentalism Provides Meaning and Certainty in Periods of Uncertainty

Fundamentalism involves the **fundamental, literal interpretation** of religious texts. Fundamentalist groups **strictly** and **fervently** follow their beliefs. Fundamentalists seek **change** to create a more **conservative** society and advocate a return to '**traditional values**'. These groups often have **charismatic leaders**.

In both of the following examples, **fundamentalism** provides **certainty** and **meaning** in periods of **uncertainty**.

1) Islamic Fundamentalism in Iran

Iran was a **traditional** society that **quickly modernised** under the **Shah**. **Women** wore **Western clothes**, alcohol was freely available and there was **secular education**. There was also **inequality** in society — the upper class were **very rich**, and working class areas were **neglected**.
Traditional Muslims were **unhappy** about the direction that Iranian society had taken, and saw the Shah as **corrupt**. They started to oppose the Shah, led by a **fundamentalist** religious leader called **Ayatollah Khomeini**. There was a revolution in 1979 and the Ayatollah came to power. He established a society based on **Islamic Sharia law** — alcohol was banned, there were harsh punishments for crime, and women were required to cover their bodies in public.

2) Christian Fundamentalism

The **New Christian Right** in **America** argues that American society is in **decline** and in a state of **moral crisis**. They think this is caused by **liberal reforms** — e.g. easy **divorce**, legalised **abortion**, **gay rights** and **secular education**. The New Christian Right **oppose** the teaching of **evolution** in schools, because it disagrees with their fundamentalist interpretation of the Bible. They started some **universities** that offer not only degrees, but also a strict **Christian education**. They promote their views through **mass communication**, e.g. TV and Christian publishing.

Practice Questions

Q1 What do sociologists mean by 'religious commitment'?

Q2 Give the key characteristics of a cult.

Q3 Give two examples of fundamentalist religious movements.

Exam Questions

Q1 Identify and explain two features of a church. (6 marks)

Q2 Identify and explain two features of a denomination. (6 marks)

Lots of religions don't condone sects before marriage...

*Don't assume you already know what a church is, what a sect is, etc. Sociological definitions can be a bit different from the everyday definitions. So **learn them**. Obviously, not all religious groups will fit neatly into one of these categories — but most will.*

Religious Organisations

The term "new religious movement" (or NRM for short) includes a huge range of movements from diverse sources. They've increased significantly in number since the 1960s. They don't always fit the old church-sect-denomination-cult divisions.

New Religious Movements *can be* Affirming, Rejecting *or* Accommodating

Sociologist **Roy Wallis (1984)** identified three types of new religious movement:

World-rejecting movements cut themselves off from society — similar to sects

1) World-rejecting movements are very **critical** of wider society and are often in conflict with the state.

2) **The Unification Church**, better known as the **'Moonies'**, is one example of a world-rejecting movement.

3) World-rejecting movements require **total commitment**. They demand **significant lifestyle changes**. Members often turn away from family and friends — world-rejecting movements have developed a reputation for **"brainwashing"** members. It's often hard to leave a world-rejecting movement.

World-affirming movements are tolerant of other beliefs — similar to cults

1) They're similar to **self-help** and therapy groups — they try to **"unlock spiritual power"**. **Transcendental Meditation** is an example of a world-affirming movement.

2) World-affirming movements seek **wide membership**.

3) World-affirming movements **don't require** especially high levels of **commitment**.

World-accommodating movements are traditionally religious — similar to denominations

1) World-accommodating movements often come from **traditional** religions.

2) They try to rediscover **spiritual purity** lost in traditional religions. **Pentecostalism** is a movement within Christianity that aims to bring the Holy Spirit back into worship.

3) World-accommodating movements allow people to carry on with their **existing lifestyle**.

The Growth *of* New Religious Movements *isn't Easy to Explain*

The **interpretivist** idea is that **new religious movements (NRMs)** provide **certainty** in times of **uncertainty**. When there's uncertainty, new religious movements have **greater appeal** and **grow** in numbers. Here are some of the **uncertainties** that people face:

1) **Marginality** — inequality, immigration and racism may **marginalise** some groups. So, some new religious movements may help marginalised people **make sense** of their situation, and may promise a better life after death as **compensation**. **Weber** called this the **"theodicy of disprivilege"**.

2) **Relative deprivation** — the concept of marginality doesn't explain why **white, middle class groups** join new religious movements. Although they aren't absolutely poor or deprived, some middle class people may see themselves as **deprived in comparison to their peers**.

3) **Social change** — transformation of society can result in **anomie** and **uncertainty**. The breakdown of **community**, the process of **secularisation** (see p.110), **cultural diversity** and bad news such as **terrorist attacks** may generate uncertainty.

anomie = a state of confusion where there is a lack of agreed norms and values.

4) **Modernity and post-modernity** — the **alienation** of capitalism, the increasing amount of **red tape**, bureaucracy, and disillusionment with work may create **uncertainty**. The choice people have in constructing their identity may create **uncertainty** and a **crisis of identity**.

Melton (1993) didn't agree that NRMs emerged in periods of uncertainty. He looked at the founding dates of non-conventional religious organisations in the US. **Rapid growth** took place in the **1950s** — in a period of **stability** and **certainty**. Why do these sociologists never agree...

Wallis (1984) explains the appeal of the three different kinds of new religious movement

1) **World-rejecting movements** grew in numbers in the 1960s. There was a lot of **freedom** for people, but also **uncertainty**. It was a period of **radicalism** with lots of alternative world views — often called the "sixties counterculture". Some people got **disillusioned** with this counterculture and wanted more **concrete** beliefs.

2) **World-affirming movements** develop as a means of coping with a **crisis of identity** in more successful groups (e.g. the middle class). They try to unlock **human potential** and help people solve their problems. **Bruce (1995)** claims that they're a response to the **rationalisation** of the modern world where it's hard to find satisfaction from work.

3) **World-accommodating movements** appeal to those who are dissatisfied with existing religion.

Religious Organisations

Millenarian Movements Look Forward to the Apocalypse

1) **Millenarian** movements are a type of NRM that claim that members will achieve **salvation** through a **cataclysmic** event — a major disaster. Millenarianism is connected to **apocalypticism**, which is the belief that **divine forces** will **overthrow** the existing social order.

2) The **Ghost Dance** of the indigenous **Plains Tribes** in **North America** is a traditional example of a **millenarian** movement. The tribes believed storms and earthquakes would return the buffalo to the prairies and end ethnic divisions.

3) Millenarian movements are associated with **deprived groups** or areas where there has been **radical social change**.

The return of Changing Rooms.
Enough to make anyone believe the end is nigh.

New Age Movements are Cultural

1) **New Age movements** are close to cults and world-affirming movements. New Age ideas often aren't linked to an organisation, but spread through a **culture**, e.g. **dowsing**, **feng shui**, **crystal healing**, **neopaganism** and **reiki**.

2) **Heelas (1996)** claims that New Age beliefs are dedicated to "**self-spirituality**" and the development of the self.

3) **Bruce (1995)** highlights **three themes** to New Age movements: **New Science** rejects many claims of traditional science, **New Ecology** is concerned for the environment, and **New Psychology** sees the self as sacred.

New Age Movements Appeal to People Already Examining their Identity

1) New Age beliefs appeal to people who have **turned away from traditional religion**. New Age beliefs say that people can find salvation, peace or perfection **inside themselves**. Modern society is more **individualistic** than before — **individual beliefs** are **trusted more**, and **authority** is **trusted less**.

2) New Age movements help some people cope with the **uncertainties** of modernity. In the modern world, people have a lot of **different roles**. New Age beliefs can help people find a sense of **identity**.

3) New Age beliefs often appeal to middle class people working in "**expressive professions**" — actors, writers, social workers, counsellors, therapists etc. New Age beliefs appeal to **women** more than men, and **middle class** more than working class.

4) New Age movements may also reflect a **cultural change** in mainstream society. People are surrounded by non-conventional ideas like horoscopes, feng shui and homeopathy. **Mass communication** gives us an awareness of different movements.

5) New Age is quite a **postmodern** thing. In a **postmodern** society of **choice** and **diversity** people can **pick and mix** from all kinds of New Age philosophies to help them construct their own identity.

> There are more and more belief systems in society. "**Spiritual shoppers**" are people who **sample** different systems of belief to find the **best fit**. This is an **individualistic** and **consumerist** attitude.

Practice Questions

Q1 What are the three types of New Religious Movement that Wallis identified?
Q2 Give two examples of New Religious Movements.
Q3 Give two of the 'uncertainties' that help make New Religious Movements popular.
Q4 What three themes did Bruce identify in New Age movements?

Exam Questions

Q1 Identify and explain two characteristics of New Religious Movements. (6 marks)

Q2 Assess the view that New Religious Movements are created in periods of uncertainty. (33 marks)

Yup, moving your furniture around counts as religion...

It's not just going to a traditional place of worship that counts as religion. Deranged groups who think the world's going to end tomorrow, and all sorts of wishy-washy lifestyle stuff is also seen by sociologists as evidence of religious belief.

Religion and Social Position

Religiosity is related to age, gender, ethnicity and social class.

Religiosity varies by Age

Age affects how religious people are.

1) People **under 15** and **over 65** are more likely to be involved in religious activity. However, participation by those under 15 usually takes the form of **Sunday school** and **religious playgroups**.

2) The **over 65** group is the **most religious** in terms of **belief**. They aren't necessarily the most likely to practise their religion by going to church, because of difficulty with mobility.

3) However, some recent studies claim that the **elderly** are **increasingly losing faith** in God.

4) **Middle-aged** groups are more likely to get involved in **world-affirming movements**.

5) **Sects** and **cults** are more likely to be populated with **young adults**.

> - **Sects** often appeal to young adults by messages of **friendship** and **companionship** — this can be attractive to those who are experiencing forms of **anomie** (lack of social/moral standards) and **detachment** from the world, and those who have few responsibilities (e.g. marriage).
> - **Cults** appeal to the **inner thoughts** and **feelings** of young adults who are often alienated from the primary cultures of society. **Cults** are attractive to individuals who are often already engaging in **counterculture** activity.

6) Young adults may be less religious than older people because of the way that society is changing. An increase in **rationalisation** means they feel less **need** for religion to explain things.

Religiosity varies by Gender

1) **Women** are **more likely to attend church**, and more likely to say they belong to a religion (**British Social Attitudes Survey, 1991**). This has often been explained by women's traditional role as **primary caregiver**. Going to **church** and **raising children** to be **religious** is traditionally seen as an **extension** of that role.

2) **Differential socialisation** is also a factor. The argument goes that girls are socialised to be **passive** and to **conform** — which fits in with the behaviour of more **traditional** and **conservative** religious groups.

3) Another argument is that **women** simply **live longer**. More women are on their **own** as they get older, and they may **turn to religion** for a sense of community. **Older** people are **more religious anyway**.

4) More **men** than **women** have **turned away** from organised religion in the 20th century.

> **Feminists' view of religion**
>
> 1) **Beauvoir (1949)** claimed that the **images of gender** in Western religion deceive women into thinking they're **equal** when they're not. Women are sometimes portrayed as **"nearer to God"** than men by religious imagery and so are **duped** into believing their **sufferings** on earth will be rewarded with **equality** in heaven (see p. 103).
>
> 2) **Jean Holm** (Holm and Bowker, eds., 1994, *Women in Religion* London: Continuum) outlined how many contemporary religions both **exploit** and **subordinate** women and give men **dominant organisational roles**. She suggested this secondary status has its origins in **biology** and **sexuality** — "Menstruation and childbirth are almost universally regarded as polluting."

Women often have Significant roles in New Religious Movements (NRMs)

1) Women generally **participate** in **sects** more than men.

2) Also, many sects and NRMs were **established** by **women**, e.g. one of the founders of the Seventh Day Adventists was Ellen White, and the Christian Science movement was founded by Mary Baker Eddy.

3) **Glock and Stark (1965)** have argued that the gender difference in membership of NRMs is because **deprivation** (social, physical and mental) is **disproportionately** experienced by **women**.

4) **Bruce (1995)** suggests that men are more interested in NRMs that advocate **esoteric knowledge**, — women are more interested in subjects that can be classified as **New Science**, **New Ecology** and **New Spirituality**.

esoteric = elitist and specialist

5) Some sociologists claim that **New Age** movements appeal more to women, because they emphasise **"feminine"** characteristics such as healing, caring and cooperation.

Remember, some NRMs have **narrow beliefs** about **women's role** in society, and therefore may **not appeal** to women. For example, some new evangelical right-wing Christian movements believe that women should not work outside the home.

Religion and Social Position

Religiosity Varies by Ethnicity

The 1994 PSI Fourth Survey of Ethnic Minorities (**Tariq Modood et al**, published **1997**) found that, in England and Wales, nearly all **ethnic minority groups** are **more religious** and participate more in religion than white groups.

1) Religion maintains a sense of **community** and **cultural identity** within ethnic minority groups.

2) **Johal (1998)** claims that in a multi-faith society such as the UK, **religious identity** has become of key importance to members of ethnic minorities.

3) **Davie (1994)** argued that identification with a **religious organisation** was important to Indians, Pakistanis and Bangladeshis in the UK because it gave a sense of cultural identity and a feeling of **belonging**.

- **Modood** found that Pakistani and Bangladeshi Muslims in the UK identified themselves primarily as **Muslim**.
- Many young Muslims have a deeper **knowledge of Islam** than their **parents** do.

  i.e. rather than British, Pakistani, or Bangladeshi
- Many Muslim girls feel more **liberated** by wearing headscarfs and dressing modestly because they are not subjected to the same **stereotypes** and values as non-Muslim girls.

4) **Afro-Caribbeans**, who are mainly Christian, attempted to incorporate themselves into the established churches of the UK but found **racism** within many congregations. One way to tackle this was to develop their own churches and ways of worshipping — e.g. Pentecostal churches.

5) **South Asians**, however, had to establish their faiths in a country with **radically different** systems of belief. Religion acted as a **support mechanism** for new immigrants, allowing them to share their culture. South Asians **quickly established** religious organisations — mosques, Sikh gurdwaras, etc. **Bruce (2002)** calls this **cultural transition**.

6) **Modood (1994)** and **Saeed (1999)** found some evidence for a decline in religious practice among Asians in the UK.

Religiosity Varies by Class

1) The **middle class** is disproportionately **Anglican** and **Quaker** compared with a more **Roman Catholic** or **Methodist** working class (this can be partly explained by their popularity in Victorian industrial areas). This pattern can be seen across many countries such as the US and this would seem to back up Marx and Weber's opinions on Protestantism and capitalism.

2) Religious participation is greater in the **middle classes**, partly because religious affiliation is seen as a **desirable** social characteristic. Church is an opportunity for **social networking**.

3) Some argue that participation in **denominations** and **sects** is based on **class position** — they claim that there are middle-class denominations and working-class denominations.

4) **Bruce (1995)** found that cults are primarily middle class — in his opinion because they fulfil spiritual needs for people who have little financial pressure.

Lisa follows the cult of the Flying Spaghetti Monster. Well, it's hard not to believe in the thing when it's sitting on your head.

Practice Questions

Q1 Suggest why young adults participate more than other age groups in sects and cults.

Q2 What role does religion play in upholding patriarchy, according to feminists?

Q3 Suggest why middle-class people participate more in cults.

Exam Questions

Q1 Identify and explain two gender-based differences in religiosity. (6 marks)

Q2 Assess the view that religious identity is of key importance to ethnic minorities. (33 marks)

"Ah no, this is the women's church. Men's church is next door"...

Well, obviously it's not quite like that. The examiners will expect you to know how religion relates to age, gender, ethnicity and class, and also how religious participation relates to those things. You should mention a few studies too — no, don't kid yourself that you can remember them all — what did Glock and Stark argue? What about Johal? Davie? Saeed? Ha!

Religiosity in the Contemporary World

As the world changes, so too do religions and patterns of religiosity.

Globalisation affects religion in Different Ways

Peter Beyer (1994) claimed that **globalisation** has had three very different impacts on religion.

1) **Marginalisation** — religion has been **pushed out** of politics and public life and into the **private sphere**.

2) **Particularism** — religion has been used by groups who feel **threatened** by globalisation. They use it to express a sense of identity through a mix of **fundamentalism** and **nationalism**.

3) **Universalism** — globalisation can result in the emergence of an understanding of **common values** between religions. Beyer gives the example of **religious environmentalism**, in which many faiths come together in **common concern** for protecting a 'God-created' world.

Secularisation is When Religion Loses Its Influence Over Society

Bryan Wilson (1966, *Religion in Secular Society,* London: CA Watts) defined secularisation as a "**process whereby religious thinking, practice and institutions lose social significance**". Secularisation is said to be a result of the social changes brought about by **modern, urban, industrial society.**

Elizabeth worshipped
bureaucracy...

The "founding fathers" of sociology **predicted secularisation**.

1) **Auguste Comte** claimed that **science** was the **final stage** in the **development of human thought**. He said modern society would be dominated by **science** and not religion.

2) **Max Weber** believed that **modern society** would be the age of **technology, rationality** and **bureaucracy**. He said rationality and efficiency **sweeps away magic, myth** and **tradition**.

Church Attendance and Membership is in Decline

Counting bums on pews gives **supporting evidence for secularisation**:

1) **UK church membership** and **attendance** has gone down — the number of people who **go to church** has fallen by almost 1 million in the last 20 years.

2) Attendance at ceremonies such as **baptisms** and **marriages** has also dropped. Just **27%** of babies were baptised in 1993, compared to **65%** in 1900.

Measuring secularisation by counting **bums on pews** has **limitations**:

1) People may **attend church** but **not believe in God**. They might attend a service, baptism or wedding out of friendship for the people involved, for respectability or because of family duty. Or even to get their kids into a certain school.

2) **Davie (1994)** argued people may **not attend church** because of their **lifestyle** even though they believe in God. Church attendance **doesn't** tell you about **belief**. The 2001 census found 72% of people identified themselves as Christians.

3) To make comparisons with the past you have to use **old statistics**, which may not be reliable.

Pluralism Gives People Choice

Religious pluralism means **diversity** in types of religious organisations and beliefs in society. As a result of this diversity the **established, national church loses its influence** in integrating people into **shared values**. **Multicultural** societies are more likely to have **religious pluralism**.

> **Some sociologists see pluralism as evidence against secularisation**
>
> 1) The increase in **New Age movements** since the 1980s can be seen as proof that the **sacred** is becoming **important** again — this is called **resacrilisation**, by the way.
>
> 2) It can be argued that pluralism is evidence of religion being **transformed**. It shows a trend towards **individuation** — people being free to search for their **own religious meanings** (to become "**spiritual shoppers**").

> **Other sociologists see pluralism as supporting evidence for secularisation**
>
> 1) Pluralism gives people **choice**. People might feel freer to choose to **reject religion altogether**.
>
> 2) Although some people in modern society have joined **new religious movements**, they are still a **small proportion** of the population. Some sociologists claim the **growth** in NRMs has been **overestimated**.

Postmodernists like **Lyotard (1984)** argue that people have lost faith in the old **metanarratives** of organised religion and politics. A metanarrative is a 'big' explanation that **makes sense** of the world, such as communism or Christianity. Postmodernists argue that organised religion has become **less influential** in postmodern society. **Zygmunt Bauman (1992)** suggested that a **religious vacuum** has been left behind — a "**crisis of meaning**". He argued that this vacuum is being filled by **new and diverse types of religiosity** such as New Age movements.

Religiosity in the Contemporary World

Desacrilisation is Where Supernatural Belief is Less of a Force in Society

1) **Weber** predicted **desacrilisation** (see glossary) in his idea of **disenchantment**. He thought that magic and myth were less important in modern society. Similarly, **Bruce (1995)** sees **science** and rational explanations as **undermining religion**.

2) Instead of turning to the supernatural or religion to **explain our problems**, we might turn to **science**. We demand pills when we are ill and we use science to explain natural disasters.

3) However, the **death** of a loved one, **injustice**, **natural disasters** and **terrorist atrocities** still sometimes lead people to prayer and faith in the supernatural. Modern science **can't explain everything** to everyone's satisfaction.

4) **Postmodernists** claim that we've moved **beyond scientific** rationality and we now **mistrust science**.

The Church May have Lost Some Functions and Become Disengaged

1) **Differentiation** is where **society becomes more specialised** so each **institution** in society has **fewer functions** than in the past. For example, the **church** used to have an important **educational** function. But since the 19th century separate institutions have taken over this role and state involvement has increased. **Bruce (1995)** argues that religion becomes less important in society as some of its previous functions are taken over.

2) **Disengagement** is when the church becomes **separated from the state**. As a result, it has **less influence**.

3) **Parsons (1974)** claims that although the church may have lost its functions and become disengaged from the state and politics, religion can still be **significant in everyday life** and encourage **shared values** in society.

4) Religion is still closely linked to **politics** in the **Middle East** and **Northern Ireland**.

Some religious institutions have become 'secularised'

1) **Secularisation** of **religious institutions** is when the church becomes **less religious** in its beliefs to **fit in** with the rest of **society**. For example, many churches will now allow divorced people to marry.

2) American sociologist **Herberg (1956)** thinks church attendance shows **commitment to community** and not religion — people go to church to **meet up with friends** and to feel like **part of something**.

3) Remember that **not all religious institutions** have become more **secular**. The **New Christian Right** don't compromise their beliefs to fit in with society — they're against divorce, homosexuality and premarital sex. The more extreme end of the religious right are also against women working outside the home.

Secularisation is Very Difficult to Measure

There's more about sociological research methods in Section 7.

1) There are lots of different **measures of secularisation**. Some are more valid and reliable than others. **Surveys** show **high levels of religiosity**, but **quantitative measurements** of **church attendance** are **low**. **Different religious groups** measure membership in **different ways**, anyhow.

2) The term **secularisation** is a general term that's sometimes applied just to Christianity. It's important to know **what's being measured** — the decline of **religion in general** or the decline in **Christianity** in particular.

3) It's difficult to measure the significance of religion and make comparisons because sociologists use **different definitions of religion**. Some sociologists use **substantive definitions** which say **what religion is** — e.g. "religion is belief in the sacred". Some sociologists use **functional definitions** saying **what religion is for** — e.g. "religion is for creating value consensus".

4) To measure whether society has become **more secular** you have to compare it to **the past**. Some sociologists argue that we see the past as a **golden age** of religion where **everyone** believed and **no one** was sceptical. This is **far too simplified**.

5) Research into secularisation can also be rather **ethnocentric** — e.g. focusing on **Christianity** and what the **predominantly white British mainstream** does. Islam, Hinduism and Sikhism are also changing and developing in different ways.

Practice Questions

Q1 How does religious pluralism provide supporting evidence for secularisation?

Q2 What is meant by desacrilisation?

Q3 Define the term disengagement, with reference to religion.

Exam Question

Q1 Identify and explain two problems with measuring secularisation. (6 marks)

Bruce (1995) sees surnames as completely unnecessary...

There are lots of different sides to secularisation, and lots of ways to measure it. There's some clear evidence both for and against the secularisation thesis — which you need to learn. Oh, and by the way, the Bryan Wilson with the theory on secularisation isn't the Brian Wilson who was in the Beach Boys. Not that you thought he was. I'm just saying, like.

Theories of Development

There are different ways of defining and measuring development and underdevelopment, and tons of theories to explain why some countries are more developed than others.

The Exact Words used to Describe Development are Important

1) The term '**development**' is used to mean economic growth, industrialisation, and high living standards, e.g. high life expectancy and universal education. Countries which have achieved this are called **MEDCs** (More Economically Developed Countries). Countries which haven't are called **LEDCs** (Less Economically Developed Countries).

2) Richer countries are also referred to as **developed**, poorer countries as **developing**. **Underdeveloped** countries have developed less than other countries with the same resources.

3) All these terms are **ethnocentric**. They define development in terms of 'Western' ideals.

4) Another set of labels that's often used is '**First World**' and '**Third World**'. These expressions are **out of date**. The First World was wealthy countries like the USA and Japan. 'Third World' was used to describe the poorest countries.

> If someone says a theory is ethnocentric they usually mean it looks at everything from a Western viewpoint and assumes Western values are superior to the values of other cultures.

5) The terms **North** and **South** are also used to describe differences between countries. These terms are more neutral. They don't imply that it's better to be Northern or Southern. They're not very accurate though. Australia is a 'Northern' country in the Southern hemisphere and China is a 'Southern' country in the Northern hemisphere.

Development is Measured in Different Ways

1) Capitalists argue that **economic indicators** such as **Gross Domestic Product** (**GDP**) are the only effective ways of defining a country's potential for developing (along capitalist lines).

> GDP = the total economic value of goods and services produced by a country over a year.

2) However, GDP doesn't tell you how wealth is **distributed**. In a country with a high average GDP per capita (per person) there may be a **minority** living in **deprivation**.

3) Economic indicators also ignore **externalities** (effects on third parties) caused by economic progress — e.g. pollution.

4) Some claim development is better measured by **social factors**. They measure development using **lists** of **basic human needs** — e.g. the Human Development Index (HDI), Human Poverty Index (HPI) and Physical Quality of Life Index (PQLI). Unlike economic indicators, these can show that there is deprivation even in 'developed' countries.

Development Theories have their foundations in Marx, Durkheim and Weber

1) **Marx** said that capitalism and industrialisation were about obtaining the **maximum** amount of **profit**. Capitalists in developed countries **exploit** underdeveloped countries to get **raw materials**, and to get a wide **market** for the goods produced by capitalism. Marx thought that capitalism would give way to **communism**.

2) **Durkheim** argued that societies would **progress** through **industrialisation** and that the most developed nations were those which had industrialised first. Durkheim saw the West as the most advanced society, and thought underdeveloped countries could improve their progression by taking on the **characteristics** of Western countries.

3) **Weber** argued that society was becoming more **rational** and **bureaucratic** — people needed to make more choices and come up with new, scientific ideas to solve social problems like deprivation. Less developed societies would need to copy Western **attitudes** in order to allow progress and economic development.

Modernisation Theory says countries Progress towards Liberal Capitalism

Modernisation theory says that **all countries** move **towards liberal capitalism**. Undeveloped countries are seen as **inferior** to **developed** countries that have achieved a higher rate of **production**, **consumption** and **wealth**.

Rostow (1971) suggested that all countries go through a five-stage process of development:

1) Basic, **agricultural** society.

2) **Transition**, or preparing for 'take-off' — farmers produce a surplus and make money from selling cash crops. Small towns develop, and there's some industry on a very small scale.

3) **Industrialisation** or 'take-off' — rapid growth of manufacturing. People move from rural to urban areas.

4) **Drive to Maturity** — lots of investment, and the right social conditions for growth. Large cities develop.

5) **Mass consumption**, or 'developed economy' — wealth spreads, people buy more and the service sector grows.

The explanation for poverty and underdevelopment is insufficient agricultural surplus to fund investment, insufficient investment in technology, and not enough hard-working business people to create opportunities.

Kerr (1962) focused on **cultural factors** — he believed that countries need Western-style politics and social values in order to develop, and they should replace traditional culture with Western values.

Theories of Development

Neo-liberalism believes in using Free Trade to help countries Develop

1) Neo-liberalism says that government intervention **distorts** the natural economic processes of the **free market**. Neo-liberals like **Friedman (1962)** believe **free market trade** can be used to help countries develop.

2) Organisations like the International Monetary Fund and World Bank favour neo-liberalism. They point to **Newly Industrialised Countries** (NICs) such as the 'tiger economies' to prove that removing tariffs (charges for importing and exporting) and encouraging free trade can lead to development. 'Tiger economies' are South East Asian countries including Singapore and Hong Kong that have experienced a period of growth over the last 20 years.

Modernisation Theory and Neo-liberalism are both criticised

Both theories are criticised for being **ethnocentric** (arguing for the superiority of Western culture and industrialisation), and critics say this leads them to distort the true history of Western involvement in developing countries.

Neo-liberals and modernisation theorists also argue that Western methods of development are easily imitated and likely to succeed — which isn't necessarily true. In fact, the tiger economies got into serious economic trouble in 1997 after attempting to **extend too far** and **too fast**.

Dependency Theory says Developed countries Exploit Underdeveloped ones

1) **Dependency theory** was a reaction **against modernisation theory**. The key dependency theorist is **Frank (1967)**.

2) The theory says that developed countries **exploited** underdeveloped nations during colonial times (especially in the 1800s) when they controlled them as part of an **empire** (see p.116), and prevented them from industrialising.

3) When the underdeveloped nations got political independence, they were often still **economically dependent** upon their former imperial rulers. The poor nation's main trading partner is often its former colonial ruler. The theory says richer developed nations organise trading relationships in their favour. They set the price for goods.

4) **Dependency theory** is Marxist — it argues that **workers** in the poorest nations are **exploited** by the **ruling class**. They're paid very low wages, so the profits from the goods they make and grow go to the ruling class. Developed nations pay a low market price for the goods, and the goods are sold in the developed nation for a profit.

5) The theory goes on to say that profits pass from **workers** in **satellite areas** (less developed agricultural areas), to the **ruling class** in the **metropolis** (major cities, the former outposts of colonial power), and out to **developed nations**.

The theory doesn't fully define what development is or give realistic suggestions for how the situation can be resolved. It also doesn't explain why **socialism also exploited** and created dependency — e.g. the Eastern European satellite states depended on Russia. Dependency theory is criticised for being **deterministic** — it assumes that **everyone in LEDCs** will be **exploited**, and it doesn't accept that some LEDCs might **choose** capitalism, instead of being pushed into it.

World Systems Theory says there's One Global Economy

1) **Wallerstein (1974)** suggested World Systems theory, which treats the entire world as one economy, rather than looking at development country by country. World Systems theory divides the world into **core** (developed countries), **semi-periphery** (e.g. South Africa, Mexico) and **periphery** (e.g. Ethiopia).

2) According to the theory, **core** countries make **full use** of the global economy, and can affect any other country — in other words, they have a global 'reach'. Core countries are the ones which get the most out of capitalism.

3) World Systems theory says the **semi-periphery** countries are **exploited** by the core countries, but they also **exploit** the **periphery** countries. In the theory, because they exploit as well as being exploited, they aren't fully "on the same side" as the periphery countries — no unity amongst the exploited means no united action to change the system.

This theory is also criticised for being too **deterministic**. It doesn't allow for **individual countries' characteristics**, and it still holds up the **core countries** as the model for perfect development.

Practice Questions

Q1 What are the five stages of development according to Rostow?

Q2 What is the central idea of dependency theory?

Exam Question

Q1 Compare and contrast dependency theory and World Systems theory as explanations of underdevelopment. (18 marks)

Singapore and Hong Kong have stripy economies that go 'RAAAR'...

And they go stalking through the jungle, swishing their tails... or they would, if they weren't just boring old economies. Important reminder — don't use the terms 'first world', 'second world' and 'third world' — the second world doesn't exist since the USSR collapsed. Pages 116-117 will help with all this — they give some of the historical background to colonialism, and its effects on trade.

Theories of Globalisation

This fine pair of pages is about international trade and globalisation. Globalisation has economic, political and cultural aspects. No, don't switch off, this really isn't that boring. Honestly. Look, there's a photo of a burger and everything.

Globalisation has resulted in a Global Economy as well as National Economies

Giddens notes that **technological change** has transformed the way people live — global **communication** and **travel** are now easy. Goods can be **transported** across the world, and **information** can be transferred across the world **instantaneously**.

1) **Globalists** (sociologists who believe that society is becoming globalised) argue that **international trade** and investment have caused national economies to blend together into a **global economy**.

2) **Transnational Corporations** (**TNCs**) operate across national boundaries. They tend to have their headquarters in MEDCs and set up production in countries where there's **cheaper labour**, in order to maximise their profits.

3) **Fröbel et al (1980)** first referred to the **New International Division of Labour** — manufacturing tends to be done in developing countries, and knowledge-intensive work is done in MEDCs. **International division of labour** also means that **different stages of production** can be done in **different countries** — the car industry is a good example.

4) **TNCs** have a **positive** effect — they bring **jobs** and **investment** to developing countries, which can help with their national strategy for development. There's also a benefit for **international consumers** — cheap consumer goods.

5) However, some argue that this is a new form of **exploitation**. **Neo-Marxist** critics of globalisation say that the people of the developing world are turned into '**wage slaves**' for the capitalist system.

6) TNCs aim to create **global markets** for the goods they manufacture. They affect cultures throughout the world.

7) **TNCs** also have an effect on the **business culture** of host nations. TNCs can be categorised as three types — **ethnocentric** (headquarters in country of origin runs everything and sets corporate culture), **polycentric** (managed locally, according to guidelines set by headquarters) or **geocentric** (management is integrated across all countries).

> **Weberian sociologist Ritzer (1993) writes about global standardisation and 'rationalisation'.**
>
> 1) He refers to a '**McDonaldisation**' of production across the world. He says products are made with the same values as a **fast food** outlet: the product is made in **assembly line** conditions, it must be **inexpensive** to make and must be **standardised** at all times, across all the countries where it's made and sold. A Big Mac® is the same everywhere.
>
> 2) Ritzer picks out five themes within this McDonaldisation — **efficiency**, **calculability** (emphasis is on quantity and speed rather than quality), **predictability**, increased **control**, and the replacement of **human** workers by **machines**.

There's also Globalisation in Politics

1) Politics is increasingly carried out on an **international** level, rather than a national level.
2) The United Nations is responsible for enforcing international law, and peacekeeping etc.
3) There's increased **international political cooperation** — e.g. the **European Union**.
4) **International** non-governmental organisations (**NGOs**) coordinate **aid** and **campaigning**.

Sweet, juicy global standardisation.

Increased Communication spreads Cultural Goods across the world

1) The increase in **international media** communication in the last few decades has meant that cultures that were once local have become international and global. British and American pop music is everywhere. American and Indian films are seen internationally. *cultural goods = films, clothes, food, music, books etc.*

2) Postmodernists argue that this allows people to consume a **plurality** of cultures. They think that globalisation leads to **hybridity** (a **pick and mix** of cultures) rather than one culture being imposed over another.

3) Critics point to the concentration of the **production** of cultural goods in the hands of a few large **TNCs** which have a lot of power in developing countries. They fear that TNCs will replace traditional culture with Western culture to try and **create new markets** for **Western cultural goods**. Critics refer to cultural globalisation as **cultural imperialism**.

4) Those who believe in the **positive** effects of cultural globalisation argue that it's a **two-way process**. Western culture is transmitted to new societies, and other identities and cultures get passed on to societies in MEDCs. An example of this would be the increase in screenings of **Bollywood films** in Western mainstream cinemas.

Theories of Globalisation

Global Organisations are seen by some as More Powerful than Governments

1) TNCs operate in **many countries** — they have a global reach. Many are as powerful as nation states in economic terms, and some critics point to their perceived lack of respect for local cultures as a key feature of globalisation.

2) National governments often find it hard to **control** TNCs and are **reluctant** to act against the interest of the TNC. The host nation **risks losing large numbers of jobs** if the TNC decides to pack up and **move to another country**.

3) **International political agencies**, such as the **United Nations** and the **European Union (EU)**, have taken some power and decision-making away from national governments.

4) Critics claim that this means nation states lose the ability to **determine their own future**, as they must constantly **negotiate** with other governments and agencies to try and get the best policy for the nation.

Leslie Sklair (2000) sees globalisation as a form of **transnational capitalism** (capitalism which crosses national boundaries). He thinks it isn't worth analysing nation states — power is held by TNCs, bureaucrats and global media.

There's Evidence to say that the role of the Nation is still as Important as ever

1) **Realists** point out that **national interest** still determines **most policies** within a nation and in international negotiations. For example, the US has so far refused to agree to the terms of the Kyoto Protocol (an international environmental strategy) **partly** because it's not in the interests of the US because of the potential effects on employment.

2) **Hall (1995)** argues that in a globalised world, **national identity** becomes very **important** to people as a way of ensuring there are still differences between the countries of the world. As a result, the nation state can be strengthened.

3) Increasing fears over the loss of power from national government to the EU has meant that many people in the UK are even more determined to protect the **sovereignty** of the nation.

4) There's a trend towards **devolution** — i.e. giving power to local bodies, as has happened with the Scottish Parliament and Welsh Assembly. Nations **within** the UK have reasserted their identity and control over key issues and policies.

You can protect her from the EU — but you can't protect her from this year's floral trends...

Practice Questions

Q1 Explain why some theorists say we now have a global economy.

Q2 What is the New International Division of Labour?

Q3 What is McDonaldisation?

Q4 Why do critics of cultural globalisation refer to it as cultural imperialism?

Exam Questions

Q1 Discuss the view that we live in a 'McDonaldised' world. (18 marks)

Q2 Critically evaluate the argument that economic globalisation benefits less developed societies. (18 marks)

Q3 "Despite globalisation, identity, culture and power are held by local communities and nation states rather than international organisations and agencies." Explore the arguments for and against this statement. (33 marks)

So the world is turning into McDonald's? I reckon Ritzer was just hungry...

Hallucinations and bizarre fantasies are common during extreme hunger. But seriously, globalisation is a big thing in Sociology. Giddens is obsessed by it. It's a many-armed beast, is globalisation, with cultural, technological, political and economic aspects. Pretty much everything we buy has some kind of global connection. Think of how much stuff has 'Made in China' stamped on it.

Strategies for Development

There are different sociological perspectives on development strategies. And unfortunately, you have to know them all.

The **History** of **Colonialism** has shaped **International Trade Relations**

1) A colony is a territory that's **controlled** by a **foreign power**. Back in the 16th and 17th centuries, **European** countries began to **colonise Asian**, **African** and **American** territories. The height of colonialism was in the **19th century**.

2) European nations colonised foreign territories for three main reasons:

- Colonies were **economically important**. **Raw materials** and **food** were sourced in the colonies, and taken back to Western Europe to fuel **industrial-capitalist development**.

- Having **colonies** and building up an **empire** added to a nation's **power** and **influence** — the colonising country could put military bases and trading ports in the colony.

- Europeans also saw colonialism as a way of "**civilising**" native people. They saw traditional Asian, African and American cultures as **inferior**, and tried to **replace** them with Western values, including Christianity.

3) Colonialism strongly shaped **economic development** in the colonies. The colonisers set up plantations to grow **cash crops** such as coffee and cotton. They used slaves and low-paid labour and sold the crops for high prices in Europe.

4) Former colonies are often **under-industrialised**, because they were used only for primary sector industries such as agriculture and mining. Former colonies didn't get the chance to develop **manufacturing** industry.

5) Former colonies which rely on **agricultural exports** are hit hard by **global recession** — when the **market price** of cash crops drops, their **national income drops**.

Many **LEDCs** face a **Debt Crisis** — they spend more on **Debt** than **Investment**

Throughout the 20th century, **LEDCs** have had to **borrow money** from **richer nations** and **international organisations** both for survival and for development. The **World Bank** and **International Monetary Fund** (IMF) have lent large sums of money to LEDCs to fund development projects.

The World Bank and IMF are groups which loan money to fund development projects in member countries. It's not just LEDCs who borrow money — the UK has taken out loans from both organisations.

1) If you ask for a **loan** from your **local bank**, it'll come with a set of conditions — you have to pay **interest**, and you have to pay a certain amount **back** each month. If you don't pay enough off each month, the **interest** starts to **pile on**, and you can find yourself in **financial trouble**. If you stop paying altogether you could even **lose your home**.

2) It's exactly the same with **nations**. Many poor countries spend **more** repaying **debts** and the interest that's built up on their debts than they spend on their own **infrastructures**. As **Hayter** points out, that's **not good** for **development**.

Dependency theory puts the crisis down to colonialism, corruption and greed

1) Dependency theorists argue that many countries are poor because **colonialism** restricted their economic development. Countries that gained independence were forced to **borrow money** to fund development.

2) Dependency theorists also argue that **aid** doesn't go to the right place — much of the money that's donated disappears, either because **governments embezzle** it (i.e. steal it for themselves) or invest in products that **don't help** a country to develop (e.g. **weapons**). This leaves an **investment gap** that has to be filled with **loans**.

3) In the 1980s and early 1990s, the **richest nations** and the **international lending organisations** significantly raised levels of **interest** paid on loans. Countries had to **borrow more** to meet **interest payments**. Dependency theorists think this rather suited the West as they saw an **increase** in the **debt owed** to them — they were suddenly looking at receiving a lot **more money** in debt repayments from the poorer nations.

There's an ongoing **campaign** to **reduce debt**, or **scrap** debts entirely. Many countries have had their **total debt** reduced, but this hasn't **yet** made a significant impact on the absolute poverty experienced by people within the poorest nations.

International Trade and TNCs can help Development

A recent view is that **trade** is more productive in development strategies than **aid**. This view is influenced by the New Right (p. 117). Not all trade-based strategies are due to New Right theorists, though — e.g. the **fair trade movement** aims to **insulate** agricultural workers in developing countries from the **ups and downs** of the world market. Fair trade businesses pay farmers a fixed '**fair**' price for their crops, whatever the global market price is. Neo-liberals claim that fair trade is just **aid under another name**, and say that **subsidies** don't encourage producers to be efficient and enterprising. They'd rather leave it to the free market.

1) **TNCs** can have both **positive** and **negative** impacts on development in LEDCs and NICs. They **provide investment** to developing countries, which can help with their own national strategy for development. They also provide **jobs**, which increases the host nation's **wealth**. Workers in the host nation have increased **spending power**.

2) TNCs can cause **rapid economic growth** which can be **too fast** for a host nation's **infrastructure** to cope with.

3) Those who define development in **quality of life** terms are concerned about **working conditions** in TNC factories.

Strategies for Development

Aid can be given in Three Different Ways

> The United Nations recommends rich countries should give <u>0.7%</u> of their <u>GDP</u> in aid. In fact, <u>very</u> <u>few</u> developed countries meet the UN target. The UK gives around 0.4% of GDP.

1) **Bilateral Aid** is where a **government** gives **direct financial support** to another **government** that needs help (e.g. Malawi).

2) **Multilateral Aid** is from **international bodies** such as UNESCO, the World Health Organisation, the International Monetary Fund (IMF) and the World Bank. Multilateral aid can be either **grants** or **loans**. The IMF and World Bank give **loans**, and charge **interest** on the loans.

3) **Non-Governmental Organisations** (NGOs) give logistical support and direct financial donations. They get their money from the **public**. Examples of NGOs are Oxfam and Christian Aid.

Different Theories have Different Views of Aid

Modernisation theory says aid helps LEDCs 'Westernise'

1) **Modernisation theory** believes that developed countries should give **aid** to countries that are prepared to accept Western styles of development, i.e. **industrial capitalism**.

2) Modernisation sees aid as having a **'trickle-down effect'**. The argument is that aid goes to the elites of LEDCs, and the elites create wealth and prosperity. Associated factors such as **employment** and **increased standards of living** should **filter down** to **local economies** and **local people**.

3) Modernisation theorists were largely justified in the mid-20th century, as many poor countries (newly independent from colonialism) received aid and experienced **growth** and **success**. However, growth stalled later, and in some countries the poverty gap increased rather than decreased.

Neo-Marxist dependency theorists see aid as a tool to serve capitalism

1) Aid is often **tied** (given with conditions attached). A common condition is that local markets should be opened up to **free trade**, allowing foreign companies (including TNCs) to import and export goods without trade or customs levies. Neo-Marxists view this very **negatively**, believing that LEDCs are often exploited economically by TNCs.

2) **Bilateral aid** often requires the **recipient** nation to **buy goods** from the **donor** nation, or employ **technical experts** from the donor nation. These requirements help the **donor** nation.

3) Critics of Western aid such as **Teresa Hayter (1971, 1981, 1989)** see it as a tool for the richest countries to **politically influence** LEDCs. **Western** countries tended to give aid to countries with **right-wing** governments rather than to countries with **socialist** or **communist** governments. This happened a lot during the Cold War.

4) To get a loan from the World Bank or IMF, LEDCs have often had to agree to make **political** and **economic changes** called 'Structural Adjustment Programmes'. These are often **industrial-capitalist** in nature (e.g. privatisation of state-run services). Evidence shows that some of these programmes **haven't succeeded** in developing poor nations.

New Right theory says that aid creates dependency

1) **New Right theorists** generally don't believe in giving anyone 'something for nothing'. They argue that aid teaches LEDCs to be **dependent** on MEDCs, rather than standing on their own two feet. They say that LEDCs start to see aid as a right, rather than as a safety net, or last resort.

2) **Neo-liberals** believe that aid mucks about with the proper operation of the **free market** — they think that the free market is the best way of encouraging development, through **enterprise** and **investment**.

Practice Questions

Q1 What are the causes of debt, according to dependency theorists?

Q2 What are the three categories of aid that are given to less developed countries?

Q3 Explain how the 'trickle-down effect' works, according to modernisation theory.

Exam Question

Q1 "Aid is merely a tool for spreading capitalism across less developed countries."
Assess sociological views on this statement.

(33 marks)

Lend us 20 million euros, would you...

You've probably heard Bono banging on about debt in developing countries, unless you've been in a cave on the moon with cushions strapped to your ears. You might even have heard him there — being a rock star, his voice does carry a fair way. You probably haven't heard of all the theories and sociologists' names on these pages, though, so you'll need to learn them for later.

NGOs and International Bodies

These pages look at the impact that international organisations have on the developing world — and it's a bit of a mixed bag.

NGOs and Charities used to provide mainly Emergency Aid

NGOs (non-governmental organisations) are private organisations carrying out campaigning, aid and development work. They are economically and politically **independent** from **government**.

1) **NGOs** and **charities** such as Oxfam, Save the Children® and the Red Cross/Red Crescent mainly respond to **emergencies** — e.g. the 1984 **famine** in Ethiopia, the crisis in the **Darfur** region of Sudan and the 2004 **tsunami** in South East Asia.

2) **Disaster and emergency relief** is obviously a **short-term** thing. It's different from **long-term development strategies**. That being said, economic and social development **can't take place** where large numbers of people are starving or homeless. It's essential to **fix** the **immediate damage** before going on to **plan strategies** for the long term.

3) NGOs also participate in **development**. They develop **local communities** through education and village clinics, and work with **governments** and **businesses** to coordinate national development.

Four stages of NGO and charity involvement

1) Relief and aid	**Food** programmes, **urgent** medical care
2) Community development	Community **health centres**, community **education**
3) Systems development	Working with **government** and **private business**
4) People's movements	Encouraging **locally managed development**

NGO Activity has Increased over the last 50 years

The number of NGOs has grown massively in the past 50 years, as has the range of their different aims and structures. **Robbins (2005)** suggests a number of reasons for this:

1) **Better communications** — for example, the **internet** has made it easier for NGOs to organise, publicise and plan.

2) **Raised public awareness** — the extensive **mass media coverage** of global development issues and crises has raised public awareness of global humanitarian issues.

3) **Funding** — some national governments have increased funding to NGOs as an alternative to taking action themselves on development issues. This is because of a **neo-liberal** belief in **private** over state action. The increase in funding has also been driven by the belief that NGOs are more likely to **deliver results**.

4) **Expertise/Responsiveness** — NGOs have **developed networks and expertise**. They have a reputation for getting assistance where it is needed quickly, and for being **less likely** to be **corrupt** than some government bodies.

International Agencies try to help countries Develop

1) The **IMF** (International Monetary Fund) is an organisation made up of 185 countries which provides **loans** to states going through **financial difficulties**. It also provides **advice** to the governments of LEDCs on handling their economies.

2) The **World Bank** provides **grants and loans** to help developing countries build **infrastructure** (the things that society needs to function and grow — roads, electricity, a telephone network, etc.) and alleviate **debt problems**. It also advises LEDCs on how to make their **economies grow**.

The main criticism of these agencies is that they attempt to impose an **ideologically biased** model of development on poorer countries. They favour **neo-liberal free market economics** (see p.113) — but this **may not** be the best approach for all the countries they try to help.

To get Loans countries have to accept certain Conditions

Structural Adjustment Programmes (SAPs) are designed to promote **private-sector economic growth**. The World Bank and IMF link aid and debt-repayment assistance to the country's willingness to make free-market economic reforms, including:

1) The **deregulation** of private-sector business and industry to remove limits on foreign investment and competition.

2) The **privatisation** of state-owned industries.

3) **Currency devaluation** to encourage foreign investment.

4) Tight **restrictions on government spending** on education and health.

5) **Reducing taxes** on businesses.

6) Gearing the economy for the **export market** rather than the domestic market.

SAPs were introduced in the early 1980s. From 1999, they have been partially replaced by **Poverty Reduction Strategy Papers (PRSP)**. These are documents, agreed with the **IMF** and **World Bank**, which outline the country's **social and economic strategy**. PRSPs put more emphasis on the country's sense of **ownership** and **involvement** in the policies adopted.

NGOs and International Bodies

SAPs have been criticised as an Ideologically Driven development programme

Hong (2000) has argued that the impact of SAPs has been negative on LEDCs. She argues it's led to:

1) **Increased poverty** — the result of **low pay** and **regressive taxation** (tax that hits the poor harder than the rich).
2) **Poor social conditions** — caused by **low funding of state health** and **social care provision**. Also caused by low pay and poor working conditions due to **lack of regulation**.
3) **Corruption** — liberalisation has **reduced** the amount of **regulation**, and provided an **open door for corrupt practices**.
4) **Environmental damage** — production for the **export market** rather than the domestic market has resulted in damaging practices such as **monoculture** (growing one crop exclusively), **deforestation** to make way for plantations of '**cash crops**', and increased **carbon emissions**.
5) **Social unrest** — Hong cites the example of **Sierra Leone** where the combination of grinding poverty and the lack of services and welfare led to serious upheaval in the 1990s.

Not all the activities of International Organisations are so Controversial

1) In 2005 the **G8** — an organisation made up of eight of the richest countries in the world — **wrote off the debts** of 18 of the poorest developing countries.
2) **Dalmiya and Schultink (2003)** argue that the work of the **World Health Organisation** (WHO) — the section of the UN that deals with public health matters — has significantly **reduced disease** and **improved nutrition** in the developing world.

Transnational Corporations are huge businesses operating across borders

Some **transnational corporations** (**TNCs**) are richer than many nation states. The **impact** of such corporations on LEDCs can therefore be **immense**. There's more about TNCs on p.114 and p.129.

TNCs have been **criticised** for their activities in LEDCs. Harmful practices include:

- **Driving down prices** paid to producers in LEDCs followed by **profiteering** when these lower costs are not passed on to consumers in the developed world.
- **Exploiting their workforce** in LEDCs, by using unregulated markets to pay very low wages for very long hours.
- Having a **negative impact** on the environment.

Isabella wasn't colouring outside of the lines — she was just 'operating across borders...'

There are Potential Benefits to TNC activity

Contreras (1987) suggests that TNC activity in the developing world can lead to **significant benefits**. For example:

1) Increased government revenue through tax increases, which can in turn be spent on **health and education**.
2) The **advanced technology** that TNCs bring with them can provide a **catalyst** to further economic growth in the economy.
3) TNCs increase **employment opportunities** and therefore income.
4) TNCs need **skilled workers**, which provides an impetus for improvements in education and training.

Practice Questions

Q1 Give four reasons for the growth in the number of NGOs in the last 50 years.
Q2 List the potentially negative effects of Structural Adjustment Programmes according to Hong (2000).
Q3 What are the potential benefits to the developing world of the activities of TNCs?

Exam Question

Q1 Evaluate the arguments for and against the model of aid and development pursued by the IMF and World Bank. (18 marks)

You're gonna have to learn this stuff — you can bank on it...

The SAPs are a big ol' bone of contention with a lot of people — while the IMF and World Bank would claim they're just trying to help, some see them as part of a big conspiracy to spread Western values throughout the globe. For me they're another crazy acronym to learn and love. It's worth getting to grips with both sides of the argument — no matter what your opinion.

Urbanisation and Industrialisation

Some sociologists say that cities are a focal point for modernisation, investment and economic development. Others say that development in cities doesn't help the poor, and damages the environment too much. The rest just live in them and leave it at that. Those last ones are my favourite type of sociologist. There don't seem to be enough of them.

Urbanisation goes along with Industrialisation

Urbanisation means the increase in **urban populations**, compared to **rural populations**. During periods of industrialisation, people have **migrated** from rural areas to urban areas in search of **work**.

Industrialisation means the change from **agriculture** and small-scale cottage industry to large-scale **manufacturing** in factories. Factories are **centralised workplaces** — they require people to move to where the work is.

In Western Europe, there was a **rapid increase** in urban populations in the **19th century** as a result of **job opportunities** offered by the **Industrial Revolution**. In Mexico, industrialisation and urbanisation happened in the **20th century**.

Modernisation theory argues that Urbanisation is key to Development

1) In modernisation theory, the growth of cities symbolises the triumph of Western models of development and Western ideals. The city is seen as a place that rejects traditional goals and aspirations and replaces them with notions of **meritocracy**, **activism** and **individualism**.

2) **Hoselitz (1964)** argues that the **cities** encourage people to **work**, and contribute to the economy, because the system within **urban** areas is focused on **achieved status** (success based on achievement rather than social position) and **meritocracy** (allocation of people to positions in society based on **ability** rather than **family**).

3) Critics of this theory argue that it is **ethnocentric**, because it's based on Western cities, Western capitalism and Western ideals.

4) Additionally, it's seen as rather **unclear** in places — it doesn't say **how** power, wealth and development move from urban areas into rural areas, it just **assumes** that they do.

Some see Development as the move from Rural Lifestyles to Urban ones

1) Some sociologists, especially modernisation theorists, see development as the shift from the characteristics of **rural** life to **urban** life.

2) Taking this view means that it's **easy** to measure development — it's just a calculation of how **urbanised** society has become. This can be measured by counting the number of **cities** and urban townships, and the numbers of **people living, working** and **socialising** within them, and comparing it to the number of people who live, work and socialise in the countryside.

Dual Economy theory says that Rural and Urban economies are Separate

1) **Dual economy** theorists argue that urbanisation leads to two very **different** types of society within one country — **rural** society and **urban** society. They function as **two separate economies** with little connection between them.

2) The **rural** economy is **localised** and focused on **subsistence**. The **urban** economy is **national** and **international** and focused on **economic growth** and development.

3) The theory is based on the idea that **colonialism** pushed progression in **urban** areas at the expense of **rural** areas, which became marginalised.

See p.116 for more on colonialism.

4) It's a useful theory to explain the point that the needs and problems of **urban** areas are very **different** to **rural** areas.

5) However, **critics** point to the fact that dual economy theory still assumes that rural economies are '**backward**'.

Dependency Theory — Poverty in LEDC cities is caused by Colonialism

1) Dependency theorists believe the cities described by modernisation theorists don't exist. They say cities in LEDCs aren't success stories of meritocracy and achieved status, where hard work always brings big rewards. They're actually polarised between the '**haves**' and the '**have nots**'. They blame **colonialism** for this.

2) Dependency theory says that urbanisation doesn't bring solutions to the developing world, just more problems, e.g. **inequality**, **urban poverty**, **bad public health**. The developing world doesn't have the infrastructure to deal with them — there's poor health care, limited access to education, and little social security (if any at all).

3) According to the theory, only the parts of the city where **capitalist elites** live and work are anything like the modernisation theory model of a city. Those parts were **designed** under colonialism to house the **colonial elite**.

4) The theory says LEDC cities depend on trade with rich nations, and serve rich nations rather than their own people.

5) Dependency theory **ignores** countries where urbanisation actually **has** brought **economic benefits** for the people.

Urbanisation and Industrialisation

The *Two Main Approaches* to *Industrialisation* are *ISI* and *EOI*

ISI is short for **Import Substituting Industrialisation**. The developing nation works to substitute **home-grown alternatives** for goods it used to import. **Trade tariffs** and **taxes** are used to **protect** the locally manufactured goods from **foreign competition**. A state applying ISI has to be **interventionist** — protecting markets, patrolling borders and overseeing the industrialisation process.

EOI stands for **Export Orientated Industrialisation**. The developing country focuses on producing **consumer goods** for **export**. There is **high demand** for the goods in MEDCs, which have **moved away** from labour-intensive manufacturing. LEDCs have **cheaper labour costs** and can sell their products at attractive prices.

ISI has *Advantages* and *Disadvantages*

On the plus side, **ISI** helps LEDCs become **less dependent** on the developed world.
They can **target** and **plan** their own economies and **invest the profits** they make in further development.

But on the down side...

1) With **no foreign competition** local industries have no incentive to be competitive. Businesses can become **inefficient** and **corrupt** or even fail.

2) **Protectionist policies** (i.e. refusing to buy goods from abroad) can **aggravate potential customers**, who may in turn **refuse to buy** the developing country's goods.

3) With **no real incentive to expand** their business, some firms **cut wages** as an easy way of boosting profits. This can drag down wage levels in the country as a whole.

EOI has *Positive* and *Negative Effects* too

EOI has worked very well for some Newly Industrialised Countries (NICs) like **South Korea**, **Hong Kong**, **Taiwan** and **Singapore** — sometimes referred to as the **'tiger economies'**. People living there now enjoy a much **improved standard of living** and **health**.

But the focus on export markets can mean the manufactured goods are **too expensive** for the domestic population to buy. **Fierce competition** in international markets can lead to **wage cuts**.

Saving for one of these?
That's fierce tiger economy...

Industrialisation can bring *Too Many People* to the *Cities*

Rapid industrialisation can lead to **massive social problems** as workers move from the countryside to work at new city factories. **Webster (1984)** described this as **over-urbanisation**. Over-urbanisation is caused by **push** and **pull factors**.

Push factors	Pull factors
Poverty	Chance of employment in new factories
Loss of land	Better access to education in towns
Natural disasters	Perception that there are better opportunities
War and civil war	Escape constraints of family, religion, culture
RESULT: people leave the countryside	**RESULT: people move to the city**

Newcomers often can't afford ordinary city housing and build temporary homes in **shanty towns**. The shanty towns don't get any of the usual city **services** like a proper **water** supply, **health care** or **policing**. Standards of living are **extremely low**.

Practice Questions

Q1   What is industrialisation?
Q2   What is the dual economy theory?
Q3   Give examples of two 'push' and two 'pull' factors which can contribute to over-urbanisation.

Exam Questions

Q1	Outline and explain three features of urbanisation in the developing world.	(9 marks)
Q2	Evaluate the effectiveness of two different strategies for industrial development in the developing world.	(33 marks)

And the city streets are paved with gold and diamonds — honest...

When you look at interpretations of urbanisation, remember that modernisation theory and dependency theory are pretty much opposite. So, given that modernisation theory says that cities are wonderful and promote development, dependency theory must say they're awful. If modernisation theory says something is black, dependency theory says it's white. And so on.

The Environment

There's a major downside to LEDCs attempting to become more economically developed — the negative impact it has on the environment. Sociologists have suggested different ways of managing the damaging effects of industrialisation, but they mostly agree that it's hard to balance building a successful economy and being environmentally friendly.

LEDCs Contribute to and Suffer from Environmental Problems

Deforestation

Rainforests are logged for **hardwoods** or to make way for **agriculture**. They are disappearing fast — a **fifth** of the **Amazon** rainforest has already been **deforested**. Rainforests **release oxygen** and **absorb carbon**, which helps hold back climate change. Deforestation also causes **species loss**.

Water pollution

The World Health Organisation (WHO) estimates that an average person needs **20 litres of clean water** a day for drinking, cooking and washing. In 2001, one billion had **no access** to piped water. **Kingsbury (2004)** suggests that water is scarce in some areas due to **industrial pollution**.

Desertification

Poor farmers may have no choice but to **over-cultivate** and **over-graze** their land. Eventually the land is **exhausted** and turns to desert. The process is called **desertification**. It can lead to **famine** and **species loss**.

Climate change

CO_2 **emissions** have increased as the developing world becomes industrialised. **Fossil fuels** (oil, coal and gas) are used to power the **industrialising economies**. As countries become wealthier and more industrialised there is more use of **motor vehicles** and more CO_2 is emitted.

Decline in biodiversity

If present trends continue, one, or even **two thirds** of the world's plants, animals and other life forms could be **extinct** by the end of the century. This could lead to total **ecosystem collapse**, making food production impossible and leading to widespread starvation.

Industrialisation is a major cause of Environmental Damage

1) Industrialisation creates air, water and land **pollution**, and uses up **natural resources**.

2) Rapid urbanisation results in **overcrowding**. Urban **infrastructures** often **can't cope** with the influx of people. Rural-urban migrants settle in makeshift **squatter** settlements without proper **water supply** or **sanitation**.

3) Urban areas are polluted by **industry** and by **motor traffic**. This affects **public health**.

4) The new **international division of labour** means that polluting heavy industry is concentrated in LEDCs.

5) LEDCs don't have **equal access** to "clean" technology — e.g. equipment to reduce air pollution from power plants.

There are different Theoretical views on how to Manage the Environment

The neo-liberal view

According to **neo-liberalist** theories, countries need to calculate the **costs** and **benefits** of any development strategy. If a country works out that the **environmental cost** of a development strategy is **too high**, then neo-liberalists expect that they'll decide not to pursue that strategy. But this may make them **less competitive** in the **global market**.

The structuralist view

Structuralist theories argue that the developing world would do more about environmental issues if it was **debt-free**. As long as the developing world is struggling to **catch up economically** the economy will always **take priority** over the environment.

Structuralist theories are the ones that say the structure of society is responsible for social problems. Marxism is a structuralist theory.

Some sociologists argue that Sustainable Development is the solution

Sustainable development is development that aims not to harm the environment.

The Neo-Marxist **Redclift (1987)** points out that the idea of sustainable development is **only needed** because development is defined in **economic** terms and characterised by trading **natural resources** for **money**. Redclift also says that some environmentalists **claim** to support sustainable development but don't give enough priority to relieving **poverty**.

War and Conflict

If you're worried that pollution and global warming might destroy the planet in the next hundred years or so, don't panic—there's a good chance we won't have to wait that long. A good, old-fashioned war could destroy the planet in no time at all. Wars tend to take place in LEDCs — and make it even harder for those countries to develop.

War and Violence are widespread in the Developing World

1) Since the end of the Second World War around **25 million people** have died in warfare. The vast majority of these deaths have taken place in **LEDCs**.

2) In 1993, there were **52 wars** taking place, involving 42 countries. In another 37 countries, **violence** (often **political**) was widespread. That makes a total of 79 countries involved in wars or other widespread violence. Of these **79** countries, **65** were **LEDCs**.

3) **Dan Smith (1994)** suggested that **MEDCs** are much **less likely** to be engaged in war and violence. The countries in the lower two thirds of the development tables were **most likely** to be **involved in violence** or conflict.

4) Smith concluded that **development aimed at generating wealth** is essential to reduce the threat of war and violence in developing countries.

5) Smith also highlighted **links** between **national debt** and the **likelihood of being involved in war** or conflict. Of those LEDCs with national debt it was the 85 per cent with the worst levels of debt that were also most affected by war, violence and conflict.

Conflict creates long-term problems

- Infrastructure (e.g. transport and communication networks) is often damaged, setting development back by many years.
- People flee their homes and can no longer work or grow food.
- In camps for displaced people, diseases often spread quickly.

KPA / Zuma / Rex Features

A camp for internally displaced people (IDPs) in the DR Congo.

Poverty, Social Division and Weak Government can lead to war

1) **Frances Stewart (2002)** says that while many conflicts may have an ethnic, cultural or religious dimension, the underlying causes of most are **economic**.

2) Economic causes of war could include **political**, **economic** or **social inequalities**, **poor government services**, high **unemployment**, **land disputes** and disputes over **resources** like water that have become scarce due to environmental degradation.

3) According to Stewart, a possible solution to these problems is **inclusive development** with the aims of **reducing divisions** between rich and poor, and **tackling unemployment**.

The conclusions of Smith and Stewart contrast sharply with neo-liberal theories of development. Neo-liberals would favour free markets, low taxes, and encouraging enterprise and wealth generation over actively intervening to tackle the causes of conflict.

Practice Questions

Q1 Name three types of environmental damage caused by industrialisation.

Q2 What is sustainable development?

Q3 Since the end of the Second World War, have more people died in conflicts in developing or developed nations?

Q4 List three economic factors that can cause wars and conflicts to break out.

Exam Questions

Q1 Assess the view that economic development must come before environmental issues. (18 marks)

Q2 Critically evaluate the argument that economic development can be an effective strategy for reducing conflict in developing countries. (33 marks)

Make tea not war...

Ross Kemp and John Simpson seem to get on alright in war zones, but I think I can safely say the rest of us would rather sit at home with a cup of tea and a biscuit. When sociologists look at war and conflict they're interested in a) what causes the violence, and b) the effects conflict has on future development. There's an easy short answer to b) — not good.

Aspects of Development: Demography

Demography is the study of population change. It's been a big thing in World Sociology since, well, forever.

Population is growing Fast in the Developing World

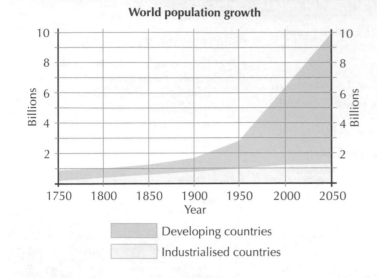

World population growth

Billions / Year / 1750 1800 1850 1900 1950 2000 2050 / 10 8 6 4 2

Developing countries
Industrialised countries

This chart* shows **world population growth** since 1750, and predicts what could happen between now and 2050.

Population is growing much **more quickly** in the **developing world** than in the industrialised nations.

* Based on a 1997 graph by Philippe Rekacewicz, UNEP/GRID-Arendal from http://maps.grida.no/go/graphic/world_population_development

Malthusians and Modernists say High Population Growth must Stop

Malthus (1798) thought that population growth could cause **problems** — a population could grow faster than its capacity to feed itself. He pointed out that limited resources would cause death, which would balance the birth/death equation.

Neo-Malthusian **Ehrlich (1968)** believed that the '**population explosion**' was putting too much stress on the resources of the world, leading the developing world in particular to experience problems such as famine and malnutrition. He believed over-population was damaging development and the environment.

1) The work of Malthus and Ehrlich has been used by **modernisation theorists** who argue that over-population in the developing world is one of the biggest obstacles to development. Any economic surplus has to be spent on feeding the population and building an infrastructure to cope with increased population, instead of on industry.

2) Modernisation theorists argue that the solution is to persuade governments to **promote birth control**, and for **Western governments** and **international organisations** to **fund birth control** programmes.

3) Modernisation theorists also suggest that money should be spent on **educating women**, because educated women tend to have fewer babies.

4) Ehrlich has even suggested that men in the developing world who have had 3 children or more should be **sterilised**.

5) **USAID** (The United States Agency for International Development) currently spends around US$425 million a year on **family planning programmes** worldwide.

6) Countries like **China** and **Singapore** have used **legal restrictions** and **economic incentives** to encourage their citizens to have fewer children.

Most attempts to Lower Birth Rates have Failed

1) Some religions, including **Islam** and **Roman Catholicism**, discourage or do not approve of using contraception. Many people who practise these faiths prefer not to use contraception.

2) **Harrison (1990)** notes that the fastest rates of population growth in the developing world are found in **Muslim** countries where traditional ideas about **women** and the **family** predominate.

3) **Feminists** have suggested **significant progress** will not be made on population control until developing countries become **less patriarchal** and the position of **women** in society improves so they are able to **take control over their own bodies**.

4) Much of the evidence does suggest that making contraception and contraception advice available is not enough. It needs to go hand in hand with **changing the position of women in society**.

Aspects of Development: Demography

Ehrlich's Theory of over-population has been Criticised

Carnell (2000) showed that Ehrlich's predictions about population growth were wrong. The population is growing more **slowly** than Ehrlich thought.

Harrison (1990) points out that the **birth rate** isn't the cause of population growth. Population growth is actually caused by a **decline** in the **death rate**, especially the infant mortality rate. People are having the same number of babies, but **fewer** are **dying**. Harrison does agree with Ehrlich that population growth threatens the environment, though.

People are having the same number of babies — only now they take up less space...

Marxists say Population Growth is Not the Problem

1) **Marxists** would say modernisation theorists blame the wrong people for population growth. Modernists say over-population is the fault of the **governments** of the developing world, **religious organisations** and the **people** themselves. Marxists blame the **global capitalist system**.

2) Modernists believe over-population is a problem because they assume Malthus was right when he said growing populations can outstrip food supplies. Marxists believe the real cause of starvation and famine is not over-population but **unfair distribution of world resources**. There is enough food for everyone, but capitalist market forces mean food goes where the money is and not where it is needed most.

Other theorists also Support Redistributing Resources

1) There's not a lot of evidence that **food resources** aren't coping. **Food production** has **increased**, and the world has the capacity to produce **more** food than it produces now, although it might be difficult to do this sustainably. **Boserup (1965)** said that **population increase** determines **agricultural change**, so that agricultural production always keeps up with the population.

2) **Dependency theorists** argue that the West continues to take the very best resources a developing nation has, leaving the inhabitants with little land of any quality. **Land reform** and **redistribution** to the poor would be a better solution than population control.

3) **Adamson (1986)** says focusing on population growth can distract us from the **real causes** of poverty and starvation. He believes the real causes are an unfair distribution of resources. We should look at the developed world's contribution to these problems, e.g. **over-consumption**, **environmental damage**, and **economic exploitation** of the developing world.

Adamson points out that, in 1986, an American used up on average 300 times more energy than a Bangladeshi.

4) **Adamson** also suggests that poverty **causes** high population. Poverty forces parents to see children as **economic assets** who will bring money into the household and support them in **old age**. Where there are high levels of infant mortality parents have more children to increase the chances of at least one surviving into adulthood.

Some believe Population Growth can Encourage Development

1) Some theorists see population growth not as a problem but as a **cause of development**. As population growth creates pressure on resources it encourages people to **innovate** and find ways to be more **productive**.

2) A good example would be **Britain** in the 19th century where many historians see population growth as a major **cause of industrialisation**.

Practice Questions

Q1 Why do modernists believe over-population is an obstacle to development?

Q2 Why have policies aimed at reducing population in the developing world had limited impact?

Q3 What positive effects does an increasing population have according to some theorists?

Exam Question

Q1 Evaluate the view that rapid population growth is a significant obstacle to development. (33 marks)

Malthus thought we had problems in 1798...

... imagine if he could see us now. The world's population was only about 1 billion then — it's over 6 times that now. Sociologists disagree about what's to blame for over-population — too many babies, too few deaths, capitalism...the list goes on. Anyway, soon we'll have bigger issues than arguing about the causes 'cause the world will be full and there won't be any room to lie down.

Aspects of Development: Education

You might not be in the mood to believe this, but good education has been proven to improve standards of living, raise participation in civic activities and make for a happier, harder-working populace. In the last 50 years, developing countries have spent more of their budgets on improving the education of their people — with mixed results.

Good Education *improves the* Living Standards *of people in LEDCs*

Education is necessary for **development**. In Rostow's model of development (see p.112), an educated workforce is necessary for industrial take-off. Many other sociologists, in particular **functionalists** and **modernists**, also think education is very important for development.

1) **Economic development** requires expert, technical knowledge on a local level. Not all expertise can be brought in from other countries. International organisations and MEDCs are generally keen to see LEDCs **train** their own people in the **specialist skills** required for the long-term development of a country.

2) Education also gives people the **values** and **attitudes** required in the process of development. Literate, numerate people can fully understand what action is required for development and **participate** in deciding what action to take in their communities and their country.

3) Education can act as a **unifying force**. It can give people a common set of **values** and ideas about their country, which helps to overcome class, ethnic and religious **differences** in a country.

4) Many people in the developing world are keen to participate in education because they want to obtain **achieved status** — a qualification, improved employment opportunities, etc. Education acts as an **empowering** tool for groups in society that have traditionally been **excluded** from **social mobility**, e.g. women and the poor.

Universal Education *is still* Unavailable *for many in the* Developing World

1) **External aid** and increased **investment** in the developing world have led many countries to introduce **universal education** policies — but provision is often **patchy**.

2) Some countries have universal education for **primary school** age (up to about 11 years old), some have universal education up to 14 or 16 years old, and some still haven't introduced universal education.

3) Even in countries that have **universal education** as a policy, not every child **actually goes to school**. This is because of other **family commitments** and needs — e.g. children may be required to **work** on the **family farm**.

4) In many countries, parents still have to **pay school fees** to get their child into school. Also, **school supplies** aren't provided by the state like they are in the UK. Families have to **buy** books and other resources.

The Growth *in* Education *doesn't mean* Quality Education

Much of the **increase** in education has had to be supplied by education **systems** that were designed to meet the **basic needs** of a **few**. Basic education systems have been put under **strain**.

Lessons aren't always of **high quality**. Some education doesn't provide enough **useful knowledge**.

The Growth *in* Education *has raised problems with* Employment

1) While young people are in schools and colleges being educated, they're not out **working** and contributing to the **local** and **national economy**.

2) Because more people are studying and fewer people are working, governments get less revenue from income tax. Governments have less money coming in but have to **pay out more** to **provide education**.

3) Bright, educated people from rural areas tend to **migrate** to the **cities** to look for jobs. This contributes to **over-urbanisation** and urban **overcrowding** (see p. 121-122).

4) The more educated citizens **sometimes struggle** to find **employment** in their own country, or they can simply earn a lot more by moving away to countries that have **better job prospects** — this is called the "**brain drain**", by the way. The end result is that the country **fails to develop** because the educated have **left**, to use their education elsewhere.

Marxist Dependency Theorists *see* Education *as Cultural Imperialism*

Dependency theorists really frown on the idea that education **trains** people for **development**. They **strongly disapprove** of education that gives people the **values** and **attitudes** that are needed for "imperial-capitalist" (i.e. Western) development — they call this **cultural imperialism**.

Dependency theory sees **education** as a potential **tool** for keeping people **culturally** and **economically dependent** on the developed world — it trains them to get the kind of **jobs** that **benefit TNCs** and the **developed world**.

Aspects of Development: Health

At the start of the 21st century, health in the developing world is still poor compared to the developed world. Good health care provision is essential for the protection of people and for a developing country's future prospects.

Physical Quality of Life Index (PQLI) Measures Health and Education

1) **David Morris** developed the PQLI in **1979**. It measures **infant mortality**, **literacy** and **life expectancy**. It's useful for sociologists concerned with development as a social issue rather than an economic issue.

2) The PQLI also allows you to compare trends across countries. However, there are problems in collecting reliable data.

Education, Poverty and the role of MEDCs all impact on Health in LEDCs

1) Poverty forces people to suffer a **bad diet** and **poor public health**.

2) It also prevents them from gaining a good quality of **health care**. Universal free health care is **rare** in the developing world — people usually have to **pay** to see a doctor. There are also **not enough doctors** and **nurses** to go around.

3) The lack of good **health education** in the developing world means many people (particularly those in traditional, rural areas) do not know how to **prevent disease** and are not aware of **basic treatments**.

4) Some drugs companies sell drugs in the developing world that are **banned** in the West for **safety** reasons. Or they may set the **price** of life-saving drugs so **high** that many people in LEDCs can't afford them.

5) **Western products** may be used **inappropriately**. For example, **baby formula milk** is heavily advertised in LEDCs. But some mothers don't have access to **clean water** to make the milk with, so many babies die from **infections**. And poor mothers may **water down** the formula too much (to make it last longer), resulting in **malnutrition**.

6) Also, TNCs that have set up in developing countries often pay little attention to the environment, or health and safety. For example, the Bhopal poison gas leak of 1984 happened because safety procedures were inadequate.

> **Example: HIV/AIDS in South Africa**
> - **Insufficient health education** in poor areas meant people **didn't know** how HIV was transmitted.
> - Clinics could be a **day's walk** away.
> - **Transnational drugs companies** refused to allow local drugs companies to make **cheap versions** of anti-HIV drugs. This practice was banned by the courts in 2001.
> - In the 1990s, the **South African government was reluctant** to **distribute** anti-HIV drugs.

They doubted that HIV caused AIDS.

There are different Theoretical Views about Health Inequalities

Modernisation theorists and **functionalists** believe **Western** medicine is **superior**, and that Western medicine and **health education** can **solve** the problems of **high infant mortality** and **low life expectancy**. **Rostow (1971)** said **high-tech medicine** used in the developed world should be **transferred** to developing nations so that **quality health care** can be provided.

Marxist **Navarro (1976)** believed that high-tech Western health care is not the immediate priority for the developing world. Poor nations need to focus on **basic health procedures** to **save lives** and **improve quality of life**. Doctors from these nations need to be encouraged to stay and work in their own countries, not to migrate to MEDCs for better pay.

Dependency theory blames **colonialism** and **exploitation**. Colonialism introduced European diseases to Africa, America and Asia. Colonialism also replaced food crops with cash crops, resulting in malnutrition. Dependency theory also blames the developed world for **poverty** and **debt**.

Practice Questions

Q1 What are the advantages and disadvantages of universal education?
Q2 What is the PQLI?
Q3 What do modernisation theorists argue is crucial for development in health?

Exam Questions

Q1 How can education be used as a tool for development in the developing world? (18 marks)

Q2 Critically evaluate the argument that the health concerns of the developing world have largely been caused by the policies of the developed world. (33 marks)

This subject is certainly draining my brain...

With every page my head feels emptier and emptier, and soon there'll be nothing left. Anyway, it's those dreaded words 'cultural imperialism' again. It's really hard to think about development without slipping into some kind of 'them and us' thinking — either assuming that the West knows best, or assuming that the West is all bad, and that poor countries should be left to get on with it.

Aspects of Development: Gender

Recently, sociologists (particularly feminists) have pointed out that women and men experience development and under-development in different ways. And you know what that means — more radical feminists. Should be interesting.

There's **Gender Inequality** in the **Developing World**

Evidence from studies into gender in LEDCs shows that in many cases women get a worse deal than men.

- Women have **lower life expectancy** than men in **some countries** (usually women live longer than men).
- Women are **paid less** than men.
- Women get **less education** than men.
- Women's **health** is **poorer** than men's health, and women have **less access** to health care than men do.
- There's even a **greater chance of abortion** if a foetus is **female**.
- Women have very poor **reproductive rights**. They don't get to choose whether to have children, or how many to have, because local **religious attitudes** are against contraception and abortion.

The Gender Empowerment Measure (GEM) is an indicator of the progress made by women in a society

1) The GEM focuses on **social indicators** of gender equality — female and male participation in **decision making**, **economic participation** and **economic power**.

2) In other words, it monitors whether women have the right to **vote**, how many women there are in **parliament**, how many women have **top management jobs** and the **GDP per capita** of the **female population**.

3) This measure has continually shown that women haven't reached **social equality** with men.

The Gender-related Development Index (GDI) measures several development-related factors

1) The GDI measures **life expectancy**, **literacy**, years in **school**, number of **women in work** and **women's income**.

2) It has a more **positive** story to tell about women and development. Sure, men still generally have better income, literacy and so on, but women have **improved** in most of the categories measured.

3) **Women's literacy** and **numeracy** has improved, and the chance of **death** during or after **childbirth** has **fallen**.

Women may feel the Negative Side Effects of development More than Men

1) According to Marxist feminists, women experience a **dual burden** of **paid work** and **domestic responsibilities**.

2) When a country **industrialises**, men go from **one** form of work (agriculture) to **another** form of work (manufacturing industry), but women go from **one** form of work (housework and childcare) to **two** forms of work (housework and childcare plus a paid job outside the home).

3) Women in LEDCs often work **longer hours** than **men**, in poor conditions.

This is quite simplified, and it's a broad generalisation anyway.

Technology can change Women's Employment Patterns

1) **Swasti Mitter (1995)** writes about the impact of **ICT** on **female employment** in LEDCs. She says that computer technology can be a real **boon** to women — it allows them to work from home and work **flexible hours**.

2) Many ICT jobs which have been outsourced to NICs from MEDCs go to women — e.g. **call-centre jobs**, **data entry**, **medical transcription services**.

3) Mitter points out that many women in LEDCs like India, Malaysia and Brazil now work in ICT, but they're concentrated towards the **bottom end** of the work ladder.

Radical Feminists argue that Development Benefits Patriarchy

1) Some radical feminists see development as a tool to make women more **dependent** upon men.

2) Radical feminists say TNCs actively seek to employ women as they are cheaper, more efficient and more docile.

3) If women do experience **improvement** in their position in society, e.g. **greater life expectancy** through better **health care** or **increased income**, it's because the **patriarchy** of the developed **world** allow it for **productivity** reasons.

Radical feminism can be **criticised** for failing to see the **exploitation** experienced by **men**.

Socialist Feminists believe Socialism can bring Equality to poorer countries

1) Socialist feminists argue that socialism can bring about a society that **isn't gendered** — i.e. that treats men and women **equally**. They push for **socialist revolution** that totally **changes** the way people see 'men's jobs' and 'women's jobs', as well as moving ownership of the means of production from employers to workers.

2) Socialist feminist **Mies (1986)** argues that traditional Marxism and capitalism both **undervalue** the work women do.

Aspects of Development: Employment

Employment is another thorny development issue. Big international companies often move their factories, call centres, or whatever it is they need, to developing countries because wages are cheaper there. That means jobs for local workers, but many people would say the workers aren't treated fairly. Looks like nothing is ever straightforward in sociology.

Developing Countries Encourage TNCs to Relocate

> TNCs (see p.114) are <u>large businesses</u> that operate in <u>several countries</u> around the world. TNCs are a feature of <u>globalisation</u>.

1) **Labour costs** are much much lower in LEDCs than in the developed world. As a result, many **TNCs** (transnational corporations) prefer to set up factories in LEDCs, or pay companies in LEDCs to make goods on their behalf.

2) Many LEDCs have actively encouraged TNCs to do this by setting up **Export Processing Zones** (EPZs), also known as **Free Trade Zones** (FTZs).

3) In the EPZs, companies may be offered **tax breaks**, **training grants**, **low regulation** and **low wage costs**. **Trade unions** are often banned.

4) There are now **more than 800** of these zones in the developing world. Most are in Asia, South America and Central America, with over 100 in Mexico and over 100 in China.

KPA / Zuma / Rex

Busan in South Korea — a free trade zone and the world's fifth busiest port.

Conditions *Favour the TNCs*, not the *Workers*

Typical EPZ industries include **garment-making** and assembling **electronic goods**. Workers are not usually directly employed by the TNCs. They work for **local manufacturers** who have to **compete** to win contracts from the TNCs. The manufacturers' main concern is to **keep costs down**. This can lead to very **poor working conditions**.

1) Often **hours are long** and **pay is low**. In the garment industry, workers in Bangladesh received the lowest wages in 2008 — US$0.22 per hour. Mexican workers were better paid, earning $2.54 per hour. In Europe, workers in Hungary doing similar work earned around $4.45 per hour.

2) **Health and safety** issues, and basic comforts like breaks or washrooms, may be **ignored**.

3) Many firms use **flexible** or **casual labour**, which means that workers have almost **no job security**. They are employed on **short-term contracts** — often on a weekly or even daily basis.

4) Highly paid jobs like marketing and design are usually done at the TNC's sites in MEDCs. Workers in the LEDC factories tend to have **basic unskilled jobs**. There's very little training or chance of progression.

5) In EPZs, **women** usually make up the majority of employees. In garment making it can be up to 90%. Because women usually earn less than men in LEDCs, it can be argued that the TNCs are **profiting** from women's **lower status**. Some companies in EPZs also use **child labour**.

6) When **trade unions** are **banned** or restricted, it's hard for workers to campaign for better pay or conditions. Governments are scared of losing the TNCs so come down hard on **strikes** and **demonstrations**.

7) Even though wages are low there are plenty of people willing to work. In this situation employers have **no incentive** to offer a better wage.

There are *Arguments For* and *Against* the special *Zones*

1) Marxists like **Fröbel** (**1980**) are highly critical of EPZs. They see them as a new version of **exploitative colonialism**.

2) **Globalists** say that EPZs benefit world consumers as a whole by **keeping prices down**.

3) **Wages** in EPZs look low compared to what people are paid for the same work in industrialised nations. However, they're often **relatively good** when compared to average wages in the developing world.

Practice Questions

Q1 What do the GEM and the GDI suggest about gender inequality? Why do they differ?

Q2 Why do TNCs locate manufacturing in LEDCs?

Exam Question

Q1 Assess the argument that women are disadvantaged in the developing world. (18 marks)

Relocation, relocation, relocation...

Employment, health, education, gender issues, the environment, demography... There can't be many issues that global development doesn't touch on. The most important thing to get straight about this section is the difference between Marxist, modernist and dependency theories. Once that's clear you can pretty much predict what they'll say on a particular issue.

Ownership and Control of Mass Media

The mass media is one of the most powerful influences in modern society because it's part of all our lives.
The study of the mass media has had to change just to keep up with new developments.

The **Mass Media Communicates** with a large **Audience**

1) **Traditionally**, the **mass media** is defined as "the methods and organisations used to communicate to a large audience". That definition covers things like radio, television, cinema and newspapers quite nicely.

2) However, since the 1980s there have been **huge changes** in the media. There are a lot more **specialist** media outlets communicating with smaller, **niche groups** rather than to the whole "mass" of the public — e.g. subscription TV channels for fans of particular football teams, special interest magazines, podcasts about special interest topics.

3) Also, new media such as blogs, email and texting allow audiences to **interact** with the media. Communication isn't **one-way** any more. Some media are more of a **multi-way network**, e.g. mobile phones and the internet.

4) We still use the term "**mass media**", though. There's some debate about what counts as mass media — for example, some theorists would count all mobile phone technology, but others would only include it when it's used to communicate to a large audience. So, sending a text to a friend wouldn't count, but **subscribing** to a service that sends you football scores by text **would** count, and so would reading an online news site on your phone.

5) Some theorists include a lot more things when they talk about "media". **Marshall McLuhan (1964)** included **any** kind of technology that helped people communicate — even cars and clocks.

> Well, OK, I suppose a car lets you drive from A to B to have a meeting, and a clock lets you be on time.

Some messages get **Removed** from the **Media**

> The process of **controlling** the content of the media is called **censorship**.
>
> Media messages which are considered **harmful** or **offensive** to society can be **removed** before the audience receives them. Censorship can be done for moral, political or security reasons. There's loads more about censorship on pages 136-137.

Sociologists **Analyse** and **Research** the **Mass Media** (and its effects)

Content Analysis — measuring how often a word, phrase or theme is used in a piece of media

1) In the social sciences, content analysis means **formal**, **quantitative** measuring. For example, you could **count** how many times a news report used the words "economic crisis". It's most suited to **written texts**, or to **transcripts**.

2) Content analysis can also be used to investigate the **relationship** between two phrases or themes (e.g. by looking at how often they appear together).

3) The main **downside** of content analysis is that it **takes a long time**. It also doesn't take **context** into account.

Semiotics — studying the signs and codes of media

1) A sign is **anything** that can be used to **mean something else** — e.g. a word or an image. Semiotic analysis looks at the **meanings** of the signs in a piece of media.

2) **Advertisements** are particularly open to semiotic analysis. Ads use **signs** to associate their product with **positive ideas**, e.g. attractiveness, happiness and success. They don't **directly** say, "buy this product and you will be happy".

3) Semiotic analysis is open to **subjectivity** and **bias**. The **values** of the researcher may influence how they **interpret** a sign, or the **relative importance** they place on different signs in a piece of media.

> 1) A sign can have a very <u>simple meaning</u>, e.g. the written word "cows" means, well, the idea of cows (the technical term for this kind of meaning is <u>denotation</u>).
>
> 2) A sign can also <u>suggest meaning</u>, e.g. a photo of a couple holding hands on the beach at sunset means the idea of romance (this kind of meaning is <u>connotation</u>).

Experiments — studying how an actual audience responds to media

1) One example would be to monitor people's **behaviour** after viewing a violent film.

2) Short experiments like this don't tell you about **long-term media effects**. People also tend to **behave differently** when they know they're in an **experiment**.

3) **Audience research** means things like showing media to a **sample audience**, then **interviewing** them or giving them a questionnaire. You have to **formulate good interview questions** to get useful and **meaningful** results and **avoid bias**.

Ownership and Control of Mass Media

The Media is **Owned** by a **Few Powerful Companies** and **Individuals**

The **same companies** often own **different forms of media** — e.g. film studios, TV stations, radio stations, newspapers, social networking websites. This is called **cross-media ownership**. It's often not publicised.

1) Media companies **diversify** — they buy other companies that make **different kinds of media**, and they also buy companies in **other business sectors**.

- Rupert Murdoch's **News Corporation** owns TV stations, newspapers, book and magazine publishers and websites including myspace® and Photobucket.
- In Italy, **Silvio Berlusconi** owns three national TV channels, an advertising agency and a magazine publisher. He part owns a banking company and a cinema firm. He also owns football club **AC Milan**.

2) Some media companies **own media** in **several different countries**. News Corporation owns newspapers in Australia, Britain and the USA. It owns TV networks in Australia, Europe, Asia, North and South America.

3) Over the last 30 years, media ownership has become concentrated into fewer and fewer hands. Research by **Bagdikian (2004)** found that the American media was now mostly owned by just **five huge corporations** — TimeWarner, Disney, News Corporation, Bertelsmann and Viacom®.

The individuals who own and control those companies have **huge power and influence** in society. They can **control** the information we receive **if they want to**. A **great example** is **Italy**, where media company owner **Silvio Berlusconi** was voted in as prime minister for the third time in 2008. **He owns a lot of media outlets** and some people claim he is able to use them to **control the reporting** of his political party and the opposition.

Marxists say **Media Ownership Controls Media Content**

1) **Traditional Marxism — media owners control what we see in the media**
The idea is that the owners of the media **exploit their power position** to **manipulate** the content of the media. Capitalist media owners **tell news editors** what **stories** to cover and what **views** to put across. There's a lot of anecdotal evidence about newspaper proprietors **personally telling** the **editors** of their newspapers **what view to take on important stories**. The media ends up putting across views that **serve the interests of capitalism**.

2) **Neo-Marxism — the media reflects the ideas of the ruling class (including media owners)**
Neo-Marxist theory is **more complicated** — it says that control over the media is **indirect**. Neo-Marxism says the **world view of the elite class** is **broadcast** and **reinforced** by the media. The **values** and **ideas** of the **ruling class** are presented as the **natural, common-sense** views to have. This is called **"cultural hegemony"** — i.e. one set of ideas **dominating** over other ideas.

Pluralism says the **Media Reflects** the **Values** and **Beliefs** of Society

The pluralist view is that **society gets the media it wants** — media outlets have to **respond to market demand** or they'll go out of business. In other words, it **doesn't really matter** who **owns** the media — it's the **market** that matters. Pluralists do realise that the media will express **some opinions more than others**, though. Pluralists reckon this isn't because of bias from journalists, editors or owners — it's only a reflection of the **most common** views in society.

Practice Questions

Q1 What does 'censorship' mean?
Q2 Give one drawback of semiotic analysis.
Q3 What is cross-media ownership?
Q4 Describe the traditional Marxist view of media ownership and control.

Exam Question

Q1 Assess the view that media owners have little control over media output. (18 marks)

I own my own TV — I've got the receipt for it and everything...

All through this section there are examples of sociological media research using the methods described on the last page, and there's tons more about sociological methods in Section 7. The debate on media ownership is interesting. I've got to say — if I owned a newspaper I'd be awfully tempted to use it to spread my own views. Just casually like, nothing blatant.

Theories about Mass Media

*These two pages focus on ideology and theory and mention things like "neo-Marxism" and "pluralism". They concentrate on the ways in which **ideology influences the media** and its content.*

Traditional Marxists *say media serves the* Economic Power *of* Ruling Classes

1) According to **traditional Marxism**, the media presents what's **important** and **relevant** to the **ruling class**. For example, stocks and share prices are featured on national news bulletins but only a small percentage of the population have a lot of shares. Marxists say that the poor are ignored by the media because they don't have money to buy the things that capitalism sells.

2) Marxist theory says that it's the "**logic of capitalism**" that the institutions in society will always be used as instruments of power by the capitalist class. It's all about serving the interests of capitalism.

3) For example, advertising is in magazines and on TV to **create the demand for goods** produced in the **capitalist economy**. Advertising also gives the idea that there's a wide range of choice for the consumer when, in reality, a few companies own the vast majority of products.

4) **Herbert Marcuse (1964)** was a Marxist who reckoned that the media promotes **consumerism** and gives people "**false needs**" — the belief that they "need" things that they don't really need.

There's more about Marcuse on page 157.

> Marxist sociologist **Miliband** (**1969**, *The State in Capitalist Society,* London: Weidenfeld and Nicolson) thought that the media encourages the proletariat to be **subordinate** and happy to serve the bourgeoisie. Remember what Marx said about **religion** being the **opium of the people** — keeping the working class **subdued** and in support of a system which works against their interests. Well, Miliband reckons that the mass media is "**the new opium of the people**".

Some Neo-Marxists *say the* Ruling Class Indirectly Control *media content*

In Marxist thought, one of the key powers of the ruling class is the power to **control ideas**, **values** and **attitudes**. The mass media is a useful tool for doing this. The values of the ruling class have dominance in society — this dominance is called **hegemony**.

This theory says that the **ideas** and **values** of the ruling class are **spread** by the mass media, and presented as if they're the most natural, obvious, common-sense things to assume and believe.

> "The ruling ideas are the ideas of the ruling class." Marx and Engels (1985, *The Communist Manifesto* Harmondsworth: Penguin, first published 1848).

1) Media content is controlled by an **approval process** — articles written by journalists are given the OK by editors. **Editors** are mostly from **white, middle class backgrounds** so they **select content** which **reflects** their own values. The idea is that they do this **subconsciously** — they **don't even realise that they're doing it**. Which is a bit odd and a bit scary. (Journalists also tend to come from middle class backgrounds — that's who newspapers and broadcasters tend to employ.)

2) Some events are given **less media coverage**, and some are **left out completely**. Marxists believe that people who work in the media are **trained** to present a **certain view of the world**. This view becomes natural and "obvious" to them and the audience. Neither the media workers nor the audience are conscious that the media are pushing a certain view.

3) This neo-Marxist view doesn't say that **alternative** views are **suppressed** — it says they're **allowed**. This gives the impression that all views get a fair shout — which makes it seem OK and perfectly fair for the dominant view to stay on top. Alternative views are often made to look silly or immature.

4) Marxist sociologists say the control of ideas **doesn't just happen in news** or factual programmes. For example, family entertainment programmes are presented as light-hearted fun but they present a specific **idea of British family life**.

Gerald liked to get good press.

Critics of Marxism don't think all journalists think the same way, and they point out that not all media stories are covered from the same viewpoint.

They also say that the media **doesn't** always **reflect** the opinions of the **dominant class**. For example, some people thought the BBC reports about government evidence for weapons of mass destruction in Iraq undermined those in power rather than supported them.

Pluralists point out that media audiences aren't completely stupid, and don't all believe everything they see on TV and read in the papers.

Theories about Mass Media

Pluralism — media content Reflects Diversity in society

The pluralist view is that society is made up of lots of **different** and **interacting** parts and the state oversees them to keep them in check. Pluralists think that the **content of the media reflects the values of society**. The **free market economy** is the key to a pluralist media — any media which reflects the values in society will be **popular** and stay in business, any that the public doesn't like will go ti... er, bosoms up. This is how pluralist theory says the media **regulates itself**.

Nick Jones (1986) studied reporting of strikes

Jones studied the reporting on **industrial disputes** by the **UK media**. He concluded there was balanced and equal reporting. Individual reports may have been biased but the overall picture was **neutral**. He said apparent bias was down to the opposing sides managing to get good media coverage — the media were happy to publicise any relevant view.

Pluralism is criticised for **assuming** the diversity and neutrality of the mass media and **not showing evidence** for it.

Critics of pluralism point out that studies are often **carried out by people who work in the media**. Jones is a BBC Radio news journalist. This means that the research **might not be impartial**.

Katz and Lazarsfeld (1955) studied media before a US election

They wanted to find out how much the **media** influenced people's **political opinions** and votes. They concluded that the influence of the media is rather **unpredictable** and is often severely **limited**. They believed it was difficult to influence people through the media. People don't all get exposed to media messages, and don't always pay attention. People's attitudes can completely distort their understanding of a message. People also paid more attention to what their spouse, parents, co-workers and friends said than what the media said.

There's more on this on pages 142-143.

Postmodernism — media content gives society a Consumerist Identity

1) Postmodernism says that **consumption** is **more important** than **class** identity. It sees Marxist views about economic power as irrelevant nowadays.

2) The postmodern view says that people's **identity** comes from **what they buy** and what kind of **culture and media** they **choose to consume**. Postmodernists think the media has a very important part to play in **showing people what they can buy** and what kind of **lifestyles** they can choose from.

Many sociologists don't trust postmodernism because it's mainly theoretical — there's not much evidence to support it.

3) Postmodernists also say that there's **no dominant set of ideas**. Postmodernism sees society as presenting many choices and many alternative opinions. There isn't a "unified culture" but many voices adding their opinions and one view is not seen as better or worse than another. Therefore there is **no dominant ideology**.

French postmodernist theorist **Jean-François Lyotard (1979)** said that the key thing about the postmodern condition was the rejection of what he called "**grand narratives**" (or **metanarratives**). Grand narratives are large-scale theories and philosophies — ideas like "progress is inevitable" or "a Marxist revolution will end capitalism".

4) French postmodernist **Baudrillard** believed that media images actually **take the place of reality** — see p.145.

Practice Questions

Q1 What do traditional Marxists think advertising is for?

Q2 What is hegemony?

Q3 Why do neo-Marxists think that alternative, anti-establishment views are allowed on TV and in the papers?

Q4 What do pluralists think regulates the media?

Exam Question

Q1 Identify and explain two criticisms of the Marxist view of the relationship between media and audience. (6 marks)

CGP — subconsciously disseminating Cumbrian values since 1995...

Hmm. Subtle. Anyway, the big difference between Marxist and pluralist views is to do with whether the media controls the audience or whether the audience controls the media. You've got traditional Marxists, who think the media's all about making profits for capitalism, and you've got neo-Marxists who say it passes on ruling class values without even meaning to.

Selecting and Presenting the News

Sociologists have studied the news as an example of how the media works because it reaches so many people. It's the main source of information on the World for most of the population. The news is a social product full of ideas and values — it's not an objective reality out there waiting to be discovered by journalists.

News is influenced by **Practical Constraints** — time, space and money

The news is **presented** to us as the most **factual**, **objective** form of media — the reporting of what's happened in the world that day. In reality, newspapers, radio and television run to very tight **deadlines** and **constraints**, which **influence** what finally appears as the news.

1) **Time constraints** mean the most **easily available stories** make it onto the TV/radio news or into the newspaper. Editors and journalists have **contacts** they use **again and again** for convenience, meaning a **limited number of viewpoints** are used. Also, all news organisations have a "news diary" of regular events. This means they can plan coverage of regular events in advance.

2) **Technical constraints** influence the news. Some places are **easier** to get **cameras**, **microphones** and **journalists** into and these are the places **top stories** will tend to come from. A story will rise and fall in significance **partly** on **how easy it is to report**.

> This can lead to, for example, disasters in far-flung places being ignored or under-reported.

3) News organisations all run to a **budget**. Stories and reports from **places where they already have reporters** or **established contacts** are **cheaper to produce**. Many newspapers **can't afford** to have **many reporters** of their own so they **buy stories from news agencies**. These agencies then have a **huge influence** over what becomes news.

4) **Competition** affects the **selection** of the news. Newspaper editors are more likely to publish stories that they believe will make their newspaper the most **popular** that day. It's very important for newspaper editors that their paper **sells more** than their rivals. News stories that can be **sensationalised**, or **celebrity gossip** are often popular.

It's common these days for celebrities, politicians and groups in society to issue **press releases**. Press releases give the story **straight to the newsroom**, which makes it much more likely to be used because it **saves time and money**.

Also remember that stories have to shrink or expand to **fit the space available**. The same story could be on page 2 one day and page 17 the next, depending on **what else has happened** or what else is available to report.

Key studies are **Cohen and Young (1981)** and **Grossberg et al (1998)**. Both refer to the above as common practices in the media.

News is influenced by the **Values** and **Practices** of **Journalists**

Journalists who report the news learn to follow **certain rules** and ideas, which tend to be based on what they believe the general public want to hear about. Sociologists have referred to these as **"news values"**. There are different types of news values which influence the news the media chooses to report.

Bureaucratic news values:
News should be **current**.
News should be **simple**.
News should be **brief**.
Big news is better than **small** news.

Cultural news values:
News should be **unexpected**.
News should focus on **important people**.
News should be **relevant to the audience**.
Bad news is preferred to **good news**.

> The relative importance of the different news values to an individual journalist will depend partly on the type of publication or programme they work for.

Two key practices used by journalists which you must know are **agenda-setting** and **gate-keeping**.

Agenda-setting

Journalists and **editors** "control the news agenda". News **only becomes news** when **journalists** and **editors** **select it** as news. When a story is selected, journalists choose what **angle** to take when reporting it. This has a **direct effect** on how the audience will **perceive** the story. Agenda-setting may not be **conscious**. It comes from **learnt practices** of journalism — usually based on what **catches the audience's attention**.

Gate-keeping

This comes from work by **Gans (1979)** which describes how the editor decides **which stories are featured** and **how much space** is given to each story. Gans says it's like a gate — the editor opens it for some stories and closes it for others. **Dutton** (**1986** *The Media*, London: Longman) concluded from his research: "editors fulfil a filtering role since there is usually an excess of material available to fill limited newspaper or broadcasting space".

Selecting and Presenting the News

Case Study of Selection and Presentation of News

The Glasgow University Media Group studied television news

The Glasgow University Media Group (GUMG) studied **television news** over a long time span (1970s and 1980s) to look for evidence of bias. They focused in particular on coverage of workplace **strikes**. They used **detailed content analysis** of **television news bulletins**.

GUMG have a neo-Marxist perspective.

Finding	Examples
The **selection of news** was biased in favour of dominant class values.	**Picket line violence** was **reported more** than police violence.
The **voice-overs** were biased in favour of dominant class values.	**Leading terms** such as "**trouble-makers**" and "**pointless strike**" were used.
Management were given **more access** to the media than strike leaders.	Television interviews with management were **more frequent** and longer than those with strike leaders.
The **filming** and **editing** was biased in favour of the police.	Cameras were often placed **behind police lines** showing the police viewpoint.

The work of the GUMG is used to demonstrate **bias in the news** and in the **values and assumptions** of the people who **produce** and **construct** the news. Their work is **highly respected** because they've studied **a lot of news** in **great detail**. Remember though, this study was done in the 1970s, so think before you start blithely applying it to the news today.

The **image** of the news as **objective** reporting of fact makes this bias more **important** and more **powerful**. When people **think the news is unbiased**, they're **more likely to believe it**.

This is linked to postmodernist ideas about reality, see p.145.

New Media have had an Impact on the Selection and Presentation of News

1) People don't sit down and spend a whole coffee break reading an **online** newspaper — they tend to click on what look like the most **intriguing, juicy headlines**. Editors therefore tend to **select interesting**, **scandalous** or **wacky** stories and present them with a headline that makes them appear **even more** interesting, scandalous or wacky.

2) Audiences can "**have their say**" on news stories via text and email. This **interactivity** seems popular with news editors. They may **select** stories that will **stir up** a big response, and **invite audience response** when **presenting** them.

3) TV news can feature **viewers' own photos** or **video footage** of news events — taken on mobiles and emailed in.

4) An online or TV news provider with a **global audience** has to try to select news items that are globally **relevant**.

There's more about new media on p.146.

News is Influenced by Society — it's Socially Constructed

1) All media sociologists agree the **news is socially constructed** but they disagree over whose values are behind the social construction of news — those of the dominant class or those of the majority of society.

2) From a **pluralist** perspective, **practical constraints** are more significant in influencing the content of the news than ideological bias. The values of journalists are the **common values in society**.

3) From the **Marxist** perspective, the **ideological influences** are most important, and practical constraints can't be separated from ideology. Journalistic values are part of the **dominant ruling class ideology**.

Practice Questions

Q1 Describe what is meant by "news values".
Q2 Explain how the process of gate-keeping takes place in news production.
Q3 Give two examples of ways that new media technology has influenced the presentation of the news.
Q4 What is meant by the term 'socially constructed' in relation to the news?

Exam Question

Q1 'Journalists create rather than discover the news.' To what extent does the sociological theory and evidence you have studied support this viewpoint?
(33 marks)

It's funny how the day's events always exactly fill the newspaper...

You think you know what news is, and then you read these pages. Suddenly, you know a lot more about news, but it isn't so clear-cut any more. News is as much of a social construct as anything else. People choose what to put in the papers and on the telly, and people aren't unbiased and neutral — they're affected by all sorts of social factors, and all sorts of ideas.

Censorship and Violence

All governments control the media to a greater or lesser extent. The media reaches a large section of the population on a regular basis and it's influential in changing behaviour and attitudes — so it's not surprising there's some control and regulation over media content to protect the public from being misled or manipulated.

The **Media** can be **Self-Regulating**

Different branches of the media have different ways of **making sure content and practices** are kept to a **good standard**.

1) In Britain the press is "free". This means all **newspapers** and **magazines** are **commercial**, not funded by the state. There's **no obligation** for the press to be **impartial** or **unbiased** — in fact many daily newspapers **openly support** a particular **political viewpoint**.

2) The press set up their own organisation, the **Press Complaints Commission (PCC)**, to monitor standards and to deal with complaints. The PCC can order newspapers to print apologies if a complaint's been upheld. A **frequent beef** people have with the PCC is that when apologies are printed they're often in tiny print at the bottom of an inside page — even when the initial story was on the front page with a **MASSIVE HEADLINE**.

3) **Broadcast media** (TV and radio) are **more regulated by the government**. They also often publicise **standards of their own** which **their journalists** have to stick to.

The **Media** must **Obey** the **Law**

Both **public** (BBC) and **commercial** broadcasting are subject to **legal guidelines** and **restrictions**.

1) There are **laws** restricting **what can be shown on TV and when**. There is a **"watershed"** of **9pm**. Before 9pm you can't show **nudity**, **sex**, **violence** or **bad language**. After 9pm a **warning** must be given before programmes that have nudity, sex, violence or bad language.

2) UK television is required by law to be **impartial** — unlike the press. For example, in 2004, a public inquiry strongly criticised the **BBC** for its **reporting** of issues relating to **Iraqi weapons of mass destruction** (WMDs). The reporter involved, as well as the Chairman and Director General of the BBC, resigned as a result.

3) In **1989** TV and radio broadcasters were **banned** from using **words spoken by members** of **11 political and paramilitary groups** in **Northern Ireland**, including **Sinn Fein**. The ban was in place for **five years** — during that time the words of Sinn Fein politicians were spoken by **actors**.

4) The **law of libel** makes it **illegal** to make **defamatory** or **damaging** comments about **anyone**. Anyone and any organisation can be **sued** for **writing** (libel) or **saying** (slander) defamatory or damaging comments. This includes newspapers, magazines, internet sites, TV, emails — even repeating comments initially made by someone else. Media providers often use **lawyers** to check **controversial material** before it is printed or broadcast.

Charters and **Legal Contracts** restrain the media

1) The **BBC** was established by a **charter** which all its TV and radio content has to stick to. The BBC has to be **"independent, impartial** and **honest"** at all times.

2) The BBC has to **follow the rules** of its charter to get **funding** from the government. It has 12 **governors** to make sure it sticks to the charter.

3) **Commercial TV and radio broadcasters** don't have to follow this charter. Before they can broadcast they have to get **legal contracts** which tie them to certain standards. These contracts run for several years and are **issued by the government**.

4) In January 2004 **Ofcom** was established as the **new government regulator** to oversee the conduct of **all communications industries**. It deals with complaints and it can **fine** or **close down** broadcasters who break the rules.

After cracking her knee on the desk, South West Tonight's Sheila Green struggled to time-delay a torrent of foul language until after the sport and weather.

Ever heard a presenter **panic** if a guest swears on TV or radio — this is because broadcasters are **heavily fined** for breaking regulations "regarding **standards of taste and decency**". One way to avoid this problem is to broadcast on a **time delay** so you can bleep out the swearing.

The **Power of Advertising** is a **Restraint** on **Commercial Media**

Commercial media outlets need **funds from advertising** to **survive** — they'll always be careful not to have **bad publicity** or content which advertisers don't like. If content doesn't fit with an advertiser's image the media outlet is likely to **adapt the content** rather than **risk** losing the advertiser.

Censorship and Violence

There are **Several Arguments** about **Violence** in the **Media**

Some sociologists argue that violence in the media has an effect on people

1) Early studies by Bandura, Ross and Ross (see p.142) show that children would **copy violent behaviours** they'd seen on film. This is often called "**copycat violence**".

2) Some sociologists say that violence on TV and film **desensitises** viewers to real violence. Seeing violence in the media makes people **less shocked** by violence in **real life**.

Other sociologists disagree with these ideas

1) **Catharsis theory** says that watching violence on screen **gets violent thoughts out of the viewer's system**. Watching a good gore-fest makes you **less likely** to grab a chainsaw and rampage through your own neighbourhood. So said **Feshbach and Singer (1971)** in their study of boys aged 8-18. Boys who watched aggressive and violent TV were less aggressive themselves.

2) **Buckingham (1993)** said that audience members actively interpret film and TV violence, and **make their own minds up** about the rights and wrongs of what they see on screen. Even young kids do this.

3) Some sociologists think that watching violence is a "**rite of passage**" for young people, especially boys. It's a phase they go through to prove they **aren't kids** any more.

4) **Morrison (1999)** makes a really important distinction between **serious, disturbing violence** and **light-hearted comedy violence**. For example, a photo of a prisoner of war getting shot in the back of the head is serious while *Jackass* and the cartoon *South Park* contain light-hearted violence. It's a darn obvious difference when you see it like that, but a lot of research has ignored it.

Cohen (1973) first used the term "**moral panic**" to describe how media reporting identifies something as a **serious threat to society**. **Martin Barker (1984)** analysed a 1980s moral panic about low-budget violent horror films known as "**video nasties**". These videos were **blamed** for violent crime, and the tabloid press predicted an **epidemic of violence** if they weren't banned.

Ferguson (2008) claims that the **generation gap** fuels moral panics about **video games** — most anti-game campaigners are **older** than most gamers, and often have **never played** the games they are complaining about. He says that research linking video games and violent behaviour is **flawed** and even **biased**.

For more on moral panics see page 141.

Censorship of **Violence** in the media is a **Tricky Area**

1) There are clear regulations for public broadcasting which all programmes and films have to follow. Films can't be shown on TV or in cinemas in the UK, or released on video or DVD until they've been **passed by the British Board of Film Classification (BBFC)** and given a **grading** which tells you **how old you have** to be to watch the film — U (Universal), PG (Parental Guidance), 12, 15 or 18.

2) Classification of most **video games** is **voluntary**. Video game producers often choose to submit violent games to the BBFC for classification, as a way of showing that the game is not intended for children. Games containing human sexual activity or extreme violence have to be submitted for classification.

3) Censorship doesn't actually stop material being produced. The **internet** has been used to distribute **violent** and **pornographic** material which would be banned from other media outlets.

Practice Questions

Q1 Explain the difference between public and commercial media.

Q2 Name two legal controls which both public and commercial media have to adhere to.

Q3 What differences are there in how print and broadcast media are regulated?

Q4 Describe the regulatory arrangements for the BBC.

Q5 Explain what Feshbach and Singer (1971) said about the effect on boys of watching violent TV.

Exam Question

Q1 "The media is regulated to protect the public from biased and inappropriate media in Britain today."
Evaluate this statement with reference to at least two forms of media. (33 marks)

TV makes me violent — I have to slap the telly to make it work...

Imagine — TV might be even worse if there weren't any controls or regulation... The question of whether violence on TV makes kids more violent and aggressive is an old one. There are those who say it does, and those who say it doesn't necessarily. Kids can be a lot more clever at telling the difference between real and pretend than you'd think.

Media Representations

The role of the media in representing social groups is very influential. These pages look at the images of particular social groups, how they're formulated and what effect they might have.

Stereotypes *are* Inaccurate Generalisations

Stereotypes are **generalisations** about **social groups**. They are **inaccurate** and often **derogatory** — e.g. "Women can't read maps", "Gay men are camp", "Chinese women are submissive".

Stereotypes *are* Socially Constructed — *often with* Binary Opposition

Binary Opposition means looking at the world in terms of pairs of opposites

1) We like to see the world in terms of **opposites** — e.g. male/female, gay/straight, good/bad.

2) According to **Levi-Strauss (1963)** we apply this system of **binary opposition** to the world in such a subconscious way that it **appears** to be entirely natural. However he suggested that it isn't natural at all — instead the sets of binary opposites have **socially constructed meanings**.

3) Levi-Strauss pointed out that these pairs of binary opposites aren't equal. One half of the pair is culturally marked as being **more positive** than the other. For example, in the binary opposition of male/female, male is culturally determined as positive. It's the dominant half of the pair. Levi-Strauss thought that we subconsciously relate **all binary oppositions** back to the two opposites **good/bad**.

4) The **media** often **perpetuates** these binary oppositions — e.g. by portraying stereotypes of women as caring and men as macho breadwinners.

Defining something as "the other" means saying it's different and foreign — and it implies it's a bit inferior

1) **Edward Said (1978)** suggested that academics in the West define the East as "the other" when they study Eastern culture. He said when they do this, they imply that Eastern culture is somehow inferior to Western culture.

2) A social group can define another group as "other" in order to **promote social cohesion** within their **own** group. It's **them and us**. The media often do this, e.g. in newspaper stories about immigration.

3) The idea of "the other" goes with the idea of **binary opposition**. The **dominant** half of the binary pair is seen as the **normal**, standard, regular version. The half of the binary pair perceived less positively is the **"other"**.

Media Messages *go through* Four Stages *from* Production *to* End Effect

In "sociology speak" this is called the **process of message trajectory**.

Stage 1 — Media Message is formulated by editors

Media messages are **formulated** (put together) by those in **powerful positions** in media institutions. These individuals aren't usually members of the social groups which the media stereotypes. For example, very few media editors are female, disabled, black, working class, openly gay, under 25 or over 65.

Stage 2 — Media Message content reflects groups in power

The content of the media **reflects the values** of the people who **formulate** it. Groups who aren't in power have **limited representation** in the media.

Stage 3 — Media Message is received by the audience

The messages are then **received** by the audience and **interpreted** in different ways — depending on **context** and **experience**.

"Look," said Saskia. "Do you see what I see?"
"Golly," said Rupert. "Working class people on the telly. Whatever will they think of next?"

Stage 4 — Media Message affects the role and treatment of social groups

Opinions and behaviour of **individuals** and **institutions** in society are **influenced** by **messages in the media**. The **impact of the media** depends on how you view the **interaction between media and audience**. It's all very theoretical.

~ There's plenty of detail about this on pages 142-145. ~

You need to **know these four stages** and to be able to give **examples** for the **social groups on the following three pages** (gender stereotypes, class stereotypes, disability stereotypes, ethnic stereotypes, age stereotypes and sexuality stereotypes). You can choose other groups but you'd need to **do your own research** to find your own examples.

Media Representations

Media Messages about Gender are Stereotyped

1) Most **editors** are **men**. **Croteau and Hoynes (2000)** found that in the mid 1990s in the US only 6% of top newspaper management were women and only 20% of top TV management.

2) Women **don't appear on the media as often as men**. Research by **Cumberbatch** (**1990**) found 90% of all advertising voice-overs were male and 66% of all people in adverts were male.

3) Women in the media are often presented as **ideals** for other women to aspire to. **Naomi Wolf (1990)** and **Susan Orbach (1991)** both reckon that the rise in eating disorders in women is a direct result of this.

4) The media tends to portray women in a limited range of roles. **Tuchman (1978)** argued there were only two female roles portrayed in the media: **domestic** and **sexual**. **Ferguson (1983)** researched **women's magazines**, and found they gave **advice and training** on being (stereotypically) **feminine** — i.e. **sexual**, **domestic** and **romantic**.

5) Some advertising portrays men as **incompetent** at the stereotypically female **domestic tasks** of housework and cooking.

6) Women are often represented as **victims** by the media — of sexual violence, domestic violence etc.

7) Action films portray **men** as **violent**, and show male violence in a **positive** way.

8) **Gauntlett (2002)** identified a **change** in media portrayal of masculinity — he found that some **men's magazines** mirrored the format of **women's magazines**, with advice on health, looking good, and attracting the opposite sex.

9) Postmodernists like **Hermes (1995)** think people can **reject media messages** about gender.

Some sociologists say there are Class Stereotypes in the media

1) Media **editors** and **executives** are almost all **middle class**.

2) **Middle class** people **appear on TV** more often than working class people, both on **dramas** and on **news** programmes.

3) **Drama roles** for working class characters are mostly limited to **soap operas**. **Upper class** characters are often seen in **historical costume dramas** — which tend to give a **romantic** picture of life and class.

4) **News** often represents **working class** people as a **source of trouble** — "anti-social behaviour", riots, strikes, crime, etc. From a neo-Marxist standpoint, the **Glasgow University Media Group (1982)** suggest that the media are perpetuating the view that the working class are trouble to ensure the dominance of capitalist ideology (see p.135 for more on this).

Glennon and Butsch (1982) looked at 40 years of families on TV in the USA

They found that only **4% of sitcoms** featured a family where the head of household was a **manual worker**.
In real life, **36%** of American families were like this. Nearly **half** the **TV families** had a **professional** as head of household.
In real life, only 25% were like this. Most of the TV families were wealthy and glamorous.

Glennon and Butsch thought that most **working class dads** were portrayed as **stupid** and **comical**, for the audience to laugh at.

Research from **Medhurst (1999)** showed that when middle class students were shown the programme 'The Royle Family' they thought it was an **accurate** portrayal of **working class life**.

This is <u>their opinion</u>, not necessarily what the TV audience thought.

Stuart Hall (1982, 1992, 1996) thinks that the media has always portrayed the **middle classes** in a **positive** light and the **working class** in a **negative** light. He says that the media has reinforced people's class identities — which keeps the divide between the classes going strong.

Practice Questions

Q1 Write a summary of the four stages of a media message in no more than four sentences.

Q2 Give two examples of social groups which have been identified as being subject to stereotyped media portrayal.

Q3 List two pieces of research which illustrate the argument that the media is a patriarchal institution.

Q4 What are Stuart Hall's views about the portraying of class by the media?

Exam Question

Q1 With reference to sociological studies, assess the view that the mass media is biased in its portrayal of women. (18 marks)

Learn the studies — you'll need them...

Remember, it's not just women who are stereotyped by the media. Men are also portrayed in a limited way, which tends to be as a strong, capable breadwinner. Most dramas which contain violence generally portray men as the aggressors, and they're more likely to be shown as criminals too. So, if a question asks about gender stereotypes, remember to talk about men as well as women.

Media Representations

The media sends out stereotypes about disabled people, ethnic minorities, young people, old people and gay people. That's a lot of people.

Disabled people are Under-represented in the media

1) Disabled people are **poorly represented** in **powerful positions** in the media. Those who do hold powerful positions tend to have specialised in disabled issues — e.g. Peter White, the radio journalist.

2) There's really **very little representation of disabled people** in the media at all. Government statistics show that about 20% of the adult population has some form of disability, yet the Broadcasting Standards Commission (1999) reported that people with disabilities only appeared in **7% of television programmes** and had only **0.75% of all speaking roles**.

3) **Roles** for disabled people are very **limited**. Research by **Cumberbatch and Negrine (1992)** looking at British television over six weeks found the roles for disabled people were based on **pity** or **comedy**. They found that **disabled actors** never appeared **just as actors** playing a person who **just happened to have a disability**, only in **roles particularly about disability**. However, there are **some positive portrayals** of disabled people in films and on TV — e.g. of deafness in *Four Weddings and a Funeral*.

4) **Audience response** depends on people's **actual experience** of disability. Cumberbatch and Negrine researched audience responses as part of their study. They concluded that people with limited or **no real-life experience** of disability **accepted** the media images with **little concern**. People **with experience** of disability were **critical** of the media and **rejected** stereotyped images.

Media representations of Ethnicity are often Stereotyped

1) New technology means there are more satellite and digital TV channels. Lots of small specialised channels have developed. Many of these **cater for specific ethnic minorities** and they're managed and controlled by people from those ethnic minorities (e.g. Zee TV, Bangla TV, Punjabi TV). However, there aren't many people from ethnic minorities in positions of **power** in **mainstream media**.

2) **The Broadcasting Standards Commission (1999)** found that terrestrial and satellite television portrayed ethnic minorities in **42% of programmes**, and ethnic minorities made up 7% of all people with speaking parts. However, the range of roles was **restricted**. The highest percentage representation was in **children's programmes**.

3) A government report **'Viewing the World' (2000)** suggests that media coverage of less economically developed countries (LEDCs) often tends to portray them as **starving** or in **conflict**. The stereotype here is that people in those countries are unable to solve their problems and need the West to "**rescue**" them.

4) Tabloid newspapers sometimes stereotype some ethnic minority groups as being a **problem** or a **threat**. **Van Dijk (1991)** made a detailed content analysis of **headlines** in five British national newspapers. He argued that there was often an **association** in the headlines between **ethnic minorities** and **violent** and **negative language**.

5) Media portrayal of ethnic minorities can also be part of a media representation of **multiculturalism** (e.g. TV and newspaper coverage of the Notting Hill carnival). Some representations of multiculturalism are **utopian** (i.e. suggesting that everything's perfect) and some admit there are problems, e.g. *Bend It Like Beckham*.

6) **Cottle (2000)** points out that media portrayals of ethnic minorities reinforce views of non-whites as the "**other**" (see page 138). He also criticises media portrayals of multiculturalism, saying that they gloss over problems such as power imbalances between different ethnic groups, and the historical effects of colonialism and racism.

7) **Audience response** to ethnic minority stereotypes varies depending on the **real-life experience** of the audience. People don't swallow media stereotypes if they know better themselves.

Hartmann and Husband (1974) analysed children's response to media

They compared the responses of children in two parts of Britain and found that in the **area with low ethnic mix**, children **believed negative media content** and thought of "race relations" in terms of conflict. In the **area with a high ethnic mix**, children **rejected media stereotypes** in favour of their own experience.

Media Representations

Images of Young and Old are Stereotyped in the media

1) The **people with power** in media organisations tend to be **older**. It takes **time** to get **experience**, so this makes sense.

2) There's often a sexist **double standard** in the way older people are represented in the media. The **older** a **woman** gets, the **less likely** she is to get a leading film role or a TV presenting job. It's a different story for men. In films, older male actors like Sean Connery and Harrison Ford are "allowed" to be romantically paired with cute young women. There are lots more **older men presenting TV programmes** than there are older women.

3) **Biggs (1993)** focused on entertainment programmes and found lots of representation of older people. However, they were often in stereotyped roles of "forceful", "vague" and "difficult" — especially in sitcoms. In America, **Signorelli (1989)** studied television characters and found that both young and old were under-represented on prime-time television. TV was biased towards **middle-aged** people.

4) **Featherstone and Hepworth (1995)** found that magazines aimed at older people tended to push an image of "youthful" old people — enjoying holidays and sports, wearing fashionable, "young-looking" clothes, etc.

5) There are also **stereotypes** relating to **young people**. **Children** are represented as **innocent**. Slightly older "**youth**" are often seen as a **social problem** — prone to drug abuse, binge drinking, petty crime and unplanned pregnancy.

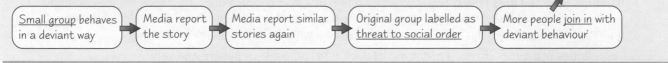

Stan Cohen (1973) described how **media reporting** of expected "trouble" could **create a moral panic**.

Moral panic — public demands that something is done about it

Small group behaves in a deviant way → Media report the story → Media report similar stories again → Original group labelled as threat to social order → More people join in with deviant behaviour

Cohen used the example of the **Mods and Rockers** in the 1960s. The media reported that there would be **fights** between two youth subcultures — the Mods and the Rockers. Lots of people turned up to fight or watch, partly because of the **media publicity**. The public then **panicked** over reports of how many people turned up to fight.

You can easily find **contemporary** examples of a moral panic — e.g. the concern over trouble at **So Solid Crew** gigs. The possibility of **gun violence** led to some shows being cancelled because **media reporting** of the concern led to **panic**.

The Mods and Rockers struggled to make contact amongst the horde of onlookers.

Representations of Sexuality in the media are Stereotyped

1) Gay men are often stereotyped as "**camp**". TV shows often use "camp" gay characters as **comic relief**.

2) Homosexual relationships and heterosexual relationships are shown differently in the media. For example, much more explicit heterosexual sex is shown on television than homosexual sex. **Coronation Street** and **EastEnders** have both had storylines involving a **gay kiss** which got widespread media attention. You don't get any outcry in the papers when a **man and a woman** kiss on a soap opera.

3) There was a **political** aspect to early **media reporting** of **HIV/AIDS**. It was initially openly characterised as a "gay disease". A tabloid newspaper headline in the 1980s referred to AIDS as a "gay plague". However, according to **Cricher (2003)**, later representation of AIDS and gay men changed from the anti-gay message to a safe sex message.

Practice Questions

Q1 Briefly explain the findings of Cumberbatch and Negrine (1992) about disabled people and the media.
Q2 Give an example of newspaper bias in relation to ethnic minorities in Britain.
Q3 How does real-life experience affect how people respond to stereotypes in the media?

Exam Question

Q1 Assess the view that the media are biased in their representation of ethnic minorities. (33 marks)

Learn these studies... in fact learn ALL the studies... in the world... EVER...

If you do a question on media audiences and ethnicity, disability, age or sexuality, you have to be prepared to mention some sociological studies to back up your points. It's the only way to get the marks. The stuff on these pages makes you think a bit. British society, and the media especially, has a way to go before it treats everyone equally.

Mass Media and its Audience

The media constructs and sends out messages to the public — but the impact of the messages depends on how the audience responds. People can accept media messages, or dismiss them as complete rubbish.

The **Hypodermic Syringe** Model — Media **Directly Influences Audience**

Way back in the **1920s**, when **radio** and **newspapers** were just starting to get **important** in society, sociologists developed theories about how the media affected people.

1) The **hypodermic syringe model** says the media **injects** its message into the mind of the audience in the same way as drugs are **directly injected** into the body. The idea is that the media is **so powerful**, its message **directly influences** the individual and they're **powerless** to **resist** the message or **reject** it.

2) This theory says that **all individuals** in the audience are **affected** in the **same way**.

> In **1938**, Orson Welles recorded a radio production of H G Wells' story *The War of the Worlds* in which Martians invade Earth. The broadcast included fictional news bulletins reporting the Martian invasion. Some radio listeners believed the fake bulletins were true, and panicked. This was used as evidence of the dangerous and direct power of the media, and it created concern in society. For the people who believed in the hypodermic syringe model it was proof enough.

3) Some sociologists decided that the hypodermic syringe model was **too simplistic** to explain how adults view media content. It did stay popular as a theory of how the **media** can **influence children**, though.

4) **Bandura, Ross and Ross (1963)** played children a **film of a man hitting a doll**. They then left the children to play with the **same doll** which they'd seen on the film. The children who'd seen the violence on film hit the doll, while those who hadn't seen the film played with the doll in a non-violent way.

> Critics of the hypodermic syringe model think it treats people as **passive** and very easily led. They also point out that **not all audience members react in the same way** to the same piece of media. Studies showed this as far back as the 1920s.

> Don't assume that this theory is dead in the water. Think about the concern that fictional TV and film violence can cause violent acts in society. In 1993, two boys were convicted of killing two-year-old James Bulger when they were ten years old. When the judge was summing up he said that "exposure to violent video films may in part be an explanation" for the boys' actions. Media reporting of the murder case created a moral panic about violence in films and the effect of the media on children. Barker (2001) criticised this panic, and pointed out that there was no actual evidence to show that the two child murderers had actually seen the video in question.

The Media Message is **Interpreted** and **Passed On** by **Key Individuals**

The **two-step flow model** was developed in the 1950s. It says that the media does influence people, but **not everyone is influenced directly**.

> 1) The **first step** is the **media message** reaching an audience member. All simple so far.
>
> 2) The important **second step** is how their **understanding** of the message is **shaped** by **social interaction** with other audience members. For example, if workers in an office chat about a soap opera during their coffee break then these discussions affect individuals' opinions of the storyline and characters.
>
> 3) **Katz and Lazarsfeld (1955)** said that there were **key individuals** in each community whose reaction **directly influenced others**. These "**opinion leaders**" openly expressed their reaction and opinions, and others **followed** their lead. Katz and Lazarsfeld studied **media influence on American voters**. They concluded that most people followed the opinion leader's views on who they should vote for, but the opinion leaders themselves often got their **ideas straight from the mass media** messages.
>
> 4) It doesn't have to be just two steps — a message can go through several stages of interpretation. **Hobson (1990)** studied an office environment and found that a few **key individuals** influenced what the others watched on television and their **reactions** to the programmes. These opinions were **passed on** to another bunch of colleagues. A **social norm** of what to watch **spread** through the **whole office**. **New recruits** had to **conform** to fit in.

Did you see X Factor?

It's easy to imagine this happening in a school or a workplace: "Did you see Big Brother?" "Isn't she such a COW?" "He loves himself, doesn't he?". If you don't watch the programme, you're left out of the conversation. If you don't agree with the ~~big-mouth~~ opinion leader, you're made to feel a bit of an outsider.

Mass Media and its Audience

Social and Cultural Context affect how an Audience Responds to the Media

1) The **Cultural Effects theory** introduced the idea that **social context** is important when looking at the effects of the media. In short, it claims that **different people** interpret the media in **different ways**.

2) The idea is that an audience **interprets the media** in the **context** of the **culture** they already belong to. This means that the effect of the media is quite complex — it's not the same for everyone.

3) "**Culture**" refers to the **small, subcultural groups** an individual belongs to and also to the **wider, general culture of society**. For example, in England an individual's response to Arsenal winning the Premiership will **depend** on whether the **individual** supports Arsenal. But audience response to media reports of **England winning the World Cup** would be broadly **similar** for most of the population because there's a **cultural norm** of supporting your country's sports teams.

> Here's a **second look** at the audience response to the *War of the Worlds* broadcast — this time from a **cultural effects viewpoint (Cantril, 1940)**.
>
> 1) The response was **caused** by the **cultural context** in which it was heard. If it was on the radio **today** it wouldn't create the same response.
>
> 2) At the time of the broadcast there was **insecurity** in American society because of a **financial crisis** and the move towards **war in Europe**. Radio programmes were **frequently interrupted for news reports**, and there was a general expectation of bad news.
>
> 3) People **wouldn't have been surprised** to hear a **real report** of bad news interrupting a drama programme on the radio. This made it **more likely** that some members of the audience would **believe** the story.

We interrupt this A2 Sociology Revision Guide...

The neo-Marxist **Stuart Hall (1980)** argued that the media has **dominant ideological** messages '**encoded**' into it, but that people of different backgrounds can, to an extent, '**decode**' these messages in different ways — with varying degrees of **agreement** or **opposition** to the ideology expressed.

The Effects of media messages Build Up Over Time

1) Media effects can build up over time to **create** or **reinforce** cultural **norms**.

2) For example, **images of women** in the media create **stereotypical images** and place **expectations** on girls and women. There's been a long-running campaign by some feminists to remove pictures of **topless women** ("Page Three Girls") from national newspapers, because they argue that these images reinforce the dominant view that it's OK to objectify women as sex objects.

3) Some theorists think it's not just the **content** of the media that has a long-term effect on society — the **technology** of the media has an impact on society too. E.g. internet technology has transformed the way people communicate, shop, apply for jobs, etc. **Marshall McLuhan (1964,** *Understanding Media* New York: McGraw-Hill**)** claimed that media technology actually had a **greater effect** on society than media content.

4) It's **difficult** to **objectively measure** long-term media effects, so the discussion of long-term effects is mostly theoretical.

> The big catchphrase to remember from McLuhan is "**The medium is the message**".

Practice Questions

Q1 Briefly explain the hypodermic syringe model of media influence.

Q2 In which study did psychologists show children a film of a person hitting a doll?

Q3 Define the two steps in the two-step flow model of media influence.

Q4 Explain what's meant by the term "opinion leader"

Q5 Briefly explain cultural effects theory.

Q6 Explain what is meant by the statement: "the medium is the message".

Exam Question

> Q1 Evaluate the claim that audiences are passive in their response to media messages, with reference to at least two sociological theories.
>
> (18 marks)

The hypodermic syringe model — it gets right under your skin...

You read one theory and think, "ah, that explains it", then you read the next theory and think, "ah, that explains it" — and they're two totally contradictory theories, so they can't both be right. I suppose they can both be right some of the time, or they can give you a part of the picture. The most important thing is that you can write about them in the exam.

Mass Media and its Audience

Here's more about how people interpret what they see and hear from the mass media. Some sociologists think people can be quite active in deciding what media messages they want to see and hear.

Audiences *Actively Use* and *Interpret* the Media to *Suit Their Own Needs*

Some theories argue that the audience responds **actively** to media content and messages.
There's a switch from "what the **media** does **to** people" to "what **people** do **with** the media".

Uses and Gratifications Theory

1) This theory was developed by theorists such as **Blumler and Katz (1974)** and says that people **use** the media to **meet their needs**. The audience **actively chooses** what media to experience, using such cutting-edge tools as free will and the remote control. Everyone chooses for themselves, so each person's media diet is **unique**.

2) A good example is the study of **soap opera audiences** by **McQuail (1972)**. He looked at how audiences used **Coronation Street** to fulfil a need for **social companionship**. Many audiences felt part of the characters' lives and felt interest and concern for what would happen next in a storyline.

3) **Lull (1990)** listed the social uses of television in the UK — and found men, women, young and old all used the media to meet different needs.

4) Uses and gratification theory is **functionalist** — it says the media exists to serve the **needs** of the public.

> In media language "to engage with" a piece of media means to find it interesting and pay attention to it — to be "into" it.

Selective Filter Model

1) This theory says the audience **choose** which media to **experience** and also **control** which parts of the media message to pay attention to and **engage with**. The audience pick out the parts of a message which **fit in with their view of the world** and **ignore the rest**.

2) **Fiske (1988)** says individuals become very **experienced readers of the media**. He says that individuals can understand one **"media text"** in several **different ways** on several **different levels** — and in relation to other **"media texts"** on the same subject.

3) **Klapper (1960)** argued that to get its message across, the media has to go through **three selective filters: selective exposure** — people only consume the media they want and are able to get, **selective perception** — people ignore messages they don't want to hear, and **selective retention** — people tend to remember only what they agree with. Klapper argued that this means it's easier for the media to **reinforce** what people think than to **change** their minds about something.

> "Media text" means a piece of media — a TV programme, a newspaper article, a magazine article, an advert. Academics really like to call things "texts" for some reason. Oh well, if it makes them happy...

4) This model emphasises the **power of the individual** to control his / her experience of the media and says that people use media in a **sophisticated** way. It's kinda postmodern in that way. However, it's been criticised for **overestimating** the control of the individual over very **powerful media messages**.

Structured Interpretation Model

1) This theory says there's a **dominant interpretation** of media messages which audiences go along with. Like the other two theories, individuals actively **pick** which media they **engage with**, but this theory says the process takes place in a **social context**. The social context creates a **"preferred reading"** of the media message (by "reading" they mean "interpretation"). For example, a film is written, presented and promoted with a **preferred reading** in mind — the makers of a film like *Slumdog Millionaire* want you to find the love story **moving** and **convincing**, not stilted and laughable.

2) **Different social groups** have **different dominant interpretations** of the same text. So, this theory isn't the same as earlier theories which saw the audience as a mass who all respond in the same way.

3) **Morley (1980)** studied how the television audience responded to one **news programme** — *Nationwide*. He showed the same programme to several **different social groups** and found that their responses to the programme **varied** hugely, **but within each group** most **individuals responded in the same way**. Trade unionists saw it as biased towards management, and management trainees saw it as pro-union.

Mass Media and its Audience

Postmodern Theory says the audience gets Lots of Meanings

1) **Postmodernists** say that there are **many, many meanings** to any social or cultural aspect of life. They say there **isn't any aspect of life** where there's one single, objective **truth** or **reality** that absolutely everyone experiences.

2) The **postmodern audience picks** and **chooses** between a range of images, messages, ideas and meanings.

Postmodern Theory also says the Media Takes the Place of Reality

1) The development of the mass media and technology have meant everyday life is **chock-full of images** and messages competing and **conflicting** with each other. The media presents so many different images and stories **woven into everyday life** that the boundary between **reality and the media** is **blurred** — the **media becomes reality**.

> The explosion of **reality TV** and the **obsessive interest** people have with **soap stars** are good examples of this. With **reality TV, real** people get put in an **unreal situation** which is presented as **real**, and the audience follows it like a **soap**. With a soap, **pretend** characters get treated by the press and by audiences **as if they're real**.
>
> There's an example with **news media** — when something's on the news, it seems like that **"proves"** it's real and true. Images on the news can be taken out of context, though. And news is **influenced** by all kinds of factors (see pages 134-135). The news isn't **objective truth**. But the news is presented as reality, and **becomes reality**.

2) This idea is related to a philosophical idea of a thing called a **simulacrum**. A simulacrum is something that **looks real**, but **isn't**. It's like a copy but **without any kind of connection** to the **original**. Postmodernist theorists say that these simulacra actually replace reality.

Postmodernism can kind of make your head swim.

3) French postmodernist **Jean Baudrillard (1981, 1994)** suggested that **everything** had been replaced by simulacra. He called this replacement of reality **hyperreality** — he said that hyperreal images seemed **more real than real** and that meant they took over from reality. He suggested that **obviously made-up images** were used to give people the impression that they could **tell reality from a simulacrum** when in fact they **couldn't**.

> "Disneyland is presented as imaginary in order to make us believe that the rest is real, when in fact Los Angeles and the America surrounding it are no longer real, but belong to the hyperreal." — Jean Baudrillard (1994 *Simulacra and Simulation* Ann Arbor: University of Michigan Press, originally published in French 1981).

4) In *The Gulf War Did Not Take Place*, **Baudrillard (1995)** argued that the 1991 Gulf War existed more as images on TV screens than as actual fighting. The Gulf War as media **spectacle** or video game type **simulation** became reality.

5) In the media a piece of information or an image can be **distorted** intentionally in order to **make it appear correct** to viewers. So it's actually **made less true** in order to **appear more true**.

Critics say Postmodernism's too Theoretical and too Obscure

Postmodernism is criticised for being too theoretical. It's really **hard to find** (or even think of) any kind of **evidence** which would **prove** postmodernism **right** or **wrong**. I mean, if you're starting out from the premise that no idea has a straightforward meaning and individuals create their own reality so that there's no one definition of what's 'real' or 'true' and that reality has been replaced with something that just looks a lot like it — *where on earth do you go from there...*

Critics of Baudrillard say his writing is **deliberately obscure**, and that it **dismisses** the reality of **suffering** and **inequality**.

Practice Questions

Q1 What do sociologists mean when they refer to an audience actively responding to the media content?

Q2 Give an example of a criticism of the selective filter model of audience response.

Q3 Explain the term "preferred reading" in relation to the media.

Q4 What are simulacra?

Exam Question

Q1 'Media audiences actively select and filter the content and messages they receive.' To what extent do the sociological theories and evidence you have studied support this viewpoint? (33 marks)

Whenever I fancy feeling like I've shoved my head in a blender...

... with an Amazon tree frog and a shot of ouzo, I read some postmodernism. There is kind of a point behind it, though. If you limit it to "people treat media images as if they're real when they're not" and "it's hard to tell images from reality" it's not so bad. Having said that, I dare you to read Baudrillard in the original, or Jacques Lacan or Jacques Derrida. I double dog dare you.

New Media

New technologies like digital TV, the internet, blogging and new fancypants mobile phones are changing how we communicate and how we consume media images and messages.

New Media has Grown Massively — here are some Statistics

1) In 2001/02, **49%** of UK households had a computer. In 2007, it was **70%**.

2) **61%** of **UK households** had **internet access** in 2007 — up from 57% in 2006. In 2007, the proportion of adults who accessed the internet every day or almost every day was 67%. This was up from **59%** since 2006.

3) The proportion of households with a **satellite**, **cable** or other **digital TV** receiver increased from 43% in 2001/02 to 70% in 2006 and to 77% in 2007. By **2012**, **all UK households** will **have** to be digital if they want to watch TV.

4) There is **inequality of access** to the new media. For example, in 2007 **97%** of households in the **highest income group** owned a home computer and 95% had an internet connection. This is in comparison to the **lowest income** group where **35%** of households owned a home computer and 24% had an internet connection.

All these lovely stats are from the National Statistics Omnibus Survey.

New Media appears to offer More Choice

1) **Digital multichannel TV** offers **hundreds** of channels, both UK-based and foreign. Some are subscription-based, others are free to watch. There are channels broadcasting to 'niche' markets — e.g. DIY, motor sport, shopping.

2) However, **Negrine (1994)** suggests that broadcasters fill their channels with cheap imported programmes which are constantly repeated, which actually **reduces** consumer choice.

3) There are hundreds of **news websites** from all over the world. You can get more news than ever before, and you can **compare and contrast** how one story is presented in different places. Some news stories are **exactly the same** on lots of websites, where several news providers have used the **same press release** or the **same news agency feed**.

4) There's tons of **user-generated content** on the internet — photos, blogs, videos, etc. Even user-generated content can be a bit samey, like when you get a link to the same cute kitten video from **everyone on the bloomin' internet**.

> The sheer **amount** of new media content and the **global** nature of new media makes **regulation and control difficult**. It's hard for a state to regulate the content of **foreign digital channels**. Regulation of the internet is extremely hard.

Consumers can become Producers of New Media

1) Anyone can publish their thoughts and opinions on a **blog** (short for web log) for other people to read and comment on. A few popular blogs about celebrity gossip, and some blogs about politics, are very **influential**. Twitter is like a blog but all posts are limited to 140 characters in length. So it's called "microblogging". Cute.

2) **Wikipedia®** is a **user-written**, **user-edited** encyclopedia. **Anyone** can edit Wikipedia® articles — so anyone can insert completely **made-up garbage** into an article. You just have to hope that any rubbish gets **edited out again**.

3) People can submit homemade videos to sites like **YouTube**, for anyone to watch. New **mobile phone technology** makes it easy to take video and upload it straight to YouTube, or email it.

4) In *We Media*, **Bowman and Willis (2003)** describe **citizen journalism** as the public "playing an active role in the process of collecting, reporting, analyzing and disseminating news and information" — this can mean taking **photos** and video and posting them on the internet, or posting **analysis** of news and its coverage on a **blog**.

> **Web 2.0** is a trendy term for the way that web design and development have evolved to make communication and networking easier on the internet. Web 2.0 sites make it easy for users to **search** for content, **add** content and **"tag"** existing content. **Social networking websites** such as **Facebook®** and **photo album sites** are good examples of Web 2.0.

People also socialise on the internet by using **virtual worlds**, e.g. Second Life®, and games like World of Warcraft®. Postmodernist **Turkle (1996)** reckons that individuals can relate to a **simulated virtual world** as easily as they can to **real life**.

Old Media have taken Advantage of New Media — this is called Convergence

1) Producers of **traditional commercial media content** such as **music** and **film** use the internet to advertise and market their products, and **sell** their products online both as "hard copy" and as a digital **download**.

2) Big "old media" companies **form partnerships** with new media companies, e.g. NBC partnered Microsoft® to form the **MSNBC** online news service — or **buy** new media companies, e.g. News Corporation bought **myspace®**

3) **Broadcasters** can interact with their audience through **social networking** and microblogging sites.

4) News organisations make use of **citizen journalism** by asking the public to send in their stories, photos and video. It actually stops being pure citizen journalism then, and becomes **collaborative journalism**.

Globalisation and Popular Culture

The global nature of the media has an effect on society. This all links back to the Culture/Identity AS module.

The **Media** is a **Global Industry** and creates a **Global Culture**

1) There has been **concentration of media ownership** — a few media corporations dominate the global market. See p.130-131.

2) **Devereux (2003)** points out that most of the large media corporations are based in the West, so images from **Western** societies **dominate** the global media market.

3) **McBride (1980)** suggests that there is **media imperialism** — Western media products flow into less developed parts of the world and **change local cultures**. This makes a **ready market** for Western consumer goods. People in many parts of the world share the **same consumption patterns** as the result of **global advertising** from companies such as Disney, Sony, Coca-Cola® and Virgin. **Klein (2000)** says there's increasing **cultural homogenisation** — everyone's culture is becoming the **same**.

> **Global mass media has created a "global village"**
>
> 1) The idea of the **global village** comes from **McLuhan (1962)**. He suggests that new technologies bring people closer together — our neighbours aren't just next door, they're on the **other side of the world**.
>
> 2) We hear **news and gossip** about people all over the world, and we can **talk to people** all over the world. Remember — at the time McLuhan was actually writing, this was only on the **phone**, but **new media** technologies like email and blogs are a great example of his ideas.

4) Some theorists claim that globalisation is specifically **Americanisation** — it's American culture that gets copied.

5) However **Sreberny-Mohammadi (1996)** suggests that many local cultures have **resisted media imperialism**. She points out the strong and **growing media industry** in Asia and South America which actually **exports media products** back to the West — e.g. **Bollywood** films influence Western culture, and Brazilian soap operas are sold to TV stations all over North America, South America and Europe. Also, it is in the interests of a Western media owner to **promote local cultures** to gain **bigger audiences** and even secure the approval of the local **government**.

Media Culture is Popular Culture — some say the media is "Dumbed Down"

1) Culture can be divided into **high** and **low** culture. High culture is seen as "good" for society — the division of culture is often considered an elitist **binary opposition**. Other theorists refer to **mass culture**, which is passed on by the **media**.

2) **Popular culture** is another way of looking at the culture of the "masses". Some theorists prefer it as it's a more positive term than low culture. Also, the idea of popular culture is based on an **active audience** who can shape their culture, unlike the concept of **mass culture** which relies on a **passive media-controlled audience**.

1) There's a debate about **"dumbing down"** in the media — simplifying content and avoiding intellectually challenging the audience. For example, the news contains more sensationalism and celebrity gossip than it used to.

2) Popular classical artists such as Katherine Jenkins, Il Divo, etc. can be seen as popularising high culture and bringing it into mainstream popular culture — or as replacing high culture with a dumbed down mass culture substitute.

3) The dumbing down argument isn't new — back in 1869, Matthew Arnold feared that high culture was under threat.

4) Pluralists argue that audiences get the media they want. So dumbing down can't be the fault of the media.

5) Frank Furedi (2004) claims that intentionally simplifying cultural content is itself an elitist activity — it's not done by the "masses" but done for them, and it assumes that they are too stupid to understand complex content.

Practice Questions

Q1 Give two examples of new media.

Q2 Roughly what proportion of households have a satellite, cable or other digital receiver?

Q3 What did McLuhan (1962) mean by a global village?

Q4 What do the terms high culture and popular culture mean? Give an example of each.

Exam Questions

Q1 'The development of new media has led to increased choice for all.'
To what extent do the sociological theories and evidence you have studied support this view? (33 marks)

Q2 Assess the view that media globalisation is damaging indigenous cultures. (33 marks)

There'll be no dumbing down around here...

Hmmm. These arguments about dumbing down sound a lot like the old arguments about high culture versus low culture. I mean, who's to say that people shouldn't watch Britain's Got Talent instead of a performance by the Royal Ballet anyway...

The Nature and Distribution of Power

Power is a tricky beast. Different theorists think power comes in different varieties. And it's not only governments or states that hold power — businesses, individuals, transnational corporations and the media all do too.

Power *is about the ability to* Control *and* Influence

The pluralist **R A Dahl** (**1961** *Who Governs?*, New Haven: Yale University Press) gives this **definition** of power: "**A** has **power** over **B** to the extent that s/he can **get B** to **do something** s/he **wouldn't otherwise have done.**"

This is a **useful starting point** for understanding power. From this definition of power, you can see that power relationships can involve processes such as **coercion** (**force**), **manipulation**, **bargaining** or **persuasion**. You also need to think about this definition in terms of **society as a whole** and the way that **some social groups** and **institutions** have **power over others**.

Authority *is* Legitimate Power

Most sociologists agree that there's a **difference** between **power** and **authority**. **Authority** suggests a sort of power relationship which is **accepted** by the people who are ruled over — they give their **consent**. It's useful to remember the phrase "**authority is legitimate power**".

E.g., most drivers obey **traffic lights**. This isn't because anyone directly **coerces** us — there's no one standing over us with a gun. It's because we know the **law** says we must stop at a red light, and we recognise the **authority** of the law, and know that the law is sensible, so we obey it. We give our **consent** to the government that makes laws governing the rules of the road.

Max Weber *said there are* Three Types *of* Authority

1) Charismatic	People give their **consent** to a **charismatic leader** because of the leader's **exceptional qualities**. The leader inspires great **loyalty** and **devotion**. **Religious** leaders are often charismatic. Examples of charismatic leaders might include: Napoleon, Gandhi, Barack Obama and Fidel Castro.	
2) Traditional	People give their **consent** because they **always have**. Established customs and practices are seen as "right" because they've always been that way. For instance, a traditional society might accept their elders as rulers because the elders have always been the rulers of the society.	
3) Rational legal	People give their **consent** to an **impersonal legal framework** (a set of rules). The rules are **rational** because they **make sense** and have a particular and **obvious aim**. A modern example would be stopping at a red light to avoid vehicle crashes.	

These types are **ideals** — pure theoretical ideas. Weber suggested that in **real life**, authority could be a **mixture** of these "ideal" types. So in our traffic light example, Jim Random might obey them because it's part of a **legal system** of understandable rules (rational legal), because we've **always** obeyed them (traditional), and because he **loves** the Prime Minister (charismatic).

Stephen Lukes *has a* Radical *view* — *he says there are* Three Faces *of* Power

1) Decision-making	The power to **make** and **implement decisions** which **affect other people**.
2) Non decision-making	The power to **set agendas** — i.e. **limit** what's being **discussed**. If a topic isn't even discussed, **no decision** can be made about it.
3) Shaping desires	The power to manipulate what people **think they want** — powerful groups can make people think they **want** or **consent to** something which actually **harms their interests**.

Lukes suggests that the **third face of power** (shaping desires) is the strongest, because it's never questioned. He suggests that power is exercised **invisibly** by controlling what people **want**. This is related to the idea of **Marcuse (1964)** that capitalism creates **false needs** — things that people **don't really need**, but **think** they do.

Karl Marx *said only* One Group *holds power in society* — *the* Bourgeoisie

1) **Karl Marx (1818-1883)** believed that power in society is **finite** (in other words there's only so much of it), and that it can only be held by **one person** or **group** at a time. This view of power is called the **Zero Sum Model**.

2) Marx saw society in terms of social classes **competing** for power. Under capitalism, the **capitalist** class (**bourgeoisie**) hold **all the power** and use it to their advantage and to the detriment of the **working class** (**proletariat**).

3) Marxists tend to reject the idea of authority as legitimate power, suggesting that the working class are **falsely persuaded** to consent to the rule of the capitalist class. They saw authority as just **disguised power**.

4) Marxist sociologist **Miliband (1969)** suggests that **political power** is held by the same class who hold **economic power**.

5) **Neo-Marxists** like **Gramsci (1971)** emphasise the power of **ideas** in perpetuating capitalism. Bourgeois **'hegemony'** (see p.99) turns bourgeois ideas and values into the '**common sense**' of the age. This means the working class **consent** to the **power** of the bourgeoisie over them.

The Nature and Distribution of Power

Elite Theorists *see society as ruled by a small, powerful* Elite

1) **Classical elite theorists** like **Vilfredo Pareto (1848-1923)** and **Gaetano Mosca (1858-1941)** saw society as divided between the rulers (**the elite**) and the ruled. The **elite** take all the **important decisions** in society and these decisions are almost always in their **own interest**. So far, they agreed with the Marxist viewpoint.

2) The big difference between elite theorists and Marxists is that the elite theorists thought **elite domination** was **desirable**, **inevitable** and **natural**. They said the elite become the elite because they are **better** than the rest of us. They saw the **rest of society** as a disorganised and apathetic **rabble**. This is **very different to Marxists** who thought that elite domination was unfair and exploitative.

1) In a more **modern** and **radical** study of the power of elites, **C Wright Mills (1959)** studied three important institutions in American society — the **business community**, the **military** and the **government**.

2) Mills claimed that the elite in all three institutions formed a **single ruling elite**, which he called the **power elite**. Military, industrial and political power were all intertwined in the power elite.

3) He concluded that **unelected elites** sharing the same **social background** dominate American society and run economic and foreign policy in their own interests. Mills argued that the power elite **weren't accountable** to the people. He saw **little difference** between American political parties, so no chance to vote for **alternative** policies.

Statistics show the **majority** of British **MPs**, high ranking **civil servants** and **business leaders** come from the same **social** and **educational** background — this phenomenon has been referred to as the "**Establishment**".

In a study of top decision-makers, **Lupton and Wilson (1973)** found that connections between them were strengthened by close **marital** and **kinship ties**. Strong internal ties within the elite group make it harder for outsiders to break in.

Functionalists *and* Pluralists *see power as* Dispersed *through society*

1) **Pluralist R A Dahl (1961)** found that instead of one elite group dominating society and hogging all the power, there were actually "**multiple centres of power**" — lots of small groups competing for power. Pluralists believe that all sorts of political parties and interest groups can have **power** over political **decision-making**.

2) **Functionalists** believe that the amount of power in society can **increase** or **decrease** depending on how many people see it as legitimate. This is the **Variable Sum Model**. Pluralists mostly believe the amount of power is **constant**.

3) Pluralists are **criticised** for focusing on only the **first** of Lukes' **faces of power** — the power to make decisions.

Postmodernists *claim that* Power *is related to* Knowledge

1) The philosopher **Foucault (1967)**, who was linked to postmodernism and poststructuralism, argued that power is to be found in all **social relationships**, and is closely linked to **knowledge**. Power and knowledge are linked, with any extension of power involving a corresponding extension of knowledge, and vice versa.

2) Foucault suggests that it's always possible to **resist** power by **questioning** the knowledge it's based on — he gives the example of a psychiatric patient **questioning the validity** of a psychiatrist's diagnosis.

3) Foucault argued that to **understand power** we need to look at its expressions in the **everyday activity** of people, rather than just its relationship to **class** (Marxism) or **politics** (elite theories).

The 'British Ceramics' course Bernard took had had no impact on his personal best.

Lyotard (1984) sees postmodernist politics as being about a **loss of faith** in **big political ideologies** that say what society should be like (see p.157 for more). Lyotard sees power as belonging to whoever has the most **useful knowledge** — individuals, corporations, governments, etc.

Practice Questions

Q1   What is the difference between power and authority?

Q2   What are Stephen Lukes' "three faces of power"?

Q3   Explain what is meant by the Zero Sum Model and Variable Sum Model views of power.

Exam Question

Q1   Assess the Marxist view that the bourgeoisie hold power in society.   (33 marks)

Three faces of power and five Mighty Morphin Power Rangers...

... who don't seem to be on the syllabus this year for some reason. Before you can get anywhere with politics and protest, you've got to have an idea of what power is, and who has power in society. Of course, different sociological schools of thought have very different ideas about power. Learn a few names so that you can drop them in your essays — but make sure you keep it relevant.

The Modern State

These pages have definitions and theories about the modern State.

Most sociologists Agree with Weber's Definition of the Modern State

Weber (1946, 'Politics as a Vocation,' *Essays in Sociology*, New York: Oxford University Press) says the modern State is "a **human community** that (successfully) claims the **monopoly** of the **legitimate use** of **physical force** within a **given territory**".

In other words: ⟹

1) The State is **created by people**.
2) The State can **use force legitimately** — **other** violence in society is **illegitimate**.
3) The State **rules** over a **clear geographical area** — in our case the UK.

The State is traditionally made up of Four Main Institutions

1) The **government**, who **make laws**.
2) The **Civil Service**, who **implement laws**.

THE STATE

3) The **police**, who **enforce laws**.
4) The **Armed Forces**, who **protect** the **territory** from threats from outside.

Government is often divided into **three branches** — the legislature, the executive and the judiciary:

1) The **legislature passes laws**. In the UK, **Parliament** (the House of Commons and the House of Lords) is the legislature.
2) The **executive** suggests new laws, and **runs the country**. The executive is often called "the **government**". Confusing.
3) The **judiciary interprets laws**. The **courts** are the judiciary.

In modern times, the State has extended its role into **health care**, **education** and **nationalised** (state-run) **industries**.

Pluralists see the Modern State as a Neutral Arena for debate

1) Pluralists see the power of the modern democratic State as **legitimate** and acting in the interests of society in general. Pluralists see the State as a **neutral arena** where competing interest and pressure groups lobby for **influence**. They say the State **arbitrates** (settles arguments) between competing interest groups, but is neutral itself.

2) Pluralists say the modern State is democratic because of the **multi-party system**, and because of the participation of **interest groups** and **pressure groups**. **Dahl (1961)** looked at the role of interest groups in local politics in the USA, and found that **several groups** had influence. An important study by **Hewitt (1974)** shows the **crucial role** of interest groups and pressure groups in **influencing Parliament**. Hewitt said that no one group got its own way all the time.

3) A study by **Grant and Marsh (1977)** showed that business interests in the form of the CBI (Confederation of British Industry) didn't have massive influence over British government policy. A **plurality** of **other interest groups** influenced policy away from what the CBI wanted.

Critics of pluralism claim that **some interest groups** have **more influence** than others. **Marsh and Locksley (1983)** found that the CBI were successful in getting their own way in key decisions (completely the opposite of what Marsh had found in his earlier study with Grant — Sociology is a funny old thing).

Marxists say the State Supports the interests of the Bourgeoisie

Marx and Engels said: "The State is but a committee for managing the affairs of the bourgeoisie," (1985, *The Communist Manifesto* Harmondsworth: Penguin, first published 1848).

Marx and **Engels** asserted that the State only became necessary when society became **divided** on grounds of **class**. They said that in primitive society there were no classes and therefore no need for a State.

Marxists claim that the role of the modern State is to **maintain**, **preserve** and **perpetuate** the rule of the **capitalist class** over the **workers**. This is achieved in the following ways:

Engels was Marx's friend and worked with Marx on the Communist Manifesto.

1) **Coercive force** — the **police** are used to contain or suppress **demonstrations** and **riots**.

2) The **illusion of democracy** — universal voting makes it **look** as though everyone has a say and that society is **fair**. This creates the **false consciousness** that the current system is legitimate. However, political parties only represent the interests of **capitalism**, so there's **no real choice**.

3) **Ideology** — a set of ideas by which the State gains approval and consent by persuading people to accept ruling class values. The neo-Marxist **Gramsci (1891-1937)** called this kind of domination **hegemony**. **Gramsci**, **Althusser** and **Poulantzas** all extend the definition of the State to other institutions which pass on values, e.g. **churches**, **mass media**, the **family**.

Althusser called the army, police and courts the <u>Repressive State Apparatus</u>, and the church, family, education and media the <u>Ideological State Apparatus</u>.

Critics say it's **hard to prove** Marxist theory. Concepts like **ideology**, **hegemony** and **false consciousness**, which are key to the Marxist viewpoint, are **difficult to define** and even more **difficult to research**.

The Modern State

Some sociologists argue that the State can act in its Own Interest

Nordlinger (1981) complicates both the pluralist idea that the state reflects the wishes of society and the Marxist idea that the state reflects the views of a minority dominant class, by claiming that a state can act **independently** in three ways:

1) By directly pursuing its **own policies** against the **wishes of the people** — it can do this by using state resources, bribery and secrecy to divide opponents.
2) By **manipulating public opinion** to support its own policies.
3) By asserting control when **public opinion** is either **unsure** or **apathetic** about an issue or policy.

Skocpol (1985) also claims that the state can act autonomously to **increase its own power** and **follow interests** which are not necessarily those of any group in society other than itself.

Neo-liberals are Opposed to State Intervention in the Economy

1) Neo-liberals argue that the keys to lasting economic prosperity are **individual economic enterprise** and a **market** (economy) which is **free** from **state intervention**. Neo-liberal theorists, like **Hayek (1944)**, argue that state intervention in the economy can **stifle capitalism** and make the economy **less efficient**.
2) Neo-liberals therefore believe that **state interference** in the economy such as high taxes, state ownership (nationalisation), or generous welfare benefits should be **rolled back** (i.e. reduced).
3) The influence of neo-liberal thinking, along with **New Right** ideas (see p.164), can be seen in the **Conservative governments** of Mrs Thatcher (1979-1990) which **privatised** state industries, **lowered taxation** and **reduced universal benefits**.
4) The **traditional challenge** to the neo-liberal view is the **reformist socialist view** — the view that the State **should intervene** in the economy in order to improve **social welfare** and **equality**. The reformist socialist view is associated with Old Labour, e.g. the post-war Labour government which created the Welfare State.

Third Way theorists want a State with Social Welfare and Capitalist Economics

1) The "**Third Way**" was an idea put forward by the sociologist **Anthony Giddens (1998)** and later adopted by Tony Blair's **New Labour Party**. Giddens has described it as "the modernising left".
2) Third Way theorists argue that the **world is changing**, for example through globalisation, and that **political ideologies** need to **change** and **adapt** as well if they are to remain relevant. The Third Way therefore includes **elements** of **both** traditional **left-wing** (socialist) and **right-wing** (neo-liberal capitalist) approaches.
3) Third Way theory suggests that the **traditional Welfare State** should be **reformed** because it **encourages dependency** (a neo-liberal idea). However, it also argues that the State should reform and manage the **global economy** to such an extent that it is able to **intervene** to **invest in its citizens**, e.g. through **education** and **social policy**. They argue this will **empower the population** to lead more prosperous, healthy and fulfilling lives.

Globalisation has changed the role of the State

1) As part of the process of globalisation (see p.162-163) **transnational corporations** (**TNCs**) have developed and become very powerful economically. **Sklair (1995)** claims that there's a **transnational capital class** who have gained power at the expense of nation states — he claims the State just isn't as important any more.
2) There's a trend towards **internationalisation** of politics, which has reduced the influence of nation states. For example, some important decisions are taken by the **European Union** rather than by its **member states**.

Practice Questions

Q1 Traditionally, what four things make up the State?
Q2 Briefly summarise the Pluralist view on the role of the State.
Q3 Briefly summarise the Marxist view on the role of the State.

Exam Question

Q1 Evaluate the view that the people in positions of most power in society have not been directly elected. (33 marks)

No need to get in a State about it...

There are a lot of strong opinions on these two pages. You need to be able to evaluate these different views fairly and objectively, whatever your own personal opinion. And I bet you do have a personal opinion. If you find yourself taking sides and thinking "stupid liberal do-gooders" or "blimmin' Tories" then take some deep breaths and start again.

Political Parties and Participation

These pages have descriptions of the main parties, and a bit on why party politics in general may be struggling.

The UK is a **Representative Democracy**

1) In a representative democracy, the people vote to **elect representatives** to make decisions on their **behalf**. These representatives (**MPs** in the UK) are accountable to the voters at the next election — they can get voted out.

2) **Joseph Schumpeter (1942**, *Capitalism, Socialism and Democracy* New York: Harper and Brothers**)** defined democracy as a system where there is a "competitive struggle for the people's vote". For a government to be a democracy, there must be **more than one candidate** or party standing in an election.

3) **Politics** in modern representative democracies like the UK is where **belief systems** (represented by **political parties**, e.g. the Liberal Democrats, Labour, the Conservatives) **compete** for **power**.

4) Citizens can participate by **supporting** and **voting** for a particular political party that they share beliefs with. They can also join that political party — and help out with **election campaigns**, or become an **activist** (someone who attempts to influence the party's policies or who supports their policies and campaigns on their behalf).

The **Mainstream Political Parties** have a number of **Important Functions**

Garner and Kelly (1993) suggest that political parties carry out a number of **essential functions**:

1) **Governing Function** — British governments are formed out of political parties. The party with an **overall majority** in the House of Commons becomes the government and its leader the Prime Minister.

2) **Electoral Function** — Elections are central to a democratic system, and depend on parties to put up **candidates**.

3) **Policy Function** — By forming distinct policies, parties offer the electorate **choice** — an essential feature of a **democracy**.

4) **Representative Function** — Political parties represent the views of a wide range of the electorate and therefore allow the views of people to be **heard** and be **influential**. In order to win, parties must represent a **broad base** of opinion.

5) **Participation Function** — Parties are important vehicles through which the people can **participate** in politics.

6) **Ideological Function** — Political parties allow for a debate to occur between **competing principles** and **ideologies**.

The **Conservative Party** is the traditional party of the **Right**

The Conservative Party is the main **right-wing** or **centre-right** party in British politics.

It is made up of three distinct parts — the **Parliamentary Conservative Party** (the elected MPs), the **Constituent Associations** (made up of volunteers) and the paid party professionals (workers at **Conservative Campaign Headquarters**).

All party members elect the **leader**, whose role includes the appointment of the party Chairman and the cabinet (or shadow cabinet). The leader also has the **final say** on what goes in the Conservative **manifesto**.

1) The Conservatives were in power from 1979 to 1997 — Margaret Thatcher was the leader through the 1980s.

2) Thatcherism emphasised **low public spending**, **privatisation**, **low taxes** and **individual responsibility** and the then government presided over periods of high unemployment and cuts in public services.

3) More recently, the Conservative leader David Cameron has **distanced** himself from traditional Conservative ideas on tax, the environment, NHS spending, gay marriage and public spending. He's used the idea of **'compassionate conservatism'** to rebrand the party as more **centrist** with a new logo, a new style and a softer and more **inclusive image**.

Labour is traditionally the largest mainstream party of the **Left**

1) The main components of the Labour Party are Labour Party **branches**, **Constituency Labour Parties** (CLPs), the **Parliamentary Labour Party** (PLP), the **National Executive Committee** (NEC), and the **leader**.

2) The leader of the party is elected by an **electoral college** made up of three parts, each with an equal say — affiliated trade unions, the PLP and the CLPs. The unions and the CLPs ballot their members before casting their votes.

3) On paper, the Labour leader has **less power** than the Conservative leader. In practice, however, modern Labour leaders have been successful in **managing** the party in such a way as to **get what they want**.

4) The Labour Party was created as the party of the **working class**. It's **never** been a **revolutionary** socialist organisation, but from 1945 through to the 1970s it was heavily influenced by **reformist** socialist ideology. Socialism aims to work towards **equality**, and favours a strong and generous **welfare state** and the **state ownership and control of industries**. Socialism says industry should be run for the **common good**.

5) Since 1979, the Labour Party has gradually changed or removed most of its reformist socialist ideas. During the 1990s, the party redesigned itself as '**New Labour**' under Tony Blair. New Labour talks in terms of a '**Third Way**' between the party's **traditional** ideals and the necessity to **maintain economic growth**. They gained power in 1997.

6) In 1995, Labour reworded Clause Four of its constitution — the clause that committed them to **state ownership** of industry.

Political Parties and Participation

The **Liberal Democrats** are the **Smallest** of the mainstream parties

The Liberal Democrats are the newest of the big three parties, formed in **1988** by a merger of the old **Liberal Party** and the **Social Democratic Party** (SDP). They frequently poll around 20% of the national vote but they rarely get many MPs because of the **'First Past the Post'** electoral system.

1) The Liberal Democrats are a **federal party**, which means local and regional parties have a lot of freedom and autonomy.

2) **Delegates** are sent from every local party to the federal conference. The biannual (twice yearly) federal conference has the **final say** on Liberal Democrat policy issues, **not the leader**.

3) Liberal Democrats are influenced by **progressive liberalism**. This is a move away from **classical liberalism**, which emphasised free markets, individualism and self-help.

4) **Progressive liberalism** calls for **state intervention** to provide services like pensions, hospitals and schools. At the same time it champions **traditional liberal values** of **individual freedom** and **choice**.

The **Influence** of **Political Parties** on the **Political Process** is in **Decline**

1) For many years the UK was seen as the classic model of the **two-party system** — i.e. a system where two **big**, **powerful** and **distinct** political parties compete for power. Other parties exist in a two-party system, but they don't have a **realistic chance** of winning an election and forming a government.

2) Sociologists have been writing about the decline of the influence of the main political parties since the 1960s. In this view, the fact that political parties have **fewer members** and **fewer activists** shows that they're **less likely** to **inspire** people to go and **vote**.

There's some powerful evidence that the influence of political parties is in decline:

1) **Party membership** and **activism** is declining among Britain's three major parties. For instance, **Labour Party** membership peaked at over 400 000 with Tony Blair's victory in 1997, but had fallen to less than half this in 2005. Conservative Party membership is also declining.

2) Young people especially are turning to **New Social Movements** to participate in politics (see p.157).

3) The differences between political parties appear to be **less pronounced**, resulting in voter "**apathy**", e.g. only **61.3%** of the electorate **voted** in the 2005 **general election**.

However, **Reiter (1989)** is **sceptical** of the claim that political parties are in decline. He says there isn't enough evidence across different countries and over a long enough period of time.

Neo-Marxist **Martin Jacques (1997)** suggests that because of the decline in political parties, British politics should move away from the **"Westminster model"**, which focuses exclusively on the mainstream parties. Jacques suggests that we need to develop new forms of political participation.

Ideologically, British **Political Parties** appear to be becoming **Less Distinct**

1) "**New Labour**" under Tony Blair dropped many of the **traditional**, **left-wing** policies and commitments of the Labour Party, e.g. **democratic socialism**, **nationalisation** and **redistribution of wealth**.

2) New Labour now competes in elections as a party who could **manage the capitalist economy** better than its traditional managers, the Conservative Party.

3) Policies on **taxation**, **foreign affairs** and **economic management** have become very **similar** in the **Conservative Party** and the **Labour Party**. This gives voters less choice, which may make them less bothered to go and vote in elections.

Vote Peter Baffin
— your Labervative candidate.

Practice Questions

Q1 Explain the differences between Thatcherism and 'compassionate conservatism'.

Q2 Give three pieces of evidence which suggest that the influence of political parties is in decline.

Exam Question

Q1 Identify and explain two key aspects of the role of political parties.   (6 marks)

See if you can spot these guys at the next General Election...

...or on Radio 4 of a morning (if you can face it before your porridge). The fact that a lot of people don't bother with them is what you'll come to know as the decline of the political parties. Make sure you know who the main parties are and what sort of things they believe in. You could always read some of the leaflets they shove through your door.

Voting Behaviour

This page focuses on the work of psephologists — they're people who study elections.

Psephologists have identified **Three Main Periods** of post-war voting patterns

1) **1945-1974** — a period of **clear ideological differences** between the parties, with strong **class alignment** (working class Labour and middle class Conservative) and strong **voter identification** with their party — **"partisan alignment"**.

2) **1974-1997** — a period of more **"voter volatility"** with **class** and **party loyalties** seemingly **breaking down**. This period also saw a **big decline** in the **Labour Party vote**, with four successive **Conservative governments**.

3) **1997-2005** — a period marked by the emergence and success of **New Labour** — the Labour Party moved to a more **centrist** position, with **fewer clear differences** from the Conservatives, which won them many **middle class votes**.

Post-war voting patterns have been explained with **Partisan Alignment Theory**

Butler and Stokes (1974) argued that **class alignment** was the main factor influencing voting behaviour. The **working class** supported **Labour**, who **represented their interests**, and the **middle class** supported the **Conservatives**, who represented theirs. Voters tended to have **strong identification** with their **particular party** (**partisan alignment**) and the result was a fairly stable **two-party system**. Butler and Stokes argued that such **predictable voting patterns** were caused by **political socialisation** — children **learnt** and **copied** the voting **loyalties** of their **parents**.

Traditional Loyalties have become **Less Important**

If all voters had voted in the way Butler and Stokes suggested there would have been a **permanent** Labour government. The fact that there wasn't led a number of psephologists to investigate the phenomenon of the '**working-class Tory**'.

1) **Bagehot (1867)** first identified the tendency of the working class to be **deferent** to those in authority. The idea of **'deferential' voting** (voting for one's "betters") has been used to explain deviant working class Conservative voters.

2) **Butler and Rose (1960)** used **embourgeoisement theory** to explain working class Conservative voters — they argued that the working class was **changing**, adopting **middle class values** and **aspirations**.

3) **McKenzie and Silver (1968)** suggested that some working class voters were becoming '**secular**', i.e. not voting on established traditional loyalties, but on **policy preference** lines — this idea has been popular in more recent studies.

4) **Sarlvick and Crewe (1983)** argued that during the period of voter volatility, **economic change** and increased **prosperity** weakened the link between class and party — **"class dealignment"**. The **old working class** based in highly unionised **industries** in northern England declined. A **new aspirational home-owning** working class emerged in **south-eastern England**. In this period Labour **maintained** the support of the **shrinking** 'old working class', but **didn't win the loyalty** of the '**new working class**'. This led to the disastrous **election results** for Labour in **1983**.

5) **Denver (2002)** argued that **policy preference** (how much voters like a party's policies) is now **more important** than broader social factors like class, gender, region, age etc. He argues that in recent Labour victories **voters' views** have simply been **closer** to **Labour policies** than Conservative policies.

6) There are **other factors** that shape voting patterns. The **region** people live in can have a big impact — Scotland, Wales and the North have majority Labour support — the South and South East majority Conservative support. **Ethnicity** is also important — **Saggar and Heath (1999)** have shown how Labour has consistently won over 70% of the **ethnic minority vote**. **Norris (1997)** showed that **women voters** are more likely to vote **Conservative**.

"Voter Apathy" is when people **Don't Bother** to vote

Voter apathy is particularly marked amongst the **young** and amongst **ethnic minority** groups. Several measures have been proposed to tackle this apathy. Some have already been adopted.

Already adopted:

1) Making voting **easier** by making it easier to apply for a **postal vote**. ←

The postal vote system in the UK has been criticised as open to fraud. Researchers and journalists have shown it's possible to register a postal vote in someone else's name. This accusation has damaged trust in the electoral system.

2) Making it easier to **register** to vote — you can register online in some areas.

3) **Educating the voters**, e.g. **Citizenship** is a **National Curriculum** subject in schools.

Not yet adopted:

1) Making **voting** easier by using **new technology**, e.g. internet voting and text message voting.

2) Extending polling day to several days.

3) **Redesigning ballot papers** to make them easier to understand.

4) Giving people the option to register a positive abstention — i.e. a box to tick that says "none of the above" or "abstain".

All the measures seem to focus on **voters** rather than the **decline** and **ideological convergence** of the political parties.
Some countries, e.g. Australia, have tackled the problem by making **voting compulsory**. This hasn't yet been adopted in Britain.

The Influence of the Media

This page is all about what the papers say, and how they control your mind.

The UK Mass Media were Pro-Conservative until the late 1990s

1) Up until 1997 the only mainstream paper that ever expressed consistent support for the Labour Party was the **Daily Mirror**. The rest tended to support the Conservatives.

2) In the late 1990s "New Labour" made it a **priority** to win the support of **big media owners**, particularly **Rupert Murdoch**. Murdoch's News International controlled the **Times**, the **Sun** and **Sky Television**.

3) The results can be illustrated by the contrasting ways in which the **Sun** treated two Labour leaders — **Neil Kinnock** in 1992 and **Tony Blair** in 1997. The Sun's 1992 election day coverage suggested that a victory for Labour under its then leader Neil Kinnock would be a **disaster** for Britain. Whereas in 1997 the Sun switched sides to **back** Tony Blair.

4) The support of significant sections of the **mass media** has been cited as a crucial factor in the **continued electoral success** of New Labour. "**Spin doctors**" are party public relations (PR) officers whose job is to **manipulate** the media and make sure that the party is presented in a sympathetic light, and that the party's opponents are presented negatively.

Marxists suggest that Media Ownership makes the media Pro-Capitalist

1) Traditional Marxism claims that the media **directly** presents news stories which serve the **interests** of the ruling class, because the media is itself **owned** by the **ruling class**.

2) **Miliband (1969)** said that the mass media was the "new opium of the people" — it keeps the proletariat subdued by showing them nice mindless entertainment. **Marcuse (1964)** said that the media gives people "**false needs**" which keep them consuming the goods that capitalism produces.

3) Neo-Marxists suggest that the world view of the capitalist class is broadcast and reinforced by the mass media through an **indirect approval process**. Editors are from middle class backgrounds, so they tend to select material which reflects their own ideas.

False need or no, Nina just had to have that brass chamber pot.

4) **Gramsci**'s idea of **ideological hegemony** (see p. 99) really applies here. Ruling class values are portrayed through the mass media as natural and common sense. Ideas that question capitalism are ridiculed as crazy.

5) An **example** of this was an attack on the policies of the Liberal Democrats by the Sun in which they superimposed former Liberal Democrat leader **Charles Kennedy's face** on the label of a **bottle of whisky**. The accompanying article suggested that the Liberal Democrats were **socialists** and that Kennedy had a drink problem.

The work of the GUMG suggests that News is Politically Weighted

	The GUMG studied news reports of industrial disputes in the 70s and 80s
Method:	The Glasgow University Media Group studied television news over a long time span to look for evidence of bias. They performed detailed content analysis on television news bulletins. See p.135 for more on their work.
Finding:	The selection of news and voice-over scripts were biased in favour of dominant class values. During industrial disputes, management had more access to the media than union leaders. Filming and editing were biased in favour of the police.

Practice Questions

Q1 Explain what is meant by political socialisation.

Q2 What does 'policy preference' mean?

Q3 Give three ways in which Marxists say the media promotes the interests of the ruling class.

Exam Question

Q1 "The most important factor affecting voter behaviour is partisan alignment." To what extent do you agree with this statement?

(33 marks)

I vote we all should do some more Sociology revision...

It's worth thinking about just how powerful the media are. The newspapers you read — or the news programmes you catch on TV and the radio — choose what events and whose opinions are worth covering, and how much coverage they deserve. If you get a couple of different papers one day, you'll be able to see how different they are. And you'll also have loads of crosswords to do.

Old and New Social Movements

These pages are on the different types of social movements.

Old Social Movements (OSMs) are Pressure Groups or Interest Groups

Bagguley (1995) argues that **Old Social Movements** (OSMs) are influenced by **economic** and **class factors**. They focus their attention on **public policy issues**, attempting to influence **decision-makers** and **law-makers**. Many OSMs are **occupationally based** (e.g. trade unions), whereas others are concerned with **single issues**.

Pressure groups can be either **protective** (also called **sectional**) or **promotional**. **Protective** groups seek to protect the interests of a particular group, e.g. trade unions protect groups of workers, the CBI protects the interests of business, and the British Medical Association looks out for doctors. **Promotional** groups promote causes, e.g. Greenpeace and Friends of the Earth promote environmental causes.

> **Pluralists argue that pressure group activity is an essential feature of modern democracy.**
>
> 1) Pressure groups give **valuable input** to government policy and provide expert opinion.
>
> 2) Pressure groups provide a vehicle for many **views** to be **represented**.
>
> 3) **Pluralists** say pressure groups have **equal access** to government. The State is seen by pluralists as a **neutral arbiter** between **pressure groups** with different opinions (see p.150).

> **Marxists suggest that pressure group activity doesn't enhance democracy at all.**
>
> 1) Pressure groups tend **not** to be **democratic**. Members have little say in the running of the group.
>
> 2) Pressure groups are **not equal** — some have more resources and therefore much more influence than others. Marxists claim that the most powerful groups are always the pro-capitalist ones.
>
> 3) Marxists think pressure groups shouldn't be powerful as they aren't **accountable** to the people.
>
> 4) Marxists think the State **isn't neutral** and can't be a neutral arbiter between pressure groups.

There are Insider and Outsider Pressure Groups

1) **Insider groups** are those which are perceived to be **expert** and **respectable**. They can get close to **government** and **decision-makers**. Governments often need the **help** and support of such groups to plan and implement their programmes.

2) Outsider groups are those who have **little** or **no access** to decision-makers because they're viewed as **extreme** or **not useful** to decision-makers.

3) Pressure groups may **change status** from outsider to insider or vice versa. In the 1970s most **environmental groups** were considered outsider groups with little influence on decision-makers — today they're largely insider groups as the major parties **seek** their advice and support. In the 1970s the trade unions were insider groups with **strong influence** over Labour governments. This changed under the Conservative leader **Thatcher**, who saw them as **dangerous**.

Pressure groups Lobby those in power to Achieve their Aims

1) Pressure groups try to gain **influence** over governments and decision-makers — this is called **lobbying**.

2) Insider groups are able to gain access to decision-makers during the **consultation stage** of legislation and right through the legislative process. Sometimes pressure groups are able to influence Parliament more generally when invited to appear before **select committees**.

3) Pressure groups also lobby politicians through the political parties. An example of this is the **close link** between the **Labour Party** and the **trade unions** which although diminished is still significant — they form a third of the electoral college which elects the party leader (see p.152).

4) Many pressure groups **don't** have **formal ties** to political parties. They are often **courted** by political parties to gain **endorsement** of their proposed policies.

> Select committees are small cross-party committees of MPs who investigate and report on important areas of policy, and who can question anybody important or expert in their field of enquiry.

There are Two Main Types of New Social Movement (NSM)

Hallsworth (1994) defines NSMs as movements which **challenge** the **established political** and **cultural order** in capitalist societies. This includes feminism, environmentalism, the civil rights movement and anti-racist movements. NSMs can either be **defensive** or **offensive** — which has nothing to do with whether they offend people, by the way.

- **Defensive** movements are concerned with **protecting** the environment or people from things they see as a threat, e.g. **nuclear power**, **genetically modified crops**, **global capitalism**, etc.

- **Offensive** movements want to **promote** and widen the **rights** of the groups they represent. Examples of offensive movements are **gay rights groups**, **human rights groups** and **anti-racist groups**.

Old and New Social Movements

The **Young** tend to participate in politics through **NSMs**

1) Hallsworth claims that most members of NSMs tend to be **young** (mainly between 16 and 30) and **middle class,** particularly from the **public sector middle class** (teachers, social workers, etc.).

This includes young people whose parents are teachers, social workers etc.

2) NSMs are **informally organised**, and **non-bureaucratic**. They tend to operate outside of traditional politics. Unlike pressure groups and political parties, NSMs tend to favour **direct action**, such as demonstrations, civil disobedience and sit-ins (see p. 158-159).

Sociologists apply different **Theories** to the phenomenon of **NSMs**

1) **Marcuse (1969)** argues that young people form and join NSMs because they are **alienated** by **capitalism**. Marcuse is a **Marxist** who says that capitalism produces a **shallow**, **superficial** mass **consumer culture** which the NSMs reject. He argues that NSMs have the potential to **liberate** people.

2) **Habermas (1987)** argues that people form and join NSMs as a response to the **intrusion of the State** into private life, and the **failure of the State** to solve problems or control industrial capitalism. He says that NSMs are deliberately non-bureaucratic.

3) **Giddens (1973)** argues that an increase in **risk** has motivated people to start NSMs. Late 20th-century peace movements responded to the increased risk of **war**, especially **nuclear war**. Environmentalist movements have responded to the increased risk of **environmental disasters**.

4) **Melucci (1989)** says that people join NSMs to give them a **sense** of **collective identity**.

Vicky and Chad show off their new social movements.

There's more about identity and protest on p. 160-161.

Some sociologists link NSMs with **Postmodernism**

1) **Crook, Pakulski and Waters (1992)** argue that **postmodernisation** is causing a shift from **old politics** to **new politics**. They define **old politics** as based on **political parties** and **class**, and belonging to a specialised **political sphere**. They define **new politics** as based on **NSMs** and moral issues, and belonging to people's wider lifestyle.

2) Crook, Pakulski and Waters say that a **decline** in the importance of **class** is partly responsible. They claim that class-based party politics is becoming less relevant.

3) The rise in importance of the **media** is another factor. They say that the media **dramatises** potential scenarios such as global warming and nuclear war, which makes people feel that they have to do something about them.

1) **Nancy Fraser (1995)** suggests that what constitutes the "**public sphere**" (where politics goes on) has changed.

2) She argues that it has **fragmented** into **several** public spheres where **special interest groups** can argue issues before trying to get their views onto the **mainstream agenda**.

3) She also claims that the public sphere has **widened**, and that the **personal** and **private** have **become political** — for example, sexual harassment was once seen as private flirting, but feminists have made it political.

1) Postmodernist **Jean-François Lyotard (1984)** claims that in the postmodern era people have lost faith in what he calls "**metanarratives**" — the big sweeping political ideologies of the modern era that say what society should be like.

2) He suggests that politics has become more **localised** and **limited** in scope, and more concerned with **single issues**.

Practice Questions

Q1 What is the difference between protective and promotional pressure groups?

Q2 What is lobbying?

Q3 What does Marcuse say about NSMs?

Exam Question

Q1 Assess the view that new social movements form because people no longer have faith in politics. (33 marks)

No need to get defensive about it — or offensive for that matter...

There's quite a bit of tricky stuff for you to remember here. Make sure you know what it is that makes old social movements old, and new social movements new — and don't you get the two mixed up. Sadly, it's not as simple as new social movements being newer — there's a whole lot more to it than that. Keep scribbling it all down without looking until you're sure you've got it...

Political Action and Protest

These pages look at forms of direct action engaged in by New Social Movements.

Direct action happens *Outside* normal *Political Processes*

Direct action is political activity which happens outside the normal political processes. It includes **peaceful demonstrations**, **sit-ins** and **boycotts**, as well as violent action such as **riots**, **vandalism** and **terrorism**.

Some direct action is **large-scale** and **public**, e.g. **demonstrations** and **marches**.
Some is **targeted**, e.g. **letter** and **leaflet campaigns**, **vandalism** and **boycotts**.

1) **New Social Movements** are far more likely to engage in **direct action** than traditional political activity. They don't have a **strong voice** in party political debate. Members of NSMs often feel they **have to take direct action** in order to get their views on the **mainstream agenda**. Getting noticed by the **media** often plays a big part in this.

2) Some say NSMs have **redefined** what is meant by **political action** — taking the political to new areas like the private sphere, e.g. by targeting the issue of domestic violence.

3) The political activity of NSMs is **deliberately** different from that of old social movements.

4) **Cyber-networking** (using e-mail lists, blogs, forums and social networking sites) makes it possible for NSMs to organise large demonstrations **quickly**, making it **difficult** for the authorities to **plan** their **response**.

> Indirect action is the more traditional form of political activity, favoured by old social movements, e.g. lobbying — see p. 156.

Direct Action is often *Against* the *Law*

1) Most illegal direct action is **peaceful**. **Civil disobedience** means non-violent direct action which breaks laws. For instance **mass trespass** is a common form of civil disobedience practised by **anti-road protestors** who put themselves physically **in the way** of developers in an attempt to protect woodlands etc. The **Reclaim the Streets** movement causes traffic congestion by organising **street parties** in the middle of busy roads, blocking the road off for the day.

2) Some **direct action** is **violent and criminal** and has been characterised as **terrorism**. Terrorist direct action has been taken against the **USA** and its allies by anti-American Islamist groups, e.g. Al Qaeda. Some Palestinian nationalist groups use terrorist actions, such as **suicide bombs**, against Israel. ETA is another group that takes violent direct action.

3) Terrorism also happens on a smaller scale. For example, the direct action of some **animal rights groups** includes sending **letter bombs** to scientists involved in testing with animals, **threatening** the **families** of scientists involved in animal testing, putting **bricks through windows** and the **firebombing** of shops selling fur goods.

Riots are a *Common* form of *Direct Action*

1) Riots are **violent** outbreaks of **serious urban disorder** on a large scale. Violence can be directed against both property and people.

2) Often riots are understood as the **desperate actions** of people not represented in any other way. In this view, social groups not represented by "Old Politics" (parties and pressure groups) resort to riots to get their **voices heard**. This view **ignores** other kinds of direct action that can be used to attract attention.

3) Riots are not a modern phenomenon, despite the fact that most sociological research has focused on the inner-city riots of the **1980s** (Brixton, Toxteth, Tottenham). Throughout the **18th** and **19th centuries** there were frequent riots in the UK in response to problems that came with **industrialisation**.

4) **Peaceful demonstrations** and marches can get **violent** and turn into **riots**.

According to *Benyon (1987)* there are *Four Types* of *Explanation* for *Riots*

1) Conservative	Conservatives see rioting as a primarily criminal and unjustifiable activity. Rioters are seen as selfish, greedy, envious and lacking moral fibre. New Right sociologists like Murray suggest the subculture of the underclass which embraces criminality is to blame for rioting. The solution from this perspective is to break the "dependency culture" (reliance on state benefits) which breeds such deviant values.
2) Liberal	Liberals identify factors like unemployment, poverty, poor housing and limited opportunities as the main causes of riots. When added to discrimination (e.g. black youths discriminated against by the police using "stop and search" in Brixton), riots are likely to take place.
3) Radical	Radicals like Marxists suggest riots are conscious legitimate political acts by groups with no other way of expressing their grievances. Marxists see rioting as a reaction by the working class to the injustices and exploitation of the capitalist system. The involvement of black working class people in riots has been seen by Marxists as an expression of anger at the way white society has discriminated against black people.
4) Feminist	Feminists have suggested that rioting by young working class males is an attempt to assert masculinity at a time when traditional male roles and male jobs are in decline.

Remember also that in large **demonstrations** that have developed into riots, **anti-capitalist NSMs** have played a part in organising and coordinating activity on the internet, e.g. in Genoa at the 2001 G8 Summit.

Political Action and Protest

Riots in Oldham and Bradford have been linked to Ethnic Tension

1) A series of riots occurred in the Northern, mostly working class towns and cities of **Oldham**, **Leeds** and **Bradford** in **2001**. The riots all involved serious clashes between **young Asians** and the police.

2) These riots differed from the inner-city riots of the 1980s because they took place in a context of a rapid increase in political activity of **far-right organisations** like the **British National Party** (BNP) and the **National Front** (NF). Both the BNP and NF have concentrated in recent years on Northern towns, especially **Oldham**, to recruit members and mobilise public opinion.

3) The **BNP** is a political party which wants to **end immigration**, and has suggested offering immigrants money to leave the UK. Some people believe the BNP is **racist**, although the BNP **denies** this.

4) Also, **socio-economic deprivation** among both white and Asian groups, housing segregation (the council estates were mainly white), and resulting **educational segregation** have all been put forward as explanations of the riots.

5) The government blamed the riots on the activities of **"thugs"**. Community leaders offered a similar response — blaming the **decline** of **"traditional Muslim values"**. **Kundnani (2001)** argued such responses ignored the deeper social causes of the riots.

Strikes are a form of Direct Action taken by Trade Unions

1) Strikes are where workers deliberately **withdraw their labour**, under the direction of trade union leaders.

2) Strikes are **direct action** by **workers** against their **employer**. Large scale strikes can also be used to influence governments.

3) There were **frequent strikes** in the **1970s**. Trade union law was changed by the Conservative government in the 1980s to make it more difficult for workers to go out on strike, and since then strikes have become much rarer.

Strikes are heavily <u>class-based</u>. The <u>working class</u> (i.e. the workers) are protesting against either their boss, or the state.

A trade union is a <u>pressure group</u>, rather than a New Social Movement. Still, strikes count as a form of direct action.

Direct Action involves issues of Class, Gender, Ethnicity, Disability, etc.

Direct action has been taken by many different groups for many different reasons.

1) Women have participated in "**Reclaim the Night**" rallies against male sexual violence.

2) Disabled people have chained themselves to Downing Street railings in protest against government social policy.

3) Muslim groups have organised **demonstrations** against the Iraq war. **Moderate** groups also engaged with the political process by **voting** for MPs who opposed the war. **Radical** groups **rejected** the traditional political process.

4) **Peaceful direct action** such as **sit-ins** and **marches** characterised civil rights protests in 1960s America. Racist groups sometimes responded with violence. The **civil rights** movement started with **civil disobedience** and a **boycott**.

In **1955**, a **black** woman, Rosa Parks, from Montgomery, Alabama, **refused to give up her seat** on the bus to a **white** person. At that time, black passengers were supposed to sit at the back of the bus and give up their seats to white passengers if the bus was full. She was **arrested**. Local church minister Dr Martin Luther King called for a **boycott** of the bus company by all black people in Montgomery, which lasted until the **bus segregation laws** were **removed**.

Practice Questions

Q1 Give five examples of types of direct action.

Q2 Give two reasons why NSMs use direct action rather than indirect forms of protest.

Q3 Give four types of explanation for why riots break out.

Exam Question

Q1 'Rioting is just a crime like any other.' To what extent do sociological arguments and evidence support this view? (33 marks)

Political action — what a riot...

New Social Movements have all kinds of ways of making their feelings heard. Occasionally they resort to violence (rioting, terrorism, firebombing etc.) but mostly they stick to peaceful methods like demonstrations, marches, boycotts or plain old striking. The French are dead keen on all that malarkey. Even their sixth-formers sometimes go on strike. Not at exam time though, alas.

Protest and Identity

Protest and direct action can be part of the process which constructs a person's identity.

An individual may create their own *Identity* through *Protest* and *Political Action*

1) Identity is the sense a person has of who they are. A person's identity can have many sources, including their class, gender, sexuality or ethnicity.

2) **Personal identity** is how a person sees themselves, and **social identity** is how an individual is perceived by others. **Personal** identity and **social** identity are not always the **same**.

3) Identities can be influenced by **politics and protest**. Belonging to a political movement based on class is likely to heighten the part of your identity that's based on class. The same goes for **gender**, or **sexuality**, or **ethnicity**.

There are several different kinds of feminism within the broader feminist movement. Liberal feminism aims for equality of opportunity for women, and works towards changing the law to make things equal for men and women. Radical feminism stresses women's identity as women. They blame men, rather than socialisation, for women's disadvantaged position.

Ken Plummer (1995) has written about new social movements based on sexuality, e.g. the lesbian and gay rights movement. He's also written about queer theory, which says that gender and sexual identities are very fluid, and can keep changing. Queer theory disapproves of the division of the world into strict categories of gay and straight.

Stephen Whittle (2000) has written about transgender identities, and transgender rights.

There are NSMs based on ethnicity. The Black Power movement in 1960s America aimed to find a distinctive identity as black Americans and emphasised the common experience of oppression. The civil rights movement aimed to get black people equal opportunities in society.

Identity Politics is politics that comes from a *Shared Experience* of *Injustice*

1) Identity politics is based on **differences** between people. Identity politics is the politics of movements which represent the interests and identity of a particular **oppressed group** within a society, rather than society as a whole. Members of the group unite around a **shared identity**. Feminism, Disability Rights, Black Power, and Gay Pride are all varieties of identity politics.

2) Individuals who feel they are **oppressed** or **discriminated** against may create a positive sense of **personal identity** through **protest** and **political activity**. This sense of **positive personal identity** helps to counteract the **negative social identity** that they feel society has given them. In other words, **society** may see an individual as **inferior**, but **protest** and **politics** can give them the sense of being **just as good** as anyone else.

3) For example, LGBT (lesbian, gay, bisexual and transgender) people who feel oppressed by **homophobia** may gain a positive sense of identity by joining a **Gay Pride** group. **Black Power** creates a positive personal identity for black people who have felt oppressed by **racism**.

Some critics **question** the idea of shared experience. Not all women are the **same**, for example — a black woman may have a very different experience of society to a white woman, and a working class woman may have a different experience to a middle class woman. Commenting on **Betty Friedan's (1963)** statement that women should get out of the house and into the workplace, African-American feminist **bell hooks (1981)** pointed out that the **experience** of being a **stay-at-home housewife and mother** was pretty much limited to **white middle class women**. African-American working class women had been doing paid jobs for years.

It can be argued that identity politics **excludes** people who aren't part of the group, e.g. a lesbian activist group would exclude men. Identity politics can also **marginalise** groups — i.e. keep them **away** from **mainstream politics**.

Identity Politics can be linked to patterns of *Consumption*

1) **Consumption** is spending on goods and services. Some sociologists argue that in the **postmodern era** there's a **link** between **consumption** and **identity**.

2) Identity politics can involve the rejection of **global brands** in favour of products chosen on **moral grounds**, e.g. out of environmental, human rights or animal rights concerns. Examples of such strategies include **boycotts** of environmentally unfriendly products and of products produced in countries with poor human rights records.

There's more on globalisation on p. 162-163.

3) An example of such consumption focused protest is the network of **anti-NIKE websites** which campaign against the employment practices of NIKE in South East Asia. These websites are used to **promote boycotts** of NIKE products and **demonstrations** at NIKE offices.

Protest and Identity

Postmodernists say *Identity Politics* is more important than *Party Politics*

1) Postmodernists like **Lyotard (1984)** argue that people have lost faith in "metanarratives" (see p.157) and party politics.

2) Postmodernists such as **Nancy Fraser (1989)** say that political life has become de-centred — this means people's political goals reflect their personal and social identity, instead of an ideology that applies to all of society.

3) This process has been amplified by **globalisation** and **world travel**. People can consider themselves part of a global social group of say, women, or deaf people, or gay men, or Muslims.

1) **Stuart Hall (1992)** claims that identity is **fragmented**. According to Hall, people no longer have a **single identity** linked to a class or ideology. Instead they possess a **number** of sometimes **contradictory** identities, which he calls "**fragmented identity**".

2) Hall suggests that the increase in number of **New Social Movements** concerned with a huge number of **identities** and **issues** (e.g. feminism, ethnic minority issues, national liberation, environmental concerns, sexuality) have helped to **fragment** people's identity. An individual could be a **Green**, **Welsh Nationalist**, **lesbian feminist** and sometimes identify as **Welsh Nationalist**, other times as **Green**, etc.

Class-based *"Old Politics"* may *Not* be *Quite Dead Yet*

1) Despite massive interest in the growth of **New Social Movements** (**NSMs**), **protest**, and **identity politics** in the last 30 years, it would be **inaccurate** to suggest that the **old politics** represented by the political parties and pressure groups is **dead and buried**.

2) It's true that some rather high profile NSMs have been able to exert significant pressure on governments, e.g. **environmentalism**, but many NSMs have had limited success.

3) It would also be easy to exaggerate the importance and growth of NSMs. Whilst **most** people **know about NSMs**, very **few** are active **participants** in them. NSMs have recruited well amongst the educated young middle class but they haven't shown much evidence of a more broad-based appeal.

4) People may grumble about party politics, but most people still go out and vote.

So, not the last resting place of party politics after all...

Some social movements try to get particular social groups to participate in mainstream politics.

1) The **women's suffrage** movement campaigned to get women the vote in the early 20th century.

2) The **civil rights** movement in America fought for black people's rights, and actively encouraged African-American people to register to vote.

These groups aren't about identity — they're about equality.

3) There are campaigns to increase the number of **women in Parliament**. **Emily's List** was launched in 1993 to raise money to help **women in the Labour Party** stand as MPs. The Labour Party has enforced **all-women shortlists** of candidates for some constituencies to make sure their candidate will be a woman. Some feminists find this **patronising**.

Practice Questions

Q1 What's the difference between personal and social identity?

Q2 Describe three types of political movements people might use to create their own identity.

Q3 What is identity politics?

Q4 Explain the link between consumption and identity politics.

Exam Question

Q1 Assess the view that falling voter turnout in elections is evidence of the decline of class-based politics and the growth of new social movements.

(33 marks)

She's the only Green Welsh Nationalist Lesbian Feminist in the village...

This identity stuff's a bit complicated. I guess you could sum it up by saying that some people define themselves by what they're protesting about, and the group they protest with. Some criticise identity politics and say it creates inward-looking groups who exclude outsiders. Supporters of identity politics say it gives people a sense of power. I say just learn it.

Globalisation

It's a whole new world — everything's globalised these days, with companies trading across borders, all sorts of media available worldwide thanks to the web, and all sorts of products, made in all sorts of places, available everywhere.

Globalisation is the trend of National Boundaries becoming Less Important

1) Globalisation has been seen to **weaken** the power of nation states to **control** their own **economies**.

2) Because of improvements in communications, consumers are able to purchase goods from all over the world. This has changed a system of national economies into a **global economy**.

3) **Transnational corporations** such as NIKE, McDonald's and Coca-Cola® have tremendous power.

4) Global corporations, with their brands, logos and associations with **lifestyles**, are shaping a global culture.

5) The effects of **global economic activity** such as **pollution** don't respect national boundaries.

6) A highly mobile global population means that **diseases** such as **HIV** are global problems.

7) **Politics** and **political action** have become more globalised, e.g. the anti-capitalist movement.

Economic Globalisation has seen the rise of Transnational Corporations (TNCs)

1) **TNCs** are big companies which operate in a **large number** of **countries** and are therefore **beyond** the **direct control** of individual nation states.

2) TNCs like NIKE, Nestlé®, Ford and GM are able to **move production** and **investment** around the world to wherever economic conditions are most favourable. For instance, in the last 30 years much **car production** has been **moved** from **Western Europe**, where **labour costs** are high and **trade unions** strong, to **South East Asia**, where labour costs are relatively low and trade unions aren't so well established.

3) Nation states individually don't have the power to **control** the **activities** of TNCs, and so have lost a significant amount of power over their own **economies**. **Ohmae (1996)** argues that some TNCs are now **more powerful** than many **governments**. There's more on TNCs on pages 114-115.

Political Globalisation has Reduced the Power of the Individual Nation State

1) Nation states are increasingly coming together to become members of **transnational organisations** which have a political element to them. For example, the **European Union** (EU), the **United Nations** (UN) and the **North Atlantic Treaty Organisation** (NATO).

2) Membership of such organisations, though beneficial to nation states in many ways, can also result in a partial **transference** of **sovereignty** from the nation state to the organisation. For example, in Britain EU law now has **precedence** over UK law.

Sovereignty is a state's ability to control what goes on within its own borders.

Cultural Globalisation has reduced the state's control over Culture and the Media

1) The explosion in **internet** and **communications technology** and cable and satellite broadcasting has resulted in consumers worldwide being immersed in **Western values**, culture and lifestyle through advertising and broadcasting.

2) The internet and the large number of TV channels now available globally make it far more **difficult** for nation states to **control access** to **information** or manipulate the media within their own boundaries.

Some sociologists argue that the Decline of the State has been Exaggerated

1) **Hirst and Thompson (1996)** acknowledge that there's been some decline in the power of the nation state due to globalisation, but they argue that it's been overstated. They point out the considerable power nation states continue to have over **foreign policy**, the **military**, the **national territory**, and their citizens' sense of **'national identity'**.

2) They also claim the spread of **economic globalisation** has been **exaggerated**. They point out that many companies labelled as TNCs still operate largely within their **'home regions'** rather than genuinely globally.

Despite globalisation, Millie had managed to work herself up into a right state.

Globalisation

David Held argues that Globalisation has Serious Implications for Democracy

1) **Held (1995)** supports the idea that the power of nation states has **declined** significantly. He points out that this has issues for democracy, with voters voting for governments who **do not** hold the **real power** over economic policy that they used to.

2) Held calls for a new **global approach** to democracy and the setting up of a **world parliament** which could hold powerful TNCs to account and **restore democratic control** over important decisions. Such a world parliament he argues would be able to tackle the **global problems** facing the world — global warming, disease, and food supply and distribution.

Globalisation's had a big impact on crime — see pages 182-183.

The Global Anti-Capitalism movement developed at the end of the 1990s

The two most quoted examples of anti-capitalist political action are the **World Trade Organisation demonstrations** in **Seattle** in **1999** and the **G8 Summit demonstrations** in **2001**. At both there was serious disorder and some rioting. **Reasons** for the development of a **global anti-capitalist movement** include:

1) **International organisations** seem to be running the world — e.g. the G8, the EU, the UN.

2) Improvements in **communications** (especially the **internet**) have allowed activists to **organise** and **network** effectively.

3) The **financial crisis** in East Asia in 1998 rocked many people's faith in the **sustainability** of global capitalism.

4) The politics of liberal democracies tend not to offer **alternatives** to capitalism.

1) Marxist **Callinicos (2003)** suggests that the apparently **diverse** interests of global social movements are linked by the **common source** of their **concerns** — what else but global capitalism (he is a Marxist after all).

2) For instance, he says it's **global capitalism** that causes pollution and therefore creates **environmental protestors**, and it's **global capitalism** which keeps LEDCs (Less Economically Developed Countries) in poverty and therefore creates protesters against **Third World Debt**.

3) It's worth remembering that global social movements cover a **huge political spectrum**. Callinicos may well be **exaggerating** their **revolutionary potential** as an anti-capitalist force.

The Global Anti-Capitalism Movement has attacked Global Branding

1) **Naomi Klein (2001)** argues that young people involved in global social movements are fed up with the global branding of **youth** and **youth culture**.

2) In *No Logo*, Klein argues that people involved in global social movements believe that political parties and "old politics" are powerless to challenge the **dominance** of **global corporations**.

3) **Global branding** gives protesters a **target** for their protests, e.g. producing a spoof advertisement or logo with an anti-capitalist message. This is called **culture jamming**.

4) The **McLibel case** shows the effects of culture jamming. Protesters produced anti-McDonald's leaflets and McDonald's sued for libel. The court case gave the protesters massive **publicity**. The judge agreed with some of their claims.

Practice Questions

Q1 List seven features of globalisation.
Q2 What are TNCs and how have they grown in power?
Q3 Give an example of how political globalisation may reduce the power of nation states.
Q4 What is cultural globalisation?
Q5 Give some evidence to suggest that the nation state is still powerful.
Q6 Explain how globalisation may be seen as harmful to democracy.

Exam Question

Q1 Assess the view that political activity is becoming globalised. (18 marks)

What do global anti-capitalists like in their sandwiches? Culture jam...

Whether you're a fan of capitalism (yay, go capitalism!) or an anti-capitalist (boo, bad capitalism!) you can't avoid the fact that politics and business are becoming more 'global'. Even issues we can all (just about) agree on, like the need to combat disease and climate change, require a global response. Make sure you know how globalisation is changing the world, and what everyone thinks.

Ideology and Political Action

These pages are about the different ideologies that motivate political groups. You don't need to learn them, but they've got a lot of really useful background info.

Conservatism has Three basic Underlying Principles

1) Conservatism emphasises the importance of the **family**, the **nation** and **patriotism** as contributors to **social order** and **harmony**.

2) Conservatism sees people as capable of good and bad — it's suspicious of any ideology which assumes people are either very **rational** or very **moral**. Conservatives therefore believe there is a strong need for a **state** and a **legal system** to **control** people and **protect** them from each other.

3) Conservatives believe that **inequalities** between people **occur naturally** and **resist** any attempts to **impose** equality on people.

Ideology is hard to define but often it's used to mean a set of ideas and beliefs about the way things should be. See p. 98-99 for more.

There are Two Main Strands of Modern Conservatism

One Nation Conservatism (or Paternalistic Conservatism) thinks the government should intervene to help the weak

1) **One Nation Conservatism** was invented in the **19th century** by Conservative Prime Minister **Benjamin Disraeli**.

2) Disraeli's ideas were a response to the **problems** and **inequalities** introduced by the industrial revolution. He described Britain as **"Two Nations"**, the rich and the poor, which could become **one nation** again if the wealthy would fulfil their **duty** of **looking after** the poor with social reforms.

3) This strand of Conservatism sees a need for some **state intervention** in the economy, to make sure the rich do their bit to care for the poor.

One Nation Conservatism doesn't call for <u>equality</u>. It calls for the privileged to <u>look after</u> the underprivileged in one <u>big happy hierarchical family</u>.

Liberal Conservatism (aka Libertarian Conservatism and the New Right) takes ideas from classical liberalism

1) Classical Liberalism believes in:
   - the **free market** and **free enterprise**
   - **minimal state intervention** in the economy
   - the idea that **individuals** should take **responsibility** for themselves

2) Liberal Conservatism has borrowed all of these ideas.

3) Where liberal conservatives differ from liberals is in their belief in **traditional values** and the need for a **strong state** to regulate behaviour and maintain **social order** and **moral standards**.

4) **Neoconservatism** can be seen as a joining of **liberal economics** to moral and social **authoritarianism** and has had a significant impact on modern British conservatism and on the American presidents Reagan and George W Bush.

This type of Conservatism is most readily associated with Margaret Thatcher. It's also referred to as "New Right Conservatism".

Liberalism was at its Highpoint immediately after the end of the Cold War

1) At the end of the 20th century **liberal values** of individual freedom, freedom of thought and conscience, tolerance, rule-based governance, and freedom of choice appeared to be **triumphant** almost **all over** the world. **Western-style democracy** was argued to be the best possible political system achievable.

2) But recently liberal democracy has come under **increased criticism** both from Marxist/anarchist inspired **global anti-capitalist movements** and from the emergence of **religious fundamentalism**.

Audrey kept her herd in the valleys below the highpoint of Western liberalism.

Revolutionary Marxism calls for the Violent Overthrow of Capitalism

1) This is the socialism of Marx and Engels which sees society in terms of a **class conflict** between the **bourgeoisie** (owners) and the **proletariat** (workers).

2) Marx and Engels argued that working class oppression would become so **bad** that eventually the workers would become **conscious socialists** and organise a **revolution** to establish a classless society.

Ideology and Political Action

Marxism influences a number of *New Social Movements*

1) There have been a number of small **revolutionary Marxist** political parties in the West for many years. However, more important perhaps is the **influence** Marxist thinking has come to have on the **global anti-capitalist movement**.

2) **Alex Callinicos (2003)** has suggested that NSMs will become more and more aware that the world's global problems — poverty, famine, disease and the environment — have their common origin in **international capitalism**. Callinicos says that **global social movements** have real potential as a **revolutionary political force**.

> **Anarchism** — which sees the **state** rather than capitalism as the source of repression and exploitation — has also had a big impact on the political activities of NSMs. **Noam Chomsky**, whose political writings are highly influential with global anti-capitalists, works within a recognisably **anarchist tradition**.

The influence of *Feminism* declined after its peak in the *1960s* and *1970s*

Heywood (2003) puts the decline in influence of the Women's Movement down to three main factors:

1) The **divisions** between radical, liberal and socialist feminism have weakened the movement.

2) The **anti-feminist backlash** seen in many parts of the world with the rise of **religious fundamentalism** (see below) has promoted a return to **strict patriarchal control** of women.

3) An anti-feminist backlash in Western liberal democratic politics from the 1980s onwards has seen many mainstream political parties focusing on **'family values'** and **traditional** forms of **family life**.

The decline in influence of the Woman's Movement on political action in the UK can also be seen as a sign of its success, as a great many of its **original aims** have been **achieved**. For example, political equality (**the vote**), anti-discrimination legislation, abortion rights, birth control, and equal access to education.

Fundamentalists see certain *Religious Ideas* as *Essential* and *Unchallengeable*

1) The late 20th and early 21st centuries have seen a rise in a new and powerful **religious fundamentalism**.

2) Fundamentalism aims to **turn the clock back** to a mythical time when people lived by the particular **sacred text** and rules they favour. The modern world is seen as **decadent** and **immoral** with its **permissiveness**, homosexuality, available abortion, pornography, etc. Fundamentalism in most of its forms tends to be **deeply conservative**, morally and socially.

3) **Andrew Heywood (2007)** points out that fundamentalists tend to take **political action** which is **militant** and often **violent** in nature, including some shocking acts of **terrorism**. He includes the examples of the **terror attacks** by **Al Qaeda** on 11th September 2001, the **bombings** of **abortion clinics** by American **fundamentalist Christians** which have continued through recent decades, and the **assassination** of the Indian PM **Indira Gandhi** by **Sikh militants** in 1984.

Practice Questions

Q1 Outline two types of modern conservatism.

Q2 Explain what is meant by anarchism.

Q3 Suggest three reasons why the influence of feminism on political action has declined.

Q4 What is fundamentalism?

Exam Question

Q1 Identify and explain two reasons why some people believe feminism has lost influence in the UK. (6 marks)

Ideology — everyone should have to carry their passport or driver's licence...

This is all about the stuff people believe. And while it would be nice to think that it was merely a private matter, some people end up in positions of power and influence — and when that happens, their ideology becomes kind of important. Make sure you know what everyone thinks and the sort of causes they stand for. Who knows, maybe one day you'll wake up a Marxist feminist.

Defining Crime and Deviance

You'll be looking at crime alongside sociological research methods — see Section 7 for all you ever wanted to know about research.

Here are some **Definitions** of **Crime** and **Deviance**

Crime = behaviour which **breaks laws** and is **punished** by the **legal system**.

Deviance = behaviour which goes against the **norms**, **values** and **expectations** of a **social group** or **society**.

Crime is mostly deviant, but **not all deviance** is **criminal**. Think about it — it's hard to think of a criminal act which isn't also viewed as deviant but it's easy to make a long list of **non-criminal deviant behaviour** — picking your nose in public and eating it, cross-dressing, barking like a dog during a job interview, swearing at the referee, cheating at poker, etc.

Downes and Rock (**1988** *Understanding Deviance* Oxford: OUP) gave this definition of **deviance**: "Deviance may be considered as **banned** or **controlled** behaviour which is likely to attract **punishment** or **disapproval**."

Crime and *Deviance* are *Socially Constructed*

1) Both crime and deviance are **culturally determined**. What is considered criminal varies less than what's considered deviant.

2) **Michel Foucault** wrote about how definitions of **criminal** deviance, **sexual** deviance and **madness** have changed throughout history, e.g. 100 years ago in the UK it was deviant for women to wear trousers, but today it's acceptable. **Deviance changes** with **time** and **place** as values, norms and social expectations change — it's **relative**.

3) Also, what's **deviant** for some groups in society is **conformity** for others. **Subcultures** have **different norms** to mainstream society.

Plummer (1979) said that the same act can be seen as **deviant** or **non-deviant** depending on the situation:

Societal deviance means acts which are seen by most of society as deviant, in most situations

- **Swearing** at an **authority figure** (it doesn't count if you're watching them on TV!) — even people who do it know it's deviant.
- Random acts of **extreme violence**. ← ⌐ Even in manga cartoons, this is the mark of a true nutcase. ⌐
- **Child abuse** — considered universally wrong by society.

Situational deviance means acts which can be defined as deviant or normal, depending on the circumstances

- Being **naked** — OK in your **own home**, deviant on the **high street**.
- Wearing **fishnet and PVC** from head to toe — OK in a **goth** or **fetish club**, deviant at **work** in an accountant's office. ⌐ Social rules can be temporarily rejected. ⌐
- **Killing** someone — OK if you're a **soldier at war** killing enemy soldiers, otherwise deviant.

Social Order and *Social Control* create a *Consensus* of *how to behave*

1) By definition, **most behaviour** in society isn't **criminal** or **deviant**. **Social order** and **social control** maintain the **status quo** and create a **value consensus** of how to behave. People are **socialised** to follow social norms.

2) Some norms become **second nature**. For example, when having a **face-to-face conversation**, most people manage to stand the right distance apart, look at each other when they're talking without staring excessively, be polite and tactful, not talk for too long — all **without really thinking** about it.

3) Other norms are followed because we're **consciously aware** that they're a norm — e.g. stopping at a red traffic light.

4) **Sanctions** are **rewards** and **punishments** that **reinforce** social norms:

	Positive sanctions — these **reward** people for **conforming** to a norm.	**Negative sanctions** — these **punish** people for **deviating** from a norm.
Formal sanctions — carried out by an **official agency**.	• A **certificate** for passing an A-level exam. • A **medal** for bravery in the armed forces. • A **cup** for winning a sporting final.	• A **fine** for breaking the law. • **Points** on a driving licence. • A **yellow card** from the referee.
Informal sanctions — carried out by the **public**.	• A **pat on the back**. • Saying "**well done**" for good behaviour.	• Deliberately **ignoring** someone. • A **telling-off** for bad behaviour.

Defining Crime and Deviance

Sociologists are interested in *Social Causes* of *Crime* and *Deviance*

Sociologists are interested in **crime** and **deviance** as a **social phenomenon** — it's part of understanding society.

The key questions about crime are: ⟶

Studying deviance is less clear-cut, because there's **deviance** and **social control** in all areas of sociological study.

- Does crime have a **purpose**?
- What are the **causes** of crime?
- **Who** commits crime?
- What is the **extent** of crime?

⌐ This is all discussed on ⌐ the next few pages.

There are *Non-Sociological Theories* of why *Crime* exists

Sociologists are not the only ones interested in understanding crime and deviance in society. The first theories regarding why crime and deviance exist in society were developed in the **19th century** and were based on the **physiological** or **psychological** characteristics of the individual deviant.

Physiological theories say that criminals are physically different

1) 19th century Italian doctor **Cesare Lombroso (1876)** became famous for his theory that criminals were **genetically different**. He stated there were **outward signs** of the criminal personality such as a large jaw or extra fingers or toes.

2) Don't dismiss physiological theories as staying in the 19th century, though. They've moved with the times. **Moir and Jessel (1995** *A Mind to Crime* London: Michael Joseph) argue **hormonal** and **chemical imbalances** make individuals more likely to be criminal. They say these imbalances affect **men** more than women, explaining why statistics show most crime is committed by men: "The male mind — whether for reasons of evolution or something else — is wired and fuelled to be more criminal."

Psychological theories say that criminals are mentally different

1) Others argue criminals are **psychologically** different from the rest of the population. Again, these theories started in the 19th century but travelled through the 20th century.

2) **Bowlby (1946)** argued that individuals who are **deprived of maternal love** in the first years of life are likely to **develop personality traits** which lead them to commit **crime**.

3) **Eysenck (1964)** concluded from his psychological research that individuals who commit crime have **inherited psychological characteristics** which **predispose** them to crime.

The **21st century** versions of physiological and psychological theories argue there are **genes** which make some people more likely to commit crimes — some individuals **inherit** these genes and others don't. Some theories say that people with **hormonal**, **chemical**, **psychological** or **brain abnormalities** (often caused by experiences when they were young) are more likely to commit crimes.

> For the **non-sociological theories** the cause of crime lies within the **individual**.
> For **sociology** the cause of crime lies in **society**.

Practice Questions

Q1 Give an example of a behaviour which is deviant but not criminal.

Q2 What is situational deviance?

Q3 Give an example of a formal negative sanction and an example of an informal positive sanction.

Q4 Give an example of a psychological theory of crime.

Q5 Give one difference between physiological and psychological theories of crime.

Exam Question

Q1 'The cause of crime lies within the individual.'
To what extent do sociological arguments and evidence support this view. (21 marks)

Naughty, naughty, very naughty...

There's something about the word 'deviance' that conjures up images of men in PVC suits cavorting in vats of custard. Or is that just me... Anyway, point being that deviance isn't limited to weird sexual deviance. It actually covers all behaviour that doesn't conform to social norms. Conformity is rewarded and deviance is punished. Remember, some deviance depends on the situation.

Theories of Crime and Deviance

All sociological theories regarding crime and deviance are trying to say why crime exists. Structural theories of crime all argue the cause of crime lies in the structure of society, but they disagree on a lot more than they have in common.

Functionalists argue crime and deviance are Useful and Necessary in society

You might well wonder how on earth crime can be useful. Functionalists say it's because it has a **function** in society:

1) Crime and deviance reinforce the **consensus** of values, norms and behaviour of the majority non-deviant population — people can join together in outrage.

2) **Durkheim (1897)** said deviancy allows for **social change** to occur. Durkheim and the **functionalists** who came after him argue that all societies need some change to remain healthy and stable. If society reacts positively to deviant behaviour it starts the process for that behaviour to be seen as non-deviant in the future.

3) **Durkheim** said crime moves from **functional** to **dysfunctional** when the level of crime is either **too high** or **too low**.
   • Too high, and it threatens social order. • Too low, and there's no social change.

Albert Cohen (1966) identified two ways that deviance maintained Social Order

1) He argued forms of deviance such as **prostitution** provide a **safety valve** for releasing tension without threatening social stability.

2) Secondly, he argued deviant behaviour is used as a **warning device** by society to **identify** emerging **social problems**, which can then be dealt with, e.g. civil disobedience, protests and truancy.

Merton said Crime is a Response to Failing to Achieve society's cultural goals

1) Functionalist **Robert Merton (1968)** concluded from his American study that the vast majority of individuals share the same goals but don't have equal access to the means of achieving these goals.

2) He identified the main cultural goals in American society as **success** and **wealth**. He said that the main (institutionalised) means of achieving those goals was through the education system. When individuals fail or are excluded from this system, this creates **anomie**.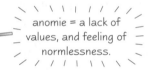

   anomie = a lack of values, and feeling of normlessness.

3) Merton argues that individuals who fail at the standard route to success **innovate** to find **alternative** and **deviant** means of reaching success and wealth — e.g. **crime**.

4) Merton says they may also **retreat** from society — e.g. by **dropping out**, **drinking** to excess or taking **drugs**.

5) They may also **rebel** against society, and engage in **protest** and revolution to try and change society.

Subcultural theories say Cultural Values of some groups Encourage Deviance

Some deviance is **conformity** to norms and values — just **different** norms and values to **mainstream society**.

Cohen said delinquent gangs provide prestige for adolescents frustrated at their lack of status in society

Albert Cohen (1955) said that working class boys suffered from a lack of opportunities to succeed in mainstream society, largely due to cultural deprivation. This leads to dissatisfaction with their position in society — which Cohen called **status frustration**.

This tension is **released** by joining or creating groups which have **alternative values** for achieving status. These values tend to be the **reverse** of those of mainstream society — behaviour deviant in society becomes **normal** and **valued** in the subcultural group. For example, **petty crime** or **drug-taking** might be valued by the group.

1) **Cloward and Ohlin (1960) combined** the ideas of **Merton** with the ideas of **Cohen**. They believed there was a **legitimate opportunity structure** (passing exams and getting a job, as Merton said), and an **illegitimate opportunity structure** (being in a gang and committing crime, e.g. theft and vandalism).

2) They also argued that access to the **illegitimate** opportunity structure is **no more equal** than access to the **legitimate** system. In some areas, there are criminal gangs which provide adolescents with a deviant route to success and status, and in some areas there aren't. This explained why **not all** frustrated working class boys turned to **crime**.

3) Cloward and Ohlin said where there's **no access** to criminal gangs, frustrated adolescents form their own **violent gangs**.

4) They also said that adolescents who have **failed** in **both** the legitimate opportunity structure and the illegitimate opportunity structure **retreat** from society and turn to drink or drugs.

The subcultural theories have been criticised for **assuming** that the majority of people aspire to the **mainstream goals** of success and wealth. **Taylor, Walton and Young (1973)** point to deviant groups such as **hippies** who **don't share these goals**.

Theories of Crime and Deviance

Miller thought crime and delinquency come from Working Class Cultural Values

W B Miller (1962) said that general **lower working class culture**, not subcultural gangs, was what encouraged lawbreaking behaviour. According to Miller, values passed from generation to generation encourage **working class men** to break the law. Delinquents are simply conforming to the **focal concerns** of their culture. 'Focal concerns' are the main things that are valued in that culture, e.g. exciting thrills and macho toughness.

Miller was **criticised** right from the beginning. **Bordua (1962)** said that the idea that the working class live their lives **isolated** from the rest of society is **flawed to begin with**.

Miller's ideas have been supported by recent **New Right** sociologists. **Charles Murray (1990, 1993)** believes that there's an underclass in both British and American society with a **distinct culture** and **value system** which **encourages** deviant behaviour.

Marxists see Crime as an Inevitable Consequence of Capitalism

1) Traditional Marxist criminology says that the **rich** and **powerful** decide what is considered deviant and criminal in society to **suit their own interests**. No surprise for Marxists that the most common group convicted of crime is the working class — Marxists say the system is rigged against them.

2) Crime such as robbery and property theft is seen by traditional Marxists like **Bonger (1916)** as an inevitable response to the **extremes** of **wealth** and **poverty** in capitalist society. They see the individual as **"forced"** into crime by the structure of society.

While not out on the beat, Nigel dreamed of the overthrow of the bourgeoisie.

Because Marxists see the 'system' as the cause of crime, much Marxist sociology has looked at the systems of **power**, **control** and **punishment**, i.e. the **police**, the **law** and the **courts**. This is covered on p.181.

Feminist Theories of crime

1) **Heidensohn (1989)** has argued that '**malestream**' sociology — i.e. mainstream sociology, dominated by men — is **gender blind**. She says most studies of crime have been researched by men who have focused on male crime and **ignored the role of women**, either as victims or as criminals.

2) Official statistics suggest women commit **fewer crimes** than men, and commit **different types of crime**. There are a number of different theories trying to explain these differences:

- **Sex-role theory** suggests that women are brought up to be passive and conformist so are less likely to commit crimes.
- **Heidensohn (2002)** argues that in a patriarchal, male-dominated society, women have less 'opportunity' to commit some types of crime. You can't commit, e.g., financial fraud unless you're in control of large sums of money, and more men are found in powerful positions in the workplace. The crimes women do commit tend to relate to their role in the home as a wife or mother, e.g. shoplifting.
- **Westwood (1999)** suggests female identities are changing and women are adopting more typically male behaviour patterns. This could be linked to an increase in female crime.
- **Carol Smart (1995)** has suggested that female crime has to be looked at as part of women's broader experience in society. For example, women are often invisible victims of domestic violence.

Practice Questions

Q1 Why did Merton think people committed crime?

Q2 What is meant by 'status frustration'?

Q3 What did Miller say was the cause of crime?

Q4 What did Heidensohn mean by 'gender blind'?

Exam Question

Q1 'The cause of crime lies in the structure of society, not the nature of the individual.'
Consider this statement, referring to Marxist and feminist perspectives. (21 marks)

Society made me do it...

Unlikely to stand up in a court of law, that one. I wouldn't recommend defending yourself by quoting Merton and Cohen. It didn't work for me after all that unpleasantness with the goat smuggling. Anyway, I'm not going into all that now. The past is the past. And I was actually doing society a favour — I was acting as a warning device that goats are not fairly distributed in the UK.

Theories of Crime and Deviance

Interpretivists (also known as interactionists) say deviance is actually defined by social reaction. Great.

Interpretivists say that Deviant folk are not that Different from everyone else

Interpretivist (also known as interactionist) study of crime and deviance starts from the standpoint that deviants are **not characteristically different** from the rest of the population. They are deviant because their chosen behaviour is **labelled deviant** by others in society.

Interpretivists therefore think that there aren't any **universal causes** of deviance or crime to be 'discovered' by sociologists.

Interpretivists stress the view that deviance is **relative** — it varies over time and place because it is defined by each society and by each situation within a society.

Becker (1963) argues deviance is behaviour which has been labelled deviant by the reaction of others

1) This may sound like common sense, but interpretivists like Becker were the first sociologists to **challenge the assumption** that sociologists should focus on what **causes** people to act in deviant and criminal ways.

2) Instead, interpretivists studied how an act or behaviour comes to be **labelled as deviant** by the rest of society, and the consequences of that label or reaction.

3) The **same behaviour** gets **different reactions** depending on the social situation. Becker thought there's therefore nothing intrinsically deviant about the act itself. For example, **nudity** is normal and acceptable in the privacy of your own home but seen as deviant (and criminal) in a public space.

4) The **reaction** of those around you is what makes you **recognise** your behaviour as deviant. Becker said, "Deviance is not a quality that lies in the **behaviour** itself but in the **interaction** between the person who commits an act, and those who respond to it." (1963, *Outsiders: Studies in the Sociology of Deviance* New York: The Free Press)

Being Labelled as Deviant can Affect Future Behaviour

Interpretivists argue we form our self-identity by **interpreting** how others respond to us and **internalising** the reaction. A **label** can have a **positive** or **negative** effect on the individual and it helps to define them in their **own eyes** as well as in others' eyes. Becker calls this a **"self concept"**.

Being labelled 'awesome' had deeply affected Edwin's behaviour.

1) Becker argued that a **self concept** of being deviant can **increase deviant behaviour**. If a person is **shamed** by the reaction of others who know they have been in trouble with the police, they may return to criminal activity or **join a criminal group** to escape the feeling of rejection. This reinforces the label of criminal — it becomes even harder to remove and a bigger part of their identity. Becker called this process the **deviant career**.

2) The **label** of **criminal** is **not easily removed** by society, whatever the actions of the individual — it becomes their **master status** (see glossary). On release from prison many individuals find it hard to obtain work, housing and positions of trust because of the reaction of others to their status as an **ex-offender**.

3) **Jock Young (1971)** used his study of drug users in Notting Hill to demonstrate the process of becoming deviant:

The marijuana users developed a **deviant self concept** because their drug of choice was **illegal**.	The **deviant** element became their **main identity** in society. They were 'hippies' first and foremost.	The **negative response** of those around them and the police made the drug-taking more **significant** to their lives.	Their drug-taking **increased**.

4) **Goffman (1961)** wrote about a deviant career in **mental illness**. He said the **negative label** of being **mad** is **imposed** on the patient by society and psychiatry, and the patient must eventually **conform** to it.

Lemert (1951) distinguished between Primary and Secondary deviance

Primary deviance = the initial deviant act

Secondary deviance = deviant acts committed after the individual has accepted the label of deviant

1) Lemert argued **most people** commit some acts of **primary deviance** in their lives but that it was of **little significance**.

2) When there's a **societal reaction** (a reaction from society as a whole or groups within society such as family, peers, police and the media) the individual is **labelled** as **deviant**.

3) Lemert argues that when the individual **feels the weight** of the label 'deviant' or 'criminal', they sometimes commit **more** of the deviant behaviour. For example, once a person is labelled an **alcoholic**, they might drink more because, well, they're an alcoholic, and alcoholics drink. Lemert called this **secondary deviance**.

Public reaction to an individual labelled deviant can be very powerful. Sometimes, individuals **commit suicide** once their deviance has been discovered — e.g. it's not uncommon for suspects in internet child pornography raids to kill themselves.

Theories of Crime and Deviance

Critics argue people are not as Passive as Interpretivists suggest

1) **Ronald Akers (1967)** criticises both Becker and Lemert for presenting individuals as **powerless** to make decisions or take control of their own identity. **Deviance**, according to **Akers**, is not something which **happens** to people but a **choice** that individuals make.

2) **Taylor, Walton and Young (1973)** argue many forms of behaviour are **widely viewed** as deviant — so deviants **know** they are breaking the law or social rules **before** any **societal reaction**, but they **still do it**.

3) Marxist critics accuse interpretivism of **ignoring the role of power** in defining crime and deviance. Certain groups have the **power** to influence what is classified as **criminal** or **socially unacceptable**.

4) **Gouldner (1973)** accused interpretivists of being **fascinated with deviance**, and even suggests they enjoy observing 'cool' deviants, and hanging out with the 'underworld'. He thinks interpretivists aren't interested in changing society.

Control Theory asks Why More People Don't commit crime

Control theory has its origins in Durkheim's belief that all societies need to have shared values. Durkheim called these values the society's '**collective conscience**'.

The sociologist **Hirschi (1969)** looked at reasons why people **don't** commit crime. He suggested that there are **four social bonds** which hold society together:

- **attachment** to society
- **commitment** to society
- **involvement** in society
- **belief** that society's rules must be obeyed

The more strongly an individual feels these bonds, the less likely that individual is to commit a crime.

Wilson and Kelling (1982) put forward the '**broken windows**' thesis. They argued that people who live in well-maintained areas with low crime rates feel like they are **part of society** and are **less likely** to commit crime. When crimes — even minor crimes like breaking windows — go uncorrected and **unpunished**, people start to feel there is no **social control** and lose their sense of belonging. This sense of detachment leads to **increasing crime rates** and a downwards spiral of decay.

Etzioni (1993) suggests that in the past poor communities **policed themselves**. In some communities, this system has broken down and a criminal underclass has taken over. The way to correct this is to create a greater sense of social integration and social responsibility, e.g. by setting up **neighbourhood watch schemes**.

Max and Christine were too hungry and Frankie was just too busy reading the small ads to commit any crime.

Postmodernists put crime down to people's Sense of Identity

1) Postmodernists argue that society is becoming increasingly **fragmented**.

2) In modern society people's **sense of identity** has more to do with what they see in the media and the brands they buy into and less to do with their family, religion or local area. People tend to think of themselves as individuals rather than part of society. Foucault called this trend the **process of individualism**.

3) As this trend continues people feel **less attached to society** and are **more likely to commit crime**.

Practice Questions

Q1 Why are interpretivists less interested in the causes of crime than other sociologists?
Q2 Explain how the reactions of others are significant in the interpretivist understanding of deviance.
Q3 What does Hirschi mean by the 'four social bonds'?
Q4 What is Etzioni's solution to the loss of social control?

Exam Questions

Q1 Assess control theories of crime. (21 marks)

Q2 Assess the view that societal reaction is a major cause of deviance. (21 marks)

Sigh. If you will insist on running naked through the streets...

It's interesting how people react to deviant behaviour. Some people scream and shout, others run away, and others pretend it's not happening. Well, according to Becker and his merry bunch of interpretivists, it's the reaction that people have to deviance that makes it deviant. They even went as far as saying that reaction can make deviants more deviant. Give a dog a bad name...

Theories of Crime and Deviance

Deviance is controlled by society, and kept to a low level. Which is good, as it means you're less likely to be mugged by a naked nose-picker. And nobody likes to be mugged by a naked nose-picker, unless of course they're seriously deviant.

Social Control keeps Order in Society

Functionalist sociologists argue that deviance must be kept to a **low level**. They say that a small amount of deviant activity can actually help maintain social order because it unites the rest of society in disapproval of the deviant behaviour. Functionalists say social control **benefits everyone** in society.

Marxist sociologists agree social control is essential to keep order. They say capitalism is an **exploitative** system which requires systems of social control over the population to **prevent rebellion and revolution**. Marxists say social control **benefits the ruling class** and works against the interests of the majority working class.

Marxists say Social Control is maintained through Hegemony

1) **Informal social control** is achieved through socialisation where individuals are **taught** to accept ideas and norms which support the status quo in society. These ideas are supported by **institutions** of the state such as the **education** and **legal** systems.

2) This ideology (set of ideas and values) is presented as **common sense** and neutral. However, according to neo-Marxists such as **Gramsci**, they're really designed in the interests of those in power.

3) Alternative ideas are overwhelmed by the **dominance** of this **ruling class ideology**.

4) The ability to **informally control** ideas and values in this way is **hegemony**.

5) Part of capitalist class hegemony is the **belief** that the legal system operates in the interests of **everyone** in society. Traditional Marxists argue the legal system is actually a method of **formal social control** over the population. They claim the legal system backs up the ideas and values of the ruling class ideology.

Marxists say the Capitalist State passes Laws which benefit the Ruling Class

1) According to Marxism, laws **aren't the will of the people**. They're a reflection of ruling class interests.

2) Other than the most serious crimes of murder, rape and violence, the vast majority of law in the UK is **property law**. **Chambliss and Mankoff (1976)** wrote that most of this law serves to keep **working class** people **away** from the property and land of the rich. The ruling class uses the law to protect **private property** because **capitalist exploitation** is built upon it.

3) The vast majority of the population have **no power** or **say** in the creation of **laws** and **punishments**.

4) The **lack of legislation** in some areas of life is also a demonstration of the law as an instrument of the ruling class.

5) Canadian sociologist **Laureen Snider (1993)** argues legislation regulating **large companies** is **restricted** in capitalist societies because it could **threaten ruling class interests**. For example, legislation regarding health and safety, pollution and fair trade are passed to a **minimum level** and often **weakly enforced**. **Tobacco companies** have put huge **pressure** on governments **not to pass laws** making them **legally responsible** for the deaths of smokers.

6) **Pearce (1976)** suggested that even the laws which supposedly protect the working class (e.g. health and safety laws, consumer laws) are really in ruling class interests. He said the system needs healthy, safe and loyal workers.

Marxists say Ruling Class lawbreakers are Less Likely to be Punished

Marxists also say the law is not enforced equally in capitalist societies.

1) **Laureen Snider (1993)** argues that working class crimes such as burglary don't cause as much harm in society as corporate crimes such as breaking health and safety law.

2) Marxists suggest that **ruling class ideology** successfully presents the burglars as the 'real criminals' and a threat to society, largely through the media. Meanwhile **corporate lawbreakers** get very **little media condemnation** and are treated more **leniently** by the legal system.

3) Also, if company bosses are charged they have the **money** to buy the **best legal advice**.

4) The work of **Chambliss (1978)** is good evidence for this. He studied crime in the American city of Seattle and found those in power were able to use their power to conduct criminal activity and to avoid prison. He found an organised crime syndicate which included elite businessmen and politicians who used money and influence to bribe officials.

Gordon (1976) argues **selective enforcement** of the law and **selective reporting** in the media gives the impression that criminals are largely working class. He thinks this not only diverts attention from ruling class crime but also **divides the working class** when the working class criminal becomes the target of anger rather than the system itself.

Theories of Crime and Deviance

Traditional Marxists are Criticised for overlooking Other Effects on Crime

1) Traditional Marxists believe that the cause of crime lies within the nature of the **capitalist system**. Their assumption that if you end capitalism you end crime is **rejected** by many. There's **crime** in **socialist societies** like Cuba, and **some capitalist societies** such as Switzerland have very **low crime rates**.

2) Feminists accuse traditional Marxist theory of **ignoring** the role of **patriarchy** in rule creation and social control.

3) More recent Marxist-influenced theory such as left-realism (see glossary) reckons traditional Marxism focuses too much on **corporate crime**. They dispute the argument that other crimes such as burglary are **insignificant**, especially as the **victims** are usually **working class**.

New Criminology argues criminals Choose to break the law

Taylor, Walton and Young's *The New Criminology* (1973) says crime is a choice

Background: *The New Criminology* was an attempt to present a thorough and considered **Marxist analysis** of crime, largely because Taylor, Walton and Young thought other Marxists, including Marx, had **failed** to do so. The main aim of *The New Criminology* was to move the sociology of crime on from the idea that society should be trying to **remove** deviant behaviour to a need to **understand** and **accept** it.

Theory: Taylor, Walton and Young argued that criminals were not **passive** individuals unable to control their economic situation as **traditional Marxists** had stated. Instead, crime was a **conscious**, **meaningful** and **deliberate choice** individuals made to try and **change society**.

Much crime is a **deliberate fight against capitalism**. Taylor, Walton and Young point to political action groups such as the **Black Panther** Movement who use criminal means to **agitate** the system. Robbery is also seen by the new criminologists as a potential means of **redistributing wealth**. (Robin Hood, anyone...)

Conclusion: Sociology needs a **"fully social theory of deviance"**. Deviance needs to be explained from **different viewpoints**, which consider how society is **organised** and at the same time **how** and **why** individuals **choose** to be deviant.

Seven Aspects of a Full Social Theory of Deviance, from Taylor, Walton and Young's *The New Criminology*:

1) How **wealth** and **power** are **distributed**.
2) The **unique circumstances** of each **deviant act**.
3) The **nature** of the **deviant act** itself.
4) **Reactions** of the **rest of society** to the deviant act.
5) Who has the **power** to **make rules** about the **treatment** of deviance or **response** to deviance.
6) The **effect** being **labelled deviant** has on an individual.
7) How all these factors **interlink**.

In **1978**, **Hall et al** applied the 'social theory of deviance' to media reports of large numbers of muggings involving black muggers. They analysed the situation in terms of:

- **Social, economic and political conditions** — The country was in **economic crisis**. Unions and militants were **threatening state power**.
- **Motivations of the state** — The government wanted to feel in **control** of the situation.
- **Motivations of the media** — The press and broadcasters wanted a **dramatic story**.
- **What happened** — The police **arrested more people**. The media reported this and presented the muggers as a **threat to society**, creating an unjustified **moral panic**.

Practice Questions

Q1 Give two examples of how Marxists argue that capitalism creates laws that disadvantage the working class.
Q2 Why do some sociologists reject the Marxist idea that capitalism is the cause of crime?
Q3 According to Taylor, Walton and Young, why do people commit crime?

Exam Question

Q1 'The law is an instrument of the ruling class.'
To what extent do sociological arguments and evidence support this view? (21 marks)

It's not my fault — capitalism made me do it...

Again, not recommended as a defence in a court of law. It didn't work for me when I insisted on running naked through the streets. Anyway, it's the usual suspects here — functionalists and Marxists. The Marxist theory of criminology is useful to learn. There are a lot of studies, and if you can explain and analyse them in the exam then you'll get plenty of marks.

Theories of Crime and Deviance

Two theories focused on finding a solution to crime have had a big influence on social policy in Britain and America — left realism and right realism. No prizes for guessing which is more right wing and which is more left wing.

Left Realists said policy must accept that crime is Real and Rising

In *What Is to Be Done About Law and Order?* **(1984)**, **Lea and Young** launched their **new theory** of crime and how to reduce it. They criticised other left-wing writers (especially Marxists) for overlooking the reality of crime in Britain by focusing on the problems within capitalism.

> **Lea and Young said left wing sociological debate and social policy on crime must start accepting that:**
> * Crimes **other than white-collar crime** are a **problem**.
> * There has been a **rise in crime** in Britain since the Second World War.
> * Being a **victim** of crime is a very **significant event** in an individual's life.
> * **Fear of crime** is a real factor in shaping modern urban lifestyles, especially for **women**.

Kinsey, Lea and Young (1986) recommend changes in Policing Policy

1) **Kinsey, Lea and Young (1986)** say that British policing policy needs to be centred on **creating** and **maintaining good communication** between the **police** and **local communities**.

> The public **report most crimes** to the police.
> The public **provide most evidence** to solve crimes.   = The police **need** the public.

2) Kinsey, Lea and Young say the public should have a **key role** in deciding **police policy**. They propose setting up **Police Authorities** which are **democratically elected** from the public. These authorities should formulate policing policy and direct police action.

3) This would create **consensus policing** where the police are acting on the instructions of the local community, rather than in isolation from them.

PCs Hillier, Samson, Costa, Armitage, Stevens, Collins and Benjamin slowly came to a consensus on where to lunch.

4) Kinsey, Lea and Young say the key role of the police should then be **"full and proper investigation of crime"** which they reckon has been reduced in recent years.

5) They say the police need to improve their **detection** and **clear-up** rates. At the time they were writing, only 12% of recorded crime was cleared up. This figure has improved since then.

Left realists say Relative Deprivation is a factor causing Crime

1) **Lea and Young (2002)** argue that a sense of **relative deprivation** is a major factor leading to crime. When an individual feels deprived in relation to similar social groups, they can turn to crime to "solve" the problem and acquire the resources to remove the feeling.

2) It's not actual deprivation but the **feeling of being deprived** relative to someone else that triggers this response. This explains why crime occurs in all social strata — the rich can feel deprived next to the super-rich.

3) **Lea and Young** says these feelings of deprivation are compounded by the **consumer culture** of modern Britain — **advertising** and the **media** present individuals with images of what they **could** have and what others have got.

4) Therefore, a rising standard of living can lead to a rising crime rate.

Left realists say Social Inequality must be fought in order to Reduce Crime

Left realists identify **deprivation** and to a lesser extent **marginalisation** as causes of crime. They say that in the long term, order will come from a **fair** and **just** society. **Left realists** stress the need for **all social agencies** to have a direct aim of removing inequality. They include the general public in this — everyone's responsible.

> Left realists use the **"square of crime"** to show the **interactions** between **four elements** which affect crime — the state, the public, the offender and the victim. Left realists argue that all four elements should **work together** to understand and reduce crime.

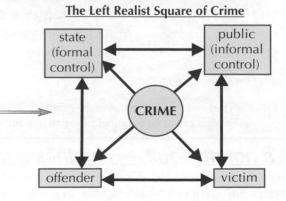

The Left Realist Square of Crime

Left realist work has influenced **Labour** government **social policy** since **1997**. Remember Tony Blair's phrase "tough on crime, tough on the causes of crime" — it sums up the left realism theory pretty well.

Theories of Crime and Deviance

Critics say that if Left Realism was Correct there'd be More Crime

1) **Hughes (1991)** says the left realists haven't explained why **some people** who experience **relative deprivation** see **crime** as a **solution** and others don't. He argues there would be a lot **more crime** if **relative deprivation** was the main cause.

2) Critics also say that Kinsey, Lea and Young didn't collect enough data to develop a full theory of crime. Their theory only focuses on **property crime**.

Right Realists have influenced American Social Policy

No one wants to end up here

1) **Wilson (1975)** believes individuals commit crime because the **gains outweigh** the chances of being **caught and punished**. In order to reduce crime, Wilson says it's necessary to issue **harsh punishments** for the smallest crimes — so the benefits won't outweigh the punishment any more. Punishment should be a **deterrent** to future offenders.

Wilson was a social policy advisor to the Reagan government of the USA in the 1980s.

2) This has been put into action in the social policy of **Zero Tolerance**, first in America and now in parts of the UK (e.g. Middlesbrough).

3) **Wilson and Kelling (1982)** say that damage to a neighbourhood has to be put right straight away, or problems of crime and delinquency quickly get out of hand. This is called the "One Broken Window" idea — their article says that tolerating just one broken window sends the message that you can get away with crime.

4) Wilson and Kelling actually advocate **taking resources and police supervision away** from areas where law and order has **broken down** — this sounds wrong, but Wilson says that once social order has gone it's almost impossible to regain it, so it's not worth **wasting resources** on trying. He recommends **diverting police** to areas which **aren't too far gone**, to **prevent breakdown** of social order in those areas.

Wilson and Herrnstein (1985) claim there's a biological predisposition to crime in some individuals — but with the right socialisation they can be trained away from it. They argue that single-parent families are more likely to have "criminal children" because their socialisation hasn't been complete.

Murray (1997) claims that the higher the **risk** of going to **prison**, the less likely people are to commit crime.

Right Realism has been Criticised

1) **Critics** of right realism have been many and varied. The argument that criminals are **biologically different** is **rejected** by many as coming from theories that have already been discredited.

2) **Jones (1998)** questions the assertion that resources put into run-down areas are wasted. He argues that investment in these areas makes a positive difference to the communities who live there.

3) **Matthews (1992)** didn't find any evidence that tolerating broken windows leads to crime.

4) Critics also say that Zero Tolerance policies have led to a big rise in the **US prison population** — e.g. the "**three strikes and you're out**" policy which means three serious offences automatically result in **life imprisonment**.

Practice Questions

Q1 Give an example of a sociological theory influencing social policy.

Q2 How does left realism differ from Marxist criminology?

Q3 What do left realists say causes crime?

Q4 Give two examples of things that right realists say would reduce crime.

Exam Questions

Q1 Assess the left realist argument that different policing strategies would reduce crime. (21 marks)

Q2 "Deprivation can trigger a criminal response."
To what extent do sociological arguments and evidence support this view? (21 marks)

A kid broke my window playing football last week — give him life in prison, I say...

Both these new approaches are quite different to the old sociological theories, which just tend to blame society. The left realists are quite harsh on Marxism, and say that it ignores the effect of crime on ordinary people. Right wing politicians and right realists have been quite firm in their claim that prison works, but just like everything in sociology, there's no broad agreement.

Measuring Crime

Measuring crime isn't straightforward. Different statisticians use different techniques and reach different, conflicting conclusions.

Police *crime figures* Don't *reflect the* Full Extent *of* Crime *in Britain*

Police crime figures are official statistics that have been recorded and published **annually** in Britain since **1857**. They're useful because they're easy to **access**, can be used to **identify trends** and show the **social background** of criminals. For 100 years, they were largely taken as an **accurate** record of all crime, but then sociologists began to **question** how reliable police stats are.

(1) Firstly, official police records only report crimes **known to the police**. Not all crime is **reported** to the police.

1) Individuals don't report crime if they **don't have faith in the police** to investigate and solve it.

2) Crime won't be reported to the police if the victim is **intimidated** by the perpetrator. Many communities have **gangs** of criminals who **threaten** anyone who reports their crimes, including witnesses as well as victims.

3) Much sexual crime is not reported because of the embarrassment, fear and shock of the victim.

4) Some victims see the crime against them as trivial — or fear the police will see it as trivial.

(2) Secondly, the police **don't record all crime** that's reported to them. Police officers use their own discretion to decide whether an incident is **worth reporting** — if there's enough evidence to say a crime has been committed, if the incident is serious enough to be a crime, etc. This makes crime reporting unreliable — some officers will record an incident, but others may consider it too **trivial** or lacking in evidence, especially as there's a lot of **paperwork** involved.

(3) Thirdly, not all offences **count** as crimes to be recorded by the police. For example, police weren't required to record all common assaults until 1989. **Official rules** and definitions **change**. In **1998, new guidelines** allowed police to record a lot more incidents as crime. This alone increased the level of crime recorded by 15%.

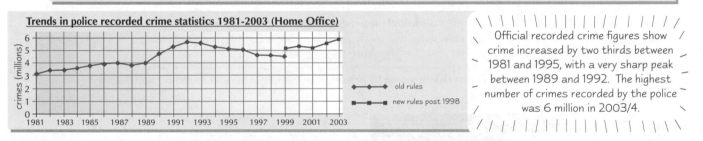

Trends in police recorded crime statistics 1981-2003 (Home Office)

◆ old rules
■ new rules post 1998

Official recorded crime figures show crime increased by two thirds between 1981 and 1995, with a very sharp peak between 1989 and 1992. The highest number of crimes recorded by the police was 6 million in 2003/4.

Victim Surveys *include crime* Not Reported *to the* Police

A **victimisation** (or victim) **survey** is an **anonymous** survey of individuals asking for details of crimes committed **against them** (even if **not reported** to the police) within a set time period, usually the last year. Because they include figures for reported and unreported crimes, they're more **representative** than police crime figures. Other advantages of victim surveys are that they use a **large sample size** and have a **high response rate**.

1) The most significant victim survey in Britain is the **British Crime Survey** (**BCS**), which interviews a **sample** of the population (approx 14 000), and asks them about their experiences of being a victim of crime over the previous year. Answers are confidential and can't be passed on to the police. The survey results are applied to the whole UK population.

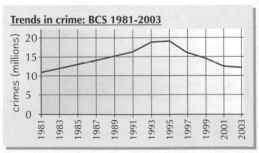

Trends in crime: BCS 1981-2003

2) In the past the BCS has indicated a significant level of **unrecorded** crime. In recent years BCS and police figures have been much closer. In 2007/8 the BCS showed **27%** of crimes were **vandalism**, with the police figures showing **21%**. The BCS showed **burglary** as **7%** of all crime, compared to **12%** of police-recorded crime.

3) Victim surveys and police figures reveal the same **broad trends**. Crime **rose** in the **1980s** and early **1990s**. Since **2002** there's been a **small drop** in crime. In 2007/8 BCS levels of crime were the lowest since 1981 when the survey began.

4) There are **problems** with the reliability of victim surveys:

- Even the largest **victim surveys** only interview a **small sample** of the population.
- BCS doesn't survey all crime, e.g. it doesn't include crimes committed against businesses.
- **No under-16s** are interviewed for the BCS.

Sociologist **Jock Young (1988)** questioned the validity of victim surveys by pointing out that **each respondent's definition** of what's criminal is **different**, so the same incident would be mentioned by one person and not by another. Also, some people are **more willing to reveal their experiences** than others. Young accepts that victim surveys have a place in research, but maintains they **don't** give a **true, full picture** of crime.

Measuring Crime

Self-Report Studies ask people about Crime They've Committed

1) **Self-report studies** ask respondents to **reveal crime** they've committed. They're **less widely used** than victim surveys.

2) Self-report studies are **anonymous** and representative of the population, like victim surveys.

3) The obvious drawback is that respondents may not believe that their crimes won't be reported to others, including the police.

4) However, they have been important in researching **who commits crime**.

> An analysis of 40 self-report studies by **Steve Box (1981)** indicated that **juvenile crime** was not a **working class** problem as had been widely argued. **Middle class** juveniles committed crime too but were less likely to get caught. Similar results have been found in the **adult** population. **Maguire (1997)** concluded **most respondents** admitted committing **some crime** at some point in their life. This is evidence against the argument that certain social groups are more likely to commit crime than others (there's more about this idea on pages 178-179).

Official Statistics show Fear of Crime is Rising

1) Statistics show that public **fear** of being a victim of crime is rising.

2) Public assessment consistently **overestimates** the actual amount of crime in Britain. People believe that the crime rate is going up faster than it really is. Also, far more people fear becoming a victim of crime than ever will become a victim of crime.

3) This stark difference between the level of crime and fear of crime has been attributed to the way crime is reported in the media. **Tabloid** papers often use **alarmist headlines** about crime and deviance to grab the attention of readers. It's been argued that these **exaggerate** the chances of being a victim of crime — which creates fear or panic in the population.

4) The **Home Office Statistical Bulletin** (2003) revealed that those individuals who read **tabloid newspapers** were twice as likely to be worried about crime compared to those who read broadsheets or didn't read any newspapers.

5) **Fletcher and Allen (2003)** identify several factors which affect the fear of crime, including locality, health, age, perception of disorder and whether a person has previously been a victim of crime.

Pantazis and Gordon found the poor are most likely to fear crime

Pantazis and Gordon (1999)* analysed household surveys and found households with the **lowest incomes** were most likely to **fear** crime, but households with the **highest incomes** were actually the most likely to become **victims** of crime.

This is due to the consequences of crime being **more severe** for people who are **too poor** to **insure** their property, or buy **replacements**.

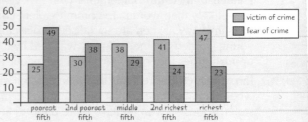

* Pantazis and Gordon (1999) 'Is Crime and Fear of Crime More Likely to be Experienced by the 'Poor'?' in Dorling and Simpson (eds) *Statistics in Society* (London, Arnold)

Practice Questions

Q1 Name two types of statistics published each year on levels of crime in Britain.

Q2 Give an example of a type of crime not covered by the British Crime Survey.

Q3 What's a self-report study?

Q4 Which social groups are most likely to fear crime?

Exam Questions

Q1 Examine the ways in which official statistics may underestimate the level of crime in the UK. (12 marks)

Q2 Examine the problems faced by sociologists trying to measure the level of crime in the UK. (12 marks)

What's that old saying about lies, damned lies and that other thing...

There are quite a lot of statistics just on these pages. Once you scratch the surface of various government statistics it's amazing just how many figures there are out there. Try not to get too bogged down in detail, but do learn the central trends and which type of study they come from. Each type of study has its own supporters and its critics — make sure you can say why that is.

Patterns of Crime

Some groups of people seem to commit more crime than others — or at least to get caught out more than other people.

Young people are Convicted of More Crime than Older People

Most crime is committed by teenagers. The peak age for criminal activity is 18 for men and 15 for women (Social Trends, 33).

1) It's argued that young people commit more crime because their **lifestyles** take them to **environments** where **crime takes place**. The vast majority of crime is **property theft** — young people are more likely to be on the **streets** or in **clubs**, which is where **pickpocketing** and **mugging** often happens.

2) This is supported by the evidence that **young people** are most likely to be **victims** of crime too — if you're aged 16-25 you're six times more likely to be a victim of crime than those aged 75 and older. It's not age itself, but the **likelihood** of being in areas where **opportunities for crime** arise which is the significant factor.

3) Young people may actually commit more crime, or it may be that they get **caught more** than older people. Crime committed by the **young** is typically more **visible**, e.g. vandalism, so it's likely to be witnessed, and the perpetrator is more likely to be caught. 'White-collar crimes' such as **fraud** are more likely to be committed by **older people**, but these offences are more **hidden** and don't take place in the public arena.

4) **Social stereotypes** that young people commit crime lead to police **suspecting** and **monitoring** young people more than older social groups — increasing their chances of being caught.

5) Young people are more likely to be **convicted** once in court — partly because they can't afford expensive **lawyers' fees**.

Men are Convicted of More Crime than Women

Women make up only **6%** of the prison population. (HM Prison Service)

58% of male prisoners released from prison are **re-convicted within 2 years**. (Social Trends, 1998)

In 2001, **167 per 10 000** of the **male** population were **found guilty** or **cautioned** for an offence, compared to **3.7 per 10 000** of the female population.

1) Men are **suspected**, **charged** and **convicted** of crime of all types more than women. This pattern crosses **all other social factors** such as **age**, **class**, **ethnicity** and **region**.

2) The subcultural theories of **Miller (1962)** and **Merton (1968)** argue that the **culture** and **lifestyles** of **young men** encourage and lead to crime (remember, most crime is committed by the young).

3) **Heidensohn (1986)** is a feminist who says gender socialisation prompts men to be more **aggressive**, which makes them more likely than women to commit violent crime. She also says that **women** are **socialised** into **not being criminal** in the same way as men are socialised into seeing criminal activity as acceptable. **Abbott and Wallace (1990)** argue young women are more closely watched by their families and given **less freedom** outside the home, reducing their **opportunities** for crime. Criminal behaviour would be seen as highly **deviant** as well as criminal for women.

4) **Ian Marsh (1986)** reckons that men commit more crime because they have more opportunities to do so. He said that where females have similar opportunities to males they seem as likely to break laws. An example of this is handling stolen goods — women have more opportunity to sell, buy or use stolen property than to steal goods in the first place.

5) There may be an **underestimation** of female crime because the police and courts are **less likely** to **suspect** women or give women a **custodial sentence**. The stereotypes of men as criminal work as a form of **sexism** against men, which allows female criminal activity to go **unchecked**. **Campbell (1981)** did a **self-report survey** which unearthed a lot **more female crime** than the official statistics. However, she did include more trivial crimes than the official statistics do.

Urban areas have much More Crime than Rural ones

According to the Home Office report ***Crime in England and Wales 2003/2004***, in 2003-2004, **metropolitan (urban) police** forces recorded **43% of all crime**. In 2002, less than 2% of people living in rural areas became victims of burglary. And, in 2003-2004, **60% of all robbery** in the UK took place in **three urban areas** (London, Manchester and West Midlands).

This table shows the percentage of households which have been **victims** (at least once) of **vehicle theft**, **burglary** and **violent crime**. The data's from the British Crime Survey, 2004.

Area type	All vehicle theft	All burglary	All violent crime
Inner city	15.3	5.3	5.8
Urban (towns and outer part of city)	10.3	3.3	4.4
All non-rural (cities, towns, suburbs)	10.8	3.6	4.6
Rural	6.5	1.9	2.7
All households/all adults	9.7	3.2	4.1

There's **more crime** in **cities**.

Sociologists argue most crime takes place in cities because there are more **opportunities** to be involved in crime in cities. Higher density populations mean more chances for **robbery** and **property crime**. Most young people live in urban areas and they are the most likely to commit crime. It's hard for criminals to remain anonymous in close-knit rural **communities**.

Patterns of Crime

Most criminal convictions are of people with a **Working Class Background**

There are more **working class** people in **prison** than any other social class. Home Office figures also show that the majority of people who appear in **court** are working class, regardless of whether they're found guilty or not.

The idea of an upper class person in prison is so rare and contrary to cultural norms that a Lord convicted of fraud can find himself on a 'celebrity' reality TV show.

1) **Subcultural theorists** such as **Miller** argue this reflects the working class subcultures which often have crime as an accepted or rewarded activity.

2) **Marxists** argue the system of law and order is run by the **ruling class**, against the interests of the working class. They say parts of the working class are criminalised by a biased system — see p.172-173.

3) Middle class crime is treated more leniently by society. Fraud and white collar crime is often undetected and seen as 'victimless crime' by the public. Consider the public response to benefit fraud compared to tax or insurance fraud. There's more about **Marxist** opinions of why this is on p.172-173.

An **Ethnic Minority Background** increases your chances of arrest and conviction

	Population of the UK	Police "stop and search", England and Wales	Arrests for serious offences, England and Wales	Male prison population	Female prison population
White	92%	74.3%	84.3%	75.7%	69.1%
Asian	4%	7.3%	4.8%	3.4%	0.8%
Black	2%	14.6%	8.8%	16%	25.3%
Mixed and Other	2%	3.7%	2.1%	4.8%	4.7%

2001 census, and the Home Office "Statistics on Race and the Criminal Justice System" (2004)

1) Some have argued that **police racism** results in higher suspicion against black people in general. The **Macpherson Report** (1999) concluded that the police were **institutionally racist**. The court system has also been accused of automatically favouring white middle class defendants. There are relatively few black people in the police or the legal system.

The stop and search, arrest and prison figures are based on what a person looks like. The census records what a person identifies themself as.

2) **Hall et al (1978)** and **Gilroy (1987)** argue that young black people have been labelled as criminal by modern British society and have become a **scapegoat** for social problems in society.

3) Hall also says that high levels of **unemployment** among young black men leads some young black men to **opt out** of **mainstream society** and turn to **crime**.

Similar in some ways, but Hall blames the system and right realists blame the person.

4) Right realist sociologists favour a **subcultural** explanation for the differences.

5) **Ethnic minority** households are **more at risk of crime** than other households — e.g. the British Crime Survey says they're more likely to be mugged than white groups, and slightly more likely to be victims of vehicle theft. Pakistanis and Bangladeshis were more likely to be **burgled**. The survey found ethnic minority respondents were **more worried about crime** in 2000 than white respondents.

Only **23% of reported crimes** in 2003 were **solved** — i.e. someone was convicted for the offence in 2003 (2004 Social Trends). The social profile of who committed the **unsolved** and **undetected** crimes could change these patterns considerably.

Practice Questions

Q1   Which social groups are most likely to be convicted of crime in Britain?
Q2   What evidence is there that crime is more prevalent in urban areas?
Q3   Briefly state the two explanations that Hall gives for increased arrest and criminality among the black population.

Exam Question

Q1   Examine some of the reasons why more men than women are convicted of crime in the UK.   (12 marks)

Avoid committing crime — be an old woman and live in the countryside...

Of course, that's easier said than done for many of us, particularly young men. But just because a task is difficult does not mean you shouldn't strive to achieve it. Being young, male, working class, black and living in an urban area puts you at the highest risk of being convicted, or of being a victim, of crime. There are loads of possible reasons for this — make sure you understand them.

Prevention, Victims and Punishment

This fine pair of pages opens with some thrilling theories about how people become victims of crime, ramps up the fun with a look at ways of preventing crime, then concludes with a spectacular grand finale on punishment.

Victimology Theories try to explain How people become Victims

There are two main sociological theories to explain how people become victims of crime — 'positivist victimology' and 'radical victimology'.

1) Positivist victimology is interested in how some people are **more likely** to become victims than others — either because their **actions** (e.g. leaving valuables on display in a car) lead them to becoming a victim of crime or because of their **lifestyle**. This approach has been criticised for 'blaming the victim'. Positivist victimologists have tended to focus on 'visible' crime, such as **reported robberies** and **assaults** — they've been criticised for ignoring issues such as **state crime** (see p. 182).

2) Radical victimology is more **left wing**. It argues that in a structurally unequal capitalist society, **poor people** are more likely to be the **victims** of crime, as part of a wider pattern of **inequality** and **disadvantage**. Radical victimologists have used the concept of 'human rights' as a more universal yardstick for measuring victimisation rather than using official statistics. This has allowed them to focus on state and corporate crimes that often go **unrecorded**.

Some Facts and Figures about Victims *

* from 'Crime in England and Wales 2002/03' and 'Crime in England and Wales 2005/06,' published by the Home Office.

- **Men** are almost twice as likely to become **victims of violence** as women. More **women** are **afraid** of becoming victims of crime.

- Young **men aged 16-24** experience the most violence — 13% in this survey.

- Men are more likely to experience violence from **strangers** and **acquaintances**.

- Women are more likely than men to be victims of **domestic violence** — 0.6% of women were affected but only 0.2% of men. People who suffer domestic violence are likely to experience **repeat attacks**.

- The 2002/03 report said that, of **mixed race** adults, 46% had been victims of crime — much higher than other groups. Just 30% of Asian and 27% of black, white and 'Chinese or other' adults experienced crime.

Feminists say Women become Victims because of Patriarchal Attitudes

1) Feminists argue that **domestic violence** is the result of an **unequal power relationship** between men and women. **Radical feminists** see domestic violence as a form of **patriarchal power and control**.

2) Some feminists argue that **fear of crime** is used to **constrain women** from taking a more active part in social life. **Stanko (2000)** suggests that women have to restrict their behaviour by taking care not to be too provocative in their behaviour and appearance.

3) **Marxist feminists** say domestic violence can be explained by the frustration and **lack of control** that men experience in the **capitalist work place**.

4) Many feminists believe the **law is biased against women** and crimes against women have been ignored. **Heidensohn (2002)** says crimes by **men** against **women** (e.g. rape and domestic abuse) often go unreported. She calls this type of crime 'gendered crime'.

5) Feminists have **campaigned** to widen the definition of what behaviour is criminal, e.g. campaigning for **legislation** against **sexual harassment** in the **workplace**.

There are Three Main Approaches to Crime Prevention

1) **Structuralists** argue that crime is caused by **inequalities** in wealth and income. They say the only way to reduce or prevent crime is to address these inequalities. **Subcultural**, **Marxist** and **left realism** theorists are structuralists.

2) The **individualist** or **interventionist** approaches argue that some groups of people are more likely to commit crime than others. They say the best way to prevent crime is to **change the behaviour** of these 'criminal types', e.g. by targeting children from a disadvantaged background. **Prison** and **community** sentences can also be seen as interventionist approaches, with the aim of discouraging other people from committing crimes.

3) The **situational approach** says society can use **changes to the physical environment** to make it harder for people to commit crimes. Changes could include creating **gated communities**, putting up more **surveillance cameras** or improving **lighting** in streets and car parks. **Zero tolerance policing** — where anti-social behaviour is tackled swiftly and strictly — is another situational approach. **Right realism** theorists favour the situational approach, advocating the development of 'community-minded' areas where there is a sense of social responsibility. Situational approaches can be effective but evidence suggests they don't always reduce crime, just move it to a less well-protected area.

Prevention, Victims and Punishment

Society tries to Control Crime through Formal and Informal Agents

1) The **police** are a **formal** agent of social control, responsible for **enforcing the law**.

2) Other formal **agents** include **Parliament**, which passes laws to say what behaviour is criminal, the **Crown Prosecution Service**, which decides who should be taken to court for a particular crime, the **courts**, which determine any punishment, and the **Prison Service**, which imposes any punishment.

3) There are also agents of **informal social control**. These include the **family** unit, the **education** system, **religion** and the **media**. All these channels help to reinforce a general sense of what behaviour is considered acceptable.

In theory the **police** should be **impartial**, but have sometimes been accused of **institutional racism** and **sexism**:

- The **Macpherson Report (1999)** into the Stephen Lawrence case said the way the police handled the case showed clear signs of **racism**.
- A report by the **Metropolitan Police Authority** (2004) found **black men** are four times more likely to be **stopped and searched** than white people.
- **Graef (1989)** said the police have a '**canteen culture**'. He thought the majority of police officers, who tend to be white males, adopt racist and sexist attitudes as a way of fitting in.

Criminals are Punished for a number of Reasons

Most societies around the world have systems for **punishing crime**. Sociologists (unsurprisingly) have different views on the **purpose** and **importance** of punishment.

1) **Functionalists** argue that punishment **keeps society going**. If crimes went unpunished the result would be anarchy and society would collapse. Durkheim said that **public punishment** of criminals was good for society. He thought it helped create **unity** and **consensus** as people came together to condemn the criminal — in other words, a public hanging was good for society.

2) **Marxists** say punishment serves the needs of capitalism by **keeping the workers under control**. They argue that the police are used to **enforce social control** in **poorer areas** whilst the rich get way with crime unchallenged.

3) The **interventionist** camp see prison as a deterrent — the very fact it exists should put people off committing crimes. The evidence suggests that this theory does not work in practice.

Labour and the Conservatives have different Attitudes to Crime

The **Labour Party** used to favour the **structuralist** approach to crime. Their main policy was to **reduce inequalities** in society.

The **Conservative Party** has tended to favour **individual** and **situational** approaches. During the most recent period that the Conservatives were in government (1979-1997) they put **more police** on the streets and more criminals were sent to **prison** — so many, that Britain had the highest rate of imprisonment in Europe.

When **New Labour** came to power in 1997, Prime Minister Tony Blair promised to be "**tough on crime and tough on the causes of crime**". The party continued to focus on reducing inequalities of opportunity (by tackling unemployment, poverty and social exclusion), while giving more emphasis to punishment.

Practice Questions

Q1 What percentage of women in England and Wales experience domestic violence, and what percentage of men?
Q2 Which sociologist said women have restrictions placed on their behaviour due to fear of crime?
Q3 Give two examples of situations in which the police were found to have behaved in a racist way.
Q4 Which political party has favoured the structuralist approach to dealing with crime?

Exam Question

Q1 Examine the arguments for and against the situational approach to crime prevention. (12 marks)

Prevention is better than cure, they say...

Unfortunately, by the time all the sociological theorists have finished debating how we become victims and the best ways of preventing and punishing crime we'll all be... no, what am I thinking — sociologists will never stop debating. The best policy for you as a conscientious sociology student is to learn what the main arguments say, and draw your own conclusions.

Recent Issues in Crime and Deviance

A global crime is one which affects national and international economies, politics or security. Globalisation (see p.114-115) has meant that different societies have become connected economically, culturally and environmentally, and has had a big impact on the nature of crime.

Trading in illegal **Drugs** and **Arms** causes huge social problems

1) According to the UN's *World Drug Report*, in **2005** the **global trade** in **illegal drugs** was worth around **$320 billion**, supplying around **200 million drug users** worldwide. This amounts to around **one eighth** of all **world trade**.

2) **Karofi and Mwanza (2006)** have outlined the **negative impact** of the trade in illegal drugs. They pointed to the consequences for **health**, the changes in **social behaviours** and the **funding** of **terrorism** and **war** with the profits.

3) The **Transnational Institute** in **Amsterdam** reported that the majority of **armed conflicts** across the globe are **funded** or **part funded** by the **illegal drugs trade**.

4) Global communications and relatively unregulated financial markets have made the illegal trade in **arms** easier to carry out and harder to trace. **Karofi and Mwanza** highlight its role in **destabilising societies** (violent crime) and making existing conflicts worse.

5) The trade in **small arms** (firearms carried and used by one person) is particularly problematic, causing an estimated 80% of conflict deaths each year. Former UN Secretary-General **Kofi Annan** called small arms **"weapons of mass destruction in slow motion"** because of their **deadly impact** in the **developing world**.

Human Trafficking creates modern day Slavery

1) **Human trafficking** is the **illegal movement** of **people** for **exploitation**. Victims are taken either with **force** or **deception**.

2) According to the United Nations Development Programme's 2007 report *Human Trafficking and HIV*, the **illegal global trafficking** of people is an industry worth between **$5 billion** and **$7 billion** a year. Human trafficking is one of the **fastest growing global crimes**.

3) According to the UN's Global Initiative to Fight Human Trafficking, an estimated **2.5 million people** are in **forced labour** as a result of trafficking. People trafficking is a global problem — it involves criminal groups from across the globe and has a **devastating effect** on its victims.

Cybercrime is crime that uses the Internet

1) Globalisation has seen a massive increase in computer use and internet use, giving rise to **'cybercrimes'** such as **data theft**, **fraud**, **credit scams**, **email scams** and **illegal pornography**. Because cybercrime breaches **national borders**, existing criminal law is often **powerless** to tackle it.

2) The extent of cybercrime is difficult to assess accurately, but some observers have suggested that it will soon **rival** the **drugs trade** in terms of **profits**.

> The **globalisation** of **communications** and the media has also aided the growth of **international terrorism**. Terrorists can now access a global audience for their **propaganda**, and are able to create **online networks** for their organisations.

Environmental or Green Crimes are those which Harm the Environment

1) Green crime might be something as small-scale as **fly-tipping**, but on a global scale it includes the illegal trade in **environmentally sensitive substances** (e.g. refrigerator CFCs), the illegal trade in **protected animals** and products derived from them, and illegal and unregulated **logging** and **fishing**.

2) The environmental impact of green crimes can be huge — e.g. illegally traded **CFCs** significantly contribute to ozone depletion. There are also severe **financial costs** — the World Bank estimated that **illegal logging** costs timber-producing countries around **10-15 billion euros** per year in **lost revenue**.

State Crimes are committed by Governments

1) State crimes are where governments break **national** or **international criminal law**.

2) State crimes include the funding of **terrorism**, **war crimes**, **genocide**, links with **organised crime**, **corruption**, use of **torture**, and **other crimes against human rights**.

3) State crime is often a controversial topic as it's states themselves that define what is **"justifiable"** and what is **illegal**.

Recent Issues in Crime and Deviance

The **Media** plays a powerful role in **Amplifying Deviance** in society

Interpretivists (also known as interactionists) such as **Stanley Cohen (1972)** argue the media helps to **create** the deviance it predicts or anticipates.

The Amplification of Deviance:

1) The media presents a **distorted view** of the level of crime.

2) This distorted view creates **public concern**.

3) Related incidents of crime and deviance are **over-reported** and given more prominence than they'd otherwise have.

4) This keeps the issue or problem **high** on the **public agenda**.

5) The public want **something done** about the problem.

6) The police are more **aware** or sensitive to the problem, so they **discover more crime**.

7) Police records **reinforce** the idea that there is **more crime** and **deviance**.

LOCAL RABBIT RANSACKS VEGETABLE BASKET

1) The perceived risk of being a victim of crime is **amplified** by **over-reporting** by the **media**. This creates a public response of **panic** or **outrage**. Cohen refers to this as a **moral panic** (see p.141).

2) Cohen developed his idea about moral panics from a study of conflicts between **Mods and Rockers** in 1964, but there are plenty of **new** examples, especially with the increased power of the media   e.g. gun crime, "bogus asylum seekers" and benefit fraud.

3) The state response to a moral panic in society is often to introduce **stricter** forms of **social control** through legislation.

4) **Hall et al (1978)** claim that the national concern about **mugging** in the early 1970s was a **moral panic**. The media claimed that mugging was a new kind of crime, but Hall et al point out that violent street robbery had been going on for a long time, and wasn't rising particularly fast at the time of the moral panic. (See p.173 for more on this.)

5) Some sociologists have suggested that the **fear** of **global terrorism** following the attacks on New York on September 11th 2001 is another example of a current moral panic, and that the terrorist threat has been exaggerated.

Ian Taylor argued **Economic Liberalisation** has caused an **Increase** in **Crime**

1) **Taylor (1997, 1998)** argued that **economic deregulation** had given some people more **opportunity** to commit crimes like **fraud**, **money laundering** and **tax evasion**.

2) He also argued that **globalisation** and **deregulation** have made employment less secure and increased economic instability by **reducing** the **control** states have over their economies. **Increased unemployment** and **cuts** in **welfare** have led to a **rise in crime** as people don't believe they will be able to secure a **reliable income**.

3) According to Taylor, **globalisation** is partly to blame for the growth of the **drugs trade** in **poverty-affected areas**.

4) Taylor also blamed **marketization** for rising crime. This is where **economic considerations** begin to **dominate** in the way people think of social life. Success becomes equated to owning **expensive consumer goods** — some people turn to crime as a way to achieve this, e.g. by stealing an expensive car.

5) Taylor argued that it's **too late** to turn the economic clock back completely, but believed that attempts should be made to **recreate** shared **values** of community and civility to **counteract** the process of marketization.

Practice Questions

Q1   What is meant by the term 'global crime'?

Q2   What is cybercrime and why is it difficult to police?

Q3   Give three examples of moral panics.

Exam Question

Q1   Assess the view that globalisation is a significant cause of crime.   (21 marks)

Can't we all just agree to play by the rules...

Of course not — especially when those who set the rules break the law themselves. State crime's like a referee who goes around kicking all the players at a football match. Another rather unhappy page for you to learn — make a cup of tea and get cracking.

Suicide

There's an awful lot of sociology on suicide, for two reasons. Firstly, it's a totally individual act, so it's a big task for sociology to explain why it happens. Secondly, it's been a focus for exploring issues of sociological methodology since Durkheim used his study of suicide to explain the "rules" of sociological research and enquiry.

Durkheim's study of Suicide is one of the most Important Sociological Works

Durkheim wrote in the **1890s**, and was one of the very **first sociologists** — right at the forefront of establishing and defining sociology as a scientific discipline. Durkheim argued that it was not only **possible** to apply **scientific principles** to **social phenomena** but that it was **essential** to do so in order to produce **useful sociology**. His 1897 book *Suicide: a study in sociology*, uses his scientific methods to explore suicide.

1) Durkheim chose suicide **deliberately**, because as the most **individual**, **private** and **psychologically driven** act it was considered by most **not** to be a **social** phenomenon.

2) If sociology could identify **social** factors and **causes** of suicide, this would demonstrate the power and impact of **society** on **individual behaviour**.

3) Durkheim followed the **methodology** laid down in his earlier book, *The Rules of Sociological Method*, in his suicide study. This methodology produced a **rigorous**, **systematic**, **detailed** and **scientific** analysis.

4) Durkheim said that if this **scientific methodology** is followed then "**social facts**" can be discovered in the same way as **scientific** research reveals laws or facts of the **natural world**.

Analysis of Statistics found some groups were More Likely to Commit Suicide

1) Durkheim's analysis of the **official statistics** on suicide revealed some **social groups** were **more likely** to commit suicide than others. He looked at a large amount of data from **different societies** and from **different cultural** and **social groups** within the same society.

2) Social **patterns** of suicide rates demonstrate suicide is **not a random individual act**. **Social factors** play a part.

> **Correlation between suicide and other "social facts".**
> - Suicide rates were higher in predominantly **Protestant** countries than in **Catholic** ones.
> - **Jews** were the religious group with the **lowest suicide rate**.
> - **Married** people were **less likely** to commit suicide.
> - **Low suicide rates** were found in some countries after a **national upheaval** or **crisis**. This might be because people feel better **socially integrated**.
> - Those with more **education** had a **higher suicide rate**.

Durkheim used "social facts" as his raw data and then analysed the data to draw conclusions on the cause of suicide. He didn't question the reliability or accuracy of the statistics — that all came later...

Durkheim concluded there were Four Forms of Suicide

Durkheim said different forms of suicide were related to how much **integration** and **regulation** there was in a society. **Social integration** means **socialisation** into the **norms**, **values** and **lifestyles** of social groups and society. **Moral regulation** means the **control** that society and social groups have over an **individual's behaviour**. Durkheim's **four types of suicide** relate to **dysfunctional** integration or regulation.

Form of suicide	Cause	Example
Egoistic	**Not enough integration**. The individual isn't successfully integrated into groups or society.	More suicide in Protestants compared to Catholics because Protestants had a **looser social network/belief system**.
Anomic	**Not enough regulation**. Society has insufficient control over individuals.	Often in periods of **economic depression** or **very rapid expansion**, the suicide rate rises. People find it hard to adapt.
Altruistic	**Too much integration**. An over-integrated individual sacrifices their life for the group.	**Followers** who commit suicide after the death of their **leader**. Terrorist **suicide bombers** are a modern example.
Fatalistic	**Too much regulation**. The individual is too highly controlled by society.	Suicides of **prisoners** or **slaves**.

Durkheim has been Criticised by some Positivist Sociologists

Positivists try to use scientific methods. See p.203.

Halbwachs (1930) largely supported Durkheim's conclusions but he pointed out that the impact of **rural** versus **urban** lifestyles on suicide rates hadn't been considered.

Gibbs and Martin (1964) argued that Durkheim hadn't used vigorous enough scientific methods even though he'd stressed how important they were. The key concepts of **integration** and **regulation** weren't **defined** closely enough to be **measured statistically**. Gibbs and Martin query how anyone can **know** what "**normal**" levels of integration and regulation are.

Suicide

Interpretivist sociologists have devised Alternative Theories of Suicide

Interpretivist sociologists say social reality isn't a series of "social facts" for sociologists to discover, but a series of different **meanings** and **interpretations** that each person brings to and takes from each situation.

Durkheim's work is **fatally flawed** from this perspective because he relies on the **unquestioning** use of official **statistics**. According to interpretivists, **statistics aren't fact** — they're a **social construction** based on the definitions of the people who compile them. In other words, statistics give you **one picture** of society, **not** the **only picture**.

Douglas (1967) said there was a need to categorise suicides according to their **social meanings** because the **triggers** and **response** to suicide are **different** in **different cultures**.

Douglas identified **four social meanings** for suicides in modern industrial societies.

1) **Transformation** of the **soul** (e.g. a way of getting to heaven).

2) **Transformation** of the **self** (e.g. a way of getting people to view you differently).

3) Achieving **sympathy**.

4) Achieving **revenge**.

Baechler (1979) used **case studies** for his research into the meanings behind suicides. He concluded suicide was an action **chosen** by individuals to **solve a problem** when all other solutions had **failed**. Suicide is one response to the social circumstances an individual is in.

Atkinson asked, "How do deaths get Categorised as suicide?"

There is a **social process** involved in a death becoming **labelled** as a **suicide**.

1) **Atkinson (1978)** studied coroners' courts and suggested that coroners use their own **interpretations** and **definitions** in order to define a death as **suicide**.

2) He thought that coroners had a **"typical biography"** of a suicide victim to compare the case against — the more factors **fitted**, the more likely they'd record the death as suicide. For example, the deaths of **young single men** were more likely to be labelled suicide than those of **middle-aged married men**.

Coroners don't have to record a death as suicide, murder or accident. They can record an open verdict if they aren't 100% sure.

3) Atkinson concludes suicide statistics are **not facts** but reflections of **coroners' interpretations**.

Critics of Atkinson have said that, although the suicide statistics are **socially constructed**, they follow a **clear set of criteria** which are **shared**, and therefore there will be **consistency** in the figures.

Taylor identified a number of Factors that influence Inquests

1) Over a twelve-month period, **Steve Taylor (1990)** studied **32 cases** where people had been struck and killed by London tube trains, **without** having left **suicide notes**.

2) The inquests into the **32 deaths** recorded **17 suicides**, **5 accidental deaths** and **10 open verdicts** (i.e. the cause of death isn't given). In cases without suicide notes, Taylor concluded that a suicide verdict was far **more likely** if the victim had a **history of mental illness** or had suffered a **recent setback** or **humiliation**. A coroner was also more likely to record a suicide verdict if it was found that the person concerned had **no clear reason** to have been **at the underground station** at the time.

3) Like Atkinson, Taylor believed that suicide **statistics** were **unreliable**.

Practice Questions

Q1 Give two reasons why the study of suicide is so important to sociology as a discipline.

Q2 What did Durkheim mean by "regulation" and "integration" in society?

Q3 What does Atkinson suggest about the social construction of suicide statistics?

Exam Question

Q1 Assess the view that suicide statistics tell us more about the values and interpretations of coroners than they reveal about the causes of suicide.

(21 marks)

On a more cheerful note, section five has just ended...

This all ties in with the stuff on sociological methods in section seven. Suicide, although a terrible downer, is something that sociologists find deeply fascinating. Never let it be said that sociologists aren't an odd bunch. The key is to understand Durkheim's theory, where he got his data from, and why he's criticised by positivists and interpretivists.

Stratification

This section is related to the Section 7 sociological methods stuff — there's tons there about applying research methods to this topic.

Societies are Stratified — divided into Layers

Stratification means the way societies are divided into **layers**. The **richest** and **most powerful** are at the **top**, the **poorest** and **most powerless** are at the **bottom**. In between are lots of **strata** (layers, like the layers in rock) organised in a **hierarchy**.

A **stratified** society can contain inequalities of **status**, **income**, **class**, **religion**, **ethnicity**, **gender** and **age**.

Social class is the main stratification system in **modern**, **Western capitalist societies** like the **UK**. Social class is partly based on **economic** factors — **jobs**, **income** and **wealth**. Social class also has elements of **power** and **prestige**.

Other stratification systems include the caste system used in India, and the feudal system used in medieval Britain.

Sociologists often talk about Four Social Classes in the UK

1) The **upper class** are **wealthy** and **powerful**. The original upper class was the **landowning aristocracy**. Their wealth is **passed on from generation to generation**. People who have made a lot of money from business or from the entertainment industry are also sometimes considered to be upper class.

2) The **middle class** earn their money from **non-manual work**. Teachers, doctors, managers and pretty much anyone who **earns their living sitting in an office** are middle class. The middle class is **getting bigger** because there are **more non-manual jobs** these days, and fewer manual jobs.

3) The **working class** make their money from **manual work**. Farm labourers and factory workers are working class. The working class have **poorer life chances** than the middle class.

4) The **underclass** get their money from **state benefits**. They include the long-term unemployed and the homeless. The underclass have **the poorest life chances**.

> Sociologists have most often focused on the division between the <u>middle class</u> and the <u>working class</u>.

Marx divided society into just Two Social Classes

1) The **proletariat** (workers) produce goods of economic value. According to Marx, they don't own the means of production — all they own and control is their own labour power.

2) The **bourgeoisie** (bosses) own the means of production. Marx said they exploit workers in order to generate profit.

3) There wasn't a clearly defined **middle class** at the time when Marx was writing his economic theories.

> See p.190 for more on Marxist stratification.

Relating Class to Occupation poses Problems

1) Occupation does bring **status** and **prestige** with it. People **judge** each other by the jobs they do.

2) Two individuals in the **same occupational class** can have very different **income** and **prestige** status — e.g. a highly paid consultant neurologist compared to a low paid junior doctor.

3) Basing class entirely on occupation misses out most of the **upper class** — a lot of them **don't have jobs** as such, but live off **rental income** from property, and income from **share ownership**.

'A job? I'm far too wealthy for one of those...'

A good social class scheme must **represent** what people in society **really think** about the **status** that goes with each occupational class — it must be **devised** and **tested** by **research**. There are far **too many occupations** for a research sample to say what they think of them **all**, so sociologists usually ask individuals about 20 or so **common** and **representative occupations**. They make inferences about the rest of the occupations in society — which is the tricky bit.

The Government used to use a scale of Five Classes called the RG scale

1) This scale is called the **Registrar General's Scale** (RG scale), and was used until 2000.

2) The **never employed** aren't included, and **unemployed** people are classified according to their **last job**.

3) The RG scale is based on the **head of household's** occupation (usually the man).

4) **Married women** were classified according to their **husband's job** — this was **sexist**.

	Class	Example
middle class {	I) **Professional**	Lawyer, accountant, doctor
	II) **Intermediate**	Teacher, nurse, manager
	III) **skilled non-manual**	Office worker, sales assistant
working class {	III) **skilled manual**	Electrician, plumber
	IV) **semi-skilled manual**	Postman
	V) **unskilled manual**	Labourer, refuse collector, cleaner

5) Also, because the RG scale only considered the head of household's job, it didn't matter what kind of job **other people in the home** had. For example, it **wouldn't distinguish** between a household made up of **two lawyers** and a household made up of a **lawyer** and a **cleaner**.

"Head of household" meant highest male earner, or if no male, highest female earner.

6) There can be **huge variations** in **income** and **life chances** between different occupations within a class.

Stratification

The Government now uses a scale of Eight Classes called the NS-SEC

Since 2000, the **government** has used a new scale — the **National Statistics Socio-Economic Classification** (**NS-SEC**). The NS-SEC has **eight classes** based on type of **employment**, rather than **skill level**:

1) **higher managerial** and **professional**	Lawyer, doctor, company director
2) **lower managerial** and **professional**	Nurse, social worker, police officer
3) **intermediate**	Secretary, personal assistant, paramedic
4) **small employers** and **self-employed**	Owner of a restaurant, self-employed plumber
5) **lower supervisory** and **technical**	Builder's foreman, sales floor supervisor in a shop
6) **semi-routine**	Postman, receptionist, sales assistant in a shop
7) **routine**	Waitress, van driver, farm labourer, cleaner
8) **never worked** and **long-term unemployed**	Last worked more than a year ago

Class 1 can be divided into a) large employers and managers, and b) higher professional.

1) The NS-SEC is based on three areas:

- **Employment relations** — whether someone is an **employer**, **self-employed** or **employed**, whether they're **salaried** or paid a **weekly wage**, and how large an organisation they work in. *This is Weberian — see p.191.*
- **Labour market situation** — income, benefits, job security and promotion prospects.
- **Work situation** — where the person is in the **workplace hierarchy**, and how much **control** they have at work.

2) The RG scale was replaced by the NS-SEC because of the recent changes in **employment patterns**. There were fewer **manual** workers and far more workers in **service industries**, so **skill level** was no longer a good way to classify workers.

3) The NS-SEC takes into account changes in social position of some occupations (e.g. shop assistants).

4) Each **individual worker** is classified, rather than classifying a whole **household** by one person's job.

5) The NS-SEC still doesn't account for the "idle rich" — wealthy **upper class** people who don't need jobs.

Class can be defined both Objectively and Subjectively

1) An **objective** definition of social class is based on something **definite** which can be **measured** or **classified**, e.g. income or occupation — the NS-SEC is an **objective** way of defining social class.

2) A **subjective** definition relies on factors which **can't be measured** — e.g. what an individual feels their social class position is. For instance a **self-made millionaire** may be **middle class** by all **objective** standards of wealth and income, but may still **perceive** themselves to be **working class**, have working class friends and share a working class culture.

Traditional Class Analysis tended to Ignore Women

The old RG scale classified the social class of all members of a family by reference to the occupation of the **head of the household** (usually the **man**). **Michelle Stanworth (1984)** suggested that by using this sociologists miss some important issues, saying that often the social class experience of women within a household is very different to that of the men.

Stanworth's ideas have been backed up by research into social mobility by **Abbott and Payne (1990)**. They concluded that women were far **less likely** to be **upwardly mobile** than their husbands and partners and that those very few women who were upwardly mobile didn't get much further than social class 3. There's more about women and social mobility on p.201.

Practice Questions

Q1 Give one problem of using occupation to measure class.

Q2 Identify two groups that were not included in the Registrar General's scale.

Q3 Give an example of a semi-routine occupation from the NS-SEC scheme.

Q4 What's the difference between subjective and objective definitions of social class?

Exam Question

Q1 Assess the validity of judging social class based solely on occupation. (21 marks)

Oh how I wish this was a classless society — there'd be less to learn...

What a lot of class schemes. For the bare basics, learn the NS-SEC, the RG scale, and the differences between them. If you want to look like you're really on the ball, you can mention that class/occupation schemes are often either Marxist (based on economics and income) or Weberian (based on labour market position and employment relations). The NS-SEC is well Weberian. Innit.

Class Inequality and Stratification

So, there's no dispute that power, status and economic assets aren't equally distributed within society. There is an awful lot of debate about why, though. A sociologist's answer depends on their fundamental beliefs about the nature of society. Off we go again...

The **Higher** an individual's **Social Class**, the **Better Chances** they have in life

This is almost **common knowledge** — but in sociology you have to give **evidence** to go along with common knowledge stuff.

1) Class affects an individual's chances from birth. The chances of a child dying before their first birthday are much higher if they're born into a lower social class.

2) When a child goes to school, their chances of achieving **good results** are better if they're in a higher social class.

3) When they go on to work they're more likely to become unemployed if they're from a working class background — **Goldthorpe and Payne (1986)**.

4) If they stay in work they're more likely to be paid less in a lower class occupation than in a middle class occupation.

5) An individual is more likely to suffer ill health and poor medical resources if they're working class. The **Black Report (1980)** and **Acheson Report (1998)** document this in detail.

6) Finally, social class affects how long a person lives.

Infant Mortality Rates in the UK (per 1000 live births)	1991	2001
Professional class	5.1	3.6
Unskilled manual class	8.2	7.2
Overall rate	5.3	4.6

Social Trends 33, (2003)

% achieving 5 or more A-C GCSE grades	2002
Higher professional	77%
Routine workers	32%

Social Trends 34, (2004)

Average Gross Weekly Incomes 2002	
Non-manual (men)	£608
Manual (men)	£366

Social Trends 33, references 2002 New Earnings Survey

Average Age at Death 1997-99	Men	Women
Professional class	78.5	82.8
Unskilled manual class	71.1	77.1
Overall	75.0	79.7

There's more on health inequalities according to class, gender, and ethnicity in the AS course.

Functionalists say the *Class System* helps society to *Run Smoothly*

1) Functionalism says that society is a **meritocracy** — the most able people rise to the top.

2) Fundamental to **functionalism** (try saying that quickly...) is the **strong belief** that the class system enables each individual to find their **right place** and **role** in society.

3) Functionalists say that the **most important** positions in society must be filled by the brightest and most able people.

4) According to **functionalism**, the people who do well in terms of the common values of society will be at the top of the stratification system. High **status**, **power** and high income are **rewards** for conforming to society's values.

5) Most people **don't object** to people in powerful positions getting **extra status** and **rewards**. According to functionalists, this shows that they support the values which underpin the system.

Talcott Parsons was an influential functionalist

1) Parsons established the functionalist position that stratification is **inevitable** and **useful** in all societies.

2) He argued that stratification systems **evaluate** individuals in terms of **common social values** — high status is a reward for **conforming** to society's values.

3) In Parsons' view, stratification **reinforces** the **collective goals** of society and establishes **order**.

I know my place

Me too. Comforting, isn't it.

I doubt Parsons was thinking about strata in rock...

Davis and Moore (1945) argue that without a stratification system, society would break down

1) According to Davis and Moore, stratification has the function of **role allocation**. It makes sure the most able and talented do the most important jobs.

2) **Inequality in reward** (pay) and **status** are essential to **motivate** the best individuals to take on the most important roles and jobs. These roles usually require long periods of training. High rewards compensate people for spending a long time in education and training.

This argument may sound familiar — it's often used to justify high rewards given to company directors and even famous sports stars.

Class Inequality and Stratification

The New Right argue that the Social Stratification system is Unequal but Fair

New Right thinking became popular in the 1980s. It's based on **19th century liberalism**, which saw the **free market** as the **best** way of sorting out everything in society from boredom to backache. The New Right say **governments shouldn't intervene in the market** or promote equality as this takes away motivation for people to **pull themselves up by their bootstraps**.

New Right thinking is sometimes known as **neo-functionalism** (or **political functionalism**) because it pursues similar themes.

1) **Peter Saunders (1990)** is a key British New Right sociologist. **Saunders** argues that societies with stratification systems based on economic differences aren't inevitable (as Parsons thought), but they are a good idea.

2) Saunders says **stratification** is a good idea because **unequal rewards motivate** people to **work hard**. He says that in a society with equal rewards, some people wouldn't pull their weight. He sees physical force as the only alternative to unequal rewards — and obviously prefers unequal rewards.

3) Saunders says that **inequality** promotes **economic growth**. Individuals are motivated to **start businesses** so that they can make money, which **benefits society** by creating **jobs** and **wealth**. He points to the rise in small businesses and entrepreneurs in modern society to demonstrate how anyone can do well if they work hard enough.

4) New Right thinkers like Saunders believe in legal equality and **equality of opportunity**, rather than **equality of outcome**. Saunders says that it's more important for society to be a **meritocracy** than for society to be **equal**.

5) In a **free market**, market forces control who earns what, according to the **supply of talent** and **demand for talent**. People whose skills are highly **demanded**, but in short **supply**, can earn a lot of money. A system based on the free market is **unequal** (some people earn a lot more than others), but it's **fair** according to New Right thinkers.

1) **Saunders (1996)** sees Britain as pretty **close** to being a **meritocracy**. He thinks that **economic rewards** match up with **merit** and **ability**.

2) He argues that what **looks like inequality of opportunity** between middle class and working class is actually caused by **inequality of ability** and **effort**. In other words, he thinks that middle class children **deserve** better jobs because they're more able, and they work harder.

Not surprisingly, this view is highly controversial...

Critics of Functionalism and New Right theory claim it Isn't Fair At All

1) **Tumin (1953)** criticised functionalism, and claimed that there's actually **inequality of opportunity** in society.

2) He also criticised Davis and Moore's ideas that some jobs are more **functionally important** than others. In any case, the usefulness and importance of a job doesn't seem to match up to the rate of **pay**. Tumin pointed out that **pay inequality** between groups may be to do with differences in **bargaining power**, rather than differences in usefulness.

3) Tumin argued that instead of **motivating** people, stratification could actually be a **barrier to motivation**.

4) Critics of functionalism also point out that the functionalist view of stratification **ignores the negatives**. Stratification is a system of haves and have nots, and people in the bottom strata can feel **excluded** from society.

5) **Gordon Marshall** and **Adam Swift (1993)** say that capitalist societies are not as **meritocratic** as the New Right claim. They argue the **free market** does not guarantee a **fair chance** for all. Opportunities vary according to which class you are born into — for example, inherited wealth makes it easier to start a business. **Luck** can play a part in success, too.

6) Evidence shows that people from **working class** backgrounds are **less likely** than middle class people to get top jobs — even when they have the **same educational qualifications**. **Class** plays a part even when people have **equal ability**.

Practice Questions

Q1 In what way did Parsons say that stratification was useful for society?

Q2 Explain what Davis and Moore mean by role allocation.

Q3 Why does Saunders say stratification is a good idea?

Q4 Give one criticism of New Right thinking on stratification.

Exam Question

Q1 Examine the view that social inequality is an inevitable product of a successful society. (12 marks)

New Wrong thinking had even more critics than usual...

There's a pattern to Sociology teaching at A-level: you study the main theories about each topic and then evaluate and compare them... It's a good approach because it teaches you to look at topics from different points of view. It can get a bit repetitive though. Functionalist, Marxist and interpretivist views come up over and over again. What about Zoroastrian views? Huh?

Class Inequality and Stratification

Surprise — some more theories of stratification! Sorry, I should have warned you on the last page. That was a cruel trick.

Marxists see stratification as a Deliberately Divisive tool for Exploiting workers

1) For Marx, **class** was the key to understanding **absolutely everything** in society. And I mean e-v-e-r-y-t-h-i-n-g.

2) Marx argued there are **only two classes** (strata) in society — the **proletariat** and the **bourgeoisie**. For Marx, a class is a **social group** who share the **same relationship** to the means of **production**.

Producers	**Proletariat** or **subject class**	**Majority**	Only own their **labour**	**Poor**
Non-producers	**Bourgeoisie** or **ruling class**	**Minority**	Own the **means of production**	**Wealthy**

The ruling class own the means of production

1) Those who own the means of production can control both the **price** at which they **sell** the goods produced, and the **wages** they pay those who produce the goods.

2) It's only by paying the workers **less** than they **sell** the goods for that they can make a **profit**. It is this profit which gives them the **wealth** and **power** to **control** the rest of society in their own interests.

The subject class are the producers

1) They **don't own** the means of production. They only own their **labour**. Because they only own their labour power they have **very little control** in society.

2) They're **completely dependent** on the **ruling class** for **wages** to live on.

1) Marx argued that all other forms of power come from **economic** power.

2) Marxism says the **education** system, **legal** system, **police** and **media** are all instruments of ruling class power. This is because those with **economic power** also have the power to **shape** and **control** the institutions in society. According to Marxism, all these institutions serve to keep the subject class in its place — powerless.

3) The ruling class also use **institutions** in society to **control ideas** and **values** in society — via the **dominant ideology**. For example, the notion that capitalist society is meritocratic and anyone can get to the top is a "false truth" according to Marxism. **Institutions** in society such as education spread this idea, and everyone's happy in the belief that society is fair. This is **useful to the ruling class** — it prevents workers from rising up and starting a revolution.

Marx thought that Workers should have a Revolution and bring in Communism

Marx thought society could be **equal** if the **means of production** were owned by **everyone**, so everyone benefited rather than a few. He was certain this would be the end result of capitalism — workers would eventually realise their power and strength, and overthrow the ruling class in a **revolution**, creating a new equal society which Marx called **communism**.

The 20th century saw the **start** and **end** of some large-scale communist societies such as the USSR. The **failure** of these communist societies, and the high levels of both **corruption** and **inequality in communist societies** have caused many sociologists to say that Marx was wrong and **egalitarian societies aren't possible**. Modern Marxists argue that the USSR and China **weren't true communism**.

China is still officially communist, but it's adopted "capitalism with Chinese characteristics", a mixture of both ideologies.

Neo-Marxist theories of stratification try to explain the Middle Class

Traditional Marxism didn't predict the growth of a large **middle class** such as the UK experienced over the twentieth century. Modern Marxists have grappled with different ways of explaining this.

1) **Erik Olin Wright (1978, 1989)** developed a Marxist analysis of class which explained the middle class of salaried professionals which grew in the late 20th century. This group have some control over the means of production, and may own bits of it, but they don't control large sections of labour power. This group is called the **petty bourgeoisie**.

2) Wright says these individuals may experience "**contradictory class locations**" — they have **things in common** with **both** classes at **different** times. For example, they may own shares (part-ownership of modern means of production) but may also lose their livelihood at the will of the ruling class (e.g. if they lose their job, or the share price falls).

3) Wright concludes that **class conflict** and **exploitation** are more **complicated** in the late 20th (and now 21st) century than Marx predicted but **class** is **still** the basis of **power** and **wealth** in society.

4) **Edgell (1993)** accuses Wright of leaving Marx behind and having more in common with **Weber**.

The **key message** from neo-Marxists is: **don't dismiss Marx's theory completely** just because he didn't focus on the middle class.

Class Inequality and Stratification

Weber argued Class is "Unequal Access to Material Resources"

Weber considered many of the same issues as Marx. Like Marx, he argued class and stratification come from an **economic** basis. Unlike Marx, he didn't go into any detailed predictions about the future, or analysis of the past.

Weber said that there are **three distinct areas** or forms of **stratification** in modern society.

Class power	Economic power to access **material goods** and **resources** in society.	
Social power	**Status** and **prestige**, and **being respected by others**.	←
Party power	**Political power** and ability to **influence decision-making**.	

These tend to be **interlinked** in real life — a person with **social power** is also likely to have **political** and **economic** power.

1) **Weber** concentrated on class power. He argued that an individual's **class power** and **class position** derives from their market position — i.e. their **economic chances**, and their ability to **control** their **wages** and **working conditions**.

2) An individual's **market position** varies partly depending on how in **demand** their skills and talents are — i.e. how much an employer is willing to pay for their services. Be careful though — market position isn't just an individual's ability to get a job. It also covers their **ownership** of **property** and **assets** (e.g. shares).

3) For Weberians, stratification isn't a case of **two classes** opposed to each other (Marx) or a **competitive meritocracy** (Functionalism and New Right) but a **complex** hierarchy of layers, each with their own class or market position.

Neo-Weberian Theory influences modern Class Schemes

The big name in neo-Weberian theory of class is John **Goldthorpe**. For his 1972 study of social mobility (see p.200), Goldthorpe categorised **seven classes** based on occupation, with **three main classes** — service class ("white collar" professionals), intermediate class and working class.

An individual's **class position** is the **market position** he or she has in the **labour market**.

When the labour market **changes**, it may be necessary to **re-categorise** the classes.

Goldthorpe has been criticised for **neglecting** the position of **women** in the labour market — e.g. by **Arber**, **Dale** and **Gilbert (1986)**.

The NS-SEC system (see p187) was developed from Goldthorpe's own classification system.

Pete was so professional he didn't even need a collar...

Postmodern theory argues that Class isn't as Important as it used to be

1) Postmodernists claim that **other differences** such as gender, age and ethnicity are **at least** as important.

2) **Pakulski and Waters (1996)** say that **cultural differences** (values, lifestyles and beliefs) are what classify individuals into particular groups or strata in current society — not economic position.

3) Crucially, they say individuals can **define themselves** as belonging to social groups or social strata and **freely move** from one to another by choosing their **lifestyle** and **identity**.

4) Pakulski and Waters **criticise** the rest of sociology for still focusing so much on **class** when they feel that other forms of **inequality** and **identity** are more relevant.

Practice Questions

Q1 What are the two classes described by Marx?

Q2 What is the "petty bourgeoisie"?

Q3 What three types of power does Weber acknowledge in his theory on stratification?

Q4 What do postmodernists say about class?

Exam Question

Q1 Assess the importance of class in British society from different sociological perspectives. (21 marks)

You should have guessed when there were no Marxists on the last page...

You knew deep inside it was too good to be true. Marx ignores the middle class, mainly because there wasn't really a middle class in the 1840s. Neo-Marxists acknowledge that society today is more complex. Weberians base everything on labour market position. And postmodernists pop up to say that class doesn't exist in a postmodern world, and that identities are all self-built anyway.

Changes in the Class Structure

The British stratification system underwent considerable change in the 20th century — alongside changes in society.

There have been **Changes** in **Work Patterns** and **Wealth/Income Distribution**

1) There are **fewer** people in **manual** jobs and **more** people in **non-manual** jobs compared to the early 20th century.

2) Service industries such as **leisure** have grown, and primary and manufacturing industry has decreased.

3) A higher percentage of **women** now work — this has risen from 56% of working-age women in 1971 to nearer 70% now.

4) Between 1945 and 1980 income and wealth became more **evenly distributed**.
   However, from 1980 onwards, the wealth/income gap has actually started to **widen** again.

5) Many state controlled industries were **privatised** in the 1980s and 1990s.

   This made private business more powerful and also increased share ownership.

6) One thing hasn't changed massively — most **wealth** is still owned by a small **minority**.

The **Ruling Class** has **Changed** — opinions differ on just **How Much**

The New Right say that the ruling class has disintegrated.
Peter Saunders (1990) argues that the increase in the number of people **owning shares** in the UK has led to power being spread more widely. The small minority in power has been replaced with a **nation of stakeholders**.

Marxists insist the ruling class is alive and kicking.
1) **John Scott (1982, 1991)** agrees with Saunders that **more and more people own shares** in the UK but argues this hasn't led to a break-up of the ruling class. Most individuals own a **few** shares but hold **very little** real **power**.

2) Scott, and **Westergaard and Resler (1976)** say there's still a **power elite** who control business and the economy.

The **Middle Class** has **Grown**, but may be **Breaking Up** into **Several Classes**

1) Functionalist and Weberian sociologists cite the rise of the **professions** (e.g. teachers, doctors, lawyers) as evidence of an expanding middle class.

2) **Embourgeoisement** means working class people **becoming middle class** in lifestyle and values as their incomes increase. It was a popular idea with sociologists in the 1950s and 1960s.

3) **Goldthorpe et al (1968)** tested the embourgeoisement thesis by interviewing car workers in Luton. They concluded that affluence had **not** made the workers middle class, and clear differences remained between them and the non-manual middle class workers — e.g. their attitudes to work and possibility of future promotion.

Some say the middle class is fragmenting into several middle classes with different life-chances and experiences.
1) **Goldthorpe** says there's an **Intermediate Class** of low grade non-manual workers who have little in common with middle class professionals. In terms of wages, perks, and relationship with employers, these groups are totally distinct.

2) Marxist **Harry Braverman (1974)** says many non-manual workers have been **de-skilled** by technology, so that they now have more in common with the working class in terms of job security and wealth. This is **proletarianisation**.

3) **Roberts et al (1977)** interviewed "middle class" workers about their view of their own class position and found wide variations in how groups saw themselves. They concluded the middle class is being fragmented into smaller strata.

4) Influential sociologist **Giddens (1973)** disagrees — he says there's a **distinct middle class**. The middle class is distinct from the working class because its members can sell their **"brain power"** as well as, or **instead** of, their **labour power**.

Postmodernists Pakulski and Waters (1996) have declared that **Class is Dead**

Pakulski and Waters give the following evidence to suggest that **class** and therefore **class analysis** in social science is **dead**:

1) **Wealth** became more **equally distributed** during the 20th century. This means not only that economic class differences are less pronounced, but that more people have more **spare cash** to spend on consumer goods. Pakulski and Waters argue that people **define themselves** and **judge each other** based on what kind of things they buy.

2) **Educational status** has become **more important** in deciding life chances, and class background less important.

3) There's a **new postmodern politics** based on non-economic issues such as ethnicity, identity, and the environment.

4) People are **less likely** to **vote along class lines** — e.g. manual workers no longer vote for left-wing parties (see p.154).

5) Pakulski and Waters claim that **globalisation** has lessened the importance of class inequality within countries.

Pakulski and Waters argue society changed from an **economic class society** in the 19th century, to a **hierarchical class society** in the first half of the 20th century, to a **status society** in the late 20th century.

However, Marxist sociologist **John Westergaard (1995)** suggests that because gaps between rich and poor are widening and big business is more powerful, class is becoming **more** significant in the late 20th and early 21st century — not less significant.

Changes in the Class Structure

The *20th Century* has *Weakened* and *Divided* the *British Working Class*

The decline in the **traditional working class** sectors of **manufacturing** and **heavy industry** in the 20th century has **reduced** the **size** of the British **working class**.

1) **Ralph Dahrendorf (1959)** argues that instead of uniting, the working class has disintegrated.

2) He said that the working class has been divided into groups of **skilled**, **semi-skilled** and **unskilled** workers, and that this is because of changes in technology.

3) Dahrendorf is criticised by **Penn (1983)**, whose research into cotton mills in Rochdale suggests that the working class has been divided into skilled, semi-skilled and unskilled since at least the **1850s**.

4) **Crewe (1983)** argues that the working class is splitting into groups with different concerns and interests, so it can no longer be considered a "real" class. He says that there's a "**new working class**" who live mainly in the South, work in the private sector and own their own homes. They have very different life experiences to the "old working class" who live mainly in the North in council houses, and work in the public sector.

The idea that the working class is on its way out has been criticised, particularly by Marxist sociologists.

1) Marxist sociologists say that the working class can change its occupation and still be working class.

2) **Beynon (1992)** points out that the old working class jobs have been replaced by new occupations which are **equally badly paid** with poor conditions and rights — e.g. call centres, fast-food outlets and hotels. Beynon says that **cooking burgers** is **manual**, **repetitive labour**, just like working on an assembly line in a factory.

3) Marxists argue what hasn't changed is the **status**, **rights** and **power** that go with the employment — the lack of these things is what makes it working class.

Remember the connection to **globalisation** (see glossary) — part of the reason that working class manufacturing jobs have vanished in the UK is because they've **moved abroad** to cheaper labour markets. There's an "**international division of labour**". Globally, the **working class** includes workers in **South East Asia** and **China** who have few rights and low pay.

Some Sociologists say there is a growing *Underclass* below the working class

The idea that the most **disadvantaged** groups in society are a **separate group** from the working class isn't **new**. Marx referred to the "lumpenproletariat" (beggars, pickpockets) and the "relative surplus" (people who aren't part of the regular labour market, but who do casual labour when needed). The idea of an underclass has gained support in the late 20th century.

1) The New Right see the underclass as dangerous to society. American sociologist **Charles Murray (1989)** defines the underclass by **behaviour** — **uneducated**, **delinquent** and **work-shy**.

2) **Runciman (1990)** defines the underclass as people who are **permanently dependent** on **welfare benefits**.

3) **Giddens (1973)** defines the underclass as the **most disadvantaged** in the job market — e.g. illegal immigrants. He says there's a **secondary job market** of **low-paid** jobs with **low job security**, which are the best the underclass can get.

4) **Dahrendorf (1987)** argued that the underclass is **growing rapidly**. This may be because of globalisation — as manual work now goes overseas, there is less demand for manual workers. Also as the labour market becomes more **flexible**, there's much more **insecure**, **temporary** or **casual** low-paid work.

Practice Questions

Q1 Identify two long-term trends which have affected the British class structure in the 20th century.

Q2 Explain Saunders' argument that the ruling class is no longer relevant in modern Britain.

Q3 Explain what sociologists mean by the terms embourgeoisement and proletarianisation.

Exam Questions

Q1 Examine the argument put forward by some sociologists that the working class has become so divided in the 20th century that it can no longer be considered a "real" class. (12 marks)

Q2 Assess sociological explanations for changes in the British class structure in the 20th century. (21 marks)

Breaking up is so very hard to do...

There are a ridiculous number of sociologists on these pages. I know it's a Sociology book, but still. I mean, for heaven's sake. It starts off OK until we reach Peter Saunders, and then they just start closing in on you. Scott starts agreeing and Goldthorpe starts testing and then Giddens disagrees and Penn criticises Dahrendorf... please, sociologists, just give it a rest. Seriously.

Inequality, Stratification and Gender

Traditionally gender and stratification was a neglected area of sociology. Feminist sociologists however have identified it as an important area which should be studied in its own right.

Sociologists say that **Sex** and **Gender** are different things

1) Sex refers to the **physical** and **biological** differences between men and women.

2) Gender refers to the **socially constructed roles** of what's considered "**masculine**" and what's considered "**feminine**".

3) Sociologists don't see gender roles as fixed. Because they're created by society and don't depend purely on a person's sex, gender roles can therefore **change over time** and can be very **different** in different **cultures**. Sociologists like to try to understand the reasons for the construction of gender roles.

Women experience **Inequalities** in the **Stratification System**

1) In the UK, women **earn less** than men and are **less likely** to be in the **top jobs**. There's still a "**glass ceiling**". In sociology-speak, the labour market is "**vertically** segregated in terms of gender" (men on one level, women on another).

'In my day, the only glass ceiling was the one in the conservatory...'

- In 1996, **23%** of board members of **British government bodies** were women.

- After the labour election win of 1997 there were many **new women MPs** (they were known at the time as "Blair's babes") but even with this increase only **18% of MPs** were women.

- In 1994-5 **93%** of all **professors** in English universities were **men**.

(Office for National Statistics, 2000)

2) Some **occupations** are almost exclusively **female** — e.g. primary school teaching. There are **more women** than men in **clerical** jobs, in **retail**, and in **catering**. There are more **male** than female **building site foremen**. In sociology-speak, the labour market is "**horizontally** segregated in terms of gender" (men on one side and women on another, on the same level of the class hierarchy). Some of these "feminine" jobs may be lower paid than equivalent masculine jobs.

3) There are also **health inequalities** between women and men

- On average **women live** five years **longer** than men, but because the chances of disability increase with age there are many **more** elderly **women** living with **disabilities** than there are men.

- In 2001, it was estimated that **women** aged **15-24** had a **higher risk** of being infected with **HIV** than men of the same age.

- Women are more likely to be **diagnosed** with mental health problems. Some sociologists say this is because of more stressful lives, while others say it's to do with sexism within the medical profession.

Liberal Feminists blame gender inequality on **Discrimination** and **Stereotypes**

1) The first liberal feminists, e.g. J S Mill and Harriet Taylor, were heavily influenced by the ideas of **political liberalism**, specifically **equal rights**, **individualism** and **liberty**. They suggest that once genuine **equal rights** have been established, 'accidents of birth' like sex will become irrelevant in society.

2) To promote equal opportunity, liberal feminists believe in campaigning to change **laws** — from votes for women in the 1920s to the more modern **anti-discrimination** legislation such as the Sex Discrimination Act (1975).

3) Liberal feminists also believe in changing **attitudes**, and overcoming **prejudice** about the roles of men and women.

4) Liberal feminists say **sexism harms everyone**, men as well as women.

Evidence suggests **Anti-Discrimination** laws have **Narrowed** gender inequalities

1) The **1970 Equal Pay Act** and its **1984** "**equal pay for equal work**" amendment helped to narrow the pay gap. The **1975 Sex Discrimination Act** made it illegal to advertise a job for specifically a man or specifically a woman.

2) Between 1970 and 1999 the pay gap between men and women narrowed. In 1970 women in full-time work earned around **63%** of average male earnings and by 2005 this had gone up to around **82%**.

3) However in **2008** the Annual Survey of Hours and Earnings reported that the gap was beginning to **widen** again. The difference in earnings of women and men in full-time employment rose slightly by 0.1% over the year.

4) Women still seem to be disadvantaged in the workplace, holding relatively **few top positions** and being over-represented in relatively **low-paid areas** of employment — administration, services, clerical and secretarial work.

5) The 1984 "equal pay for equal work" amendment says a woman should be paid the same as a man in a job of **equal worth** — but it can be very difficult to decide which jobs are equivalent to each other.

Inequality, Stratification and Gender

Radical Feminists say there is Conflict between All Men and All Women

1) **Patriarchy theory** is favoured by radical feminists. Radical feminists suggest that society is run in the interests of patriarchy — male power. According to this view, men take most of society's rewards and privileges for themselves. Men are the ruling class and women are oppressed.

2) Radical feminists argue that men also use their control of culture to create the belief that **gender inequality** and **patriarchy** are "natural".

3) Sexual oppression is seen as the most fundamental form of inequality, with all others such as class and ethnicity being seen as secondary.

4) Radical feminists want to **free women** from what they see as patriarchal control. Some radical feminists put forward the idea of **separatism**.

It had a lovely big moat to keep all the men out.

5) **Female biology** and the way it's treated by society are seen by radical feminism as a cause of gender inequality.

> **Sherry B Ortner (1974)** says that because women give birth they are seen as **closer to nature** and further from culture than men — and they're therefore seen as **inferior** in society.
>
> **Shulamith Firestone (1970)** asserts that gender inequalities are the direct result of **biology**. She says pregnancy and childbirth lead to physical, psychological and social disadvantages. She claims that gender inequality can only be put right when women take **control** of the **reproduction process**. She advocates **abortion** and **contraception** and ultimately calls for a future where human reproduction takes place in **artificial wombs**.

Marxist feminists blame gender inequality on Capitalism as well as Patriarchy

1) Marxist feminism says that gender inequality can only be understood in a **social and economic** context.

2) From this perspective, it **suits capitalism** that women are exploited by men on many levels. Engels even went as far as to suggest that the emergence of capitalism had resulted in 'the world historical defeat of the female sex'.

3) Marxist feminists say that **capitalism exploits women's work** in specific ways:

> - Employers treat women as a "**reserve army of labour**" to be hired and fired as needed.
> - Male workers try to **exclude females** from their **trades** and **crafts**.
> - Husbands **exploit** their wives' **unpaid housework**.

4) Marxist feminists see the **bourgeois family** in capitalist society as **patriarchal** and **unequal**. They say that this is because it is set up by men in order to pass **property** on from fathers to sons. Women are seen as working for the benefit of this system, rather than for their own benefit. The logic of this argument suggests that **without private property** there would be no need to do this.

5) For Marxist feminists the solution to gender inequalities is therefore the **end of capitalism** through socialist revolution.

Black Feminism and Triple-Systems theory say Ethnicity is also important

In *Ain't I a Woman?* **(1981) bell hooks** (yes, she does spell her name without capital letters) argues that because they benefit indirectly from living in a racist society, white feminists are not enthusiastic about tackling racism. She says that mainstream white feminism makes the **false claim** that black and white women face **exactly** the **same problems**.

Sylvia Walby (1990) said women are oppressed in three systems: **gender** (through patriarchy), **social class** (through capitalism) and **ethnicity** (through racism). This is known as a "**triple-systems theory**" of patriarchy.

Practice Questions

Q1   What is the difference between sex and gender according to sociologists?

Q2   Give three pieces of evidence to support the view that there is gender inequality in society today.

Q3   Briefly outline the similarities and differences between liberal, Marxist and radical feminism.

Exam Question

Q1   Assess sociological explanations of gender difference and gender inequality in society.   (21 marks)

Ah, more sociological disagreement — always fun...

If you were just flicking through, and not really bothering to revise, you probably wouldn't realise that there are so many different kinds of feminism. So make sure you learn this lot properly. Remember that you can apply these ideas to many other topics that you've studied — e.g. the family, gender inequality in health, religion as patriarchal, representations of women in culture.

Inequality, Stratification and Ethnicity

Lots of evidence suggests that different ethnic groups have different chances in society.

Sociologists make a distinction between Ethnicity and Race

1) "**Race**" as a word is usually used to refer to groups sharing a particular physical or biological set of characteristics (usually skin colour). Sociologists however **reject** the concept of "race" for two very important reasons:

   - There's **no scientific basis** to ideas of race — the genetic differences between groups of humans are tiny.
   - Ideas of race were largely **discredited** in the early to mid-20th century with pseudo-scientific ideas such as Social Darwinism being used to justify horrendous persecution in places such as Nazi Germany.

2) Instead, sociologists prefer the concept of **ethnicity**, which places emphasis on **culture** (shared norms and values) rather than on spurious biological differences. **Ethnicity** is therefore something which is **socially constructed**.

3) There are still **difficulties** in using the concept of ethnicity, though. Many ethnic groups are **huge** and subdivided into very different subgroups, e.g. "Asian" covers an enormous range of different cultural experiences.

Ethnic Minorities are more likely to experience Discrimination and Inequality

1) **8%** of the current UK population belong to an **ethnic minority** — Social Trends 33 (2003).

2) People in households headed by someone from an **ethnic minority** are more likely to be at the **bottom** of the **income scale** than those where the head of household is **white** — Social Trends 33 (2003). *It's important to distinguish between different ethnic minority groups.*

3) **Bangladeshi** and **Pakistani** groups have the **highest unemployment** rates in the UK.

   > In the UK in 2001-2002, **21%** of working-age **Bangladeshis** were unemployed and **16%** of **Pakistanis**, compared with **4%** of the **white** population, **6%** of the **Chinese** population and **7%** of the **Indian** population.

   (Annual Labour Force Survey, reported in Social Trends 33, 2003)

4) **Bangladeshis**, **Pakistanis** and **Black Caribbeans** were **least likely** to be in the **highest socio-economic group** (higher managers and professionals).

   > In 2001-2002, of people in employment, **3% Bangladeshis**, **4% Pakistanis** and **5% Black Caribbeans** were in the highest social economic group, compared to **11% Chinese** and **34% White** (made up of **8% White British**, **10% White Irish** and **16% Other White**).

   (Annual Labour Force Survey, reported in Social Trends 34, 2004)

5) People of **Bangladeshi**, **Black African** and **Other Black** origin were **most likely** to live in housing in the **social rented sector** (rented from the council and housing associations). Whites and Indians were most likely to own their home.

   > In 2001, **48%** of **Bangladeshis**, **50%** of **Black Africans** and **50%** of **Other Black** were in social rented housing, compared to **8% Indian** and **17% White British**. **79%** of **Indians** and **71%** of **White British** were owner-occupiers.

   (2001 census)

Important **public inquiries** have found evidence of **racism** in modern Britain, in many areas of life. The **Gifford Report (1989)** found evidence of **widespread racism** in the police force. The post-Brixton riot **Scarman Report (1981)** said Britain wasn't institutionally racist, but public policy often had **unintended consequences** that **disadvantaged ethnic minorities**. The **Macpherson Report (1999)** into the investigation of the Stephen Lawrence murder said that the police force was **institutionally racist**, and said the recommendations of the Scarman Report had been ignored.

You can use Examples of ethnic inequality from Other Units you have studied

Education	According to research by **Modood et al (1997)**, Black Caribbean boys are the group most likely to be excluded from school, and Chinese and Indian pupils are the least likely to be excluded. The same research shows Black Caribbean boys are the lowest achievers, and Chinese and Indian pupils the highest achievers.
Health	Pakistani and Bangladeshi people report the **highest** levels of ill health, and Chinese and Indian people the lowest. Government statistics from 1999 show **Bangladeshi men** are more likely to **smoke** than other groups.
Crime	The **British Crime Survey (2000)** shows ethnic minorities are more likely to be **victims** of crime than the majority population, and also more likely to be **arrested** or **imprisoned**.

Patterns of ethnic disadvantage are Changing and in many cases Decreasing

Andrew Pilkington (1999) gives the following as evidence:

1) Large numbers of people from ethnic minorities have **high status jobs** in non-manual/professional occupations.

2) The **labour market position** of all ethnic minority groups has improved at a faster rate than whites.

3) The **continuing disadvantage** of some ethnic groups (e.g. Bangladeshis) has a lot to do with **cultural** factors — e.g. attitudes to women working outside the home, and linguistic deprivation (not having fluent English) in new immigrants.

Inequality, Stratification and Ethnicity

Functionalists believe Ethnic Inequality is only Temporary

Functionalist **Sheila Patterson (1965)** suggests that disadvantages will gradually melt away as the immigrant communities and the host communities **adjust to each other** and the meritocratic principles of society start to take effect. Patterson says racism and disadvantage are therefore only **temporary** — eventually and inevitably the immigrants take on the values of the host culture and **assimilate** into the host society, and the hosts **accept** the immigrants.

Functionalists cite as evidence the successful assimilation of minority groups in the UK and USA. They have been **criticised** for assuming that assimilation is somehow inevitable and **ignoring** the obstacles of **racism** and **class conflict**.

Marxists suggest that Capitalism Benefits from Ethnic Inequalities

1) **Castles and Kosack (1973)** say that capitalism benefits from having a working class **divided** by ethnic inequality and racial tension — a divided class is easier to rule.

2) They argue that ethnic differences are used to **distract** the working class from the real cause of their problems. For instance, ethnic minorities get the blame for problems such as **unemployment** and **housing shortages**. The power of the working class is diminished so long as some ethnic groups see themselves as **superior** to others. Instead of uniting to start a revolution, the working class **fights amongst itself**.

3) Castles and Kosack say that ethnic division also creates a **reserve army** of **relatively cheap ethnic minority labour**. Capitalism therefore encourages ethnic division and disadvantage.

Weberians see Ethnic Inequalities in terms of Labour Market Position

1) Weberians like **John Rex (1970)** use the term "**underclass**" to mean people who have the lowest social class and lowest social status. They say the underclass are **beneath** the rest of the working class, and **alienated** (cut off) from the rest of the working class. They feel this describes Britain's **ethnic minorities**.

2) **Rex and Tomlinson (1979)** state that there are **two types of job** and **two types of worker**. In the **primary labour market**, workers have secure jobs, good wages, opportunities for training and high status. In the **secondary labour market**, jobs are less secure, wages are low, there are few opportunities for training, and workers are not valued by employers. Their evidence shows a disproportionate number of people from ethnic minorities are in the secondary labour market.

New Right sociologists use Cultural Explanations of ethnic disadvantage

1) New Right theorists like **Charles Murray (1984)** and **Peter Saunders (1996)** believe that most of Western society is meritocratic — in other words, individual ability is rewarded, and lack of ability means lack of rewards.

2) The New Right agree that the **underclass** is disproportionately made up of people from **ethnic minorities**. Because they believe society is a **meritocracy**, they blame ethnic minority groups rather than society, or racism.

3) Murray suggests that the distinct **subculture** of some ethnic minorities causes their disadvantage. He believes that this subculture contains an **unwillingness to work**, a tendency to value criminal activity and a tendency for **single-parent families**. He says this leads to dependency on State welfare benefits and ultimately leads to poverty.

4) New Right ideas have been challenged by sociologists who argue that in "blaming the victim" they **ignore** both the damaging influence of **racism** and the **structural causes** of poverty. **Giddens (1973)** says that **poor access to education** means people from ethnic minorities are often **underskilled** and **underqualified**.

Practice Questions

Q1 Why do sociologists use the term ethnicity and not race?
Q2 Give three pieces of evidence that there are differences in life chances between different ethnic groups.
Q3 Briefly outline the Marxist explanation for ethnic inequality.
Q4 What does Charles Murray blame for ethnic disadvantage?

Exam Questions

Q1 Assess the evidence that some ethnic minorities are disadvantaged in society. (21 marks)

Q2 Assess New Right explanations of ethnic inequality. (21 marks)

Sociologists blame the usual suspects...

In other words, it's the fault of the labour market, capitalism or the victim. Functionalists even suggest that ethnic inequalities serve some purpose in society, although I must admit their definition of "purpose" seems to be stretching it a bit. Remember that not all ethnic minorities are poor, or trapped in low-paid work. One of the richest people in Europe is an Indian steel baron.

Inequality, Stratification and Age

People are also treated differently based on how old they are.

Age Categories *are* Socially Constructed

Views about age **aren't fixed** or **universal** — they can change with **time**, and vary between different **societies** and cultures.

1) **Age** is part of social **identity**. People are **socialised** to accept the **norms** and **values** of the **society** they live in. So the way a society **views** certain age groups affects **people's behaviour** and **treatment of each other**.

2) Assumptions about at what age someone becomes an "**adult**" or at what age someone is "**old**" can **vary** between different societies and cultures.

3) The **law** affects how different age groups are treated. For example, legally **65** is the retirement age in the UK. People over 70 **can't** do **jury service**.

There is Stratification *by* Age — *both the* Young *and the* Old *face* Inequality

Older people face disadvantages in society

1) Retirement is frequently accompanied by a **loss of status**, self-respect and influence. Old people may become **socially isolated**, because of the decline of the **extended family**.

2) After retirement, old people are vulnerable to money problems which can lead to **poverty** — particularly for old people who rely on the **state pension**.

3) Historically, older people have faced inequality in the workplace — being **forced to retire** before they want to, or being passed over for promotion or training opportunities due to **stereotyped** views of their **capability**. The **Employment Equality (Age) Regulations 2006** makes it **illegal** to discriminate on the grounds of age.

> The law says employers can still discriminate if they really need to in order to meet a "legitimate aim"...

Children and young people also face inequality

1) In work, young people are **paid less** than older workers — this is partly to be expected, as they lack job experience. The **minimum wage** is **lower** for workers under 22 than workers over 22, and lower still for workers under 18.

2) Students in higher education face large **debts** after they graduate. **Student loans** have to be paid back once you're in full-time work and earning over a certain amount.

3) Young people in work often experience **low pay**, low responsibility, and **low status** work. In 2001 around a quarter of a million young people were being paid no more than the **minimum wage**.

4) State benefits such as **Income Support** and **Housing Benefit** are paid at a lower rate to the under 25s.

5) Children and young people experience **discrimination** in society. They are often **stereotyped** as **irresponsible** and lacking the knowledge and experience to make judgements and choices.

6) There are **changes** to patterns of stratification by age. Young people today stay **dependent** for far longer than in earlier generations. Before 1944, people could leave school and start a full-time job at the age of **14**. Recently there's been a big increase in the number of people going on to **further or higher education** rather than straight into full-time work.

There are Different Sociological Explanations *of* Age Inequality

Functionalists see age inequality as useful to society

1) Functionalists like **Parsons (1977)** say that passing through age groups has the important function of **integrating people** into society. The **role sets** of the different age groups allow a person to develop **full functioning** in society.

2) There's a criticism — functionalism doesn't explain the role of the **elderly**, who tend to **disengage** from society.

Marxists see age inequality as helping capitalism by providing cheap labour

1) Capitalism benefits from treating young workers differently because they can be **paid less**, and **hired and fired** more easily than more mature workers — and society tends not to object. Paying young people less means more profits can be made. Also the low pay of the young can help to **keep general wages lower**.

2) From a Marxist standpoint the elderly become **irrelevant** and **marginalised**, especially if they are poor. Richer old people who have been able to plan a relatively **affluent retirement** can maintain status in a capitalist society. Once again, Marxist sociologists see **class inequality** as the inequality that takes precedence over all the others.

Weberians explain age inequality by reference to labour market position

1) Both the young and the old have a **poor labour market position** compared to people in middle age.

2) For Weberians, social status and political power are also important in social stratification. Both the old and the young have relatively low **social status**, and may find it difficult to influence **political decision making**.

Inequality, Stratification and Disability

Although it's illegal, people with disabilities are still discriminated against.

Disability affects Life Chances and Social Position

Despite being **overlooked** by sociology for many years, **disability** has a serious impact on a person's life chances.

1) Registered disabled people are around **seven times more likely to be unemployed** than able-bodied people. This is despite recent anti-discrimination legislation which **in theory** makes it **illegal to discriminate** against disabled people. The result is that large numbers of disabled people suffer poverty and live on state benefits.

2) Disabled people in work are more likely to be in **low-paid**, low-skill, **low-status** jobs than the general population.

3) The Low Pay Commission Report (2007) says **disabled women** are more likely to be **unemployed** than disabled men.

People with disabilities have Unequal Access to Education and Leisure

1) Traditionally, disabled people went to **special schools** instead of mainstream schools. At these schools, opportunities and facilities were sometimes limited.

2) Nowadays, many people with disabilities do attend mainstream schools. However, in some cases disabled pupils can't get the **support** they need to get the best out of mainstream education.

3) **Attainment levels** amongst disabled people are considerably **lower** than for able-bodied people, and less than 50% of disabled people continue their education after the school leaving age.

Remember there's a bunch of stuff about disability stereotypes in the AS Culture and Identity section.

1) Despite the Disability Discrimination Act of 1995 making discrimination **illegal**, disabled people still encounter **practical difficulties** in accessing cultural and leisure amenities — e.g. lack of wheelchair ramps, signs that aren't clear enough for the visually impaired etc.

2) They may also experience social **stereotyping** and **social exclusion** from clubs and activities — due to able-bodied people's prejudices about their abilities.

3) Some children and teenagers with disabilities don't have the opportunity to **socialise with other kids** without **adult** carers being present.

Recent Sociology of Disability focuses on Disability as a Social Construct

Traditionally, a **medical model** of disability has shaped society's attitudes towards disabled people.

1) The medical model focuses on the physical impairment and tries to "fix" it.

2) Treatment is **interventionist** — it's something that's done to the disabled person.

3) The medical model can **label** disabled people as **dependent** and **weak**, or "**faulty**".

More recently, sociologists in the disability movement have suggested that disability discrimination and disadvantage doesn't actually have much to do with actual impairments and is more to do with disabling **social** and **environmental factors** — e.g. attitudes, **stereotypes**, lack of access, and lack of rights. They suggest disability is a **social construct**.

1) This **social model** of disability suggests that it's **society** that needs to be fixed, not people with disabilities.

2) It has prompted changes in **social policy**. The most important is the **Disability Discrimination Act** 1995, which makes **equal access** a legal requirement for employers, shops, schools, bus and train stations etc.

Practice Questions

Q1 Give two ways in which the elderly may face disadvantage in society.

Q2 Give three ways in which children and the young may face disadvantage in society.

Q3 Give two examples of how disability impacts on life chances.

Q4 Explain the difference between the medical and social models of disability.

Exam Question

Q1 Assess sociological explanations of age inequality in society. (21 marks)

Not to be ageist or anything, but it's the same "old" story...

Just like with gender inequality and ethnic inequality, there are now laws to make age and disability discrimination illegal. It's not as simple as passing a law and *boom* the inequalities instantly vanish, though. People try to find loopholes in the law to let them carry on doing things the old way. And you still have to change attitudes and stereotypes, which can be a toughie.

Social Mobility

Social mobility is about how easy it is for people to change class, e.g. if you want to go next door and start A2 history.

Learn these **Definitions** of **Mobility**

Social mobility = the movement from one stratum (class) to another.

Intra-generational mobility = social mobility of the same person within their **lifetime**.

Inter-generational mobility = social mobility **between generations** (i.e. does a person stay in the same class as their parents).

Absolute Mobility = how much social mobility there is in the society as a whole.

Relative Mobility = how much social mobility different social groups have relative to each other.

Ascribed status = status given to a person at birth either through family (e.g. being a prince) or through gender or ethnicity.

Achieved status = status resulting from hard work, merit and effort.

Societies which allow for **achieved status** are called **open systems of stratification**. ⟵ *Open systems have a lot of social mobility, and they're meritocratic.*

Societies where social position is **ascribed** are called **closed systems of stratification**.

The **First** major study of **Social Mobility** in Britain was in **1949**

Glass (1954) compared social class of fathers and sons

David Glass used statistical data and analysis to compare the class of fathers and sons. He found there was a high level of social mobility — two thirds of sons were in a different social class from their father. This mobility was equally split — one third upward and one third downward.

This study was done in 1949, but not published until 1954. Yes, that's a long time ago, but it's a classic study — and a springboard for all the research that's happened since.

But, the social mobility was mostly short-range. Most sons moved to the next class up or the next class down. (Glass categorised seven classes.) The study also found that the upper class had fewer people moving in or out of it than the other classes.

Conclusion: The evidence showed that Britain was a society with unequal opportunities for individuals of all classes to reach the top.

The **Oxford Mobility Study** found **Higher** rates of **Social Mobility** in **1972**

This study was conducted by **Goldthorpe et al** and used Goldthorpe's seven-class scheme (see p.191). You'll see this referred to as the **Oxford Study**, the Goldthorpe Study or the Nuffield study. Whatever the name, it's the same study.

Goldthorpe et al. (1980) also compared social class of fathers and sons

	This study was done in 1972, but not published until 1980.
Results:	There were higher rates of social mobility than in 1949 — half of all sons were in a different social class from their fathers. More of this movement was to a **higher social class** than down to a **lower** one.
Conclusion:	Opportunities for working class individuals had improved in the second half of the 20th century. This has been used by functionalist sociologists to show that Britain has become a more open and meritocratic society.
However:	Closer analysis showed that the chances of getting into the higher classes were much greater for those whose fathers were already there. There was some movement but relatively those born upper class were still better off.

A neat summary of the probabilities of upward mobility and downward mobility is given by **Kellner and Wilby (1980)**. The data revealed a **1:2:4** rule of "relative hope" — whatever the chance of a **working class** son being in the **professional class** as an adult, it was **twice** as much for an **intermediate class** son and four times as much for an **upper class** son.

So, this study has also been used by sociologists to show Britain is an unfair society.

Upper class people tend to be *Born Upper Class*

There's a much greater chance of **higher class** individuals **staying** in that class than **working class** individuals **moving up**. The top classes in the UK remain very **static** — the majority of members come from families who have been in the upper class for **generations**. The elite recruit the sons of those already in the elite (**elite self-recruitment**).

1) **Stanworth and Giddens (1974)** found that of the top company positions in over 400 British companies, only 1% were occupied by individuals with working class origins.

2) **Goldthorpe and Payne (1986)** did a follow-up to the Oxford study, looking at mobility rates during the **economic recession** of the 1970s. They concluded that mobility rates had **increased generally** but the chances of reaching **top classes** remained **unequal** in favour of those whose parents were upper class.

3) The **Essex study** of social mobility by **Marshall et al (1988)** looked at 1984 data and found that social mobility was increasing, but it was mainly short-range. Working class children are less likely to get top jobs. The **Essex study** also showed that working class people who got upper class jobs were less likely to retain them than upper class people.

Social Mobility

Other sociologists say the Social Mobility Data shows Britain is Meritocratic

There **aren't many** sociologists who interpret the data as evidence of **equality of opportunity**, but there are some.

1) The main man is the New Right thinker, **Peter Saunders**. He uses the Essex study and the National Development Survey to conclude that the **opportunities** are there for social mobility but the **individual** has to get off their backside and take them.

2) Saunders argues the inequality that exists results from differences in the **talent** and **hard work** of the individual — not their class of origin.

> "Class destinations reflect individual merit much more than class background."
> **Saunders** (1996, *Unequal but Fair? A Study of Class Barriers in Britain* London: IEA)

3) Saunders has been **criticised** by many sociologists. His **methodology** is criticised — he **doesn't include** the **unemployed** and **part-time employees** in his analysis.

4) Saunders' views have also been criticised because **class bias** at school could mean that school achievement reflects class background rather than ability. **Labelling** and **stereotypes** at school might discourage **working class** pupils from applying themselves to their studies. *See the AS course.*

Savage and Egerton (1997) analysed the **same** development survey as Saunders, but came to a very different conclusion. They found that those with the same ability didn't all have the same chances of ending up in the higher classes. Other factors such as **social networks**, **confidence** and **cultural advantages** helped upper class children get to the top — e.g. Savage and Egerton argue that educational qualifications and tests are based on middle and upper class culture and values.

What about the girls — Women's Social Mobility wasn't studied until 1981

1) One of the biggest problems with the usefulness of the study of social mobility is that almost all major studies failed to take any account whatsoever of the class position of **girls** and **women**.

2) The first time women were included in a study was in 1981. **Heath (1981)** went back and looked at the statistics for 1971 and 1975 and compared **fathers'** and **daughters'** social class positions (still no mothers). He found that in classes I and II (see p.186), **daughters** were much more likely to be **downwardly mobile** than sons.

3) **Goldthorpe and Payne (1986)** concluded that women's mobility rates varied according to which class they were in — just the **same as men**. They argued from this that the non-inclusion of women in previous studies didn't affect the overall results. Class overrode gender.

4) The **Essex study (1988)** looked at male and female mobility and found that women moved both up and down into the **routine non-manual** group — most routine non-manual work was done by women regardless of their class of origin.

5) **Savage and Egerton (1997)** looked at male and female mobility and found that class affected opportunity less for daughters than it did for sons. This may be because middle class sons can access an "**old boys' network**", or because of sexism in traditional upper middle class jobs.

Upward mobility is fun.

A woman's class used to be defined by the class of the **male** she lived with (see p.186-187). **Feminist sociologists** used to argue that as long as that was the case, social mobility studies **couldn't reveal much** about the impact of gender on social mobility. In **2000**, government statistics switched from a scheme that measured women by the **man's job** to a scheme which measured women by their **own job**. So, some **more useful studies** might come along soon.

Practice Questions

Q1 What's the difference between ascribed status and achieved status?
Q2 What did the Oxford mobility study find out about social mobility?
Q3 What's meant by saying that the upper class is "static"?

Exam Question

Q1 Assess the usefulness of social mobility studies that exclude women's social mobility. (15 marks)

I'm upper class — I have to go up three flights of stairs...

This may not be your favourite topic. You may be pining for the heady days of 'Section One: Beliefs in Society'. Thing is, you've got an exam coming up, and this could be a good opportunity to get some marks squared away. Learn the studies — the Oxford study, Goldthorpe and Payne's follow-up, and Savage and Egerton are three good ones to learn and remember.

Research and Sociological Theory

Depending on who you believe, sociology may or may not be a science. Of course whether sociology's a science or not comes down in large part to what science actually is.

Science uses Experiments and Observation to Test Theories

1) Scientists collect data through **experiments**, **observation** and **measurement** in order to **test hypotheses** (a hypothesis is an unproved theory).

2) Science values **objectivity** (an unbiased viewpoint). Scientific statements are **based on evidence** which has been collected using **systematic, logical methods**.

There is more about theories of science on pages 100-101.

There are Different Philosophies of Science

Obviously, it couldn't all be that simple. There are **different views** about **what science is all about**.

The Logical Positivists believe that scientists go off in search of scientific laws

1) The researcher **observes** something, and decides it needs to be **explained**.

2) The researcher thinks up a **hypothesis** to **explain** the observed phenomenon.

3) The hypothesis is **tested** by **experiments**.

4) If the experiments **agree** with the hypothesis, then the hypothesis becomes a **scientific law**. Scientific laws are **universal** — they explain all phenomena which are similar to the one which was observed in the first place.

This process is called verification, which means checking that something is true.

Rudolf Carnap (1936, 1966) and Carl Hempel (1966) are examples of logical positivist philosophers.

Popper (1959, 1963) argued that experiments should try to prove the hypothesis wrong — this is called "falsification"

1) The idea is that you can't ever **prove** a hypothesis **100% correct**, no matter how much evidence you've got — but you can prove it **wrong** with just **one** piece of evidence that **contradicts** it.

2) For example, the hypothesis "all swans are white" isn't proved correct by seeing one flock of white swans. You'd have to look at **every single swan in the universe** and see that they were all white to do that. But if you see just **one black swan**, that proves that "all swans are white" **isn't true**.

3) Popper believed that it wasn't possible to know **absolute truth**, because you can't prove things are correct.

Popper's view has been **criticised** by later philosophers of science who point out that an experimental result that disagrees with a hypothesis may be because of **experimental error** and **silly mistakes**. In Chemistry practicals, you may not get the **predicted result**, but that doesn't mean you've **proved chemistry wrong** — it usually means you've made a **mistake**.

Thomas Kuhn (1962) disagreed with both the logical positivists and Popper

1) Kuhn believed that science uses an **accepted body of knowledge** to solve puzzles. He called this "normal science". He was pretty critical of it...

2) He thought that scientists took a lot of **assumptions** about the world **for granted**. This assumed **way of looking at the world** is called a "paradigm". He said that what scientists do is **constrained** by the **paradigm** they take for granted. For example, for hundreds of years people thought that the Sun went around the Earth, and astronomical observations were interpreted according to the paradigm that the Sun went around the Earth.

3) Kuhn argues that **big leaps** of scientific progress come about when **evidence** which **doesn't fit the paradigm** builds up to the point where it **can't be ignored**. Then, scientists come up with a **new paradigm**. This process is called **scientific revolution**.

Paul Feyerabend (1975) went even further, and claimed that there **weren't** any **hard and fast rules** of scientific method. He argued that scientists make all kinds of **tweaks** to theories to make them work. He also disagreed with the idea that science tests hypotheses according to whether they fit observed facts, claiming that already-accepted theories **influence** the way scientists actually **observe** facts.

There's Disagreement about whether Sociology is Scientific

1) **Auguste Comte** (1798-1857) was one of the founders of sociology, and he thought of it as a science. He thought sociology should be used to develop a **rational theory** of **society**.

2) **Popper** (see above) said that some sociological concepts **weren't scientific** as they couldn't possibly be **proved wrong**. Sociology could only be a science if it made **hypotheses** which could be **falsified**.

3) **Kuhn** argues that sociology **doesn't have a paradigm** — there isn't a consensus as to what it's about and how it's done. So in his view, it doesn't count as a science.

Research and Sociological Theory

Sociology is More Subjective than Traditional Science

1) **Objective knowledge** is the **same** no matter what your **point of view**. **Objective** methods provide **facts** that can be easily **verified** or **falsified**. Objective research is also **value-free** (see below), and doesn't have any bias.

2) **Subjective knowledge** depends on your **point of view**. **Subjective** methods give data that **can't** be easily tested. Subjective research requires **interpretation**.

3) Sociology is **more subjective** than the physical **sciences**, but it aims to be at least partly objective.

4) Some **postmodernists** like **Lyotard (1984)** claim that it's **impossible** to be objective at all. Lyotard sees **knowledge** as something that people **construct**, not something that people **discover**.

Positivist Sociology tries to be as Objective as Possible

1) **Positivists** think sociology should be **scientific** and **analyse social facts**. Positivists define social facts as things that can be **directly observed and measured**, e.g. the number of followers of Christianity in Britain. Positivists claim that social facts are **external** to individuals, and constrain their behaviour.

2) Positivists look for **correlations in data**, and **cause and effect relationships**. To do this, they use **quantitative** methods like **questionnaires** (see p.218) and **official statistics**, which are **objective** and **reliable**.

1) **Interpretivist sociologists** (also called **interactionists**) reckon sociology **doesn't suit scientific methods**. They try to understand human behaviour from the point of view of the **individual**, so they use methods that let them discover the **meanings**, **motives** and **reasons** behind **human behaviour** and **social interaction**.

2) **Weber** (see p.246) said it's important to use **empathy** to figure out **why** an individual is doing what they're doing. He called this "**Verstehen**". Interpretivists take this idea very seriously — they're big on empathy.

There's Debate over whether Research can be Value-Free

1) **Value-free research** doesn't make **judgements** about whether the things that are researched are **good** or **bad**.

2) Value-free research doesn't let the **researcher's own beliefs** get in the way. For example, questionnaires mustn't ask questions that **lead** the respondent towards a particular answer.

3) In order for this idea of **value freedom** to work, the researcher must **interpret** all data **objectively**.

4) Value freedom means that the **end use** of the research **shouldn't matter**. Research should come up with **knowledge**, and how that knowledge is **used** isn't up to the researcher.

5) Positivists argue that **quantitative** research methods are, in general, **more value-free** than **qualitative** methods. Qualitative methods, such as unstructured interviews, mean the researcher is **more involved** and so there's **more risk** their attitudes and feelings will **influence** the respondents. Quantitative methods, such as closed questionnaires, allow the researcher **less opportunity** to influence their respondents. They allow the researcher to **keep their distance**.

Some sociologists say **sociology can't be value-free**.

1) The decision to research in the first place is **value-laden** — someone has to decide that the research is worth spending money on. Some say that research which the **state** or **businesses** want to see is most likely to get funding.

2) It's difficult to **completely avoid bias** and interviewer effects (see p.222). Researcher bias may interfere with structured questionnaires as it's still the researcher who chooses the questions respondents answer.

3) Some Marxist and feminist sociologists **deliberately choose research** with an **end use** that they **approve** of. They believe that sociology **should** make **value judgements** about society and **suggest** ways it could be **better**.

Practice Questions

Q1 What is a hypothesis?

Q2 Why do some sociologists say sociology can't be value-free?

Exam Question

Q1 Evaluate why some sociologists say that the study of sociology is scientific. (33 marks)

Don't even get them started on "What is art?"...

*If you're flagging, remember that Sociology can lead to all sorts of **good jobs** — researcher, writer, lecturer, civil servant, NHS manager, housing officer, social worker... If you want to be a lion-tamer though, you're in the wrong book.*

Consensus Structuralism

*Structural perspectives analyse society as a whole system made up of different parts that mesh together. Structural approaches can be either consensus or conflict based. Consensus structuralism is pretty much the same thing as **functionalism** (which you already know and love). It stresses the harmonious nature of society, something Durkheim called "**social solidarity**".*

Functionalists use the "Organic Analogy" to describe the Nature of Society

1) The **organic analogy** is used by **Talcott Parsons (1951)** to show how society acts like a **living organism**. An organism has a series of **organs** that are **interconnected** and **interdependent**, and Parsons says that likewise **society** is a set of parts that are all **interconnected**, and all **interdependent**.

2) Functionalists describe change as "**evolutionary**", which means that if there's a change in one part of society, other parts will **slowly evolve** to adapt to this change.

3) **Social ills** (such as excessive crime) have a **disabling** effect on certain parts of the organism (society), and they can gradually "infect" other parts.

> According to functionalism, interrelations between the various parts of society can only happen because all members of society **agree** on **values** and **norms**. In other words, **society functions by value consensus**. These agreed values and norms are passed down from generation to generation through the process of "**socialisation**".

Functionalism says Society's Needs are met by Four Major Subsystems

1) **Functionalism** says all members of society have **needs** and **desires** that the **social system** must cater for. These needs can be broken down into **instrumental** needs and **expressive** needs.

2) **Instrumental needs** are **material** — e.g. the need to be fed, the need to have a home. These needs are supported by the **economic subsystem** (**industries**) and the **political subsystem** (**political parties** and **trade unions**).

3) **Expressive** needs are **emotional** — e.g. the need to **belong**. They're looked after by a **kinship subsystem** (marriage and family) and a **cultural subsystem** (which includes schools and churches).

Functionalism tries to Explain Everything

1) Functionalism, through the work of **Comte, Durkheim and Parsons**, was the first real attempt to create a theory to explain the operation of the **whole of society**. This kind of theory is called a **macro-theory** — i.e. a **large-scale theory**, as opposed to a **micro-theory** or **small-scale theory**.

2) It's useful in showing how all the main institutions of society, such as the **education** system and the **family**, are **linked** to each other.

3) It helps to explain activities and actions that superficially seem **unusual** or strange. An example of this is **Durkheim's** study of **suicide (1897)**. In this study, Durkheim argues that **social structure** and problems in the modern world cause people to commit suicide. In this case, what seems to be an **individual act** is actually part of a **wider social picture**.

There's plenty more about suicide on p.184-185. Go and read it — it's relevant to this section.

Functionalism is Criticised for Ignoring Conflict and Maintaining Inequality

1) Functionalism is criticised for its focus on **harmony** and **cooperation**. It fails to take into account the **differences** and conflicts between groups in society.

2) It tries to see a **positive purpose** in **all aspects of society** — even aspects which many people would view as harmful and negative. Durkheim claimed that if a **social phenomenon** didn't fulfil a **function**, it wouldn't **exist**.

3) Functionalism has been seen by critics as a **conservative** approach to society that **upholds inequality** and injustice. Critics say the problems suffered by the working classes, women and ethnic minorities have not been adequately explained and justified by functionalism.

Functionalism says that this hairstyle has a purpose in society.

4) Functionalism has an almost **fatalistic** approach to the nature of **inequality** in society — it's seen as **inevitable**. Functionalists such as Parsons talk about "**meritocracy**", which is the idea that people succeed or fail based on their own merits. This suggests that society is **already fair**, so it's pointless to make things more equal.

5) According to functionalists, **conflict** in society is **minimal** because people **accept** the **inevitability** of inequality. **Conflict theorists** (see p.205) definitely disagree on this.

Conflict Structuralism

Marxism is conflict structuralism. Marxists acknowledge that society is made up of institutions that work together. However, they believe that there is a conflict of interests between two different groups in society: the bourgeoisie and the proletariat.

Marxism says **Capitalist** society has created **Two Classes** with **Different Needs**

1) According to **Marx (1867)**, the ruling class owns and controls the means of production, and the working class work for the ruling class.

2) Marx explained change in society as the result of a **conflict of interests** between the **classes**.

3) According to Marx, the ruling class owns the **infrastructure** (the means of production) and sustains its control over it by utilising the **superstructure** (the **institutions** within society, e.g. religion, the education system).

4) In Marxist thought, the job of the superstructure is to legitimise the position of the ruling class through **ideological messages** within the institutions of society — i.e. society's institutions are set up to stop the working class gaining power, and also to make it seem okay for the ruling class to own and control everything.

5) Marx claimed that the proletariat (working class) are lulled into a **false consciousness**, which means they aren't fully aware of the **oppression** they suffer and how to **break free** from it. Marxists argue that only through **revolution** will the proletariat see how they have been oppressed, and then a socialist/communist society will emerge.

Neo-Marxism focuses on **Ideology**

1) Neo Marxists such as **Althusser (1969)** and **Gramsci (1971)** redefined the focus of Marxism by developing the theory of **ideology**.

2) For example, Gramsci argued that the ruling class can only maintain power through **gaining the consent** of the working class by manipulative use of **ideology**. Althusser talks about **ideological state apparatuses** — e.g. the education system. See page 99.

Marxism is criticised for its **Structural Focus** and **Determinism**

1) Marxism is **deterministic** — it assumes that oppression is inevitable for the working class, until a revolution happens.

2) Marxism fails to see everyday life in any other terms than "**class conflict**". **Ethnicity** and **gender** are largely **sidelined**.

3) Additionally, the fall of Communism in Eastern Europe has been used as evidence for flaws in Marxist theory. However many people argue that Eastern Europe didn't have **true Communism** anyway.

4) The increased affluence and consensual nature of many Western societies highlights the **lack of conflict**.

Weber was **Critical** of **Marxism**

Weber said that there could be **conflict** between **all kinds of groups** in society. He **rejected Marx's idea** that the division between **owners** and **workers** was the **only important division**.

Weber claimed that people were divided by **class**, **status** and **political** grouping. Weberian conflict theorists such as **Dahrendorf (1959)** argue that conflict is **much more complicated** than Marx had claimed. Dahrendorf argues that conflict is based on **power** and **authority**, not **economics**.

Practice Questions

Q1 What are the four subsystems in society, according to functionalists?
Q2 What is the main difference between neo-Marxism and traditional Marxism?
Q3 Why are Marxist methodologies likely to be similar to functionalist ones?

Exam Question

Q1 Compare and contrast functionalist and Marxist theories on the nature of society. (33 marks)

I'm barely functional before my first cup of tea...

You'll probably be at least a little bit familiar with these theories from other sections. It helps to have it all here, so that you can revise what you need to know for the sociological theory and methods questions without getting it mixed up with other stuff. Make sure you know the differences between consensus and conflict structuralism — and the main criticisms of both.

Social Action Theory

Social action theorists focus on the interaction between individuals and small groups, rather than on the big structures of society. Social action theory is pretty much the same thing as interpretivism or interactionism (which you already know and love...).

Social Action *sees individuals as* "Social Actors" *who* Act *rather than* React

1) Social action theorists see people as **making their own choices**, and taking their own **action**, rather than being **controlled** by **social structure** or **reacting** to social structure. They see people's actions as key to studying society.

2) Social action theory claims society is **constructed** from people's meanings, interpretations, behaviours and negotiations.

The process of labelling is important for understanding how people interact on a daily basis. People observe the behaviour of others and classify that behaviour into various categories — e.g. responsible, or delinquent, or deviant. Social action theorists see labelling everywhere — in the family, in education, in health care, in the sociology of deviance, etc.

Social Action Theory *sees* Social Order *as a* Social Construction

1) Social action theorists argue that social order isn't something generated by **institutions**, either through consensus or conflict. Social order is **part of everyday life**, and they see everyday life as a series of **interpretations**.

2) They say social order is a social construction — a **product** of individuals' minds. They say people want to believe that there's order in society so they behave towards others in a way that **convinces** them that there **is** order. For example, they **follow social norms**, e.g. being **polite** to each other, **not stealing** from each other.

Social Action Theory *rejects the idea that* Sociology *is* Objective

1) The idea is that if you believe that people put their own meanings and labels on the world, you also have to accept that they can all put **different labels** and **meanings** on the **same action**. Every person will interpret an action (e.g. drinking alcohol regularly) slightly differently to others depending on the meaning they attach to it, e.g. one person might think it's a normal part of relaxing after work, and another person might think it's the first sign of alcoholism.

2) This means that sociologists **can't predict** people's behaviour as easily as structural approaches would suggest. People don't passively react to external stimulation in exactly the **same way** every single time. They act differently according to the **circumstances**, and according to their own **personal opinions**.

3) In other words, social action theory says sociology **isn't an objective science**. It's all very, very subjective.

Social Action Theory *is* Criticised *for being so* Subjective

1) Social action theory is **criticised** for its **subjective** and **relativist** nature. Critics worry that if the world is seen as subjective and based on assumptions and interpretations, then **nothing is true or false** — this would reduce sociology to a **mess of individual opinions**.

2) Structuralists argue that social action theory fails to properly address the **large-scale structure** of society. They accuse social action theorists of concentrating too much on the **small scale**, and ignoring the **wider social context** that individuals act (or react) in.

3) Critics of social action theory also point out that social action theory doesn't really **explain social norms**. They're taken-for-granted as something we believe in, maybe because we want there to be some kind of social order.

This is a simplified version of Giddens' theory. The real thing is pretty abstract.

Structuration *combines* Structuralism *and* Social Action

1) Structuration theorists such as **Anthony Giddens (1984, 1987)** believe that there's a place for a strand of sociological theory and research that looks at both the **relationship between individuals** and their **social setting**.

2) Structuration theorists say that individuals are subject to **restrictions** and **pressures** generated by **social structures** and **social systems**, e.g. laws. But... they also argue that individuals **respond** to these in **different ways**. Individuals have an **awareness** of the social rules and structures and have **some level of choice** about how to react to them.

3) Structuration theorists say social structures are **open to change** — they can be **changed** by the actions of individuals.

Critics of structuration theory point out that institutions can **severely restrict** people's actions — not just affect them a little bit. Structuration theory assumes that if people want to change the world, they can manage it fairly easily. This is something that Marxists and feminists would disagree with.

Modernity and Postmodernity

Modernity refers to the Modern, Industrial, Ordered world

1) Modernity refers to the industrial world. It's linked to **urbanisation**.

2) It's also linked to the rise of **state bureaucracy**.

3) Modernity refers to a period of time when studies of the world were guided by **ordered**, **rational scientific** thinking. **Science** was seen as the answer, rather than the **traditional** sources of knowledge, such as religion.

4) Modernist sociological theories aim to **investigate** the world **scientifically**. They explain why societies have **evolved** to be the way they are, and explain why they're **arranged** in the way they are.

5) The modernist theories are the **structuralist** theories of **Marxism** and **functionalism**. These are also called "**grand narratives**", which is a fancy way of saying "**big stories**", and "**metanarratives**", which is a fancy word for "stories that **make sense** of **other stories**". They're **big**, **all-encompassing stories** that explain **how** the world got to be the way it is.

6) Modernist theories like Marxism claim a **monopoly of truth** — they claim that they're **objectively right** about the way the world is.

Postmodernism argues that Society has Progressed from Modernity

Postmodernists say that society today has **moved on** from the ordered industrial world of modernity. They point to various **changes** in society:

1) **Work** has become more **flexible**, and service industries have partly taken over from manufacturing industries.

2) **Globalisation** has affected both **production** and **communication**. There's been globalisation of **consumption** and **culture**.

3) There's an emphasis on **consumption of cultural products**.

4) There's **pluralism** of culture, and **pluralism** of roles. People **interpret** society, and their own identities, in **different ways** according to the **circumstances** they're in (i.e. the same woman could have labels and roles of "mother", "wife", "friend" and "employer").

Work had become increasingly flexible for Jeffrey

Postmodernists argue that sociology has moved into a time when "**metanarratives**" don't answer all the problems of the social world. Postmodernists say that there's a whole range of **competing theories** out there, which all have **something** to say about society. They argue that no one theory can claim a monopoly of the truth.

Postmodernism is Criticised by Structuralists and Social Action Theorists

1) Postmodernists emphasise the role of **culture** and the **media** in driving the creation of **identities**, **norms** and **values**. People no longer seek one answer to life but are happy to **pick** and **choose** values and identities.

2) This approach largely ignores the interactions between **individuals**, which **upsets social action theorists**. It also ignores the relationships between **social institutions**, which **upsets structuralists**.

3) Some sociologists **disagree** with the claim that we're living in a postmodern society. **Giddens (1990, 1991)** argues that we're actually in a state of "**high modernity**", with **high risk** of war, economic collapse or environmental disaster. He sees high modernity as like a **juggernaut** — a massive force which we can collectively try to direct, but which could go **out of control**.

Practice Questions

Q1   Which is more important to social action theory — social structure or personal circumstance?

Q2   How does structuration theory combine both structuralism and social action theory?

Q3   List three ways in which society has progressed from modernity according to postmodernists.

Exam Question

Q1   Assess the usefulness of structuralist and social action theories in a study of society.   (33 marks)

When crossing the road, look both ways for the juggernaut of modernity...

Postmodernism is a lot easier to understand when you look at modernism. Modernism has all these ideas about how the world should be, and how sociology should be, and postmodernism decides to do the opposite. Remember that you can be asked about the usefulness of social theories in general to explain society, and that includes all the theories on these pages and on p.204-205.

Realism and Feminism

These pages cover the main schools of feminism, and also have a little section on realism.

Feminist Theory aims to explain the causes of Gender Inequalities

1) Feminists believe that society is **patriarchal** — institutions are run by, and in the **interests** of, **men**.

2) Feminist theory aims to **unmask** patriarchy and to **empower** people to campaign against it.

3) Feminists also believe that traditional sociology and its theories and methods are often patriarchal and male-orientated. They are often interested in studying issues which have been **ignored** in **traditional sociology**, for example **domestic violence**, power relationships within the **family**, and gender inequalities in **education**.

4) There are many **different strands** of feminism, including **liberal** feminism, **radical** feminism, **black** feminism, **Marxist** feminism and **socialist** feminism.

Liberal Feminists want Equal Rights for Women

After completing her degree in engineering, Phyllis was delighted to find work within existing power structures.

1) **Liberal feminists** believe that the **main cause** of inequality is a lack of legitimate **opportunities** for women in **education**, **employment** and **politics**.

2) Liberal feminists believe the most effective way to bring about greater gender equality is to work within **existing power structures** to create **equal opportunities**.

3) An example of this is the introduction of laws that prevent sex discrimination, such as the **Equal Pay Act (1970)**.

4) Liberal feminists have been criticised by radical feminists for failing to recognise that **patriarchal values** are rooted in other areas of social life such as the **family**, as well as in formal institutions.

Radical Feminists want to Change Society Itself

1) **Radical feminists** argue that the very **structure** of **society** is based on the **oppression of women**. **Revolutionary change** is needed to bring about **new 'gender roles'** and **real equality**.

2) **Kate Millett (1970)** argued that **partriarchy** was the **first** and is the **most fundamental** form of **inequality**. She argued that, **regardless of class**, **all women** are expected to be **subservient** to **all men**. While it may be **difficult** to **change** your **class**, historically at least, it has been all but **impossible** to **change** your **sex**.

3) Millett argued that there's a form of **politics** in all **relationships** featuring an **imbalance** of **power** — such as **at work** and **in the home**. Sexual politics for Millett was the **working** of that **power** to keep **women** in a **subordinate role**.

4) Millett saw the **ideology** of **patriarchy manifest** and **maintain** itself in:

   the family — where women are brought up to **expect** and **assume subordinate roles**.

   education — where women **aren't expected** to **study subjects** which **lead to high powered** or **highly paid jobs**.

   religion — which uses its **authority** to **strengthen patriarchy**.

5) Millett believed that women largely **internalise patriarchy** and come to **see themselves** as **inferior** — but that the **final guarantee** of **male dominance** is **force** and the **threat of violence**.

6) Millett **analysed** well-known **literary texts** by **D H Lawrence**, **Norman Mailer** and **Henry Miller** to show how they promote **sexist patriarchal ideology**.

Friedan blamed the Feminine Mystique

1) Influential feminist **Betty Friedan (1963** *The Feminine Mystique* New York: Norton**)** argued that women were limited by ideas of **'femininity'**, and that women were victims of an ideology she called the **'feminine mystique'**.

2) This promoted the idea that a **'good woman'** gloried in her own femininity, and focused her life on trying to "catch" a **man**, please her **husband**, and be a **good mother**.

3) Friedan argued that this limited the possibilities in spheres outside of the home, and that women brought up only to be **wives** and **mothers** often ended up feeling **unfulfilled** with no real **identity** of their own.

4) Friedan believed women were **ashamed** of these **feelings**, and so **didn't talk** about them. This led Friedan to describe this **unhappiness** as **"the problem with no name"** — an idea she formulated after sending out an **in-depth questionnaire** to her classmates at Smith College, 15 years after graduation.

Realism and Feminism

Feminist Sociology doesn't try to be Value Free

1) Generally, feminist sociologists **don't believe** in **value-free research** — they want their work to help **combat patriarchy** and the oppression of women.

2) Feminists would argue that much sociology in the past that claimed to be value-free was in effect **biased** against women. Feminist sociology has countered **"malestream"** sociology, which largely ignored the situation of women, by focusing on previously ignored topics — such as **domestic violence**.

3) In her **1983** essay **"Do her answers fit his questions?"**, Hilary Graham suggested that surveys are often designed around the experiences and assumptions of men — even when they're specifically for women — and so women's experiences haven't really been captured. Many feminists feel that their research should be **designed** and directed to take into consideration their **respondents' needs** as much as the needs of their research.

4) Much feminist sociology has been qualitative and interpretivist in nature. **Oakley (1981)** argued that a feminist interviewing women should aim at a **more friendly**, **less hierarchical** relationship with interviewees. When researching the experiences of pregnant women she felt obliged to answer any questions they had about her work and their pregnancies — which fundamentally **changed** the normal **interviewer-interviewee** relationship.

5) Feminists also use **quantitative data and analysis**, e.g. for studying the **disparity** in average **wage levels** between the genders.

Realist Sociology argues that Sociology can be Scientific

1) **Realists** believe that sociology can be **scientific** — but they define science in a different way to positivists (see p.203). They divide science into two kinds:

- The study of **closed systems** — subjects like chemistry where the **variables** can be **closely controlled** and laboratory experiments can be done.
- The study of **open systems** — subjects such as meteorology where the variables are **difficult** or impossible to **control**. Scientists can't make very accurate predictions and can't easily test them experimentally.

2) **Sayer (1984)**, a realist, argued that sociology is the scientific study of an **open system**. Society, like the weather, is **too complex** a system to lend itself to accurate predictions and experiments, but that doesn't mean sociology's not a science.

3) Realists use **qualitative** as well as **quantitative** methods. Individual human motivations — which are investigated by qualitative methods — can't be **directly observed** or **measured**. But realists argue that science has a long and **successful history** of **researching** things that can't (or couldn't at the time) be **directly observed**, e.g. **black holes** in space.

4) Realists argue that science isn't fundamentally defined by the **collection** and **recording** of **observable data** — for them it's the **search** for the **underlying causes** of **things**, even if those causes aren't directly observable. Realists believe that the **mechanisms** behind social trends and phenomena are **real** and can be **scientifically studied**.

5) They argue that sociology **can't** be entirely **value-free**, but researchers must try to **collect** and **present data** in a **clear** and **neutral** way.

> Realism is a tricky concept. It's used in lots of different ways in all sorts of contexts — politics, international relations, criminology. Here we're just talking about sociology, and these are different realists from the right and left realists you study in the Crime and Deviance topic.

Practice Questions

Q1 Name three schools of feminism.

Q2 Why don't most feminists believe in value-free research?

Q3 What, for realists, is the difference between an open and a closed system?

Exam Question

Q1 Evaluate the usefulness of the concept of patriarchy in an understanding of society. (33 marks)

It's a real headache...

I like feminism — although it has many different varieties, it's stacked around central concepts that basically make sense. It's a school of sociology that has clear ideas about the kind of things to be researched (women, gender, etc...), and has a long history of campaigning and getting things done. Now realists, on the other hand, can't even get a monopoly on their own name.

Sociology and Social Policy

Social policy focuses on social problems and how social institutions respond to them. Social policy analysts use sociological research to inform governments and other organisations, and influence their response to social problems.

Giddens *claims the study of sociology gives* Four Practical Benefits

Anthony Giddens (2001) believes that sociological research has four practical purposes:

> 1) An **understanding** of the world.
> 2) A heightened awareness of the needs of **individual groups**.
> 3) An assessment of **"what works"** — evidence-based policy.
> 4) An increased **personal knowledge** of ourselves and others.

Social Policy *is the area of* Government *that tries to* Help People

1) **Social policies** are those parts of **government** policy that deal with the **well-being** of their **citizens** — pensions, unemployment benefits, education, health, etc. **Social Policy** has also come to be the name of the **academic subject** that **studies** this area of government.

2) New ideas for social policy are generated by **governments**, **political parties** and **pressure groups**. Social policy **varies** with the **party** in power — i.e. in the UK most likely either **Labour** or the **Conservatives**.

3) Most **research** into social policy issues is carried out by **government agencies** such as the departments for **education** and **health**, but some is done by **charities**, such as the **Joseph Rowntree Foundation**, and **university departments**.

4) Governments use **quantitative statistical social research** to **discover** basic **social trends** such as the levels of **population growth**, **unemployment**, **income** and **inequality**. More in-depth, **qualitative social research** can give governments an **insight** into the **causes** of **social problems** such as **poverty** and **crime** — and can **help** in the **search** for **policies** to deal with them.

Sociological Research *gives* Policy Makers *insight into* Poverty *and* Inequality

1) The creation of the **Welfare State** after the Second World War gave many the **impression** in the late 1960s that **poverty** had been largely **eradicated** from the UK.

Empirical evidence means data that's from observation and experience.

2) However, **empirical evidence** from **Peter Townsend (1979)** and **Mack and Lansley (1985)** showed that poverty was a hidden problem. Later research by the **Child Poverty Action Group** reported that some groups experienced poverty more than others.

3) Sociologists then did more research to come up with theories of **why** certain groups were more vulnerable to poverty. **Social Democrats** blamed an **inadequate** welfare system, the **New Right** (e.g. **Marsland (1989)**) blamed **reliance** on an over-generous welfare system, and **Third Way** thinkers emphasised **citizenship** (two-way responsibility between the citizen and the state).

4) These theories, plus **empirical data**, guided **social policy** about welfare, poverty and inequality.

This link between sociology and social policy was particularly close in the case of **Frank Field (1989, 1996)**, who wrote about the underclass as a group denied citizenship rights, and suggested **social policy changes** to improve the living standards of the elderly and unemployed, and to get the unemployed back into work. Between 1997 and 1998, as a **Minister** in the Labour government, he actually **was** a **social policy maker**.

Weber *believed* Sociology *shouldn't tell decision-makers* How *to* Fix Society

1) Weber believed that sociology **shouldn't make value judgements** — it shouldn't tell policy makers **how to fix society**.

2) Weber argued that sociological research can tell decision makers whether a particular policy is likely to have the **desired result**, and what **social costs** the policy will incur. Weber thought that the policy maker should come up with the **policy first**, and **then** the researchers should go away and find evidence to work out the best way of doing it.

3) Weber thought it was important to have **good methodology** to give the most **useful information** to policy makers.

4) Critics of this view say policy should come **after evidence gathering**, not before. There's a danger that only evidence which **backs up** the policy will be found. Evidence which might suggest a **much better policy** might be ignored.

Postmodernists *have* Diverse Views *on the link between research and policy*

1) Postmodernist **Zygmunt Bauman (1990)** believes that sociology **should** inform social research, and worries that society may **get worse** if sociological theories about **poverty** and **welfare** aren't listened to. He argues that **postmodern consumer society** is **marginalising** the Welfare State, and believes this to be a bad thing.

2) On the other hand, Lyotard is worried that **"scientific"** methods of sociological research could be used to construct **oppressive metanarratives**. **Lyotard** sees **modernist metanarratives** (see p.207) as leading to **strict doctrine** and **oppression**. (Go back and read about metanarratives on p.207 if you're getting confused...).

Sociology and Social Policy

Marxists *think sociology is* Too Close *to the* Capitalist System

1) Marxists believe that sociology is too closely intertwined with the **capitalist system** to make a difference to society. Since Marxists believe that capitalism is inherently flawed and oppressive, they suggest that sociological study is a **tool** used to **justify unjust social policy**.

2) Marxists believe that research is **controlled** by **ruling class interests**, which prevents it from being used to change the system to socialism. They point to the amount of **funding** for sociological research which comes from the **state** and from **industry** — they claim sociology is being **bought**.

3) An example would be the use of empirical data to show that the poorest in society are over-represented in prison. Marxist commentators argue that sociology is being used here to **justify social policy** designed to **further oppress** and **marginalise** the working classes by focusing on crimes committed by the poor rather than looking at the underlying reasons for crime (i.e. the nature of capitalism, according to Marxist theory).

Some Feminists *believe Sociology* Can't *affect* Gender Inequality

Feminists are in **disagreement** over whether or not sociological research can actually improve the lives of women in a patriarchal society.

1) **Liberal feminists** believe that sociological research and analysis has influenced governments and had **beneficial results** for women's lives. For example, the UK has developed social policy designed to improve the status of women and make them equal in all spheres of social life including employment and benefits.

2) However, **radical feminists** argue that liberal feminist sociology can't **make much difference** to the lives of women because society is **inherently patriarchal**. Radical feminists such as **Shulamith Firestone (1971)** believe that patriarchal society must be dismantled before women's lives can ever be improved.

3) **Socialist feminists** claim that social policy oppresses women in particular. They argue it **undervalues women's labour** (e.g. in the voluntary and informal welfare sectors) and assumes they will bear a double burden of work and housework. Socialist feminists propose changes to social policy based on their own research and ideology.

Some believe the Link *between* Sociology *and* Social Policy *isn't all that strong*

Governments take account of research, but they're **constrained** by **other factors**.

1) Firstly, governments often seek to implement social policy that's **popular** with the **electorate**. It's argued that policies which aren't clear vote winners don't get implemented.

2) Some groups in society may be marginalised because they **don't vote** in **large numbers**. Even if sociology focuses on these groups, they may still find themselves neglected if they don't have electoral power.

3) Governments must consider the **financial implications** of any policies they introduce. If a policy is **too expensive**, then no matter how persuasive the sociological research behind it is, it **isn't going to happen**. Also, **expensive policies** tend to make **voters worry** that **taxes** might have to **increase** to pay for them.

Practice Questions

Q1 What four practical benefits does sociology have for society, according to Giddens?

Q2 What role did Weber think sociology should have in relation to social policy?

Q3 How do Marxists criticise the link between sociology and social policy?

Q4 What other factors affect government decisions on social policy, other than sociology?

Exam Question

Q1 "Sociology has no effect on social policy." How far do the sociological perspectives and evidence you have studied agree or disagree with this statement? (33 marks)

Sociology, eh — what's it all for...

In an exam, remember that all arguments in this topic are broken into three camps: 1) sociology should actively try and influence policy, 2) sociology should try to change and replace the system, and 3) sociology shouldn't influence social policy. Some people criticise sociologists such as Giddens for overplaying the ability of sociology to influence government decisions and actions.

Stages in the Research Process

The first step in sociological research is figuring out what you're going to research. The second step is condensing your topic down into a single question, or a single hypothesis.

Sociologists pick a **Topic** based on their own **Preference** and **Knowledge**

Well, obviously. But there's slightly more to it than the obvious, so here you go.

1) Sociologists often **specialise** in different fields of the subject and therefore will often choose a topic that they have experience or knowledge of — for example, **Steve Bruce** specialises in **religion**.

2) Sociologists try to pick a topic that they think they'll find **enjoyable** and **interesting** to research. It's best not to try a piece of research that you won't enjoy — it only leads to a poorly constructed report that may be either flawed or just plain boring.

3) Also, certain topics become popular in sociology at different times. For example, research in the **mid-twentieth century** often focused on **stratification** and the **class system**. **Nowadays**, the focus of sociologists has moved on to other topics such as **World Sociology**. To gain **prestige**, **funding** and public or academic **interest**, sociologists are more likely to focus their research on topics that are currently **in vogue**.

People often asked Francis what it was that first made him focus on the sociology of coastal leisure in the Caribbean.

4) Sociologists and other academics who want to make a **change** in society prefer research that could help develop **solutions** to **social problems**.

5) Sociologists may feel that a particular issue is **neglected** by other researchers, so they'll research the issue to try and "**plug the gap**" — and encourage others to embrace the issue as well.

Funding and Cooperation for Research have an impact on the choice of Topic

1) There are a wide range of potential **sources of funding**. Some research is funded by **charities**, e.g. the Joseph Rowntree Foundation. Some is funded by **industry**. Some is funded by the **government**. A lot of quantitative studies are done **directly** by **government agencies**.

2) The organisation which funds the research is sometimes called a **gatekeeper**, because it often has the final say in the **choice of topic**, the **way** that the topic is **researched** or whether a topic gets researched at all. Government agencies often do research into areas covered by current or proposed **government policy**. **Industrial** grant providers tend to fund research that gives their industry some **practical benefit**.

3) Additionally, a researcher needs to decide whether or not they will be able to get the **cooperation** of the groups they'll be studying if they choose a particular topic. If potential subjects refuse to give their help for the research, then the topic may not be viable.

The researcher's Career in Sociology is another factor in selecting a topic

1) Sociologists have their eye on their **careers**, just like everyone else. Researchers would jump at the chance to conduct a study that improves their **employability**. Interesting, original or popular topics that are well researched, with good clear results, improve an academic's chance of having their work **published**. Getting work published, particularly in one of the **big sociological journals**, really **improves a researcher's standing** in academia.

2) A quick way for a sociologist to progress in their career is to respond to another sociologist's work. The aim can be either to **prove** the other sociologist **wrong**, or to **add something** to their research. Practically speaking, this could mean investigating the same topic, but using slightly different methods, or investigating a different group of people.

3) This can mean that particular social groups are researched a lot. For example, **routine office workers** are frequently researched in order to test out **theories of stratification** — some systems classify them as working class and some as middle class. Each sociologist who wants to **disprove** or **add to** earlier research on classification has to research **yet another** bunch of routine office workers. Beekeepers **never** get this level of interest from sociologists.

Reviewing the Field is crucial to a good research topic

1) **Reviewing** and **critiquing** existing **data** and **literature** is an important feature in any sociological report. It requires the researcher to spend time reading **articles**, **publications** and other sources of information already produced on the subject.

2) The researcher then needs to **analyse** this material to help clarify the issues around the subject.

"Lush, undulating, 4/5"

3) Reviewing the field gives the researcher useful information on the types of **methodology** used in **previous studies**. They can see whether specific methods, e.g. structured interviews, worked in the past. They can see if research samples were big enough, and form ideas about how big their own sample should be.

See p.214-223 for more on methodology.

Stages in the Research Process

Research Questions give Focus to sociological research

1) Once the researcher has chosen a broad topic area, they need to **narrow down** the focus of their research so they don't spread their work out too thinly and end up with not enough detail. They do this by coming up with a **single research question** that their research aims to **answer**.

2) A good research question should focus on **one part** of the topic, and it should be **clear** and **easy** to **research**.

3) Questions should be as **value-free** as possible. In other words they shouldn't be **biased**, or **suggest potential social changes**. So, "Should governments provide vocational education to 14-year-olds?" isn't a good research question because it asks for a **value judgement** on social policy. "What are the attitudes of employers, parents and teachers towards vocational education for 14-year-olds?" is **better**.

Hypotheses are Statements that make Predictions that can be Tested

1) A hypothesis is a **statement** that makes a **prediction**. A hypothesis acts as a **starting point** for research. The research will aim to either **show that the hypothesis is true**, or **show that it's false**. Having an idea and then testing against the evidence is the traditional view of scientific research. Having a hypothesis and trying to prove it wrong is called the falsification model (see p.202).

2) A hypothesis states a **relationship** between **two factors** — e.g. "sociology teachers wear corduroy trousers" or "material deprivation causes educational underachievement".

Terms like "democracy" need to be Operationalised — i.e. Made Measurable

1) Sociology prides itself on giving names to **concepts** and **ideas** that aren't **easily explained** or measured. For example, it's **tricky** to measure things like "democracy", "development" and "culture".

2) You end up measuring these concepts by measuring **something else** that's **linked** to the tricky concept — sociologists call this an **indicator**. This is called "**operationalising**" a concept. It means making it operational, or workable, by finding a way to measure it.

3) Researchers do this **every time** they conduct a piece of research, because you **can't research** something if you **can't measure** it. Each difficult concept needs an **indicator**, e.g. electoral participation or diversity of electoral results for democracy.

4) Researchers need to be able to **justify** how they **operationalised** their concepts in their final report. This is often a **subjective** process and the way a researcher operationalises may be **criticised** by other sociologists.

Triangulation is where you Combine Methods or Data

Triangulation is when sociologists try to combine different methods or data to **get the best out of all of them**.

1) Triangulation gives a more **detailed picture** than when you only use one method, so it's more **valid** (see p.214).

2) When you triangulate, you can **check** different sets of data against each other.

3) Triangulation combines **strengths** and **weaknesses** of different types of data.

4) It can be **expensive** and **time-consuming** to do the same research by lots of methods. Sometimes it's **not possible** to use triangulation — e.g. when there's only one viable method to get the data.

Practice Questions

Q1 Give three factors to consider when choosing a topic for research.
Q2 Why is reviewing the field useful?
Q3 What is the "operationalisation of concepts"?

Exam Question

Q1 Assess the strengths and limitations of using triangulation for social research. (33 marks)

Isn't operationalising setting terms to music?

Not only is it vital you learn these pages for your exams, it's worth knowing about this stuff if you're thinking of becoming a sociologist. That's a frightening thought, isn't it. One day you too could find your name in a revision guide, with your life's work condensed into a nice maroon box. And then the following box will explain why everyone else thinks you're an idiot.

Research Design

This page is a spot of revision of AS material. There is some new stuff here too though, so don't skip over it.

Remember the **Difference** between **Reliability** and **Validity**

1)   Reliable research can be **repeated** to get the **same results**. Reliable data means data that **another researcher** would be able to get by using the **exact same methods**.

2)   **Sociological research** isn't generally as reliable as research in the **natural sciences** (physics, biology, chemistry, etc.).

1)   Valid data is a **true picture** of what the researcher is trying to measure.

2)   Even **reliable** data isn't always valid. For example, you could measure democracy by measuring voter turnout. This wouldn't always give a true picture, because it's possible to have **high voter turnout**, but **completely fixed elections** (e.g. under a dictatorship).

Research can be **Primary** or **Secondary** and **Quantitative** or **Qualitative**

Primary Data	Secondary Data
Information gathered by the **researcher him/herself** it's new, **original** and not taken from any existing data set.	Information gathered from **existing data sets** or **documents** — e.g. official statistics, diaries etc.
Primary data is as **valid** and **reliable** as the researcher's method makes it.	The researcher has to **trust** that the data is **valid** and **reliable** — this is easier if the researcher can find out the **original methodology**.
Collecting primary data can be **time-consuming** and **expensive**.	Using secondary data can **save** the researcher **time and money**.

Quantitative methods	Qualitative methods
These produce **numbers** and **statistics**.	These produce **stories**, and include people's **motivations**, and the **meanings** they give to what they do and think.
Can be **very reliable** — studies are easily repeated.	Qualitative methods **aren't reliable**.
May not be valid. Doesn't include anything subjective.	Can be **very valid**.
They allow the use of **large samples** (see p.218) so they can be **highly representative** of the population.	They're **time-consuming**, so they only use **small samples**. This means they're **less representative** than quantitative methods.

Theoretical considerations **Influence** choice of **Method**

1)   **Structural** theories like **functionalism** and **Marxism** favour a **positivist** approach and **quantitative** methods.

2)   **Functionalists** argue that the social world acts similarly to the **natural world** and therefore all study should be similar to that of "natural science" — i.e. using **objective** and **quantitative techniques**.

3)   **Marxists** explain the nature of society in **economic** terms which also tend towards "scientific" techniques of data collection — i.e. quantitative methods.

4)   **Social action** theories are interpretivist — they favour **qualitative** methods, because social action theory is **subjective**.

5)   For a social action approach, methods of data collection are more **small-scale** and **in-depth**. In order to analyse **why** people make the assumptions they make and act in the way they do, researchers **observe** and **question** them **at length**.

6)   Social action theorists prefer techniques that give detailed **stories** and **meanings** — e.g. ethnographic studies, unstructured interviews (see p.219) and observation (see p.220).

Practical considerations **Influence** choice of **Method**

1)   Some methods take a lot of **time** — **qualitative** methods tend to **take longer** than quantitative methods. Participant observation takes a very long time both to plan and to complete. But quantitative methods can also be time-consuming — social surveys take a relatively short time to **complete**, but a **long time** to **interpret**.

2)   **Funding** affects choice of method. The **researcher's time** costs money, **resources** such as computers cost money, and it costs money to send out **postal questionnaires** to large samples.

3)   **Lack of access** to primary sources would mean that the researcher has to use **secondary** sources.

Research Design

Before you can Start — you Need a Sample

1) All researchers have a **target population** in mind before conducting research, which might be anything from **everyone** in a **country** or **region**, to a select group with **specific characteristics**, such as 'all women over 50' or 'all pupils in one school'.

2) It's **too expensive** and **time-consuming** for sociologists to survey the **whole population**. They select a **sample**.

3) If the **characteristics** of the **sample** reflect the **characteristics** of the **target population** — with similar proportions of people in terms of age, class, ethnicity and gender — then the sample can be said to be **representative** of that target population. The extent to which a sample represents the target population is known as its **representativeness**.

4) If the sample is sufficiently **large** and **representative**, then it should be possible to make **generalisations** from it about the **wider target population**. The extent to which you can accurately do this is the sample's **generalisability**.

5) Some target populations may be **difficult** to **access** — e.g. criminals, the very young or very old. In these cases you can use **non-probability sampling** methods such as **snowball sampling** — see the section on non-probability sampling below.

Probability Sampling involves Random Selection

Probability sampling involves picking names out of a "sampling frame" at **random**. A sampling frame is a **complete list** of the population being sampled, which needs to be **accurate**, **complete** and without any **duplicate** entries — easier said than done. **Random**, **systematic** and **stratified random** are all kinds of probability sampling.

1) In simple random sampling, names are taken completely at random, e.g. randomly selected from a list by a person or a computer, so each member of the population has an equal chance of being selected.

2) Systematic sampling involves choosing a starting point in the sampling frame and selecting every *n*th value, e.g. every fifth name. There may be bias, if there's an underlying pattern in the sampling frame.

3) In stratified random sampling the population is put into segments called "strata" based on things like age, gender or income — e.g. age 18-24, 25-34, 35-44, 45-54, 55-64, 65+. Names are selected at random from within each segment.

Non-Probability Sampling involves Human Choice

The following are different types of **non-probability sampling**.

1) In **quota sampling**, the selection is made by the **interviewer**, who'll have a quota to meet — e.g. "interview 20 women between 25 and 34". It's a bit like stratified random sampling, but it's not random — interviewers tend to pick people who look "nice", which introduces bias. It's quick and useful, though.

2) **Multi-stage sampling** means selecting a sample from **within another sample**. It's often used to select samples for opinion polls to measure voting intention. First, a selection of constituencies is chosen to represent the whole country, then postcodes within that constituency are selected, then houses from those postcodes.

3) **Snowball sampling** means finding **initial contacts** and getting them to **give you more names** for your research.

4) **Purposive sampling** is when researchers select non-representative samples that will yield information-rich cases for in-depth study. There are many different ways of doing this. **Extreme** or **deviant sampling** means selecting the most extreme or unusual individuals for study. **Typical case sampling** involves studying those who are average or typical of a particular group.

5) Sociologists sometimes **deliberately** pick a sample that **isn't representative**, in order to try to **falsify** a hypothesis about social behaviour. E.g. feminist sociologists trying to disprove the idea that gender roles are determined by biological difference deliberately looked for samples where women's roles **weren't different from men's roles**, or weren't traditionally "feminine".

A Pilot Study is a Small-Scale Practice Run before the Real Research

A **pilot study** lets you test the **accuracy** of your questions, and check if there are any **problems** in your **research design**. You can use them to make studies **more valid** and **reliable**, test how **long** the research will take, and **train** your interviewers. Though they're **time-consuming**, **expensive** and create lots of **work**, they show that the project is **feasible**, and can help you secure **research funding**.

Practice Questions

Q1   What does it mean to say that a study is: a) reliable, b) valid?

Q2   What is a sampling frame?

Exam Question

Q1   Identify and explain two methods of sampling that you could use for a postal questionnaire on crime.   (6 marks)

I did a pilot study once — I made notes while golfing with a Wing Commander...

These pages cover the real nuts and bolts of sociological research. Every study at some point involves someone sitting down and having a good think about these things — what population to study, what methods to use, what kind of sample to select...

Ethics in Research

Ethics is concerned with appropriate behaviours and procedures that sociologists must adhere to when conducting research. The British Sociological Association publishes guidelines to help researchers to conduct ethical research.

Ethical Considerations *can be grouped into* Four Main Areas

1) **Consent** — all participants must have openly agreed to take part.

2) **Confidentiality** — the details of all participants and their actions must remain confidential and private.

3) **Avoidance** of **harm** — participants should not be physically or psychologically harmed by the research process.

4) **Avoidance** of **deception** — researchers should be open and honest about the study and its implications.

Participants *should give* Free, Informed Consent *to their role in the study*

1) The researcher should get participants' **consent** before they conduct their study. Sociologists should be **open** and **honest** about the work they wish to carry out. It's important that the respondent knows what they're signing up for.

2) **Children** or people with **learning difficulties** may **not fully understand** what participation would entail. This is problematic. It can be argued that **uninformed consent** isn't really consent at all.

3) Consent can be **difficult to obtain**, especially from **secretive** groups (e.g. Scientologists, the Freemasons, gangs) or when the research is about a **sensitive** topic (e.g. crime, sexuality).

But... studies can be **endangered** if the person studied is aware of the **real purpose** of the work.

Milgram (1974) was not honest with participants in his experiments on obedience

Background:	Milgram conducted a series of experiments in which volunteers were ordered to administer electric shocks to another person (who was actually an actor) on the other side of a glass screen, when that person failed to give the correct answers in a memory test. Many volunteers kept on giving punishment shocks until the actor pretended to pass out.
Deception:	• Milgram lied about the purpose of the experiment. He told the volunteers that they were doing an experiment about **memory**. • The electric shocks **weren't real**. The person who the volunteers were "shocking" was an actor, pretending.
Results:	The results of the experiment were **very useful**. The experiment showed how people are ready to **obey** authority without **question**. This helped people understand how **ordinary people** take part in war crimes and genocide.

The experiment **wouldn't have worked** if the volunteers **knew** the real purpose of the experiment. If they knew that their **obedience** was being tested, they might have deliberately been less obedient. If they knew the shocks weren't real, they wouldn't have behaved in the same way. Milgram **had to be dishonest** for the experiment to work at all.

The general opinion is that this experiment **wouldn't be allowed to go ahead today** — partly because of the **deception**, but mostly because of the risk of **psychological harm**. Some participants were disturbed at how **easily** Milgram had **manipulated** them. However, Milgram **debriefed** all the participants afterwards so they all **understood** the study, and did **follow-up work** to check that they weren't psychologically harmed. He found that some participants saw it as a **valuable learning experience**.

Covert Studies *are* Criticised *for not getting* Informed Consent

1) Covert methods (e.g. **covert participant observation**, see p.220) involve **not telling** the group being studied that they actually are being studied. They're often criticised for their **lack of honesty** and the absence of **true informed consent**.

2) Covert participant observers argue that to **negotiate access** into **sensitive** or **dangerous** groups such as criminals, the researcher often has to either **pretend to be part of the group**, or not inform the group of the **true purpose** of the study.

Laud Humphreys' "Tearoom Trade" (1970) was a covert observation of secretive homosexual activity	
The group:	The group Humphreys wished to study were men who engaged in homosexual activities in **public places** (especially public toilets). They were **secretive** about their activities for three main reasons — homosexuality was **taboo** in mainstream society, sexual activity in public is **against the law**, and some of the men may have been married men leading a "**secret life**".
Covert study:	Humphreys probably wouldn't have gained access to this group if he'd openly and honestly informed them about the nature of the research and then sought their permission. Even if he did gain their permission, it's likely that they'd have **acted very differently** if they were aware that they were being observed. Humphreys therefore posed as someone who watches homosexual acts for a sexual thrill. This enabled him to gain the **trust** of the group and observe **genuine actions**.

Not that sort of tearoom...

Other sociologists argue that work like Humphreys' shouldn't be conducted, even if it gives valuable insights to sociology.

Ethics in Research

Respondents have Rights to Privacy and Anonymity

1) All respondents taking part in a piece of research must have their **basic right to privacy** valued and **upheld**. The **data** gathered from them and their **personal details** must not be distributed to anyone **outside** the **research process**.

2) When the report is finally produced, respondents must be made **anonymous**. Any descriptions of people, geographical locations and institutions have to be written in a way that prevents readers from easily recognising the participants. **False names** may be used — in which case the researcher should **clearly state** that false names have been used, in case someone who **shares** the name is **mistakenly identified** as having taken part in the research.

3) Of course, if a researcher **breaches** trust and confidentiality, potential participants will be **put off** taking part in future studies. Research participants must feel they can **trust** the researcher, especially if the research is of a sensitive nature — e.g. a self-reported crime study, or a sexual health survey.

Researchers must make sure that Nobody is Harmed by Taking Part in a study

1) Emotional and physical harm is **never acceptable** in sociological research, and work is actively criticised and rejected if it has allowed harm to come to those involved.

2) Researchers studying topics such as **mental health** or **geriatric care** may stumble across **situations** and **experiences** that cause individuals **harm** — e.g. inappropriate living conditions, or abuse by carers. There is an ethical question as to whether they should **stop** or **suspend** the research in order to **remove** the individual from the dangerous situation.

3) Some topics that are discussed may be **traumatic** for the respondents — they would need to be **informed** of the possible temporary mental and emotional harm before starting the study. Remember, it's important to make sure that all consent is **informed consent** (i.e. that the person fully understands all the implications and aspects of the research before they agree to take part).

Some Sociologists can justify Bending or Breaking ethical rules

There's a lot of **good** that can come from sociological research. Many sociologists can **justify** breaking or slightly bending some of the **ethical rules** — if the data that they'll gather is likely to make a beneficial contribution to society. This justification becomes even stronger if potential ethical problems are minimised — e.g. if there's **minimal harm** and **full confidentiality**, but just a **wee bit of deception** (the basis of covert participant observation).

1) For example, **Nigel Fielding (1981)**, in a study of the **National Front** (an extreme right-wing political party with a secretive hierarchy) argues that he needed to conduct covert research otherwise he wouldn't have been able to gain access to the group and gather information.

2) **"James Patrick" (1973)** was a false name given to a researcher conducting a study on **violent gangs** in Glasgow — to ensure his **own safety** and protection.

3) **Roy Wallis (1977)** wasn't entirely **honest** when researching Scientology. He didn't say he was a sociologist when he signed up to a Scientology course. If he had been honest, the Scientologists may have told him to go away. Wallis was also forced to **name** some of his sources, during a **legal battle** between the Church of Scientology and another researcher. This broke the rule on **privacy** and **anonymity**, but in this case Wallis had **no choice**.

Practice Questions

Q1 What are the four main ethical considerations a sociologist needs to be aware of in their study?

Q2 Why are covert methods seen as unethical?

Q3 Give two reasons that sociologists might use to justify breaking ethical rules.

Exam Question

Q1 Assess the importance of ethics when conducting sociological research. (33 marks)

Danger, sociologists at work...

Well, obviously you wouldn't decide to do a covert observation of how people react to being hit on the head. Because that would be wrong. The key point is that sometimes there are justifications for breaking ethical guidelines, but only when the research is likely to provide such useful information that it's worth it. More than nine times out of ten the best option is to stick to the rules.

Quantitative and Qualitative Methods

Quantitative data is the kind you usually get from things like questionnaires — it can be turned into numbers, and put in graphs easily. Qualitative data comes from things like unstructured interviews — it's in-depth data. Although most of this was covered in the AS syllabus, it's on the A2 syllabus as well.

Questionnaires *mainly provide* Quantitative Data

1) When planning a questionnaire, the researcher must first operationalise their concepts (see p.213). Once they've come up with a bunch of indicators, they can plan questions which accurately test for those indicators.

2) **Closed questions** and standardised **multiple-choice answers** give **quantitative** data. They're appropriate for **positivist** research (see p.203).

3) You can do a questionnaire with **open-ended questions** but it's harder to quantify the data into nice neat numbers. It's not impossible though — you have to classify the answers into **categories**. This is called coding (see p.240).

4) Questionnaires should use **clear**, **simple questions** which are **easy to understand**.

5) They should give **clear instructions** and have a clear layout.

6) **Multiple-choice** questions must give an appropriate number of responses. The researcher doesn't want too many respondents to answer "none of the above" or "other".

Questionnaires have several advantages

1) Questionnaires are **easy to administer**, and they can collect a **lot of data** in a **short time**. Closed questions provide quantitative data which can be **quickly** analysed too.

2) Questionnaires are **reliable**.

3) Questionnaires are **anonymous** and don't require the respondent to sit **face-to-face with an interviewer**. This makes them suitable for **sensitive topics**. For example, the National Survey of Sexual Attitudes and Lifestyles was a **postal questionnaire** rather than a face-to-face structured interview.

4) A **large sample** can be given a questionnaire, so if the sample is representative (see p.215), the questionnaires should produce **representative data** that can be used to make generalisations.

Questionnaires have limitations — they aren't very valid

1) Respondents **may not tell the truth**. They may lie, or they may be mistaken.

2) Questions may be **misleading** or **mean different things** to **different people**. This means they may not accurately measure what you **want to measure**.

3) Respondents can't give any **extra information**, even if it would be really helpful to the researcher.

4) Because the respondent fills in the questionnaire on their own, there's no one there to **explain** the questions if the respondent doesn't understand them.

5) Postal questionnaires have a **low response rate**. If it's **too low** it won't be a **representative** sample.

Pilot studies (see p.215) are useful for questionnaires. Researchers can test if the questions make sense to the respondents.

Structured Interviews *are* Questionnaires *given* Face to Face

1) **Structured interviews** are like **questionnaires** given to **individuals** or **groups**, only an interviewer is present to ask the questions.

2) The main plus point over a postal questionnaire is that the interviewer can **explain** and **clarify** the questions.

3) Also, most structured interviews get a much **higher response rate** than questionnaires. People tend to agree to be interviewed — unless the research topic is **sensitive** or **taboo**.

4) However, they're **more expensive** than questionnaires — you need to **pay for the interviewer**.

5) In a structured interview, the interviewer has to **follow the list of questions** so they **can't ask for more detail** if the respondent says something **particularly interesting**.

Social Surveys *use* Questionnaires *and* Structured Interviews

1) **Social surveys** collect information about a **large population**, using **questionnaires** or **structured interviews**.

2) There are three main types — **factual**, **attitude** and **explanatory**. Some surveys are a **mixture** of more than one type.

Type of survey	What it's for	Who conducts it
Factual	Collects descriptive **information**	**Government agencies** and sociologists
Attitude	Collects **opinions**	**Opinion poll organisations** and sociologists
Explanatory	Looks for **reasons** and tests out hypotheses	Sociologists

Quantitative and Qualitative Methods

Unstructured Interviews give Qualitative Data

1) **Unstructured interviews** are **informal**, without a **rigid structure**. They use **open-ended questions** and give **qualitative** data, so they're quite **valid**. Interviews are **flexible** — they can be used to find out facts or attitudes.

2) In a **fully unstructured** interview, the conversation just develops **naturally**. Interviews can be **partly structured** and partly **unstructured** — i.e. the interviewer has to follow the questions in a set order, but they can let the respondent **elaborate** on any interesting points, and they can **ask** the respondent for **more information.**

3) Interviews can be done with **individuals** or small **groups**. Group interviews let the researcher observe **interaction**.

4) Because they're used with **smaller samples than questionnaires**, they're **not as representative**. However, they're **more representative** than **participant observation** (see p.220).

5) Unstructured interviews are good for researching **sensitive issues** where the interviewer has to gain the respondent's **trust** — for example sexuality, domestic violence, crime. They're appropriate for **interpretivist** research (see p.203).

6) The interviewer needs to have **skill** so they can **probe** to **find out more detail** about the interviewee's **beliefs** and **opinions**.

See p.222 for more about interviewer effects.

7) There are a lot of **interviewer effects** in an unstructured interview. The interviewee may say what they **think** the **researcher wants to hear**.

8) It takes a **long time** to write up an **unstructured interview**. You have to write down a **whole conversation**, not just the **codes** for **multiple-choice answers** (see p.218). It's possible to do some **limited coding** of responses — the researcher could code for a particular category of opinion expressed, for example the respondent saying, "I'm worried about crime."

1) Interviewers usually use a **non-directive** style — they keep their own opinions to themselves, and they don't show any approval or disapproval of what the respondent says.

2) However, some sociologists choose to be more **aggressive** and **argumentative** in their questioning — more like a journalist. **Becker (1970)** took this approach when interviewing teachers, and claimed he'd got more useful information out of them than if he'd used the traditional non-confrontational approach.

3) **Ann Oakley (1981)** included unstructured interviews in her description of a "**feminist methodology**", and contrasted them with structured interviews, which she saw as masculine. She liked the respondent to get **involved** in the research process, and sought to get more from them by becoming close to them.

Pilot studies allow the researcher to find out what kind of question gets a **substantial response**. They let the researcher find out whether they need to **warm up** with a gentle **chat** to gain **rapport** with the respondent before asking more meaty questions.

Longitudinal Surveys are done over a Long Period of Time

Longitudinal studies are done at **regular intervals** over a **long period of time**, with the same people. They're often **large-scale quantitative** surveys. Some are more **qualitative** — e.g. the TV programme *Seven Up*.

1) You can **analyse changes** and **make comparisons** over time.

2) You can study how the **attitudes** of the sample **change** with time.

3) It's **hard** to recruit a **committed sample** who'll want to **stay** with the study.

4) You need **long-term funding** and you need to **keep the research team together**, which may be problematic.

Seven Up was a TV documentary that asked 14 kids aged 7 what they thought about life, and what they wanted to be when they grew up. The programme makers came back to interview them every seven years.

Practice Questions

Q1 Give two advantages and two disadvantages of questionnaires.

Q2 Give two advantages of unstructured interviews compared to questionnaires.

Q3 What is a longitudinal survey?

Exam Question

Q1 Assess the strengths and limitations of interviews as a method of data collection. (33 marks)

Top tip: never subcontract your interviews to Trappist monks...

It's worth giving these methods a good going over, even if you think you remember them from the AS course. There's a little bit more detail here, and you're supposed to take a more critical approach at A2 level. That means you don't just learn what each method is, you have to be aware of pros and cons, and how to figure out if it might be appropriate for a particular topic.

Quantitative and Qualitative Methods

Sociologists can do experiments on people, or they can observe them — with or without the subjects knowing about it. Or they can take the opposite approach and just read about people through secondary data.

Experiments *provide* Quantitative Data

1) **Lab experiments** are done in a **controlled environment**. They analyse **one variable** in terms of **another**. This method is often used by **psychologists**. Experiments can be very **reliable** and give **quantitative data**, but on the other hand they may not be valid because it's **hard** to **reproduce real social situations** in a lab.

2) **Field experiments** are a response to the criticisms of lab experiments. They take place outside of the lab in **real social settings** and those involved are often **unaware**, which poses **ethical problems**. This method is used by **interpretivist** sociologists. They're highly valid, but much less controllable and reliable than lab experiments.

Observation *provides* Qualitative *data about* Behaviour *in* Real-Life Settings

1) In **covert observation**, the researcher **doesn't tell the group** they're being observed. The BSA advise that you should only use covert observation when there's **no other way** of obtaining the data.

2) **Overt observation** (direct observation) is when the group is aware of the research and they know who the researcher is.

3) **Participant observation** is when researchers **actively involve themselves in the group**.

> 1) Participant observation gets the researcher **right to where the action is** — so they can **check out the dynamics of a group** from **close up**. The researcher gets **first-hand insight** into people in **natural real-life settings**.
>
> 2) **Participant observation** allows you to research the workings of deviant groups (see **Humphreys**, p.216).
>
> 3) The researcher may get too involved and find it **hard to objectively observe** the group. **Whyte (1955)** became so involved with the gang members he studied that he started to see himself as **one of them** — even though his research was **overt**. The researcher in a **covert observation** may be pressurised to join in with illegal acts if they're in a **deviant** group.
>
> 4) Participant research is extremely **flexible**. The researcher can change their ideas based on what they see.
>
> 5) Participant research **lacks reliability** — it can't be repeated. A covert observer may find it difficult to **record** the study accurately, and without imposing their own subjective values on it. However, interpretivists say observation can be used to assist more objective methods. **Becker (1970)** used observation to collect information that he used to formulate a **hypothesis**, which could then be checked out in further research.
>
> 6) There are **ethical** and **practical** problems in **getting in**, **staying in** and **getting out** of the group.
>
> 7) The research usually includes a **small group** so it's not **representative** of the population. **Goffman (1968)** studied just **one** mental asylum.
>
> 8) It's **hard work**, **time-consuming** and **expensive**.

Overt researchers may have a "sponsor" who gets them into the group. Covert researchers must pretend to be just like the group members.

4) **Non-participant observation** is when the researcher **observes** the group but isn't actively a part of the group.

Ethnography *Studies the* Way of Life *of a Group*

Anthropology is the study of humans.

1) **Ethnography** is the scientific description of a specific culture by someone with first-hand experience of observing that culture. It was first used by **anthropologists** to study **traditional societies**. They joined the community, learnt the language and noted their observations.

2) Ethnography is **in-depth research** which gives **inside knowledge** about a community. You get a **valid** picture from ethnography, but it relies on the **researcher's interpretations** of what people do and say. It's **difficult** to **make generalisations** from small-scale research.

3) It is based on small-scale fieldwork that tends to produce **qualitative** data. It's **valid** because you can study behaviour in **natural settings**. You can use all sorts of methods to get **primary data**. You can use **unstructured interviews**. You can **observe** a community and see what they get up to.

Focus Groups *are a Type of* Semi-structured Observation

1) A **focus group** is a **small sample**, perhaps fewer than ten people. The sample are **put in a room together**, and asked to talk about a particular issue or to try to answer a specific set of questions. The discussion is **observed by a researcher**.

2) Because this is more like a **natural conversation**, the subjects may feel **more able to express themselves** than if they were speaking **directly to an interviewer**. Sometimes the focus group is **left alone** and a **video camera** or **audio recorder** is used to **record the discussion for later analysis**. Sometimes researchers **stay with the group** and **take part in the discussion** — they use the focus group to conduct a **group interview**.

Quantitative and Qualitative Methods

Case Studies *focus on just* **One Thing**

1) Case studies are **detailed investigations** of **a specific thing** — e.g. one person, one group, one institution or one event.

2) One particular kind of case study is the **life history**, which studies one person's whole life.

3) Examples of case studies include **Willis's (1977)** study of one group of boys in a school (p.234) and **Venkatesh's (2008)** study on the organisation and impact of one criminal gang (see p.228).

4) **Interpretivists** like case studies because they can provide very **detailed data**, and they can give the researcher great **insight** into the subject under investigation.

5) Positivists dislike case studies as they **aren't representative** of wider populations, and so they can't be used to make accurate generalisations because of the **small sample size**.

Statistics *are a Source of* **Secondary Data**

Official statistics are a source of secondary data. They're produced by local governments, central government and government agencies.

Kenny found all statistics hard.

1) **Hard statistics** are **objective**. Politicians can't fiddle with them. Statistics on births and marriages are hard statistics.

2) **Soft statistics** are more **subjective**. Politicians can fiddle with them. Statistics on **crime**, **poverty** and **unemployment** are soft statistics. In the 1980s and 1990s, the government **changed the method** used to **measure unemployment** over 20 times.

3) **Social Trends** is a collection of **regular government surveys** published every year. It's a **great source** of **secondary data**.

4) The **census** is a survey of every household every 10 years. Every household has to fill in the form **by law**.

5) The **British Crime Survey** looks at victims of crime. The data is collected by a questionnaire.

Non-official statistics are statistics collected by organisations other than the government. For example:

1) **TV ratings** collected by the **British Audience Research Bureau**.

2) **Surveys** carried out by **special interest groups**, such as charities.

3) **Surveys** carried out by **sociologists**.

Documents *and* **Mass Media** *are a Source of* **Secondary Data**

1) A document is **written text**. Documents can be **personal** — like **letters**, **diaries**, **autobiographies**, **memoirs** and **suicide notes**. Documents can also be **official**, like **school records**, **health** records, **church** records and **social work** records.

2) Documents can be **expressive** — more to do with **meanings**, like a **suicide note**. Documents can be **formal** — like **official documents**. **Interpretivists** prefer **expressive** documents because they're a big source of **qualitative data**.

3) **Max Weber** used **historical documents** when he was studying how the **religious** beliefs of Calvinism brought about a **social change**. **Michel Foucault** used **historical documents** to analyse changes in **social control** and **punishment**.

4) **Content analysis** is a method of **systematically** analysing a communication (e.g. a speech, film or letter) to understand its **meanings**. It is often used to study the mass media, e.g. research by the **Glasgow University Media Group**.

5) There are **problems** with documents. They can be **difficult to understand** if they're old. They might be **fakes**. They might contain **lies** — especially personal documents.

Practice Questions

Q1 What is the difference between covert and overt observation?
Q2 What is ethnography?
Q3 Give three examples of official statistics.

Exam Question

Q1 Evaluate the usefulness of observational techniques in sociological research. (33 marks)

Plenty of quantity and quality on these pages...

Data is to the sociologist what clay is to the sculptor, or what pigeon liver and celeriac are to the chef — you can't do great work without the best raw materials. Studying methodology may not have the Hollywood glamour of criminology or the rustic charm of politics — but without data sociologists have nothing to do. So you'd best learn where and how to find it.

Issues About Validity

The way in which data is collected can seriously affect its validity.

Data must be **Valid** — the **Collection Process** can make it **Less Valid**

1) Respondents in an interview may **forget** things, **exaggerate**, or just plain **lie**.

2) They may try to show themselves in the **best possible light**. They may say they **wouldn't commit crime** when **really they would**. They may say they **recycle all their rubbish** when **really they don't**.

3) **Criminals** interviewed by **Laurie Taylor (1984)** later claimed that they'd **made up lies** to see if Taylor **believed** them.

Asking people about their **attitudes** to an event a **long time afterwards** often isn't valid. People **change their views** over time, and may **alter their description** of the past in the light of their **current beliefs**. For example, a middle-aged person may **falsely claim** to have been law-abiding as a youth when really they were a teenage delinquent.

There is a danger in **participant observation**, particularly **covert** participant observation, that the researcher will "**go native**". This means they get **too involved** and find it **hard to stand back** and **observe** the group **objectively**.

The **Research Process** can **Alter** the way **Respondents Behave**

1) Respondents in interviews may give the sort of answer they **think** the **interviewer wants to hear** — or the **exact opposite**, if they're feeling contrary.

2) Interviewers can give **subtle direction** towards certain responses — often **without realising** they're doing it.

3) These are known as **'interviewer effects'** (or 'researcher effects').

1) Participants in experiments may try harder at what they're doing to get a **positive response** from the researchers.

2) This is called the **Hawthorne effect** — first observed in an experiment at the **Hawthorne** electricity plant in Chicago, analysed by **Elton Mayo (1933)** in his work on motivation. The experiment was **meant** to test worker responses to **changes in variables** such as **workplace lighting**, but in fact **productivity increased** with **each variable change**, positive or negative. The workers seemed to be responding to the fact that they **knew an experiment was going on**.

3) These effects mean data from experiments may not be **valid**.

Even relatively unbiased researchers have to make **decisions** about how to **present** and **interpret** the **data** they've collected. They will tend to do so in line with their own **ideas** and **values** — this is known as **researcher imposition**.

Cultural Issues have an Impact on Validity

1) **Labov (1973)** found that **black American children** were much **more forthcoming** with a **black interviewer** than a **white** interviewer. He suggested that this could lead white researchers to think that the children had poor linguistic ability.

2) Ethnicity wasn't the only factor — the children were most forthcoming in an **informal setting**, where they could bring a **friend** with them.

3) Labov's explanation was that the children didn't speak up and show their abilities when they perceived the situation as alien, or **hostile**.

4) **Oakley (1981)** thought that **women** responded to a **friendly** interview style.

The **acceptability** of some sensitive issues **varies** between **social groups**. Some social groups may be less keen on **admitting embarrassing** or **socially undesirable** things, e.g. deviant behaviour, or mental health symptoms.

Publication must be Honest and allow Criticism and Comment

1) In the quest for objectivity, researchers should be open and public when they **conduct** research and when they **publish** their findings. Being open and public enables the researcher to **avoid accusations** of **falsifying data**, **over-emphasising insignificant findings** or using **dodgy methodology**.

2) Researchers should present their data and allow other researchers to build on it, criticise it or compare it to other work. This means that results get analysed in terms of **objectivity**, **validity** and **reliability**, and it allows others to **check** the researcher's **interpretations** to see if they are correct.

3) **Accountability to participants** is **crucial**. All participants should be given **access** to the final report.

4) The report should be **fair** and **representative** of their meanings, actions and beliefs.

5) The report must not **identify** the participants without their consent.

Issues About Validity

Many people question how valid or reliable a piece of research is if the presence of the researcher has affected the results. Reflexive researchers acknowledge that their opinions affect their work, and take this into account.

Research can be affected by the **Background** or **Opinions** of the **Researcher**

1) An individual's **social background**, their **perspectives** on life, their **sociological viewpoint**, and their **culture** will all affect how they **perceive** the world around them.

2) This goes for **sociologists** in exactly the same way as it does for us **regular folk**. Sociologists **are** regular folk.

3) What the **researcher** observes or notes as relevant depends on **their idea** of what's useful, true and accurate.

Reflexive Research takes the **Researcher's Opinions** into **Account**

1) Reflexivity refers to the **understanding** that a researcher has that their research **will be affected** by their own **opinions** and **standpoints**.

2) Reflexivity forces the sociologist to see **social structures** and **norms** and ways of **interpreting** them as something they have **in common** with the people they study.

3) Sociologists aren't magically free of the effects of the social world. They can't necessarily be **value-free** or **impartial**, but they **can** keep a **sense of self-awareness** about their preconceptions.

4) **Bourdieu and Wacquant (1992)** saw reflexive sociology as a way of giving a **deeper** and more **meaningful** understanding of the social world. They thought that if the sociologist saw themselves as in the **same boat** as the people they studied, they'd understand them better.

5) Bourdieu and Wacquant argued that **reflexivity** could **help Sociology** to be **more objective** — they thought it was very important to **keep an eye** on the way that researchers **actually obtain knowledge**, as it could help researchers avoid settling for poor methods.

6) Reflexivity rejects the **certainty** of **functionalist** approaches, and rejects the "**there's no truth**" attitude of some **postmodern** approaches.

The **Reflexive Researcher** will try to **Guarantee Valid Research**

1) A researcher who's **aware** of **potential bias** can take steps to **avoid** it.

2) Reflexive work can often be found in **interpretivist** (or interactionist) **sociology** (see p.203 and 206). Social action researchers use subjective methods that involve **interpretation**. Reflexivity techniques require the researcher to put themselves **in the place** of their participants for long periods of time to seek a **fuller understanding** of the **meanings** that participants put on their actions.

3) For example, **Barker (1984)**, in her study of the Unification Church (the Moonies), spent significant periods of time with **Moonie families** to gain their **trust** and understand their lives **from their point of view**. This allowed her to understand Moonie lifestyle without excessively imposing her **own interpretations** (which may have been different to theirs).

4) **Cicourel (1968)** actually spent time as an **unpaid probation officer**, which enabled him to **interpret** the meanings attached to the definition of "**delinquency**" from the perspective of the probation officers.

1) **Respondent validation** is asking respondents for their **opinions** on the research — checking that the researcher's findings are **fair**, **accurate** and **reflect** their views. Interpretivists argue that this is a good way of **assessing** the **validity** of data collected.

2) Research may still be **valid** even if respondents **disagree** with it. Respondents might **not understand** how their experiences have been **analysed**, or may be more concerned with presenting themselves in a **good light** than with accuracy.

Practice Questions

Q1 What is the Hawthorne effect?

Q2 What are the benefits of making research open and public?

Q3 What is meant by "reflexivity" in sociological research?

Exam Question

Q1 Assess the importance of openness and honesty in sociological research. (33 marks)

If you tap my knee, I'll do an interview — the reflexive researcher...

These pages are all about how researchers can have an unwanted impact on their research — and the steps they can take to reduce it, such as using respondent validation. This is really important to interpretivist sociologists, as they want their research to be as valid as possible — even if it means joining the Moonies or becoming a probation officer for a stretch.

Sociological Research: Crime and Deviance

*The following pages are about applying sociological methods to the topic of crime and deviance. They are for students who are studying the **Crime and Deviance** topic (see Section 5).*

Crime can be looked at in a number of Different Ways

1) A sociologist's **theoretical perspective** influences both their **research topic** and the **methods** they use.

2) **Structuralist** sociologists prefer **positivist** methods. **Social action** theorists prefer **interpretivist** methods.

3) **Consensus** structuralists (e.g. functionalists) focus on the **background** of criminals, while **conflict** structuralists (e.g. Marxists) are more **critical**, focusing on the role of **elites** and **agents of social control** in the criminalisation process.

Positivists use Quantitative Data to study Crime and Deviance

1) The positivist view is that an individual is **shaped** by **society** and by their position in the **social structure**. The point of doing research is to uncover the **underlying laws** that govern human behaviour.

2) Positivists work with **official statistics** and other sources of **quantitative data** such as **police-recorded crime statistics**, the **British Crime Survey** and the **Youth Lifestyles Survey** to gain an overview of how the crime rate varies across regions and social groups. They use this data to look for **correlations** and to try and establish what the **causes** of higher crime rates might be.

3) Official statistics show that high crime rate areas are often characterised by:
   - **poverty**
   - high levels of **social disorder**
   - high levels of **rented accommodation**

4) Official statistics (**Crime in England and Wales 2008**) reveal that offenders are more likely:
   - to be **male**
   - to be aged between **16 and 24**
   - to have **parents** who have **committed crime**
   - to have had an **absent father**
   - to have a history of **truancy** and **drug abuse**

Cyndi didn't know why she loved stealing German police cars — maybe it was because they had great sandwiches in them.

5) Positivists prefer to use **official statistics** in understanding crime and deviance because they are **reliable** — they provide us with an **overview** of crime in society, and they make it easy to **compare** crime rates across regions.

Interpretivists prefer Qualitative Data

Interpretivists criticise the use of official statistics, arguing that they give us a **false impression** of the nature and extent of crime in British society. Interpretivists argue that —

> 1) Both **official police statistics** and the **British Crime Survey** are **socially constructed**. The public **selectively** report crimes and the police **selectively** record them — e.g. a member of the public might not bother to report low-level vandalism.
>
> 2) The crime statistics may reflect the **bias** of the police — e.g. if the police think **young people** are more likely to commit crime, they may **over-police** the young and uncover more of their criminal behaviour as a result.

Interpretivists prefer to use **qualitative**, often small-scale research methods such as **unstructured interviews** and **participant observation**, for the following reasons:

> 1) They can provide **in-depth insight** into the **lives** of criminals and deviants.
>
> 2) They allow for **empathetic understanding** between researcher and respondents. They enable the researcher to see how criminals **perceive their own crimes**, and what reasons they **themselves** give for their behaviour.
>
> 3) This approach has also led to the establishment of **labelling theory**. This focuses on the **agents of social control**, by looking at how **labelling** can affect the **self concept** and **behaviour** of those labelled 'criminal' (see p.170).

Interpretivist methods are often used by **social action theorists** such as **Howard Becker (1963)**. They are often **sympathetic** to criminals and **'take the side of the underdog'**. This is not value-free and can involve **'turning a blind eye'** to criminal acts while conducting research — which creates ethical problems.

Sociological Research: Crime and Deviance

Consensus Sociologists believe some people suffer Anomie in Society

1) **Consensus theories** include **functionalism**, **strain theory**, **subcultural theory** and **social control theory**.
2) They argue that the social system is **generally good** and functions well for the majority of people.
3) Consensus sociologists see institutions such as **education** and the **family** as being crucial to **maintaining social order**.
4) They argue that **crime** and **deviance** are a result of individuals becoming **detached** from **mainstream institutions**. They blame specific failings of the **institutions**, or **peer groups**, for encouraging deviance, rather than the system.
5) Consensus-based research tends to be **positivist** in nature, i.e.

- Research is usually **quantitative** and **comparative**, seeking to understand and establish **correlations** between **social conditions** and **criminal behaviour**.
- Research focuses on factors in criminals' **backgrounds** that lead them to commit crime.

Conflict Sociologists argue that Injustices in the Social System cause crime

1) **Conflict theories** include traditional **Marxism** and **feminism**.
2) Conflict theorists argue that institutions of **formal social control** maintain the power of the elite groups (i.e. the bourgeoisie or men) over oppressed groups.
3) They argue that it's the **oppressive system** and **prejudiced agents of social control** that marginalise and selectively criminalise powerless sectors of the population.
4) Conflict theorists use a mixture of **quantitative** and **qualitative** research methods focusing on —

- How the **injustices** of the social system generate criminal behaviour.
- How **institutions** work in the interests of **elite groups**.

5) Research is **sympathetic** to criminals, seeking to understand how deviant action can be **rational** for the **marginalised**.

Sociologists' Theoretical Perspectives shape their ideas about Social Policy

Theoretical perspective influences ideas about what policies should be put in place to **combat crime**:

Positivists and Consensus theorists	They believe in **'early intervention'** to stop **'high risk'** individuals from committing crime, such as putting policies in place to encourage **strong families** and **higher school attendance**.
Conflict and Action theorists	They may work with the police to **reduce prejudice** and **labelling**. They aim to **reduce inequalities** within the society. They may believe that a **complete change** of system is necessary to reduce crime.

Practice Questions

Q1 Suggest two reasons why positivists prefer to use quantitative methods when researching crime and deviance.
Q2 Suggest two criticisms an interpretivist might make of the positivist approach to crime research.

Exam Question

Q1 Explain one problem of using official statistics, such as the British Crime Survey, in researching crime and deviance. (3 marks)

Someone's only gone and nicked my clipboard...

Quite a bit there for you to get your teeth into — again it comes down to what questions sociologists ask and how they get their answers. Just remember, if there are sociologists turning a blind eye while you're busy embezzling, they're most probably interpretivists of some sort. Unless they're undercover Interpol officers disguised as sociologists. It's all so confusing.

Sociological Research: Crime and Deviance

*In their choice of research methods sociologists are influenced by ethical considerations, practical constraints, and their theoretical perspective. These pages are mainly on positivist/quantitative approaches. For students studying **Crime and Deviance**.*

Different Factors *influence the choice of* Research Topic *and* Method

1) **Theoretical factors** are important. **Positivists** tend to prefer **quantitative methods** because they're more representative, reliable and objective. **Interpretivists** tend to prefer the greater validity of **qualitative** methods (see p.224).

2) **Practical constraints** include:

   - **Time and money** — the easiest data on crime to use is *Crime in England and Wales*, which is available for free. If a criminologist wants data that's **nationally representative** they must use **quantitative** methods. Qualitative research will always **take longer** and **cost more** for the same number of respondents.

   - **Funding** — by far the largest source of funding for criminology is the **government**, which favours quantitative research as it's more **representative** and **objective**. The government's also more likely to fund research that fits in with its **current aims**.

   - **Access** — it may be difficult to gain access to some groups. Elite cadres and corporate criminals, for example, would take years of personal networking to infiltrate. **Covert participant observation** (p.220) may be the **only method available** to research criminal and deviant groups.

3) There are also **ethical considerations**. Researchers need to think about how those involved are **impacted** by the **research process**. Some topics need to be researched with **sensitivity** — researching victims usually requires unstructured interviews to ensure the setting is not too intimidating.

4) The **interests** and **values** of the **researcher** may influence what is seen as **worthwhile** or **ethical** to study in the first place. Some **feminist researchers** in the 1980s, for example, studied the victims of **domestic violence**, a group who were extremely marginalised in society. This fitted in with their theoretical perspective and concerns.

Positivists value Representativeness, Reliability *and* Objectivity

1) Positivists use **quantitative data** from **police-recorded crime** figures and large-scale surveys such as the *British Crime Survey* in order to uncover **society-wide** patterns of offending, such as the relationship between crime and locality. They believe this is necessary to ensure that data is **representative of society as a whole**.

2) Positivists believe that statistical data is **more objective** than data obtained by qualitative methods. There are three major sources of data on crime that positivists rely on —

   - **Police-recorded crime (PRC)** figures include all crimes reported to and recorded by the police. These are collected by police forces across England, Wales and Scotland.

   - The **British Crime Survey** asks ordinary people if they have been a **victim of crime** in the previous 12 months and whether they **reported the incident** to the police. This is carried out every other year, using a sample of over 40 000 people living in private households.

   - **Self-report studies** are surveys of a cross-section of the population which ask what **offences** they've committed.

The government publishes crime data in the yearly publication *Crime in England and Wales*, which contains both information on **police-recorded crime** and data from the **British Crime Survey**. This is freely available and can be used to compare the differences between police-recorded crime and the BCS data on crime.

Police-recorded Crime *figures are* Easy *to get hold of...*

1) It's easy to make **comparisons** across regions because all police forces use the **same categories** to record crime.

2) They are **readily available**, easy and cheap to use.

3) They allow the **efficiency** of the police to be **assessed**.

...but they need to be handled with Care

1) **New counting rules**, which increased the number of different offences that are counted, were introduced in **1998** and **2002**, which makes it **difficult** to make **comparisons over time** — although these new counting rules should improve the **validity** of police-recorded crime statistics.

2) The number of offences recorded will vary with **police initiatives**. If more resources are put into tackling knife crime, the police will uncover more of it. An increase in police-recorded crime may mean the police are getting **more efficient** at detecting crime, **rather** than indicating an increase in the actual rate of crime.

3) Most importantly, **not all crimes** are recorded by the police. Before a crime is officially recorded someone has to **notice** a crime has occurred and **report** it to the police, and then the police have to **record** it. At each stage, certain crimes **disappear**. This results in what criminologists refer to as the **"dark figure of crime"** — crimes that do not appear in the PRC statistics.

Sociological Research: Crime and Deviance

The **British Crime Survey** reveals the extent of the **Dark Figure of Crime**

The **British Crime Survey** shows the chance of a crime being reported to the police depends greatly on the **type of offence**. Based on the **2007/08** *BCS*:

- **42%** of incidents were **reported** to the police.
- **Thefts of vehicles** were **most likely** to be reported (93%).
- **Vandalism** (35%), **assault without injury** (34%) and **theft from the person** (32%) were the **least likely**.

The **British Crime Survey** has its own **Weaknesses**

Despite providing criminologists with a more valid measurement of crime, there are still limitations to BCS data.

1) The data is based on a **household** survey which means it will not detect crimes against the **homeless** or **prisoners**.
2) Some types of crime are **excluded** from the *BCS*, such as **corporate crime** and **fraud**.
3) Despite the survey being **anonymous**, people appear to **under-report** sexual offences.
4) Crimes against **children** are excluded, as only those **aged over 16** are interviewed.

Self-report **Studies** uncover **Hidden Crime...**

1) They **reveal information** about the kind of offenders who **aren't caught** or processed by the **criminal justice system**.
2) It is possible to find out about the age, gender, social class and even the location of these **'hidden offenders'**.
3) It is also the most useful way to find out about **'victimless' crimes**, such as illegal drug use.

...but tend to miss **Serious Offences**

1) Self-report studies are only useful for finding out about relatively **minor offences** — serious offenders would probably lie.
2) They also create the **ethical problem** of **knowing about crimes** committed, but not being able to report them due to the necessity of keeping information **confidential**.

Interpretivists deny that official statistics are **Objective**

1) Interpretivists argue that despite claims of objectivity, police statistics and the *British Crime Survey* are very much reliant on **'social processes'**. They are reliant on a series of decisions made by individuals, each with their own **motivations**, **values** and **views**.
2) Interpretivists say official statistics such as police-recorded crime are **'socially constructed'**. Before a crime is **officially recorded** a number of things must happen (it must get **noticed**, **reported** and then **recorded**), and at each stage certain crimes disappear — speeding offences **go unnoticed** on country roads, people **don't bother** to report vandalism, or may be **too scared** or **ashamed** to report domestic violence. Sometimes the police may fail to record crimes for the **sake of their statistics**.
3) Interpretivists argue against **quantitative macro-style sociology**, saying it treats human beings as though they are puppets, merely **reacting to social forces**. They believe that to fully understand why some people commit crime, you need to take an **in-depth look** at their lives. Interpretivist methods are covered on p.228-229.

Practice Questions

Q1 Describe two practical constraints on a sociologist's choice of research method.
Q2 Why might some crimes not appear in the police-recorded crime statistics?
Q3 What do interpretivists mean when they call official crime statistics 'socially constructed'?

Exam Question

Q1 Assess the strengths and limitations of using victim surveys such as the British Crime Survey to understand the nature and extent of crime and deviance.
(15 marks)

Admit it — you love criminological research methods...

Though some sociologists don't think they're great, official crime statistics are at least free to look at and easy to get hold of. Interpretivists claim the whole enterprise is riddled with socially-constructed nonsense. But at least it gives you solid numbers to play with. Make sure you know the pros and cons of police-recorded crime figures, the British Crime Survey and self-report studies.

Sociological Research: Crime and Deviance

*These pages are mainly about qualitative/interpretivist methods. They are only for students studying the **Crime and Deviance** topic.*

Interpretivists *prefer* Qualitative Methods

1) Interpretivists value **validity** — research is valid if it provides a **true picture** of what is really **'out there'** in the world.

2) Generally speaking, the more **in-depth** the research, the fuller picture we get of the **thoughts** and **feelings** of the individuals involved. Data becomes more valid when the researcher **stands back** and allows the respondents to **'speak for themselves'**. Methods such as **participant observation** and **unstructured interviews** aim to gain valid data.

Unstructured Interviews *have helped in researching* Victims of Violence

1) Unstructured interviews allow researchers to deal sensitively with difficult topics, as **Dobash and Dobash (1983)** did with their research into the **victims of domestic violence**.

2) Unstructured interviews with **victims of crime** also have the advantage of giving the **powerless a voice**.

Winlow and Hall *used* Unstructured Interviews *to research* Street Violence

1) **Winlow and Hall (2006)** used unstructured interviews to understand more about **young people's attitudes** to the culture of **drink** and **violence** in the 'night-time economy' of clubs and pubs.

2) This method allowed the young people to talk to the researchers **as naturally as possible** about their **everyday lives**, and about what violence **meant to them**.

   - Winlow and Hall **interviewed** 43 working class youths mainly aged between **18-25** in the North East of England who were in **temporary** or **casual employment**.

   - They found that the main leisure activity was **drinking alcohol** with friends in the many city centre bars and pubs. **Drunkenness** allowed normal rules and expectations to be **flouted** in a situation where there was **little policing**.

   - **Violence** seemed to be accepted as **inevitable** because of the high **alcohol consumption**. It did not put young people off going out, rather it provided an **'edge'** that was part of the **attraction** of night life.

   - Based on their findings, Winlow and Hall were able to **reject previous theories** about night-time violence being a form of **'resistance to oppression'**.

Participant Observation *means building relationships with* Respondents

1) **Participant observation** allows the researcher to gain an **empathetic understanding** with a group.

   Paul Willis (1977) used participant observation to research the attitude to school of 12 rebellious working class boys. He found they **rejected school** because they saw it as **irrelevant** to their future work plans. Messing around was a strategy that helped them **pass the time** and **regain power** by getting their own back on those in positions of authority.

2) Participant observation allows the researcher to **'follow their nose'** and **discover the unexpected**.

   Sudhir Venkatesh (2008) spent **10 years** with a gang of crack dealers in Chicago. He found that they **structured themselves** much like any normal regional sales business.

3) **Covert participant observation** may be the **only way** to gain access to some groups.

   Donal MacIntyre conducted research for the BBC by **infiltrating** the hooligan 'firm' the Chelsea Headhunters. He uncovered how they **organised** their football violence and their links to **right-wing groups**. It's unlikely they would have **opened up** to MacIntyre if they had known he was a researcher.

Participant Observation *has its* Problems

1) It's often very **difficult** and **time-consuming** to gain **access** to the group being studied — it took both Willis and MacIntyre **months**.

2) Both Willis and Venkatesh could be accused of **'going native'** as both appeared sympathetic to their key respondents. This implies a **loss** of **objectivity**.

3) The data is **unrepresentative** of wider groups. Venkatesh was especially **reliant** on JT, the leader of the crack gang, for much of his information. His findings may not be relevant to other criminal gangs — it's all specific to this one group.

4) There can be **ethical problems** with participant observation. Venkatesh **witnessed** drug dealing and several beatings during his research but decided **not to inform the police**.

Sociological Research: Crime and Deviance

Secondary Documents can be useful in research into Crime and Deviance

1) **Autobiographies** such as **Charles Bronson's (2000)** give us a valid, **in-depth insight** into the **viewpoint** of a criminal.

2) **Diaries** have been used by researchers to encourage respondents to **express themselves**. One example is the 'Freedom Writers'. **Erin Gruwell**, an idealistic English teacher at a high school in California, encouraged a class of **"unteachable, at-risk"** students to write diaries about their **day-to-day experiences**. Their diaries eventually got turned into a book. It presented the students' lives from their own **point of view** and in their **own words**.

3) Writers may be **selective with the truth** — especially where details of **criminal acts** are concerned.

4) Those documents selected for publication are likely to be the **more sensational** and **exciting** ones. Mundane crimes will be missed, giving an **exaggerated picture** of the nature and extent of crime in a society.

Qualitative Methods present their own Problems

1) Methods such as **participant observation** — where the researcher can spend **several months** or even **years** with a small group of respondents — are **not very reliable** as it's **impossible to replicate** the original research exactly.

2) These methods are also open to researcher, or interviewer, **bias**. The more **involved** the researcher, the more they may **bias the results**.

3) In **extreme** cases, the researcher may **'go native'** and start to **sympathise** with the respondents — to **share** in their point of view rather than just to **understand** it — even if they're criminals. This means the research would no longer be **value-free**.

After a decade undercover studying the links between crime and mime, Andrei struggled to communicate his findings.

Positivists argue that Laboratory Experiments can provide Useful Data

1) **Experiment-based research** can **isolate** the effects of one variable on another.

2) Positivists argue that the method is **reliable** because the conditions of the experiment are easily **repeated**.

- One classic example of a laboratory experiment is the **Bobo doll** experiment, by **Bandura, Ross and Ross (1963)**.

- In the experiment, children were split into two groups. One group was shown a **film** of a person beating an inflatable plastic **Bobo doll** with a mallet. When the two groups of children were then put in a room with a Bobo doll and a mallet, the group which had watched the video acted more **aggressively** towards the doll.

- One of the conclusions drawn was that children who **witness violent images** are more likely to be **aggressive** than those not exposed to such images.

3) Interpretivists would argue that the experiment lacks **ecological validity** as the conditions are **not true to real life**.

4) In the real world, **media violence** does not have an isolated, independent effect on children, because they rarely watch television alone.

5) The experiment does not distinguish between the effects of **different types** of violence in the media.

Practice Questions

Q1 Suggest two advantages of using unstructured interviews in researching crime and deviance.

Q2 Identify two limitations of using secondary documents in social research.

Q3 Suggest a strength of using laboratory experiments to understand deviant behaviour.

Exam Question

Q1 Assess the strengths and limitations of using participant observation to understand the nature and extent of crime and deviance.

(15 marks)

Studying research methods? Infiltrate a gang of sociologists...

Not content with studying from afar, some sociologists seem to just love getting as close as possible to their respondents — either by joining their gang (like the interpretivists) or by bringing them back to the lab (like some positivists). The interpretivists in particular seem mad for going out 'into the real world' — make sure you know why.

Sociological Research: Stratification and Difference

*The following pages are about applying sociological methods to the topic of stratification and difference. They are for students who are studying the **Stratification and Differentiation** topic.*

There are **Different Approaches** to researching **Stratification** and **Differentiation**

1) The choice of research topic and the methods employed are often linked to the particular sociologist's **theoretical perspective**.

2) **Structuralist** sociologists prefer **positivist** methods. **Social action** theorists prefer **interpretivist** methods.

3) **Consensus structuralists** (e.g. functionalists) focus on the **benefits of stratification**, while **conflict structuralists** (e.g. Marxists and feminists) are more **critical**, focusing on the role of **elites** and **agents of social control** in creating stratification.

Positivists use **Quantitative Data** to look at the **Big Picture**

1) The **positivist view** is that an individual is **shaped by society** and by their position in the **social structure**. Research can uncover how factors such as an individual's **class**, **gender** and **ethnicity** can shape their **life chances**.

2) Positivists work with sources of quantitative data such as **Census data**, the **British Social Attitudes Survey** and **official statistics** from **government departments** that use **objective measurements** of class, gender and ethnicity.

3) Official statistics show that there is often a **link** between an individual's social class, ethnicity and gender and their life chances. Some examples taken from *Social Trends 38* **(2008)** are given below:

   - In 2005/2006 there were **1.5 million women enrolments** in **higher education** compared to **1.1 million men**.

   - **Black African, Caribbean, Bangladeshi** and **Pakistani households** are **roughly twice as likely** to be **non-working** households than **white** and **Indian households** (roughly 20% compared to 10%).

   - In English state schools the **rate of truancy** among pupils **eligible for free school meals** was almost **three times** that of the other pupils.

4) Positivists prefer to use **official statistics** in understanding stratification as they provide **objective data** that is **reliable** and can be **compared** easily.

Interpretivists prefer **Qualitative Data**

Interpretivists prefer to use **qualitative**, often small-scale research methods such as **unstructured interviews** and **participant observation** to explore the **complex nature** of class, gender and ethnic identities in modern Britain.

Interpretivists **criticise** the use of **official statistics**, arguing that their reliance on **clear-cut definitions** of **class**, **gender** and **ethnicity** is **flawed**. For example, **gender identity** and **sexuality** are **more complex** than the simple **male-female distinction**.

Savage *et al.* (2001) discovered that people don't have simple ideas about class

Savage *et al.* carried out **in-depth interviews** with **178 people** living around Manchester and discovered that most people had an **ambivalent attitude** towards their **own class**. Many of the people he interviewed thought their area **contained** a particular **class**, but that they themselves **weren't defined** by it.

Connell (1995) investigated different forms of masculinity

Connell researched the **life histories** of men through **in-depth interviews**. Connell identified **different forms** of **masculinity**, such as an idealised 'hegemonic' masculinity involving **toughness** and **authority**, which **subordinates** other masculinities, including **homosexual** masculinity.

Theoretical Perspectives also shape ideas about **Social Policy**

Theoretical perspective influences sociologists' ideas about what social policies should be put in place to combat inequality.

1) **Consensus structuralists** believe sociologists should work within the **existing system** to reduce inequalities. Consensus theorists believe that **some inequality** in society can be **beneficial** (see p.188).

2) **Conflict structuralists** generally have a more critical view of inequality, and believe we need more **radical changes**, for example to the **taxation system** or even to the **system of government** itself, to bring about greater equality.

Sociological Research: Stratification and Difference

The choice of Research Topic and Method is influenced by Several Factors

1) **Theoretical factors** are important. Positivists tend to prefer **quantitative methods** because they are more representative, reliable and objective. Interpretivists tend to prefer the greater validity of **qualitative methods**.

2) **Practical constraints** influence the choice of method. These include such things as how much **time** and **money** are available.

- **Time and Money** — the easiest data for the sociologist to use is produced by the **Office for National Statistics**, which is available for **free**. If a sociologist wants data that is **nationally representative** they must use **quantitative methods**. **Qualitative research** will always **take longer** and **cost more** for the same number of respondents.

- **Funding** — by far the largest source of funding for sociology is the **government**, which favours quantitative research as it's more **representative** and **objective**. The government's also more likely to fund research that fits in with its **current aims**.

- **Access** — it may be difficult to gain access to some groups — **elite cadres** (see below), for example, may be difficult to access as they would take years of personal networking to infiltrate. On the other hand **marginal groups** such as some **ethnic minorities** and the **lower classes** may not allow access, if they think they have little to gain from being researched.

3) Research must also take into account **ethical considerations**. This involves thinking about how the research **impacts** on those **involved** with the **research process**.

4) The **interests and values** of researchers may influence what is seen as **'worthwhile'** or **ethical** to **study** in the **first place**. Marxist and **feminist** researchers might see the **role** of **social research** as **political** — about **understanding** the **plight** of the **oppressed** and giving them a **voice**, for example.

Ethics and Access are Important Factors

1) Many sociologists would like to do **more research** on **elite groups**. Powerful elite groups tend to remain **under-researched** as they are **hard to infiltrate**. This means that there is an **imbalance of data** available about members of **different social strata**.

2) Trying to do research on **unwilling groups** raises many **ethical problems** — it's generally accepted that wherever possible sociologists should get the **consent** of the participants in their research, and **shouldn't deceive** them about the **aims** of the research. This can make some groups **incredibly difficult** to research. See p.216 for more on **ethics**.

At last Dr Miriam Elstree, Professor of Sociology and Social Policy at Beanthwaite University, had found a group willing to talk to her.

Practice Questions

Q1 Suggest two reasons why positivists prefer to use quantitative methods when researching stratification.

Q2 Describe one criticism that interpretivists make of the positivist approach to research on stratification.

Q3 Briefly describe the way Savage collected data for his study of attitudes about class in the Manchester area.

Exam Question

Q1 Assess the strengths and limitations of using official statistics to understand the nature and extent of stratification in British society.

(15 marks)

Quantitative data — research that counts...

More for you here on all the little battles that keep sociology interesting — heck yes. Some of this stuff may be pretty familiar to you by now, but it's worth thinking about how people with different perspectives will end up asking different questions in different ways. Even within perspectives — like feminism — there's plenty of room for disagreements. It's never simple or straightforward.

Sociological Research: Stratification and Difference

Sociologists' theoretical perspectives have a big impact on what they research and how they do it. These pages focus on the positivist approach to researching stratification and differentiation. For students studying the **Stratification and Differentiation** *topic.*

Positivists value **Representativeness**, **Reliability** and **Objectivity**

1) Positivists believe that statistical data is **more objective** than data obtained by qualitative methods.

2) Positivists use **quantitative data** from **official statistics** and **large-scale surveys** such as the **English Longitudinal Study of Ageing (ELSA)** to uncover **society-wide** patterns of stratification. They believe this is necessary to ensure that data **represents society as a whole**.

It had the reliability Penny was after — but did it have the objectivity?

Positivists like to use **Objective Social Class Scales** in their research

1) **Social classes** are groups of people who share a similar amount of **wealth**, a similar level of **income**, type of **job** and **education**.

2) There are different '**class scales**' that group people in **different ways**.

See p.186-187 for more on class scales.

- The **Registrar General's scale** ranks people according to the **occupational skill** of the head of the household.
- The **Hope-Goldthorpe scale** classifies people according to **market position**, or how **in-demand** a particular set of skills is among employers.

3) The advantage of **objective class scales** is that they enable comparisons to be made.

These comparisons can be within the same **period**...

Data from the **Office for National Statistics** tells us that there are still variations in life expectancy across social classes. In the period 2002-05:

- **Males** in the **professional class** had a life expectancy at birth of **80.0 years**, compared with **72.7 years** for those in the **unskilled manual class**.
- **Females** in the **professional class** had a life expectancy at birth of **85.1 years**, compared with **78.1 years** for the unskilled manual class.

...or **over time**.

A recent example of a study on intergenerational **social mobility** carried out by the **Sutton Trust** in **2005** compared the mobility of people born in 1970 to those born in 1958.

- The study found that intergenerational mobility had **fallen** markedly over time in Britain.
- The **difference** between the **proportion** of people from the **poorest 20%** of households who had been to **university** compared with the proportion of people from the **richest 20%** had **increased** between these years.
- One of the explanations given for the **decline in mobility** is the growth in the relationship between **family income** and **educational achievement**. **Extra opportunities** to stay in education at age 16 and 18 **disproportionately benefitted** those from more **wealthy backgrounds**.

There are **Disadvantages** to using **Objective Class Scales**

1) Different studies use **different social class scales**, so it's **difficult** to **compare** the results across the studies.

2) Some of the **old social class scales** do not work today, as the nature of social class has **changed**.

3) Social class is a **complex mix** of education, occupation, income and values — so it's not surprising that many people don't feel as if they '**fit**' their **objective social class**. People who are objectively working class may feel that they are middle class.

4) Some argue that **ethnicity** and **gender** are more important sources of stratification.

Sociological Research: Stratification and Difference

Large-Scale Surveys provide reliable quantitative data on Stratification Issues

1) A good example of a large-scale survey is the **English Longitudinal Study of Ageing (ELSA)**, which was set up by **Michael Marmot**. It follows a group of **over 8500** people from all social classes who were **born before 1952**.

2) The ELSA is partially funded by **central government**.

3) The subjects have had to fill in a questionnaire **every two years** since **2002** about their health, work, experience of healthcare, cognitive abilities and income. In 2004, the questionnaire was combined with **a visit from a nurse** to measure things such as **blood pressure** and **lung function**.

4) A new report on the study is **published** after every set of questionnaires.

5) In 2006 the study showed that over **ten times** more participants aged 50-59 from the **poorest 20%** of the population had died than from the **richest 20%**.

6) It also showed that there is a **strong relationship** between levels of **wealth** and **mortality and morbidity**.

Longitudinal studies are ones that follow the same group of subjects over a long period of time.

Advantages of Marmot's research method

1) Marmot has generated a **huge amount** of **quantitative data**, which is helpful for **scientific** and **positivist** research.

2) **Longitudinal studies** are the most **reliable** way to analyse **changes over time** as they eliminate the possibility of **different sample groups** each being **unrepresentative** in **different ways**.

Disadvantages of Marmot's research method

1) Longitudinal studies are **very expensive** and **time-consuming** — long-term funding is essential.

2) Some of the original group inevitably **leave the study** as time progresses — either **by choice** or just because they **die** or become **impossible to contact**. This affects the **reliability** of the research.

Many sociologists use Mixed Methods

Sociologists researching **stratification** and **differentiation** will often **use a combination of methods** — both quantitative and qualitative — this is known as 'triangulation', see p.213. This gives a **more detailed picture** than you'd get with one method — so it's more **valid**.

1) **Connor and Dewson (2001)** used **focus groups**, **interviews** over the phone (both qualitative methods), and **postal questionnaires** (a quantitative method) to research the factors that influence whether school leavers from lower social class backgrounds enter higher education.

2) They identified who was from the lower classes using the **Registrar General's scale** (see p.232).

3) They discovered a number of important factors that discouraged qualified **working class** candidates from entering **higher education**:

- **Candidates from lower-class backgrounds** were more likely to want to **earn money** and be **independent** as soon as possible.
- They were **more concerned** about the **cost** of funding their studies.
- They had **less confidence** in their **ability to succeed** in higher education.

Practice Questions

Q1 Name two social class scales.
Q2 Briefly describe two criticisms made of objective class scales.
Q3 What is the name of the large-scale survey set up by Michael Marmot?
Q4 Name the different methods used for gathering data by Connor and Dewson (2001).

Exam Question

Q1 Describe one disadvantage of using longitudinal surveys to research stratification. (3 marks)

These pages are pure class...

Positivists want representativeness, reliability and objectivity — and they're prepared to go to great lengths to get data that fills those criteria. Just imagine all the data that ELSA's generated — filing cabinet after filing cabinet of the stuff. It makes a mockery of all those interpretivists, with their cassette-taped chats. You could bury all the interpretivists in ELSA generated data. All of them.

Sociological Research: Stratification and Difference

*These pages focus on the use of qualitative methods in researching stratification and difference. They're for students studying the **Stratification and Differentiation** topic.*

Interpretivists *prefer* Qualitative Methods

1) Interpretivists value **validity** — research is valid if it provides a **true picture** of what is really **'out there'** in the world.

2) Generally speaking, the more **in-depth** the research, the fuller the picture we get of the **thoughts** and **feelings** of the individuals involved. Data becomes more valid when the researcher **stands back** and allows the respondents to **'speak for themselves'**. Methods such as **participant observation** and **unstructured interviews** aim to gain valid data.

Qualitative Methods *have* Advantages *for researching* Stratification

1) Qualitative methods give the researcher **insight** into the **lived experience** of **marginalised groups**.

2) Qualitative methods allow the respondents to **speak for themselves**, which could provide them with a **sense of empowerment**.

3) The researcher may find out **unexpected things** that enable **policy makers** to more effectively **tackle poverty** and **marginalisation**.

Qualitative Methods *present their own* Problems

1) Methods such as **participant observation** — where the researcher can spend **several months** or even **years** with a small group of respondents — are **not very reliable**, as it's **impossible to replicate** the original research exactly.

2) These methods are also open to researcher or interviewer **bias**. The more **involved** the researcher, the more they may **bias the results**.

3) In **extreme** cases, the researcher may **'go native'** and start to **sympathise** with the respondents — to **share** in their point of view rather than just to **understand** it. This means the research would no longer be **value-free**.

Qualitative Methods *are appropriate for researching* Marginalised Groups

1) A good example of research into marginalised social groups is **Paul Willis's (1977)** study of a group of 12 working class boys as they made their **transition from school to the workplace**. He used a mixture of **observation**, **group interviews** and **individual interviews**.

2) He found that the group had formed an **anti-school culture** that **rejected trying hard** in favour of **disruptive behaviour**. The group had decided not to try to **gain academic qualifications**, even if they were **intellectually capable**.

3) Willis found that they transferred the same **anti-authority culture** to their **workplace**. Most of them found work as shop-floor staff in factories.

4) Willis claimed that their anti-authority nature was something they **created themselves** and not something that was **transmitted to them** by school or society.

Advantages of Willis's research method

1) Most human interactions are **instinctive** and best studied in **real situations**. Willis used **direct observation** to see how the group acted in school and in their workplace, **group interviews** to see how they acted in each other's company, and **individual interviews** so that he could get an idea of what each subject was like on their own.

2) Individual interviews gave Willis a chance to **build a rapport** with the boys, allowing him to gain an **in-depth understanding** of their behaviour.

Willis's work is an example of a mixed method study (see page 233).

Disadvantages of Willis's research method

1) A sample of just 12 working class boys is **unlikely** to be **representative**. It would be misleading to generalise about all working class boys from these results.

2) However, performing the same study with a larger group of boys would be **very expensive**.

Sociological Research: Stratification and Difference

Unstructured Interviews give insight into *Personal Experiences* of *Stratification*

1) **Simon Charlesworth (1999)** conducted **unstructured interviews** with a **mixed** male and female group of 43 **working class** people in Rotherham, Yorkshire.

2) He focused on how **unemployment** has affected the lives of many of these people, finding that they had lost their **sense of identity** and **belonging** as a result of the decline of **traditional manual labour**.

3) One of the reasons Charlesworth was successful in gaining **access** was that he was from a **working class family** from **Rotherham**.

1) **Winlow and Hall (2006)** interviewed **43 young people** who were in **temporary jobs** in the **North East of England** about their attitude to **violence**. As well as the interviews, the researchers also carried out observation work.

2) They discovered that **violence** at the weekend was an **ordinary** and **anticipated** part of their **social life**. The researchers theorised that this was because of **frustration** caused by the sense of **'going nowhere'** in temporary employment, fuelled by **cheap alcohol** in **densely packed city centres**.

3) **Winlow** came from a **working class background** in **Sunderland** — which helped in finding **contacts** in the area for the study.

"Kid, you're the best, you're number one, you're an animal. Now go get 'em."

1) An important study by **Diane Reay (1988)** based on the 33 mothers of children at two London primary schools found that the **cultural capital** of the **middle class mothers** gave their children an **advantage** at school.

2) Middle class mothers were found to be **more likely** to do such things as **help** their children with **homework**, **bolster** their **confidence**, and **sort** out their **problems** with **teachers**.

1) **William Labov (1972)** used **informal, unstructured interviews** to test the theory that **"linguistic deprivation"** was a cause of **underachievement** of **working class** and **ethnic minority children**. Linguistic deprivation — a lack of ability with **Standard English** and a tendency to use **slang** — was believed to cause them to underachieve despite the fact that they may **express** the **same ideas** as high achievers.

2) He discovered that when **working class African-American children** were interviewed by a **white person** in a **formal interview**, they became **tense** and **spoke nervously**, appearing to be **linguistically deprived**. When they were interviewed by a **black person** In an **informal setting**, they became much more **articulate**. So the **apparent linguistic deprivation** seemed to be a reaction to a **perceived hostile environment** rather than a genuine feature of the children's **communication methods**.

Practice Questions

Q1 What does participant observation involve?

Q2 Why can we not treat Paul Willis's 1977 research as representative?

Q3 According to Reay's research, what things did middle class mothers do which gave their children an advantage at school?

Q4 Describe one problem with formal interviews that was encountered during Labov's research into linguistic deprivation.

Exam Question

Q1 Examine the advantages and limitations of using qualitative methods when researching marginalised groups in society.

(15 marks)

It's no use sitting on your class — get these pages learnt...

So, what's your favourite approach? I think I'd go with using quantitative data. That way you can stay at your desk all day, making the odd cup of tea, periodically checking what's in the biscuit tin. That's clearly the way to do sociology. You won't end up bumping into crack dealers that way either. But both methods have their pluses and minuses, so learn them well.

Do Well in Your Exam

*These two pages are all about how to do well in your exams. For your A2 you'll get **two exams** — one on Unit 3, and one on Unit 4. **Unit 3** is worth **60 marks**, 20% of the whole A-Level. **Unit 4** carries **90 marks**, which is **30%** of the A-Level.*

> These pages show what the AQA exam papers should be like based on the information currently available — it's possible there'll be some changes though. So it's important that when you take the exams, you **read the instructions and questions really carefully**. Don't assume they'll always follow the same pattern.

You'll have a *1½ Hour Exam* on Unit Three

1) In Unit 3 you have four topics to choose from: **Beliefs in Society**, **Global Development**, **Mass Media**, and **Power and Politics**. You should **only** answer questions from **one section**.

2) You might have been taught **more than one topic** — it's probably a good idea to revise **two** of them and then choose the **best questions** on the day. **Read** all the questions on the topics you've studied **before** making your choice.

3) In this unit you're likely to have to answer **two questions**:
   - The first question is **compulsory**. It's likely to be a **data response question** (i.e. you'll get a short extract of sociological material to answer questions on). It'll probably be split up into parts (a) and (b).
   - For your **second question** in Unit 3 you'll get a choice of **two essay questions**.

You'll have a *2 Hour Exam* on Unit Four

1) There are two sections in this exam — one on **Crime and Deviance** and the other on **Stratification and Differentiation**. Pick the section on the topic you've studied and answer all the questions.

2) There's likely to be **three questions** you need to answer:
   - a data response question on your **chosen topic**
   - a data response question on **sociological research methods** in the context of your chosen topic
   - an essay question on **sociological theory** and **methods**.

3) The exam paper should give clear **guidelines** on **how much time** you should spend on each question — make sure you stick to the advice they give you.

You Get Marks For...

In A-Level Sociology you'll be given marks for two Assessment Objectives — **AO1** and **AO2**:

> **AO1**   **Knowledge** and **understanding** of the **theories**, **methods** and **concepts** in sociology and the **links between them**. Also included in AO1 are marks for **communicating knowledge** in a **clear** and **effective** manner.
>
> **AO2**   The demonstration of the skills of **application**, **analysis**, **interpretation** and **evaluation**.

1) There are **more AO2 marks** available in the **A2 exams** than there were for the AS exams.

2) This is significant. You must be able to draw on a wide range of studies and theories and **analyse** them in detail. However much knowledge you display, if you don't **analyse** and **evaluate** it you won't get high marks.

Take a concept and *Make It Work* for you

A way to build up those AO2 marks is to master the art of **writing about sociological concepts**. There are key concepts in every topic — here's how to **wring the marks out of them**:

1) **Define** the concept.

2) Give **examples** of it in practice.

3) Present **different viewpoints** on the same concept.

4) Present **evidence** for each viewpoint.

Kit really felt the concept "sailor" worked for him.

Do Well in Your Exam

Use what you learnt in your AS-Level

Don't make the mistake of **forgetting** all the Sociology you learnt to get your stunning AS grade. The key research and theories will be relevant to these exam questions, too. The A2 units are **synoptic** — this means you need to show awareness and understanding of how topics interlink and the subject as a whole.

Oh... and don't forget **the basics**.

The AQA examiners really care about stuff like being able to read your handwriting — they're always going on about it in their examiners' reports.

- Write as **neatly** as you can.
- Use good **grammar** and **punctuation**.
- Check your **spelling** — especially of words to do with sociology.
- Make sure you **answer the question**.

It's important to be **disciplined** about **time** in the exam. Practise answering past papers under timed conditions. Candidates often lose marks by spending too much time on questions worth relatively few marks.

Here's an example of the Source Material for the Unit 3 paper

Item A

In the UK, the number of people turning out to vote is in decline. Recent election statistics prove alarming reading for politicians. When New Labour first got elected in 1997 they did so with a turnout of around 71%. By 2001 this figure had dropped to about 59% — a staggering decrease.

The issues of voter absenteeism and voter apathy undermine the UK's democracy. A democracy without legitimacy is no democracy at all. Without a high turnout of voters in general elections it is difficult for the winning party to claim meaningful legitimacy or mandate from the people.

5

Here's an example of a Short-Answer Question for Unit 3

1 (a) Identify and explain some evidence which supports the view that the ideological differences between the main political parties are no longer significant. (9 marks)

> There has been a significant shift in the ideological positions held by the mainstream British political parties in recent years, with Labour continuing to move to the right, and the Conservatives moving left away from the Thatcherism of the 1980s and 1990s.
>
> Before its recent shift rightwards, Labour was a recognisably democratic-socialist party seeking to transform society to a more socialist model. For instance, the Labour Party favoured a strong welfare state and state ownership of key industries. In contrast, the Conservatives under Margaret Thatcher were committed to free-market economics, privatisation, low taxes and a New Right approach to social policy.
>
> Today the situation is different. Labour, following the reforms of Tony Blair, has become 'New Labour' — adopting a new set of ideas called 'The Third Way' which seek to fuse a pro-business, free market approach to economic management with some of the caring aspects of 'Old Labour' such as a continued commitment to the Welfare State. The Conservatives under David Cameron have moved away from Thatcherism to a more 'compassionate conservatism' which attempts to be more inclusive.
>
> This shows that the two main political parties now occupy similar ideological ground, which suggests that the old class-based, left-right ideological division is now less important.

Address the question straight away.

Show off relevant background knowledge.

Keep your evidence relevant to the question.

Do Well in Your Exam

Here are some more sample exam questions and answers to show you the kind of thing to aim for.

Here's another **Sample Question** based on the **Source Material** on p.237

1 (b)   Using material from Item A and elsewhere, examine the view that voters have become apathetic about participating in politics.

(18 marks)

It is clear from Item A that voter turnout in elections is falling, with a turnout of only 59% in 2001 compared to 71% in 1997. This suggests that people are less interested in participating in politics.

Make sure you refer to the source material if it's mentioned in the question.

As well as a fall in voter turnout, there has also been a decline in membership of the main three political parties. For example, Labour's membership has fallen below 200 000 (compared to around 400 000 in 1997). This suggests that people no longer feel committed to party politics.

Show an awareness of recent developments.

That the government recognises voter apathy as a problem can be seen from measures they have taken to re-engage the public with politics, such as various attempts at making voting easier. They have also put citizenship on the national curriculum.

A number of sociological explanations have been put forward to explain this apparent apathy, including class dealignment and the rise of alternative methods of political participation at the expense of the more traditional methods of 'old politics'.

Try to use the correct terminology.

Class dealignment has been studied by Sarlvick and Crewe (1983). This refers to the tendency for voting behaviour to be less obviously based on traditional class positions — the working class identifying with and voting for Labour and the middle class identifying with and voting for Conservative. This breakdown of class alignment can be seen as having also weakened the bonds between people and the political parties as a whole.

Explain why your evidence is relevant.

Similarly the ideological convergence of the main political parties may have led people to feel there isn't enough difference between them to bother voting, or getting involved.

An alternative view is that the rise of New Social Movements and participation in direct action and protest by young people through NSMs suggests that they may not be politically apathetic at all.

Discuss contrasting viewpoints.

Mention relevant studies.

Postmodernists, such as Lyotard (1984), suggest that people's political engagement has become more local and issue-based, and has moved away from the sweeping, party-based ideological politics of the past. This would imply that falling turnout suggests a change in people's political participation rather than a widespread apathy.

While the postmodernist position may well be an exaggeration, there would appear to be substance in the idea that low electoral turnout may well have less to do with political apathy amongst groups within the electorate and more to do with the changing nature of political participation in a globalised world.

Examine the view that it's time to get your revision on...

Oh exams are wonderful things. You spend ages and ages studying a whole array of topics from across the sociological spectrum and then you're expected to get that all down in just a couple of hours. But what that does mean is you need to get used to writing under exam-type conditions — make sure you practise answering questions under timed conditions as part of your revision.

Do Well in Your Exam

> **3** Assess the view that religion is in decline in the UK. (33 marks)

Mention relevant studies.

Define the key term or idea that the question asks you about.

Bryan Wilson (1966) describes a process of secularisation. This is a decline in the significance of religious belief, religious institutions and religious practice in society. Evidence about the influence of religion in society is often open to different interpretations; it is difficult to prove definitively that religion is in decline.

Evaluate how reliable data is — don't just take it at face value.

In the 2001 census, 72% of the people in the UK identified themselves as Christian. However, these 72% who identify themselves as Christian do not necessarily hold strong religious beliefs. Some may have been brought up nominally Christian, but have minimal belief in God or the teachings of Christianity.

Church attendance figures are often used to support the view that religion is in decline — the percentage of adults who go to church has fallen from 10% to 7% over the last 20 years. This is a questionable method of judging the extent of secularisation though, as it only deals with religious practice, not religious belief. It's possible to attend church without having faith, just for the social networking aspects, as Herberg suggested. On the other hand, it is possible to believe strongly in God, but never go to church. Davie (1994) claimed that belonging to a church and believing in religion are getting more and more separated.

Have separate paragraphs about different aspects of a topic.

Some argue that religious institutions have lost influence in wider society. Bruce (1995) said that the Church became less important to people as its functions were taken over by other, secular institutions. For example, the Church used to have a strong role in education and welfare — roles which are now primarily filled by secular, state organisations. On the other hand, Parsons claims that even though the Church no longer has all the functions it had back in the Middle Ages, religion can still have an influence on people's everyday lives.

Discuss contrasting viewpoints.

There has been a trend towards religious pluralism (a greater variety of religions practised in British society). This is partly because of the immigration of ethnic minorities, and partly because of new religious movements (NRMs).

Immigrant groups often have a higher level of religiosity than the settled population. Religion contributes to a sense of community and ethnic identity. Davie claimed that identification with a religion was important to South Asian immigrants because it gave a strong sense of cultural identity. Bruce refers to cultural transition — when South Asian immigrants came to the UK, they quickly set up religious institutions to act as a support structure for the immigrant community.

Bring in relevant examples.

Religious pluralism has also resulted from the growth of new religious movements (NRMs) since the 1960s. A large variety of groups and beliefs have been labelled NRMs, from the Moonies to reiki healers. Many sociologists use the growth of NRMs as evidence to argue against secularisation. Sociologists have claimed that the conditions of modernity and postmodernity create insecurity and alienation, and that the growth of NRMs is a response to this. However, it is not easy to use the rise in NRMs as evidence against secularisation. Some NRMs are very vague in their beliefs, and may not count as religions at all.

Explain your opinion on the topic, based on the evidence in the essay.

In conclusion, it is difficult to accurately measure whether religion is declining. Personal belief is a complex topic; for example, even if a person says they are Christian, they may not attend church or believe strongly in God. The rise of NRMs since the 1960s suggests that many people do want some element of spirituality in their lives, but it is arguable whether this is the equivalent of a traditional religion.

Imagine you're doing a covert participant observation study of exam candidates...

The more stuff you learn, the more you'll be able to write about. But you have to try to keep it all relevant. It's all too easy to start off answering the question, but end up waffling on about something else entirely. One of the best ways to avoid this is to plan out your answers before you write them. Go through each point you want to make and include supporting evidence.

Glossary

absolute poverty Not having the essentials needed for life — food, warmth and shelter.

achieved status Status you get by working for it.

agenda-setting A practice in journalism where an editor or journalist selects what to include in the news and chooses a particular angle to take when reporting it, so affecting how the story is perceived by their audience.

anomie Durkheim's term for a state of moral confusion in society, resulting from an absence of the common shared norms and values that bind a society together. He argued that this was bad for both individuals (who are uncertain of how to behave in particular situations) and for society as a whole. Anomie (or "normlessness") is a state that is typical of societies undergoing sudden change.

ascribed status Status you have from birth.

Bandura, Ross and Ross (1963) Conducted psychological experiments that demonstrated how boys imitated aggression in films they had watched. Their research has been used to support the hypodermic syringe theory of the media.

Bourdieu, Pierre (1930-2002) French sociologist who came up with the idea of cultural capital.

bourgeoisie Marxist term for the capitalist ruling class. They own the means of production (e.g. factories, equipment, raw materials).

capitalism An economic system based on private ownership of the means of production, distribution and exchange of commodities. In the capitalist system labour itself becomes a commodity which employers buy for wages. Capitalism is associated with free trade and individual enterprise. It started in Europe and the US and has spread to become the dominant economic philosophy in most countries.

catharsis theory This theory suggests that seeing violence on TV helps viewers release tension and violent thoughts, making them less likely to commit violent acts themselves.

censorship The control of the media (TV, newspapers, film etc.) through banning certain works, scenes, images or language from being broadcast or published.

census A government survey of all people within a defined geographical area. The British census is an obligatory survey of the entire population every 10 years. It's an important source of secondary data on the changing characteristics (housing, education, work patterns etc.) of the British population.

civil disobedience Protest action that breaks laws.

class A way of stratifying society, on the basis of people's social and economic status. Class is hierarchical — some classes are more privileged than others. The "class system" is criticised by Marxists.

classical liberalism The view that the market should be free, with minimum state intervention, and that individuals should take responsibility for themselves.

coding Numbered codes for each answer of a question on a multiple choice questionnaire. Coding makes it easy to turn the results into graphs and analyse them.

collective consciousness The shared values and norms that hold society together.

communism A system of government which is theoretically based on a classless society and where private ownership has been abolished. It is influenced by the ideas of Marx and Engels. During the Cold War, there was conflict between capitalist Western countries and communist countries like the USSR and China. With the end of the Cold War and the break-up of the USSR, many formerly communist countries have moved towards adopting capitalism. To some extent, their reasons for doing this have discredited communism as a viable political philosophy.

conformity Adherence to the norms and values of society. The opposite of deviance.

Glossary

conjugal roles Husband and wife roles — who does the paid work, who does the washing-up etc.

consensus Fundamental agreement within a society, especially about that society's basic values. Functionalist theory suggests that, as a result of socialisation, the people in a society all share the same norms and values and this contributes to consensus.

correlation The association between two variables where changes in one variable are associated with changes in the other variable, but do not necessarily cause them.

cult A religious group without a fixed set of beliefs. Cults tend to focus on the inner power of the individual and mysticism. They're often short-lived and don't usually have a hierarchy.

cultural capital The skills and cultural know-how that children learn from their parents.

cultural deprivation theory This theory says working class culture makes people disadvantaged.

culture The "way of life" of a society or group. Culture is made up of things such as language, customs, knowledge, norms and values. It is passed on by socialisation.

Davis and Moore (1945) Functionalists who believed that modern society rewards ability, effort and intelligence. They claimed that there has to be a system of unequal rewards to motivate people to train for demanding and difficult jobs. The function of the education system is therefore to allocate people to appropriate occupations.

deferred gratification Working and waiting for a while until you get your reward.

delinquency Bad behaviour and social disruption. Includes criminal behaviour and plain annoying behaviour.

dependency theory A development theory which blames underdevelopment on colonialism.

desacrilisation Religious and spiritual beliefs ceasing to have a place in society.

deviance Something that goes against society's norms and values. Deviant behaviour is behaviour that society doesn't approve of.

discourse Any kind of discussion or talk about something.

Durkheim, Emile (1858-1917) French founding father of sociology. He thought that different parts of society had different roles, like the organs of the body. The founder of functionalism, he was one of the three most influential figures in shaping the modern discipline of Sociology, together with Weber and Marx. Durkheim introduced many important sociological concepts, including the "collective consciousness of society" (the shared norms and values that bind a society together) and "anomie" (a state of being without these norms). Durkheim also wrote extensively on the subject of suicide and on the sociology of religion.

Engels, Friedrich (1820-1895) A sociologist, philosopher and co-founder of Marxism, Engels was a fierce critic of capitalism. He said women were subordinated through the institutions of private property and monogamy. Engels argued that the family had the economic function of keeping wealth within the bourgeoisie because parents pass it on to the next generation as inheritance.

ethnic group A group of people with a common culture — language, religion and way of life.

ethnocentric Centred around the values and interests of one particular ethnic group.

ethnography Research which studies the culture and way of life of a community. It is usually done by observation, and may also use interviews and case studies. Ethnography looks at social relationships, organisations, customs and practices. It is an interpretivist approach to sociological study and so produces qualitative data.

extended family Three or more generations all living together — grandparents, aunts, uncles etc.

Glossary

false consciousness Marxism says that workers are in a state of false consciousness about their place in society. They have learnt values and beliefs that support the interests of the ruling class (through their education, the media and religion), and this prevents them from realising how unfair capitalist society is.

false needs Things people think they need but which don't really satisfy them. Marxists say these false needs have been created by a capitalist culture which encourages consumerism.

falsification Proving a hypothesis wrong.

feminism A broad movement which believes that social organisations and culture have been dominated by men to the exclusion of women. Feminists claim that this has devalued and disadvantaged women into a marginalised status. Feminist sociologists think that mainstream sociology has ignored the lives of women. There are many varieties of feminism, e.g. liberal feminism, Marxist feminism, radical feminism and black feminism.

folk devil A scapegoat for things going wrong in society.

free market An economic system that lets supply and demand control prices, wages etc., rather than the government.

Functionalism An important sociological perspective about how society works, founded by Durkheim, which argues that everything in society exists for a reason. Functionalists believe that society is made up of a number of institutions, each of which has a useful function and helps society to run smoothly, e.g. the family, the education system, religion. These institutions work in harmony because of agreed norms and values, and this is essential for society to survive. Functionalists say that individuals internalise these norms and values (socialisation). Another term for functionalism is "consensus structuralism". So now you know.

gender Sociologists say that gender (femininity and masculinity) is a social construction. Being male or female is the biological sex you're born with, while masculinity and femininity are identities you're socialised into.

Glasgow University Media Group (1976) (1980) (1982) Studied bias in the media. They found that TV coverage of workplace strikes in the 1970s was biased in favour of management and against the strikers in terms of the perspective, the language and what was covered.

globalisation The breaking down of traditional national boundaries as globally people become more interconnected. This happens due to factors such as the growth of multinational companies, improvements in communications and technology, increased migration of people between societies, and the global marketing of cultural products.

Hall, Stuart (1932-) British sociologist, big on studying ethnicity and popular culture.

Hawthorne effect When participants are aware they are taking part in an experiment, it often affects their behaviour. This is known as the Hawthorne effect.

hegemony The domination of one group of people over others, or of one set of ideas and values over others. Law, religion, media, art, science and literature may all be used to make the dominant group or values legitimate and to discredit the alternatives.

hidden curriculum The social norms and values that are taught at school, but not as part of the regular curriculum. Includes conformity, respect for authority and other cultural values.

hierarchy A system which ranks people according to status. Any system where you have a boss in charge of people is a hierarchy.

household A group of people who live together. They needn't be related.

Glossary

hypodermic syringe model The idea that the media injects its message directly into the minds of the audience. It claims that all people in the audience are affected in the same way, and that they're powerless to resist or reject the message.

hypothetico-deductive model Where you come up with an idea (a hypothesis) and do experiments to test if it's true or not.

iatrogenesis The appearance of health problems caused by the medical system.

identity An individual's sense of self. This can be influenced by social factors such as class, gender, religion and ethnicity.

ideological state apparatus Institutions like the media, schools, Church and family which can spread the ideology of the state.

ideology A set of ideas and beliefs about the way things should be — often politically motivated.

infrastructure In Marxist theory, the infrastructure is the economic base of society (e.g. labour and manufacturing).

institutional racism When the policies, attitudes and actions of an institution discriminate against ethnic minorities — sometimes unintentionally.

institutions of society Things like the family, the Church, the education system, the health care system.

internalised norms and values Norms and values that have become part of who you are and the way you think.

interpretivism A sociological approach which focuses on the actions and thoughts of individuals. Society is viewed as the product of interaction between individuals. "Interpretivism", "interactionism" and "social action theory" are pretty much the same thing — so don't get confused if you see these other terms being used.

labelling theory This theory says that the labels given to someone affect their behaviour, e.g. someone who is labelled a criminal is more likely to commit criminal acts. Labels also affect how other people treat someone, e.g. teachers might treat a child labelled a "troublemaker" more strictly.

LEDC Less Economically Developed Country.

Left Realism Sociological viewpoint which developed from Marxism. The approach focuses on working within the capitalist framework and aims to direct social policy to help the poor.

longitudinal study A study done over a period of time.

Mac an Ghaill (1994) Used overt observation and interviews to study masculinity. He found that many boys formed deviant subcultures because of failure at school and a desire to be "macho" and masculine. He introduced the idea of a "crisis of masculinity" as a cause of the underachievement of boys at school.

Marcuse, Herbert (1898-1979) Neo-Marxist who wrote about leisure, its consumption by workers and the way it is presented by the mass media. He claimed that the mass media promotes consumerism and gives people false needs (things they think they want but which won't really satisfy them). He said that leisure is based around these false needs, creating "happy robots" who work hard because they're under the false impression that leisure makes them happy.

Marx, Karl (1818-1883) German social theorist who wrote Das Kapital and came up with the somewhat influential theory about power being the control of the means of production.

Glossary

Marxism A theory and political ideology based on the views of Karl Marx (1818-1883). Marxists are opposed to capitalism, which they believe is based on the exploitation of the working class (proletariat), who do the work, by the ruling class (bourgeoisie), who own the "means of production". Most of the profit from the work that the working class do is kept by the bourgeoisie. The bourgeoisie arrange society to keep the workers down. Original Marxist ideas have been developed and adapted by **neo-Marxists**. Some states have been run politically along Marxist lines, e.g. Cuba under Castro.

mass media Ways of communicating with large numbers of people, e.g. newspapers, TV, magazines, radio, internet.

master status A quality in an individual that comes to dominate the way that they are treated or viewed, to the extent that all their other qualities are disregarded. This quality then takes on the status of a label. E.g. if someone with mental health problems is given the often negative label "mentally ill", and then finds that all their other qualities are ignored, the label "mentally ill" has master status.

means-tested benefit A benefit that you can only get if you can prove you're poor enough.

MEDC More Economically Developed Country.

media text Any piece of media — e.g. a book, a TV programme, an advert.

meritocracy A system where the best (most talented and hard-working) people rise to the top.

metanarrative An overarching, all-encompassing story which gives meaning to history and events.

moral panic A fear of a moral crisis in society. Moral panics are often linked to "folk devils". The mass media have a big role in starting moral panics in modern society.

Murray, Charles (1943-) American New Right sociologist who believes that there's an underclass who are too dependent on benefits.

neo-Marxism In the 20th century, some of Marx's followers revised and adapted his ideas to make them more relevant to modern society. Neo-Marxists often stress the importance of culture in sustaining capitalism, e.g. through the hegemony of capitalist ideas. Neo-Marxists include Gramsci, Althusser and Stuart Hall.

New Right Movement developed in the 1980s. New Right theory believes in the "moral superiority" of the traditional nuclear family, and tends towards the view that sexual tolerance and single mothers are bad for society. Problems like poverty and unemployment are seen to be caused by an over-generous welfare state. New Right sociologists have also claimed that there's been a moral decline in society due to secularisation.

non-conformity Not going along with society's norms and values.

norm A social rule about what is correct and appropriate behaviour within a particular culture, e.g. queuing in a shop.

nuclear family Mum, dad and children living together.

Oakley, Ann (1944-) Feminist sociologist who studied housework and gender socialisation.

operationalisation Defining a concept and deciding how to measure it.

Parsons, Talcott (1902-1979) American functionalist sociologist who wrote about the structure and functions of society.

patriarchy A society where men are dominant. Feminists often describe male-dominated societies and institutions as "patriarchal".

peer groups People of the same or similar social status and age, e.g. a group of teenagers.

Physical Quality of Life Index (PQLI) A development index that measures infant mortality, literacy and life expectancy.

Glossary

pluralism The belief that society is diverse and reflects the needs and views of everyone via democracy and the free market.

positivism A theoretical point of view which concentrates on social facts, scientific method and quantitative data (facts and figures). The positivist view is that human behaviour is determined by external social factors, and so is outside the control of the individuals in society.

postmodernism Theory which says there is no one objective truth or reality that everyone experiences. Postmodernism rejects the ideas of modernism, such as positivism and metanarratives.

postmodernity The world after the modern age — with flexible working, individual responsibility and people constructing their own identity.

qualitative methods of research Methods like unstructured interviews and participant observation that give results which tell a story about individuals' lives.

quantitative methods of research Methods like surveys and structured interviews that give results you can easily put into a graph or table.

reflexive sociology Research that accepts that the researcher's opinions have an effect on results, and takes this into account.

reliability Data is reliable if other sociologists using the same methods on the same group collect the same data. Quantitative data is usually the most reliable.

representative democracy Rule by the people, via voting in elections for representatives (e.g. MPs).

rite of passage A growing-up ceremony that young people do to prove they aren't kids any more.

sanctions Rewards and punishments that reinforce social norms.

secularisation When religion loses its influence in society.

self-fulfilling prophecy When people behave in the way that they know others have predicted.

semiotic analysis Looking for hidden meanings in the structure of a text, image or object.

social construct An idea or belief that's created in society, and doesn't come from a scientific fact.

social democrats People who think the state should redistribute wealth, and that there should be a strong welfare state paid for out of taxes. Social democrats believe in social equality.

social policy Government decisions which affect society, e.g. raising taxes, changing the benefits system, privatisation.

socialisation Passing on cultural values and norms from one generation to the next, so that they become internalised, i.e. part of everyone's way of thinking.

stereotype A generalisation about a social group — often inaccurate and insulting.

stratification The way society is divided up into layers or classes.

stratified sample A sample with the same proportions of gender, class, age etc. as the population you're studying.

subculture A group who share values and norms which are different from the mainstream culture. A culture within a culture.

superstructure In Marxist theory, the superstructure is the institutions in a society which aren't economic (such as legal, political, cultural and religious institutions) and the beliefs and values which these institutions propagate. It has a role in maintaining and sustaining the economic infrastructure.

symmetrical family A family structure where conjugal (husband and wife) roles are equally shared.

Glossary

third-way politics A political viewpoint that combines elements of right-wing self-sufficiency and left-wing social democracy.

triangulation Combining different research methods and data to get the best results.

underclass A social group at the bottom of the social hierarchy. New Right sociologists think they're lazy and dependent on welfare. Left wing sociologists think they're disadvantaged by the welfare system.

universal benefit Benefit that everyone gets, whether they're rich or poor.

validity Data is valid if it gives an accurate picture of what's being measured.

value-free research Research that isn't biased, and isn't influenced by the researcher's beliefs.

values General beliefs in a society about what is important or what is right and wrong, e.g. freedom of speech is a value of Western society.

victim survey Survey asking if respondents have been victims of crime.

vocational education Education aimed at a particular job.

Weber, Max (1864-1920) Influential, early sociologist. Weber argued that the better a person's market situation, the better their life chances, wealth and status would be. He also suggested that as societies developed, secularisation would follow as people came to believe more in science. Weberians are followers of Weber's work and ideas.

Welfare State The British Welfare State was set up in the 1940s with the aim of wiping out the social problems of society (poor health, housing and education, poverty and unemployment). The Welfare State was designed to be free at the point where people actually needed it (e.g. a visit to hospital) and was paid for by people in work contributing to a national insurance scheme.

Willis, Paul (1945-) Sociologist who studied working class boys and their anti-school subcultures.

World Systems theory Development theory which looks at the world as a single economic system where some countries have a lot of power and others don't have power.

Index

Index

Index

Index

Index

Index